Harriet Georgina Dufferin

Irish Emigration and the Tenure of Land in Ireland

Harriet Georgina Dufferin

Irish Emigration and the Tenure of Land in Ireland

ISBN/EAN: 9783744735261

Printed in Europe, USA, Canada, Australia, Japan

Cover: Foto ©ninafisch / pixelio.de

More available books at **www.hansebooks.com**

IRISH EMIGRATION

AND

THE TENURE OF LAND IN IRELAND.

BY

THE RT. HON. LORD DUFFERIN, K.P.

—

LONDON:
WILLIS, SOTHERAN, & CO.,
42, CHARING CROSS, (OPPOSITE CRAIG'S COURT.)
1867.

PREFACE.

The greater portion of the contents of the following pages, appeared originally in the form of letters to the *Times*.

Those letters were written in the hopes of inducing my fellow-countrymen to pause, before adopting without further investigation a theory with regard to Irish emigration and what has been called "the exterminating policy of Irish Landlords," which, after having been for years industriously propagated in Ireland, had at last received the imprimatur of one or two influential Members of Parliament.

But though hastily committed to paper, the views I thus submitted to the public were the result of diligent enquiry, and long-continued observation of the changing phases of our national existence. Nothing but an uncontrollable conviction of the injustice of the accusations with which the landed proprietors of Ireland are assailed, and of the gross incorrectness of the data on which those accusations are founded, would have induced me to embark in so uncongenial a controversy,—my natural repugnance to which was enhanced by the generosity of sentiment exhibited towards our unfortunate country, in those very speeches to portions of which I felt compelled to take exception. That persons of great intelligence should fall into error on the subjects in question did not surprise me. In any country it is difficult to disentangle the threads of popular sentiment, or to follow out the intricate operation of economical laws,—but in Ireland, a hundred influences,—many of them compatible with the purest patriotism, and the most scrupulous integrity, had contrived to prejudice local opinion, and to mislead the national conscience. Yet it would be from such sources alone, that a popular champion would naturally seek inspiration, and if his view of the situation should betray considerable misapprehension of the real facts of the case—it would be unfair to doubt the genuineness of his convictions, or to receive with any other feelings than those of respect and gratitude, any suggestions he might have to offer.

Though deeply sensible of my unfitness to do more than offer a slight contribution to the investigation which has been undertaken of late by many eminent persons, into the relations of Irish tenants with their landlords, there was a certain respect in which I felt I occupied an advantageous position. On the one hand, as a northern landlord, I had no interest in refuting accusations, from which, by general consent, the landlords of Ulster have been exempted; while, on the other, the phenomena which were supposed to justify them as against the proprietors of the South and West, and the difficulties incident to estate management in Ireland, were sufficiently common both to North and South, to make me familiar with their true origin and character. On this account I was able to enter upon a review of the past, with as much impartiality, and perhaps more acquaintance with the subject than persons totally unconnected with the landed interest of the country. I may indeed be told, that because I am a landlord, I must therefore be prejudiced in favour of the class: I can only reply that I am not conscious of any such partiality, and that I do not even understand the possibility of feeling greater sympathy with the legitimate aspirations of one section of the community, than with those of any other. It has always seemed to me that a true statesman should guard the rights and promote the welfare of the diverse but inextricably associated interests of the Nation with an undistinguishing solicitude.

Even with respect to the future, if I am opposed to many of the changes in the land laws of Ireland which have been suggested, it is not merely because they are detrimental to the interests of the landed proprietors, but because they are gross infractions of the first principles of Liberty, Justice, and Government, and fraught with mischief to the community at large.

In throwing my letters into the form of a pamphlet, I have not had time to introduce into them the improvements I could have wished. Though here and there considerable additions have been made to some of the paragraphs, most of the original sentences remain as they were written. Even the new matter, only expands or explains statements and opinions which were originally conveyed in the concise form adapted to the columns of a newspaper. But though very little has been altered, there is scarcely a passage which has not been carefully reconsidered by the light of the various criticisms, with which my letters to the *Times* were honoured.

Whenever I have been able to convince myself that a correction was required, I have hastened to introduce it. Even in those cases where the ascertained facts perfectly justified a broad expression, I have frequently modified that expression in order to bring it into more perfect harmony with an opponent's view, and from first to last I have endeavoured to understate rather than to exaggerate the data on which I based my argument.

I have also carefully revised my figures, and submitted them to the scrutiny of several eminent statisticians both in this country and in Ireland.

But though I have scarcely done more than review or verify my previous composition, it is not a mere "réchauffé" I submit to those who may have patience to glance over these pages. Feeling how little claim I had on public confidence, I have endeavoured to illustrate and corroborate every statement and opinion of my own by a reference to such authorities as are held in universal esteem, and the text of my pamphlet is accompanied throughout by a running commentary of notes, and quotations from various authors.

On no work have I drawn so largely as on the Digest of the Evidence taken before the Devon Commission. I have also frequently appealed to the authority of Mr. Mill, Sir G. C. Lewis, Mr. Cobden, Mr. Thornton, Mr. Fawcett, Dr. Hancock, and other equally honoured names in support of many of my views. With regard to the agriculture of foreign countries, I have taken M. de Laveleye as my guide for that of Belgium, and M. de Lavergne for that of France.

In the General Appendix will be found the answers I have received from a great number of gentlemen living in different parts of Ireland, to whom I ventured to address a series of questions connected with the subjects under discussion, as well as some extracts from Dr. Hancock's valuable pamphlet on the alleged decline of prosperity in Ireland, and an interesting paper on the present condition of agriculture in the counties of Cork and Kerry, drawn up by Mr. Robertson, a very well informed and intelligent agriculturist, who proceeded this spring at my request, to the South of Ireland, in order to obtain precise information on one or two disputed matters of fact.

Finally, I have excluded from the present volume everything approaching to a personal allusion. Though differing so widely on many points with the gentlemen whose misapprehensions I have endeavoured to correct, I sympathize most cordially with their unmistakable anxiety to improve the condition of our fellow-countrymen; and I should only be too happy to co-operate with them in promoting such a change in the state of Ireland as would render the real origin of her misfortunes a matter of indifference to every one but the antiquary.

INDEX.

	Page.
PREFACE	i—viii
ANALYSIS	xiii—xxii

CHAPTER I.
EMIGRATION.   1—34

APPENDIX to CHAPTER I.

Vital Statistics—France . . .	34
Sir G. Lewis on Emigration . . .	34
Effect of Emigration on Population in Ireland	35
Return shewing amount of money remitted by Settlers in North America to their friends in the United Kingdom, 1848—64 (inclusive) . .	36
Condition of Irish people in 1834 . .	37
Mr. Mill on the Profits derived from large and small Farms	38
Spade versus Plough	38
Pay of the English Soldier . . .	39
Emigration from the Scotch Highlands .	39
Note as to the Reduction in the number of Persons of different Religions and Races in Ireland, from 1834 till 1861	41
Reclamation of waste Lands in Ireland, as affected by Emigration	43
The Emancipation of the Dorsetshire Labourer .	44-5

CHAPTER II.
LANDLORDS AND TENANTS.   46—84

APPENDIX to CHAPTER II.

- Emigration of Protestants from Ireland . .	85
- Return of the Emigration from the United Kingdom to all parts of the World during the years 1854 to 1858, inclusive ; shewing the trade, occupation, or profession of the Emigrants . .	86-87
- Table, shewing the Occupations, Sex and general destribution of the Emigrants in 1864 . .	88-89

b

Page.

CHAPTER III.

A RETROSPECT OF THE ECONOMICAL HISTORY OF IRELAND.   90—144

Appendix to Chapter III.
    The Difficulties of the Irish Landlord's situation . 145-6
    The Pastures of Ireland 147-8
    Progress of Belfast 149-50

CHAPTER IV.

IRELAND AND BELGIUM: OWNERS AND OCCUPIERS.   151—205

Appendix to Chapter IV.
    No. of Cultivators in Ireland 206
    „   „   „ Great Britain . . . 208
    „   „   „ Belgium . . . 209
    Length of Belgian Leases 209

CHAPTER V.

A REVIEW OF VARIOUS PROPOSALS FOR THE ALTERATION OF THE TENURE OF LAND IN IRELAND.   210—275

ANSWERS TO QUERIES AS TO RATE OF WAGES, ETC.   . . . . 276—301

Appendix to Chapter V.
    Rate of Subdivision of Land in France . . 302
    Progress of French Agriculture . . . 303

GENERAL APPENDIX.

Dr. Longfield on Valuation 304-308
The Custom of Tenant-right in Ulster . . 308-333
    (Extracts from Lord Dufferin's Evidence before Mr. Maguire's Committee.)

	Page.
Large v. Small Farms	333-340
On the alleged Progressive Decline of the Prosperity of Ireland, by Dr. Hancock	341-343
Comparison of the Rise in Wages, and in the Price of Food	343-344
Cork and Kerry in 1867	345-352
The profits of the small farmer, and the wages of the labourer compared	353
Table, shewing the Population in 1841, 1851, 1861: the number of persons attending school and the number and proportion per cent of those not attending school	355
Density of population in Ireland and other countries	356
Comparison of the mineral resources of Great Britain and Ireland	356
Deposits in Joint Stock Banks	357
Table, shewing the Acreage under crops in 1866	358
Table, shewing the gross produce of the Acreage under crops in 1866	359
Table, shewing gross value of Acreage under crops in 1866	360
Table, shewing the Tillage acres, the Tillage cultivation, and the gross annual value of the produce in proportion to acres and cultivators	361
No. of acres in each Province in 1851 and 1861; also the same reduced to proportions per cent.	362
Extent of Land in Statute Acres under crops in Ireland, each year, from 1847-66.	363
Number of holdings (classified according to the total extent of Land held by each person), and the entire extent of Land under each class of Landholders with the increase or decrease in each class	364
Total number of Holdings, and their extent in Statute Acres in 1864	365
Table of Holdings, 1841 to 1864, from the Register General's Return	366
Table, shewing the number of hands employed on various farms in England	367
Cost of Hand-Power	368
EMIGRATION: a temporary remedy	370
Number of Emigrants in each year	371

	Page.
Mr. Robertson's Report on the rate of Agricultural Labour in Co. Cork	372
NOTE by Lord Dufferin's agent on the present and former rate of wages in the County of Down	376

POSTSCRIPT.

Some observations on Mr. Butt's new work, "*The Irish people, and the Irish Land*"	377-391
Mr. Hill's Data and Statistics in relation to Ireland examined	395-402

ANALYSIS.

CHAPTER I.

The counts in the indictment against the landlords of Ireland, pp. 2, 3—The prosperity of the emigrant, 4—The former condition of the Irish labourer, 5—The present supply of labour, 6—The casual labourer, 7—Conversion of cottiers into labourers, 8—Excess of labour supply in 1846, 9—Proportion of cultivators to area cultivated, 10, 11—More cultivators are still employed than is compatible with their proper remuneration, 12, 13—The consequences considered, if no outlet had existed for the surplus population, 14, 15—Emigration no longer so imperative a necessity, 16—No extraneous influence should be used to divert the present occupying class from their avocations, 17—The effect of the potato on population, 18—The failure of the potato restricted population, 19—Present rate of increase of the nation, 20—The prospects of the rising generation, 21—Emigration from Germany, 22—Emigration suggested by Sir G. Lewis, 23—The effects of emigration on rent and on rate of wages, 24, 25—The momentum emigration may acquire, 26—The present supply of labour and waste lands, 27—Improvement has been compatible with emigration, 28—The effect of emigration on British manufacture, 29—The effect of emigration on the British army, 30—Emigration and the love of home, 31—The whole earth placed at man's disposal, 32—Checks on population, 33—Colonization, 34—Sir G. Lewis on emigration, 35—Tables on emigration, *ib.*—Money remitted by emigrants, 36—The labourer and the cottier in 1834, 37—Small farms *v.* large, 38—Plough *v.* spade, *ib.*—Pay of the labourer and soldier, 39—Emigration from the Highlands of Scotland, 40—Protestant and Catholic emigration, 41, 42—Reclamation of waste lands, 43—Emancipation of the Dorsetshire labourer, 44—Mr. Girdlestone and the Dorset labourer, 45.

CHAPTER II.

The classes that have emigrated, 47—The connection of the landlord with the emigrant, 48—The limits of the competence of Parliament, 49—The results of the investigation by the Devon Commission of most of the charges against the landlord, 50, 51—The trying nature of the crisis in 1846, 52—Judge Longfield on evictions in 1846, 53—Emigration the only possible alternative, 54—One-third of the landlords ruined in 1846, 55—The sacrifices made by the landlords to assist emigration, 56, 57—The greater proportion of the emigrants not occupiers of land, 58, 59—The extent to which consolidation has been carried, 60—The reduction of holdings between 1841 and 1861, 61—Holdings above 15 acres have largely increased since 1841, 62, 63—Emigration of the tenant class principally confined to occupiers of from half an acre to six acres, 64, 65—Many of the cottier tenants remained at home as labourers, 66—The tenant class may have contributed one-fourth to the total emigration between 1846 and 1851, 66, 67—Since then very few occupiers of land have emigrated, 68—Judge Longfield probably correct in stating that about 4 per cent. of the emigrants are farmers, 69—Comparison of the extinction of small holdings in the four Provinces, 69*—Comparison of the extinction of holdings of all sizes in the four Provinces, 70, 71—Comparison of the emigration from the four Provinces, 72—Annual number of evictions in Ireland, 73—Number of notices of evictions served on Poor-law guardians, 74—Table of notices and actual evictions, 75—Proportion of persons affected by evictions to number of emigrants amounts to about 2 per cent., 76, 77—Rate of evictions amounts to 1 per annum on every 10,000 acres of occupied land, 78—Two-thirds of the actual evictions are for non-payment of rent, 79—Comparison of the proportion of farmers who have emigrated to the total number of emigrants, 80, 81—The analysis of the Emigration Commissioners makes the emigration of Irish farmers amount to $2\frac{1}{2}$ per cent. of the total emigration from Ireland, 82, 83—Comparison of the emigration of the professional and farming classes, 84—

Protestant emigration from Ireland, 85—Emigration returns, 86—Occupations of emigrants, 88, 89.

CHAPTER III.

The responsibilities of a former generation of landlords, 91— The position of an Irish landlord 80 years ago, 92—The nature and origin of rack-rents, 93—In former days most of the land let on lease as pasture, 94—The substitution of " la petite culture" for pasture, 95—The inability of the landlord to prevent subdivision of farms, 96—His relations with his fellow countrymen, 97—The middleman often, though not always, sublet against the will of the landlord, 98, 99—The landlord could not have foreseen the curse to the country the middleman would become, 100, 101— The introduction of a middleman occasioned sometimes by benevolent motives, 102, 103—He was intended to act as a link between the peasantry and their landlords, 104, 105— It was not his economical position but his individual defects which produced the evils complained of, 106, 107—The middleman not much worse than his neighbours, 108, 109— It is as fair to take the highest rent as to employ labour at the lowest rate of wages, 110, 111—The one course as fraught with evil consequences as the other, 112—The rise of the middleman, 113—The middleman in Ulster, 114— Competition and rack-rents in Ulster, 115—The Ulster tenant-right is the creature of competition, 116, 117—Prices given for the "good-will" in Down and Donegal, 118— These prices often represent no real value, 119—The disadvantage of the system to the incoming tenant, 120—The inconsistency of restricting the rent by Act of Parliament, and allowing the "good-will" to be put up to auction, 121— The devolution of tenancies of constant occurrence, 122— The fraud on the landlord and on the incoming tenant, 123— The landlords seldom take advantage of competition but the tenants always do, 124, 125—Competition is an irrepressible force, 126—Is equally prevalent in every part of Ireland, 127—Some agency must have checked the prosperity of Ireland, 128—The commercial jealousies of Great Britain, 129—Duties on Irish produce: cattle, wool, provisions,

leather, 130—Duties on Irish manufactures: woollen and
cotton goods, leather, silk, soap, candles, 131—Prohibitions
on Irish trade, 132—The land the only resource left to the
Irish people, 133—The rapid expansion of the agricultural
population and the rise of prices of agricultural produce
during the French war, 134—The consequent pressure of the
people on the land, 135—The linen trade alone exempted
from the effect of the jealousy of Britain, 136—Expansion
of the linen trade in Ulster and the prosperity of that
Province, 137—An outlet thus afforded to the agricultural
population of the North, 138—Review of the foregoing
arguments, 139—The responsibilities of Irish landlords and
British manufacturers compared, 140—Mr. Cobden's view of
the subject, 141—Mr. Charles Greville's view of the same
subject, 142, 143—Sir G. Lewis's view of the same subject,
144—The difficulties of an Irish landlord, 145—The course
of his proceedings, 146—The pastures of Ireland, 147, 148—
The trade of the North, 149—The trade of Belfast, 150.

CHAPTER IV.

The disproportion of cultivators to the area cultivated in Ireland reconsidered, 152, 153—Table of proportion of cultivators per acre in Ireland, England, Belgium, and Flanders, 154—Comparison of results in produce, 155—Proportion of cultivators per acre larger in Connaught and Munster than in Ulster, 156—The amount of produce nearly in inverse ratio to the proportion of cultivators in different parts of Ireland, 157—The proportionate number of cultivators in Ireland about the same as in Belgium, though Ireland is less adapted to spade-husbandry than Belgium, 158, 159—The opinion of various persons on the minimum size of farms on which a tenant can live with comfort, 160, 161—The agriculture of Belgium, 162—The rack-rents and short leases of Belgium, 163—The profits of the Belgian farmer, 164—The agricultural population of Belgium most wretched where the farms are smallest, 165—Condition of the Belgian farm-servant, 166—The advantages afforded in Belgium to 'la petite culture,' 167—The market gardening of Belgium, 168

—The facilities of obtaining manure in Belgium—The amount of manure per acre applied in Belgium, 170—Stolen and textile crops, 171—The manufactures of Belgium auxiliary to her agriculture, 172—A great number of the minute holdings of Belgium held by artizans, 163—The climate of Belgium compared with that of Ireland, 174, 175—The rainfall of Ireland at harvest-time, 176—The lessons to be learnt from the example of Belgium, 177—A proportion of the farms in Ireland might be enlarged with advantage, 178, 179—Judge Longfield's opinion on the subject, 180—The definition of the relations of landlord and tenant to one another and to the land, 181—The confiscations of Elizabeth and Cromwell, 182—The ownership of an Irish proprietor identical with that of his English fellow-countrymen, 183—A tenant's position defined, 184—The hiring of land and the chartering of a ship compared, 185—The conditions of each arrangement determined by contract, 186—The rights of the Commonwealth over landed property, 187—The equitable duration of a tenancy defined, 188—The dissoluble nature of the connection between landlord and tenant, 189—Susceptibility of land to deterioration by neglect, 190—Agriculture has become a science, 191—Large farms are not suitable to Ireland, 192—The landlord must be left the liberty to give the industrious tenant sufficient scope, 193—Emigration the resource of an embarrassed tenant, 194—Cases of emigrants who have returned to the author's estate, 195—The extreme rights of the landlord should be exercised with great consideration, 196—The relations of an employer of labour to his men, and of a landlord to his tenants compared, 197—The sources of the present discontent in Ireland, 198—The opinion of the Catholic Prelates on the subject, 199—The actual occupiers of land not tainted with Fenianism, 200—No difference of tenure would have affected emigration, evictions, or Fenianism, 201—The probable result of an agrarian revolution in Ireland, 202—The absence of tenant-right agitation in Ulster, 203—The three sources of uneasiness in the mind of the Irish tenant farmer, 204—Number of Irish cultivators, 205—Note by the Registrar General of Ireland, 206—Table of English Cultivators, 207—Table of Belgian cultivators, 208, 209.

CHAPTER V.

Mr. Bright's proposition considered, 211—Difficulties in the way of establishing a yeoman class in Ireland, 212—Tendency to sublet or subdivide, 213—Impossible to prevent the tendency by mere legal restraints, 214—' La petite culture' and subdivision in France, 215—Number of small freeholders in France, 216—Their indigence, 217—The large extent of fallow in France, 218—The inferior rate of production in France, 219—The mortgages on these small properties, 220—Mr. Michelet's method of solving the difficulty, 221—The embarrassment of the French peasant proprietor occasioned by competition, 222, 223—The desire to subdivide as prominent as ever in Ireland (*note*), 224—The Farmer's Club of Cork (*note*), 225—The tendency to subdivision which seems excessive in France would be more intense in Ireland, 226—The proposals to deprive Irish landlords of their proprietary rights considered, 227—The conditions under which the state can expropriate, 228—Mr. Butt's plan, 229—The effect on the interests of the landlord, 230—The expropriation of the landlord's improvements in his property, 231—The extent of those improvements both in the North and South, 233—Amount of compensation which has been paid to tenants, 234—The duration of leases in England, Scotland, and Belgium, 237—Mr. Butt's 63 years' lease, 237—Probable consequences of Mr. Butt's plan with reference to the interests of the tenant, 238—Three standards of valuation of land in Ireland, 239—And three rents, 240—Judge Longfield's opinion of fixity of tenure, 241—Difficulties of valuation, 242—The moral aspect of the schemes to deal with the property of the country, 243—It is an easy task to persuade uneducated people that what is apparently for their interest is right, 244, 245—The objections to such an arrangement, 248—The right of contract should be left as free as possible, 249—Alterations are not always improvements, 250—An operation which is slightly beneficial to a farm may be detrimental to an estate, 251—An instance of the foregoing assertion, 252—The Government bill of 1866, legitimate and politic in principle, faulty in detail, 254—Some amendments suggested, 255—The reversal of the presumption that what is affixed to the soil is the property of the landlord, 256—An improvement executed by a tenant outside of an agreement to be presumed to be his property, 257—Registration of improvements necessary, 258—An illustration of this necessity, 259—The difficulty of identifying an improvement after a lapse of time, 260—The necessity of the landlord having an opportunity of acquainting himself with liabilities incurred on his account, 261—The consequences to a tenant of surreptitious operations, 262—Economy in improvements in the interest of the tenant, 263—Leases most desirable but should not be issued indiscriminately, 264—Leases not always desired by the tenant, 265—The reasons why some landlords hesitate to grant leases, 266—The consequences to the tenant of landlords being forced to grant leases, 267—An illustration of the result, 268—The result of such an obligation on the falling in of an old 61 years' lease, 269—Great caution is necessary in legislating on this subject, 270—A suggestion that the State should lend landlords money to compensate their tenants for existing improvements, 271—The result if such assistance were afforded, 272—The benefits to be derived from the distribution of capital over Ireland, 273—The probable effects of an alteration in the law of tenure on emigration and disaffection, 274—Conclusion, 275.

ANSWERS TO QUERIES.

Rate of agricultural wages, 276, 277—Rate of wages for unskilled labour, 278—Rate of wages at harvest-time, 279, 280—Supply of labour, 281, 282—Allowances to agricultural labourers, 283, 284—The classes which have contributed to emigration, 285—The classes to which the Irish emigrants belong, 285, 286—Emigration the only alternative for the sons of small farmers, 287, 288—Emigration not the result of evictions or landlord influence, 289—Emigration voluntary; sacrifices made by landlords, 290—Emigration not the result of pressure put on the tenant by the landlord, 291—Tillage *v.* pasture, 292—Ireland is not being converted into a cattle farm, 293—During the last decade the extent of area under crops has increased, 294, 295—The cause of the late tendency to convert tillage into pasture, 296, 297—Evidence on the subject from different parts of Ireland, 298, 299—The influence of the rise in the price of stock in promoting the change from tillage into pasture, 300, 301.

PROGRESS OF FRENCH AGRICULTURE.

Rate of sub-division of land in France, 302.
M. de Lavergne on the progress of French agriculture, 303.

GENERAL APPENDIX.

Judge Longfield on the difficulties of valuation, 304—Judge Longfield on fixity of tenure, 305—Its ultimate effect on future tenants, 306—The competition rent converted into a fine paid to the outgoing tenants, 307—The injustice done to the landlords, 308.

THE ULSTER TENANT-RIGHT.

The Ulster tenant-right, 308—The definition of the custom, 310—Its effects, 311—The proper method of compensation, 312—The position of a small tenant under the custom of tenant-right, 313—Goodwill, 314—Two views of the custom of tenant-right, 315—Arbitration, 316—The Ulster tenant's notion of tenant-right, 317—Compensation for buildings, 318—For drainage, 319—The sale and purchase of tenant-right, 320—An agricultural lease not sufficiently long to compensate the tenant for the expenditure in buildings, 321—A tenant makes an improvement more cheaply than a landlord, 322—The feeling of the tenantry of Ulster with respect to legislation, 323—Subdivision, 324—North and South are under the same law, 325—No great desire for leases in the North, 326—Different modes of assessing the rent, 327—An instance of subdivision, 328—Sublet lands are generally highly rented, 329—The anxiety to subdivide has been a little checked in the North, 330—Conditions introduced into grants of lands in Ireland by James I., 331—Counter claims of the landlord for dilapidations and bad cultivation likely to prove a formidable offset to a tenant's claim for compensation, 332, 333.

SMALL v. LARGE FARMS.

The question of small *versus* large farms considered, 334—"La petite" *versus* "la grande" culture, 335—Small *versus* large farms, 336—Evidence on the condition of the small farmer, 337—The consolidation of farms in Ireland has not brought their average size up to the average size of the farms in countries where "la petite" culture is practised to most advantage, 338, 339—Evidence on the subject, 340.

THE PROGRESS OF IRELAND.

The prosperity of Ireland has not been on the decline, 341—The effect of three wet seasons on Irish prosperity, 342—The necessity of manufactures to sustain agriculture, 343.

RISE OF WAGES v. RISE OF PRICES.

Comparison of the rise in wages and in the price of food, 344.

CORK AND KERRY IN 1867.

Cork and Kerry in 1867, 345—Mr. Robertson's report, 346—Agriculture: leases; fixity of tenure, 346, 347—Want of skill and capital, 348—Subdivision, 349—The cottier and the farmer: supply of labour, 350—The labourer cannot obtain constant employment, 351—Large fences and small fields, 352.

TABLES AND STATISTICS.

A small farmer's profits *v.* a labourer's wages, 353—School population, 355—Density of population, 356—Minerals of Ireland, 356—Deposits, 357—Acreage under crops in 1866, 358—Acreable produce in 1866, 359—Acreable value of crops in 1866, 360—Comparative tables of tillage acres, acreable value, and cultivators, 361.—Number of acres in each Province in 1851 and 1861, 362—Extent of land under crops from 1847 to 1866, 363—The holdings in 1841, 1851, 1861 classified, 364—Extent of land held by each person in Ireland. 365—Table of holdings from 1841 to 1864, 366.

NUMBER OF CULTIVATORS TO ACRES IN ENGLAND.

Instances taken from Mr. Morton's Hand Book of farming, 367.

THE COST OF HAND POWER.

The product of manual labour contrasted with that acquired by the application of steam, 368.

EMIGRATION.

The future expansion of the Irish population: The prospects of an embarrassed tenant and a prosperous emigrant compared, 370.—Number of emigrants from 1851 to 1865, 371.

AGRICULTURAL LABOUR IN IRELAND.

Rate of wages, 372—Condition of casual labourer, 374—
—Labourers often unemployed, 374—The small tenant a bad labourer, 374—Not low wages but uncertainty of employment occasions the misery of the labourer's condition, 375.

PRESENT AND FORMER RATE OF WAGES IN DOWN.

Note by Lord Dufferin's agent on the above subject, 376.

POSTSCRIPT.

Mr. Butt's New Work on Ireland.

Some observations in reply to the exceptions taken by Mr. Butt to Lord Dufferin's statements of fact, 377-379—Mr. Butt's statistics of emigration, 380-383—Lord Dufferin's statement as to the rise of wages, 384-390—Objections to Mr. Butt's version of his opponent's opinions, 390-392—Conclusion, 393.

Mr. Hill's Article on Ireland.

Mr. Hill's data and statistics examined, 395-402.

IRISH EMIGRATION

AND

THE TENURE OF LAND IN IRELAND.

N.B. The figures in the Table, p. 35, are estimates published by the Registrar-General.

CHAPTER I.

"If Ireland were a thousand miles away from us, all would be changed,—or the landlords would be exterminated by the vengeance of the people."

These are pregnant and comprehensive words: they envelope in the same stern condemnation, both the cultivators and the owners of the soil of Ireland. Their meaning cannot be mistaken: the term vengeance pre-supposes injury,—injury of as deep a dye, as the revenge it has evoked. Yet they express the genuine conviction of one of England's leading politicians, and consequently the opinion of many who confide in his judgment. By some they will be regarded as a rhetorical exaggeration of a partial truth. By others they have been resented as an ignoble calumny.

I do not myself venture to pronounce dogmatically between these conflicting conclusions; no man can hope in a hasty dissertation to determine the opinions of his fellow-countrymen on so vital a question; but, as a member of the obnoxious class referred to, I may be permitted to suggest the propriety of patiently examining the grounds which are supposed to justify these grave denunciations.

Perhaps the simplest method of conducting such an inquiry will be—first, to specify the charges against the landlords of Ireland, as set forth in the public manifestoes of such persons as may be supposed to speak with the greatest authority on the subject, and then to examine, one by one, the truth or falsehood of each. The vehement eloquence with which the wrongs of that country are invariably discussed, affords ample materials for framing the indictment,—a circumstance which relieves me from the invidious expedient of singling out any particular individual as our public prosecutor.

Stripped of all exaggerated phraseology the accusations with which the landlords are assailed may be condensed into the following series of propositions.

1. That the emigration from Ireland has been a curse to that country.

2. That this emigration has been occasioned by the eviction of the rural population by their landlords.

3. That acts of eviction in Ireland are to be attributed rather to the cruelty and injustice of the landlords than to any failure on the part of those evicted to fulfil their legitimate obligations.

4. That the present discontent in Ireland has been chiefly occasioned by the iniquity of the laws affecting the tenure of land.

5. That a change in those laws in a specified direction would pacify discontent and create agricultural prosperity.

A glance at any national newspaper or at the reports of an Irish debate, will show that I have not misrepresented the gist of the remarks to which I refer: " Millions of human beings have been driven across the Atlantic by the landlords of Ireland ;" " Landlordism is the curse of the country ;" " Emigration and the misery of the people is occasioned by the injustice of Parliament, and the iniquity of the laws which regulate the tenure of land ;" " Ireland presents us with the spectacle of a whole nation fleeing from their oppressors ;"—are the ordinary phrases in use.

Now, Sir, are these things true? That is the inquiry I propose to prosecute.

First, Has the Irish exodus, as it has been termed, been a calamity or the reverse?

We have to consider this question from two points of view, inasmuch as it has affected the condition of two classes of persons, namely, those who went away, and those who stayed at home.

There is one single fact which will probably be accepted as a safe indication of the effects of emigration on the destinies of those who took part in it. To their immortal honour, within 17 years after their departure they had sent back to Ireland upwards of 13,000,000*l.* of money,* chiefly for the

* See Appendix, p. 36.

purpose of enabling their friends to follow their example. Now, unless they had prospered, these savings could not have been accumulated; unless their new existence had been full of promise they would not have tempted their brethren to join them. But what if, instead of setting forth to reap the golden harvests of the West, these forlorn multitudes had remained pent up within their rainy valleys, would the existing population, those that have clung to the old country in spite of everything,—would they be now the better or the worse? Two obvious consequences must have followed,— wages would have been lower, rents higher than they are now, while a very large proportion of the peasantry would be occupying farms half the size of those they are at present cultivating. Now, low wages and high rents may be advantageous in a certain sense to the manufacturer, to the landlord, and to the recruiting sergeant; but how do they affect the masses—the tenant, the labourer, and the mechanic?

When I was in the west of Ireland some 18 years ago, the rate of agricultural wages varied from half-a-crown to five shillings a week.* Ever since,

---

* The following extract sufficiently describes the former condition of the Irish Labourer:

" The earnings of the Labourers come on an average of the whole class from 2*s* to 2*s* 6*d* per week or thereabouts upon the year round.

" Their food commonly consists of dry potatoes, and with these they are at times so scantily supplied as to be obliged to

it has gradually advanced—in some places it has doubled—in others it has more than doubled. In the north, the farm servant has become almost master of the market, and is certainly better off than many of the small tenants;—in the south, though still not paid as he should be, his position is much improved, while, all over the country, the navvy, the quarryman, and the drainer are receiving from 10s to 12s a week.*

Occasionally complaints are being made of a dearth of hands: it is true this outcry generally means that at particular seasons of pressure, farmers can no longer turn into their fields at a moment's notice the crowd of ill-paid cotters that used to wait their pleasure in enforced idleness during the slack seasons of the year.† But any temporary inconvenience of this kind will be more than counterbalanced by the necessity which will be imposed on the landed interest, whether proprietors or tenants, to guarantee to those they wish to retain in their service, com-

stint themselves to one spare meal in the day. They sometimes get a herring or a little milk, but never get meat except at Christmas, Easter and Shrovetide."—*Report of Commission of 1834 on Condition of the People of Ireland.* See Appendix, p. 37.

* There seems to be a difference of opinion as to what is to be taken as the present rate of wages in Ireland. This is probably occasioned by wages varying in different localities, but to the best of my belief the above is a correct view of the general state of the case. For further information on the subject see Appendix, p. 37. See also Answers to Queries, pp. 278, 280.

† See Appendix, p. 37, and Answers to Queries, p. 283, and Mr. Robertson's Report, p. 350.

fortable lodging, fair remuneration, and above all, permanent employment. It is this growing difficulty of obtaining an unlimited amount of *casual* labour at low rates during summer, that is weaning the embarrassed tenant from his yearning after land. Eventually those only will be able to engage in farming with advantage who can either reduce their need of the labourer to a minimum, or can afford to pay him good wages all the year round. Hitherto the agricultural class has been composed too exclusively of occupiers, who though able to perform the ordinary operations required on their farms during two-thirds of the year, were dependent at seed time and harvest on a half-employed labouring population, who were relegated to idleness and penury, the moment the grain was sown, or stored.* A worse distribution of industry could not be imagined. What we want are fewer

* " Of the four seasons, two—the spring and autumn—are passed by our farmers in industry, however injudiciously applied. The summer and winter are too frequently passed by them in idleness."—*Dig. Dev. Com. Summary, p.* 366.

"No fact seems established more clearly by the Land Commission evidence, than that employment for the agricultural labourers is almost universally deficient."—*Ibid. p.* 473.

" The wretched condition of the labourers in Ireland is a necessary consequence of this deficiency of employment. The supply of labourers being so much greater than the demand for them, the employers are able to rate their wages at the lowest amount which will support life."—*Ibid. p.* 474.

" Every searching inquiry shows how extensively the want of employment and the want of enlightenment in their art influence the numberless indications of social derangement in Ireland, whether resulting in the miseries or crimes by which her

indigent occupiers and more constant employment for the labourer; for it is quite evident that an area cultivated by 10 farmers and 15 farm servants in constant work, would be better managed than if it were subdivided amongst 15 farmers who gave only occasional employment to 15 labourers.*

To those who closely watch the transitional phases of our national life, it is very evident that

people are characterized. No tariff upon land or rent can possibly dry up these two copious springs of national evil; and until they are dried up our crimes and our miseries will probably continue."—*Dig. Dev. Com. p.* 76.

"In a country in which farms are in general too small to afford employment for hired labour, a peasant has scarcely a chance of being able to gain a livelihood, unless he obtain possession of land; and in Ireland the competitors for land are so numerous that the price paid for the use of it has reached a degree of exorbitancy unheard of elsewhere: such keen competition clearly shows that population is excessive, that is to say that the labouring class is too numerous in proportion to the amount of employment for it; but it would be a mistake to regard this redundancy of population as a consequence of the prevalence of small farms."—*Thornton's Peasant Prop. p.* 188.

"From these premises it may be inferred that the present misery of the Irish peasantry is of no recent origin, but has been from time immemorial an heirloom in the race. The number of labourers has always been greatly in excess of the demand for labour, and the remuneration of labour has consequently never been much more than sufficient to procure the merest sustenance."—*Dig. Dev. Com. Summary, p.* 195.

Though these observations are less applicable now than when originally made, there is still too much truth in them.

* We should probably exceed the truth if we said that a third part of the Irish labouring population were employed all the year round. The remaining-two thirds obtain work at the seasons of extraordinary demand, viz., at the potato-digging,

the foregoing and other cognate agencies are gradually emancipating the farming classes from the tyranny of competition. During the last few years many a struggling tenant has been tempted by the rise of wages to hand his farm over to his more competent neighbour, and himself to pass from a life of precarious husbandry into the disciplined ranks of labour, where his industry is both better remunerated, and employed to a better purpose than ever it was before: and in proportion as the peasant becomes aware of the existence of a more hopeful theatre for his industry, whether at home or abroad, than that presented to him and his children by the miserable patch he miserably cultivates, that morbid hunger for a bit of land which has been the bane of Ireland will gradually subside; competition will relax something of its suicidal energy; and in the same way as the Irish labourer has already risen from the condition of a serf to an equality of comfort with his employer, will the tenant farmer, relieved from the lateral pressure of his superfluous associates,

and during the harvest.—*Sir G. Lewis on Irish Disturbances, p.* 312.

The remedy wanted for this state of things is to alter the mode of subsistence of the Irish peasant: to change him from a cottier living upon land to a labourer living upon wages: to support him by employment for hire instead of by a potatoe-ground. *This change can only be effected by consolidating the present minute holdings,* and creating a class of capitalist cultivators, who are able to pay wages to labourers, instead of tilling their own land with the assistance of the grown-up members of their family.—*Ibid. p.* 319.

be able to treat with his landlord on more independent terms.

But it may be objected by those who deplore emigration, that had these vanished thousands remained among us production would have been stimulated, and the well-being of the whole community proportionately increased. Let us see how far this would be a reasonable expectation.

Had no emigration taken place from Ireland, and had the population continued to multiply at its normal rate, the additional increase to our present numbers would by this time have amounted to three millions of souls, and as there is no reason to suppose that such a circumstance would have materially expanded the restricted manufacturing operations of the country, the larger proportion of these three millions would have had to depend upon the land for their support. Now, it appears from an official Report, drawn up on the conjoint authority of Archbishop Whately, Archbishop Murray, and Mr. Moore O'Farrell, that in 1846 five persons were employed in the cultivation of the soil of Ireland for every two that cultivated the same quantity of land in Great Britain, while the agricultural produce of Great Britain was four times the agricultural produce of Ireland.* As a matter of fact, therefore, so far as the past is concerned, the addition to the agricultural produce of Ireland has not been proportionate to the excess of the agricultural population.

* See Appendix, p. 37.

It may, however, be pretended that so unsatisfactory a result is to be accounted for by the unintelligent method in which this redundancy of labour has been applied to the soil. But in the Lothians of Scotland, and in certain parts of England, the art of agriculture is neither unintelligently nor unsuccessfully practised, and probably a given space is there made to produce as remunerative a crop as the united efforts of man and nature are destined to accomplish ;* yet in those

* Probably the gross produce per acre obtained by spade cultivation in parts of Flanders is greater—*though not very much greater* than what is raised from a corresponding area in well cultivated districts in England and Scotland, but the amount of profit enjoyed by the British agriculturist on the transaction is much higher than that obtained by the Belgian cultivator. In comparing Belgium with England, however, it must always be remembered that a great part of Belgium was originally a sand-bank, and that even if the acreable amount of produce in the two countries were the same, Belgian agriculture would have evinced a greater "*energy of production.*" The comparative yield per acre of England, Belgium, and Lombardy, is thus given by M. de Laveleye.

" Sous le rapport du produit brut, la Belgique se trouverait ainsi en premiere ligne parmi les Etats européens et les chiffres de la statistique viendraient confirmer ce que nous avait fait entrevoir l'observation directe. *Elle ne le céderait qu'à l'Angleterre* proprement dite, prise indépendamment de l'Écosse et de l'Irlande, et à la Lombardie ; car la première produit, d'après M. de Lavergne, 200 francs par hectare, et la seconde, d'apès M. Jacini, 400 millions sur un peu plus de 2 millions d'hectare, c'est à dire autant que l'Angleterre."

Eco. Rurale, p. 229

It is all a question of working at high or low pressure. By putting on more steam, I can add almost indefinitely to the

localities it has been found that about 18 men, with a small proportion of women, are sufficient to cultivate in the most efficient manner 500 acres of arable land.

Were we to apply this proportion to the 15,832,892 acres of land, under cattle and crops in Ireland, we shall see that some half million of persons would be able to cultivate the entire area.* But by the census returns of 1861 the number of adult males engaged in agricultural pursuits in that country are considerably over a million. Consequently, notwithstanding the emigration which has

speed of my ship, but at so rapidly increasing a cost of fuel, that the amount of coal expended in obtaining the last half knot exceeds the entire quantity necessary to produce the total velocity previously acquired. Now, though reasonable expedition may increase the profits on my cargo, it would not pay me to buy that expedition at a cost which would reduce those profits to a minimum. In the same way, there must be a point beyond which the increase of produce obtained by the application of additional labour to the soil will be less than sufficient to cover the cost of that labour. To adopt the rate of the gross produce as an unfailing test of the prosperity of the cultivators is therefore fallacious; a high rate of production is quite compatible with small profits and low wages. Whether it is better to subsoil with a plough at £1. 10s per acre, or to trench with spade labour at from £8. to £12. an acre, must be left to the discretion of the individual agriculturist. See Appendix, p. 38.

* "The extent of land in Ireland, either already cultivated, or capable of cultivation, may be stated at eighteen millions of acres, which, at the rate of one person for every twenty-eight acres, the proportion usual in England, would furnish work for 642,000 male adults."—*Thornton's Peasant Proprietors*, p. 211.

See Appendix, p. 38.

taken place, the disproportion between the respective amounts of agricultural labour, and the area cultivated in the two countries, which was noted in 1846 by Archbishop Murray and his colleagues as being in the ratio of 5 to 2, may still be taken as about 2 to 1. Of course, as I have already observed in a previous publication,* such a comparison can only be regarded as a rough approximation. On the one hand the canon which regulates the proportion of men to acres in a country of large farms, cannot be applied without modification to an area subdivided into such small holdings as prevail in Ireland, while on the other a correction must be made for the predominance of pasture lands in the one kingdom, and of tillage in the other. Making however every allowance for these counter considerations, it is probable that at the date of our last census, some three hundred thousand persons were engaged in the cultivation of the soil in excess of those whose exertions, if directed with greater skill and energy, and accompanied by an adequate expenditure of capital, would be sufficient to ensure us as high a rate of production as is obtained in the sister country.

Consequently, even making allowance for the decrease of the agricultural population which has since been going on, it is probable that there is still in Ireland a considerable section of the inhabitants with their wives and children dependent for their support

* Contributions to an Enquiry into the State of Ireland. *Murray*, 1866.

upon the land, whose misapplied industry is as unproductive as if it were devoted to the grinding of a treadmill or the lifting of shot; but though contributing nothing to the producing power of the class with which they are incorporated, they have to be supported out of its profits, of which they diminish by so much the share to the remainder. To deny this is to assert—that you can make a vessel sail faster by doubling the complement of her crew, and that the supernumerary hands will have made no impression on the ship's rations by the end of the voyage.*

* " In all countries which have passed beyond a rather early stage in the progress of agriculture, every increase in the demand for food occasioned by increased population will always, unless there is a simultaneous improvement in production, diminish the share which on a fair division would fall to each individual."
Mill's Principles of Political Economy, Vol. I. p. 237.
" If the growth of human power over nature is suspended or slackened, and population does not slacken its increase; if with only the existing command over natural agencies those agencies are called upon for an increased produce, this greater increase will not be afforded to the increased population, without either demanding on the average a greater effort from each, or on the average reducing each to smaller ration out of the aggregate produce."—*Ibid*. Vol. I. p. 240.
" From this results the important corollary, that the necessity of restraining population is not peculiar to a condition of great inequality of property. A greater number of people cannot, in any given state of civilization, be collectively so well provided for as a smaller. The niggardliness of nature, not the injustice of society, is the cause of the penalty attached to over-population. It is in vain to say, that all mouths which the increase of mankind calls into existence, bring with them hands. The new

But if, instead of the reduced numbers at present left in this false position, the hundreds of thousands who have emigrated had remained at home to breed and stagnate on the overburdened soil, is it not evident that a state of things would now exist in Ireland such as no man can think of without a shudder ? I do not wish, however, to imply that the existing surplus of agricultural labour, need necessarily follow their example. When once the rate of wages in a country has reached a point, which ensures to the labourer the necessaries and decencies of life, emigration ceases to be of such

mouths require as much food as the old ones, and the hands do not produce as much. If all instruments of production were held in joint property by the whole people, and the produce divided with perfect equality among them, and if in a society thus constituted, industry were as energetic and the produce as ample as at present, there would be enough to make all the existing population extremely comfortable; but when that population had doubled itself, as, with the existing habits of the people, under such an encouragement, it undoubtedly would in little more than twenty years, what would then be their condition? Unless the arts of production were in the same time improved in an almost unexampled degree, the inferior soils which must be resorted to, and the more laborious and scantily remunerative cultivation which must be employed on the superior soils, to procure food for so much larger a population, would, by an insuperable necessity, render every individual in the community poorer than before. If the population continued to increase at the same rate, a time would soon arrive when no one would have more than mere necessaries, and, soon after, a time when no one would have a sufficiency of those, and the further increase of population would be arrested by death."—*Ibid.* Vol. I. *p.* 238.

paramount importance, and no man could contemplate the expatriation of so many brave hearts, and strong right arms with equanimity. The true remedy for the anomaly I have indicated, is to be found in the development of our commercial enterprize, of our mineral resources, of our manufacturing industry:* it is not bloodletting to relieve a plethora, but stimulants to restore the balance of a congested circulation that are needed.

Still less would I advocate an attempt to divert, whether by moral pressure or otherwise, any portion of the land-occupying class from their present avocations. Persons of practical experience are aware that even in the most prosperous parts of Ireland, the extension of holdings undesirably diminutive, is continually taking place by a natural process, which need never involve the violent displacement of a single individual, and at a rate which rather exceeds than otherwise, the accumulation of the necessary capital in the hands of those, to whose farms the surrendered scraps of land are annexed. Death, bankruptcy, failing health, and the hundred casualties which diversify the current of human affairs, annually place at the disposal of the landlord a number of vacated tenancies, more than sufficient to carry out any amount of judicious consolidation. To hasten,

* I have never seen this view more admirably set forth than in the last pastoral of the Catholic Archbishop of Cashel.

therefore, the transition which the agricultural system of Ireland is gradually undergoing, is neither his interest nor his practice. It is true the slower the absorption of the surplus agricultural labour of the country into other pursuits, the worse for the general body of cultivators, but each year is improving their situation, and it is better the conviction of what is for their true advantage should penetrate their intelligence of its own accord, than that their prejudices should be shocked by any extraneous influences, however well intentioned.

But to imagine that even the most scrupulous observance of this rule, by every landlord in Ireland, could ever have prevented, or can now check the departure of a large proportion of the people is a delusion. The increase of every nation must be limited by the extent and capabilities of the area it occupies, and the amount of capital it possesses.*

This law is of universal application, though one race from its more sordid habits, or lower civilization, may be more compressible than another.†

---

* " It is also evident that the quantity of produce capable of being raised on any given piece of land is not indefinite. This limited quantity of land, and limited productiveness of it, are the real limits to the increase of production."

" From the preceding exposition it appears that the limit to the increase of production is twofold ; from deficiency of capital, or of land."—*Mill's Political Economy*, Vol. I. p. 220.

† " The desire to become possessed of one of these gardens operates very strongly in strengthening prudential habits and in restraining improvident marriages. Some of the manufacturers in the canton of Argovie told me that a townsman was

But, the appointed limits once reached, either the procreative energies of the people will be artificially restricted, as has been the case in France,* or

seldom contented until he had bought a garden, or a garden and house, and that the town labourers generally deferred their marriages for some years, in order to save enough to purchase either one or both of these luxuries."—*Mill's Political Economy*, Vol. I. p. 357.

"In some parts of Switzerland," says Mr. Kay, "as in the canton of Argovie for instance, a peasant never marries before he attains the age of 25 years, and generally much later in life; and in that canton the women very seldom marry *before they have attained the age of thirty.*"—*Ibid.* Vol. I. p. 357.

* "Un jeune ménage . . . . échappant par une *stérilité systématique* aux charges du mariage pousse rapidement sa fortune, ... Ceux au contraire . . . . . *qui conservent la tradition des mariages féconds* ne sortent pas de la condition de salariés."
—*La Réforme Sociale en France par M. F. le Play. Paris*, 1866, *p.* 388.

Whether a system which discourages marriage or delays it to a later age than that intended by nature, or checks fecundity by mechanical expedients, can be justly considered beneficial, is another question: in my own opinion, a race that marries, produces children, and populates the world, enjoys a happier destiny.

The town population of France, excluding Savoy, Savoy Haute, and Alpes Maritimes, as they were not included in 1856, was 9,844,828 in 1856, and 10,644,401 in 1861, the increase per cent in the five years was 8·12 or 1·57 per cent per annum. The rural population, excluding the above new departments, was 26,194,556 in 1856, and 26,072,853 in 1861: *there was therefore a decrease in the rural population;* the *decrease* per cent of the population in the five years being ·47 or ·09 per cent per annum.

The French returns make the town and rural population to have increased as follows:—

See Appendix, p. 34.

the surplus population will emigrate, as they have done from Germany, from Ireland, and to a lesser degree from England.

Up to the year 1846 the soil of Ireland retained the capacity of producing, to an almost unlimited extent, a certain root, containing all the elements necessary for the support of human life.* The ex-

Increase per cent in the five years . . 9·60 Town.
          "   "   . . 1·53 Rural.

Thus making the rural population increase instead of decrease, but this is not correct, as they have *excluded* Savoy, Savoy Hautes, and the Alpes Maritimes, in 1856, but *included* them in 1861. See App. p. 34.

* " A close analysis of this subject would probably lead to the conclusion, that the potato is the main cause of that inertia in the population, and that want of improvement in the lands and tillage, which is so striking throughout Ireland.

" This root, as compared with other food stuffs grown in this climate, supplied the largest amount of human food on the smallest surface. Its peculiar cultivation enabled the occupier of land to plant it in the wettest soils; because the ridge or lazy bed, universally adopted in such cases, supplied the most minute system of drainage that can be imagined for that one crop, although it did not permanently drain the land, or extend any substantial benefit in that respect even to the following crop.

" The indolent occupier, therefore, passed his winter inactively, consuming this food which he preferred to all others, and neglecting to prepare his land permanently for more profitable crops, of which he had heard little, and for which he cared less. Enjoying all the while the pleasing delusion, that, as sure as the spring came round, any portion he might select of his farm would be ready to receive his favourite root, and to furnish a certain supply of food for his numerous and increasing family.

" This delusion is now broken, but its evil consequences continue."—*Digest. Devon Commission, Summary, p.* 16.

pansion of the population was proportionate to the facilities it enjoyed for obtaining sustenance. Suddenly, by the visitation of God, those facilities were withdrawn; the potato failed; no other product of the soil existed to take its place; corn crops neither supplied the same amount of nutriment, nor could they be grown in successive years on the same spot. The life-sustaining power of the soil, had become restricted; as an inevitable consequence the population of the island has become proportionately restricted; and, exactly in the same way as the working classes of Manchester would have been obliged to remove to other centres of industry had the cotton famine continued, has the surplus population of Ireland been compelled to emigrate to a more fertile soil.

Though acting with diminished energy, the same causes may be expected for some time to come to produce similar results. The natural expansion of a prolific nation, still numbering upwards of five millions and a half, must be considerable. Did this increase maintain its normal rate, we might calculate on a net annual addition of 60,000 souls to our population; but as a large proportion of those who emigrate are men and women in their first youth, we must presume it has been considerably checked: putting however the excess of births over deaths at a minimum of 40,000 per annum, we shall confront a very formidable figure.* How are these

* See Appendix, p. 35.

successive waves of fresh arrivals to be accommodated?

Even those who most deplore emigration would not recommend a resubdivision for their benefit of holdings whose size at this moment is perhaps below the desirable average:* the labour market is only too amply supplied: agitation has succeeded in burking everywhere, except in Ulster, our nascent manufacturing enterprise;† what other

* Number of holdings not exceeding 1 acre, 48,653
„   „   5 „ 82,037
„   „   15 „ 176,308
                                  ———
                                  306,998

This is more than one-half of the entire number of farms in Ireland. Of the remainder, 136,578 are less than 30 acres in extent. Census, 1864.

† "Political excitement and agrarian outrage tend to discourage the introduction of English capital, limit the competitors in the market for those mortgaged estates that are sold, prevent the relief of the mortgager by a diminished rate of interest, and therefore cripple his means of assisting his tenantry, while they at the same time estrange the feelings of the tenant from the landlord, their interest being inseparable, and the progress of improvement being entirely dependent on their mutual co-operation.

"Thus we find, that the original causes, *ignorance and want of employment*, with their numerous evil effects, act and re-act upon each other in every possible variety of ways that can be imagined, to increase the miseries and disorders of society; and these destructive consequences must continue and extend until the original causes be removed by the sound instruction and profitable employment of the people.

"The present failure of the crop, as it renders utterly hopeless the position of those classes who have hitherto depended

alternative have you to offer, if you shut up their path across the sea? During the last five or six years, the emigration from Ireland has been a little over 90,000 a year; nearly one half of that emigration, therefore, has merely harmonized with the mechanical law, which only permits the introduction of water at one end of a pipe by the expulsion of a corresponding volume at the other.

In all parts of the world similar processes are occurring, and it is absurd to talk of Ireland, as the only country from which an extensive emigration has proceeded. From Germany alone, and principally from the North and West of Germany, as many as 250,000 persons have emigrated in a single year,* while between 1851 and 1861, even from

upon an acre of potatoes for their annual subsistence, will facilitate any humane measure which may be applied with a view to placing them where their labour may afford a more certain means of livelihood."— *Dig. Devon Commission, Summary, p.* 321.

* To those who will only regard emigration as the exponent of landlord cruelty, I would suggest that inasmuch as a very considerable emigration has been taking place from countries where these evil influences do not prevail, it may not be unreasonable to suppose that some one or other of those natural causes, which are noted by M. Jules Duval in his History of Emigration, as having occasioned emigration from Germany, viz.: a difficulty of procuring subsistence at home, low wages, bad harvests, *an excessive subdivision of the land*, and the attraction of the gold fields, have also promoted emigration from Ireland.

It has been objected that the population of Germany is 40,000,000, and the population of Ireland only 5,500,000; but in Germany 30,000,000 of people did not subsist on the potato, and the failure of the potato in Germany was not the same

Great Britain, the emigration has averaged as high as 74,000 a year.*

calamity that it was in Ireland. On the other hand, it would probably be as fallacious to distribute the German Emigration over the entire German nation, as to credit England with a proportional share in the emigration from the United Kingdom. M. Duval especially notes that hardly any emigration takes place from Austria.

I give M. Duval's statistics of the German Emigration up to the end of the last decade.

Number of Emigrants from Germany from the year 1847 to 1856:—

Year	Number
1847	109,531
1848	81,895
1849	89,102
1850	82,404
1851	112,547
1852	162,301
1853	162,568
1854	251,931
1855	81,968
1856	98,573
1857 } 1858 } 1859 }	108,000 (total of the 3 years.)

I also append the Official Statistics of the Immigration into the United States for 1860.

Immigrants from Great Britain and Ireland, 107,308; Germany, 86,675; British North American Provinces, 29,189; Norway, 8,075; France, 4,950; Switzerland, 2,704; Sweden, 4,523; Denmark, 1,769; Italy, 1,028; Holland, 1,314; Belgium, 1,185.

Of late the Immigration from Germany seems to have been on the increase. The following returns have been made by the New York Commissioners of Emigration for the past year (1866).

Immigrants from Germany, 106,716; Ireland, 68,047; England, 36,186; other countries, 22,469.

* See Appendix, p. 39, Some Observations of the Duke of Argyll and Sir John M'Neill on Emigration from the Highlands of Scotland.

Still more unreasonable is it to describe the "ruling classes" as standing alone in their opinion, an opinion most unjustly ascribed to "their stupidity and selfishness," that emigration has been no calamity to Ireland.

In the first place, to call emigration a calamity, implies a confusion of ideas.

Emigration may be occasioned by a calamity: it may be followed by disastrous consequences: but it is in itself a curative process: and to confound it with the evils to which it affords relief, would be as great a blunder as to mistake the distressing accidents of suppuration for symptoms of mortification. Plans for the express purpose of stimulating emigration have been devised and advocated from time to time by such men as Mr. Smith O'Brien, Sir Thomas Wyse, Mr. Sharman Crawford, Sir George C. Lewis,* and Mr. Cobden;† while, did

* See Appendix, p. 34.

† "But, unhappily, the maladies of Ireland have taken such deep root, that legislation cannot hope, for ages to come, effectually to eradicate them, whilst here is a mode by which hundreds of thousands of our fellow-creatures are eager to be enabled to escape a lingering death. Surely under such circumstances, this plan, which would leave us room to administer more effectually to the cure of her social disorder deserves the anxious consideration of our legislature.

"Here let us demand why some forty or fifty of our frigates and sloops of war, which are now, at a time of peace, sunning themselves in the Archipelago, or anchoring in friendly ports, or rotting in ordinary in our own harbours, should not be employed by the Government in conveying these emigrants to Canada, or some other hospitable accommodation."

Extract from Cobden's Political Writings. Vol. I. p. 83.

space permit, I might furnish dozens of quotations to show how common this conviction has been to every school of politics and class of society.*

To attribute such a view to landlord stupidity and selfishness is even more gratuitous. When did a tradesman ever complain of the multitude of his customers, or a manufacturer of the easiness of the labour-market? And what is the owner of an estate other than a trader in land? His tenants are his customers; the more strenuous their competition, the higher his rents, and the denser their number, the more keenly will they compete;†

* "As a means of alleviating the distress occasioned by the removal of tenants, it was proposed by the Select Committee on the state of Ireland in 1832, that public money should be given in aid of such sums as may be paid by a landlord to a removed and destitute tenant, with a view to its being employed in emigration."—*Digest Devon Commission, Summary*, p. 1113.

† "Rent being regulated by competition, depends upon the relation between the demand for land, and the supply of it. The demand for land depends on the number of competitors, and the competitors are the whole rural population. The effect, therefore, of this tenure (cottier tenancies) is to bring the principle of population to act directly on the land, and not, as in England, on capital. Rent, in this state of things, depends on the proportion between population and land. As the land is a fixed quantity, while population has an unlimited power of increase; unless something checks that increase, the competition for land soon forces up rent to the highest point consistent with keeping the population alive. The effects, therefore, of cottier tenure depend on the extent to which the capacity of population to increase is controlled, either by custom, by individual prudence, or by starvation and disease."

Mill's Political Economy, p. 392.

emigration has a tendency to diminish rather than to increase his rental, and if it has not done so already it is because the number of those who seek to obtain their living by the land, are still out of proportion to the area capable of maintaining them.

Again, the landlord is very often a large employer of labour. Within the last 15 years I myself have paid away upwards of £60,000 in wages alone. During the last half of that period, in consequence of the rise in wages, I have got much less for my money than I did during the first half, and my consequent loss, comparing one period with another, would amount to several thousand pounds, and this has been a direct consequence of emigration. But, though a dealer in land, and a

"If the owners of land be liable to the imputation of usury in their bargains for rent, the best and only effectual corrective will be found in reducing the competition amongst the labourers and occupiers of land by removing the ignorance of our husbandmen, and also the impediments to the extension of employment."

"If these two principles should prove inadequate to establish the equilibrium of the labour market in this country on a sound basis, we have still the vast resource of emigration, which, when used upon a humane principle, will improve our condition at home with extreme and certain benefit to those who leave our shores; and no other principle of emigration ought for a moment to be tolerated."—*Digest Devon Commission, Summary, p.* 757.

"The only unobjectionable way of enabling tenants to obtain reasonable terms from their landlords, is to diminish the competition for land by lessening the number of competitors."
Thornton's Peasant Proprietors, pp. 215-16.

payer of wages, I am, above all things, an Irishman, and as an Irishman I rejoice at any circumstance which tends to strengthen the independence of the tenant farmer, or to add to the comforts of the labourer's existence.

But it is said, that though as yet no inconvenient diminution of the agricultural population has occurred, as is proved by the still inadequate rate of wages in the rural districts, emigration is acquiring a momentum which will carry it far beyond all reasonable limits.* This I admit to be a contingency deserving serious attention: but the first precaution to be taken is to fix those classes most exposed to the current, in a position of such comfort and stability as will enable them to resist

---

* " But, these things being as they are—though a judiciously conducted emigration is a most important resource for suddenly lightening the pressure of population by a single effort—and though in such an extraordinary case as that of Ireland, under the threefold operation of the potato failure, the poor law, and the general turning out of tenantry throughout the country, spontaneous emigration may at a particular crisis remove greater multitudes than it was ever proposed to remove at once by any national scheme ; it still remains to be shown by experience whether a permanent stream of emigration can be kept up, sufficient to take off, as in America, all that portion of the annual increase (when proceeding at the greatest rapidity) which being in excess of the progress made during the same short period in the arts of life, tends to render living more difficult for every averagely-situated individual in the community. And unless this can be done, emigration cannot, even in an economical point of view, dispense with the necessity of checks to population."—*Mill's Polit. Economy*, p. 246.

its influence. Such an object will be far more surely promoted by whatever tends to abate the tyranny of competition, than by offering those who are now hustling one another off the land any artificial inducements to continue the scramble.

Others suggest that the great works of irrigation and reclamation which still require to be executed in Ireland, would more than absorb all the redundant population. To this I reply, in the first place, that during the very period which has witnessed the greatest emigration, larger areas have been reclaimed, than have ever been before;* that the productive powers of the soil have been increasing in a ratio nearly corresponding to that at which the population has diminished; and that as we still have one adult cultivator to every six acres of land under crops, it is not any want of hands which hinders the island being converted into a garden from one end to the other. In the next place, the very thing I desire, is to see our surplus labour power, now frittered away in the desultory cultivation of fields which ought to produce twice as much with one-third fewer hands, intelligently applied to the development of the country's resources. All that I contend for is, that while you are collecting your capital,† and organizing your plans, for the intro-

* Between 1844 and 1862 more than 2,000,000 acres of waste land have been reclaimed. See Appendix, p. 43.

† "Self-evident as the thing is, it is often forgotten that the people of a country are maintained and have their wants

duction of that millenium of enterprise which has already disappointed the hopes of previous generations, you have no right to keep the men, whose grand-children you may perhaps eventually provide with employment, standing idle and starving in the market-place.*

supplied, not by the produce of present labour, but of past. They consume what has been produced, not what is about to be produced. Now, of what has been produced, a part only is allotted to the support of productive labour; and there will not and cannot be more of that labour than the portion so allotted (which is the capital of the country) can feed, and provide with the materials and instruments of production.

Yet, in disregard of a fact so evident, it long continued to be believed that laws and governments, without creating capital, could create industry."—*Mill's Political Economy*, p. 80.

* Mr Fawcett thus speaks of emigration in his essay on the 'British Labourer:'—" From England and Scotland, during the last fifteen or twenty years, there has been a very large emigration, although the people have not been compelled to leave these countries by so sudden and awful a catastrophe as that which caused the Irish exodus. . . . . When we reflect on the pecuniary advantages which every emigrant may reasonably expect to obtain, it seems surprising that our labourers have not left us in much greater numbers. . . . . . The ordinary wages of our agricultural labourers are not more than nine or ten shillings a week; many of them live in dwellings which do not deserve the name of human habitations. . . . . It seems wonderful that men who are in this condition do not emigrate *en masse.*"

Again, he says, " The truth, therefore, becomes irresistibly brought home to our minds, that if a man finds his labour is not wanted in one country he ought not to stagnate there in hopeless poverty. There is placed before him in other lands a great and glorious career: a great career, because he may become the progenitor of mighty nations; a glorious career, because he

Again, it is asked, what is to become of the manufacturing industry of Great Britain if the normal flow of Irish labour should suddenly run dry? How are the armies of England to be recruited if the magic shilling no longer has attractions for the Irish peasant?

With such ill-omened surmises as these I have no sympathy. However serious the contingencies suggested, it is very certain the solution must be sought elsewhere than in the maintenance of a fourth of the population of Ireland at starving point. A perennial flow of cheap labour into Lancashire and of broken Irishmen into the Queen's service, means perennial indigence and discontent in Munster and Connaught;—and discontent in her Southern provinces means the perpetual abstraction from the available forces of the Empire of a garrison nearly as large as the military contingent furnished by all Ireland. To foster, therefore, an excess of population with the intention of forcing the most desperate of their numbers to

---

will abundantly fulfil the behests of his Maker if he causes the wilderness to become the home of civilized man. This world was made for the occupation of the human race, and it never could be intended that fertile soils should grow nothing but rank and useless vegetation. It never could be intended that rivers which might stimulate production of untold wealth should always continue to flow through solitudes; it never could be intended, we may unhesitatingly say, that scenes should continue to be viewed by no human eye, which are so beautiful, that their contemplation must make man look from Nature up to Nature's God."—*The Economic Position of the British Labourer, by Henry Fawcett, M.P.*, p. 209.

embrace an existence which the gradual improvement in his condition has taught the Highland gillie and the Kentish yokel to disdain, is hardly a remunerative speculation.* Of the humanity of regarding the sister kingdom as a reservoir of impoverished war material, and stagnant labour-power, to be turned on as the convenience of England may require, I will say nothing. Even the butcher fattens his sheep before he drives them to the shambles, and to speculate on Irish destitution to man the looms of Manchester for all eternity, seems to me hardly more excusable than to advocate the continuance of slavery in the tropics, for the sake of fine cotton and cheap sugar.

Notwithstanding therefore all that has been said to the contrary, I still consider that not only has emigration been an infinite blessing to Ireland, but that for some years to come a considerable portion of the nation will continue to profit by its advantages. I am aware that this is an unpopular opinion, and I may be told that I am rejoicing in the expatriation of my countrymen, but to those who can attach such a meaning to the foregoing sentences, it would be idle to address further explanation. Both in Parliament and elsewhere I have recorded my conviction that were it not for the agitation which now scares capital from her shores, and prevents the development of her industrial resources, Ireland might be rendered capable of sustaining a population far larger than any she has ever borne,

* See Appendix, pp. 39, 44.

and no one has deplored in more emphatic terms than myself the circumstances which compel so many noble-hearted Irishmen to leave the land of their birth.* But to lament an emigration you are unable to arrest, and which is composed of those you cannot employ, is a useless waste of feeling. There are few human passions with which I have greater sympathy, or which I can better understand, than the love of home; but in this life no one can arrange his destiny altogether to his taste; and to sally forth and battle with the world is one of the most universal conditions of existence. It is all very well to talk pathetically of the hardship endured by the Irish peasant in quitting the home of his childhood, but to dwell for ever in the home of one's childhood is almost the rarest earthly luxury which can be mentioned; not one man in ten thousand expects to enjoy it; no woman desires it. Law in France, custom in America discourage such permanent arrangements, while in England they are only within the reach of a comparatively small minority.

Expatriation is undoubtedly a great calamity, but emigration does not necessarily imply expatriation. Hundreds of those who go, return, and if the greater number stay it is only because they prefer to do so. Nor, when Providence spread out the virgin prairies of the New World, or stored up the golden treasures of Australia, can it have been intended that attachment to the natal soil should

* See Appendix, p.

become so predominant a passion as to deter man from taking possession of the new territories prepared for his reception. Far then from being in itself a calamity, emigration is an essential element in the future progress of the United Kingdom, and our fellow countrymen who depart, even if absorbed by an alien community, often minister to our prosperity more effectually than when they dwelt amongst us. The transformation of an indigent and disaffected subject into a prosperous foreign customer is a change not wholly disadvantageous, and the industry which has gone forth to till the prairies of the West cheapens the loaf to millions in the old country.*

One thing at all events is certain. In the progress of every civilized community, the period must arrive when the natural increase of population overtakes the normal rate of production. The true remedy may be to communicate additional fertility to the soil: but this is seldom an immediate possibility :† as a consequence the rate of increase of

* We now import nearly 2,700,000 quarters of Indian corn a year; before 1846 our imports of Indian corn only amounted to 11,000 quarters per annum. See Appendix, p. 35.

† " Whether, at the present or any other time, the produce of industry proportionally to the labour employed, is increasing or diminishing, and the average condition of the people improving or deteriorating, depends upon whether population is advancing faster than improvement, or improvement than population. After a degree of density has been attained, sufficient to allow the principal benefits of combination of labour, all further increase tends in itself to mischief, so far as

the population must be checked; or its standard of comfort must deteriorate; or its accruing surplus must remove.* But the first necessitates an artificial and often an unnatural social system, as is said to prevail in France;† and the next is an alternative which entails the physical degradation we have seen supervene in Ireland. There remains therefore the third,—a course in perfect harmony with the laws of nature, and one which has already established the religion, the language, and the freedom of England, over one-fourth of the habitable globe. To lament the exhibition of so much enterprise, vital energy, and colonising power, in the race to which we belong,‡ seems to me more

regards the average condition of the people."—*Mill's Political Economy*, p. 239.

* " But though improvement may during a certain space of time keep up with, or even surpass, the actual increase of population, it assuredly never comes up to the rate of increase of which population is capable; and nothing could have prevented a general deterioration in the condition of the human race, were it not that population has in fact been restrained. Had it been restrained still more, and the same improvements taken place, there would have been a larger dividend than there now is, for the nation or the species at large."—*Ibid.* p. 241.

† " Le Partage forcé affecte à la fois la petite et la grande propriété rurale; il détruit les petits domaines agglomérés, à *familles fécondes,* et les remplace par ces petits domaines morcelés où la fécondité conduit fatalement au paupérisme, et où le bien-être des individus se fonde *sur la stérilité du mariage* et sur l'egoïsme."—*La Réforme Sociale en France, par M. F. le Play,* Vol. I. p. 396.

‡ Saxon and Celt have taken an equal part in emigration from Ireland.—See Appendix, pp. 41-85.

perverse than to stigmatize as a curse the blessing originally pronounced on those who were first bidden " to go forth and multiply and replenish the earth."

APPENDIX.

Vital Statistics.—France. (*See supra, p.* 18.)

" The slow rate of increase of population in France compared with that of England may, therefore, be chiefly attributed to a low ratio of births, the result of late marriages *and of hindrances to fecundity.* Early marriages have the effect of shortening the interval between generations, and tend in that way to increase the population. The spirit and character of a nation alone determine the limit to its numbers; and the increasing power and prosperity of England and her colonies, resulting from a high rate increase of population, have proved the fallacy of the doctrine " that the increase of the human race should be restricted, so that it may not outstrip the means of subsistence." The proportion of deaths to 1,000 persons living in each of the two countries, France and England, was 21·96 and 22·88 in 1853; 23·57 and 21·80 in 1857; 23·18 and 21·63 in 1861; and 21·72 and 23·86 in 1864. In France, in 1854 and 1855, the deaths exceeded the births. The mean after-lifetime, or expectation of life in England, is 40·9 years. In France it is 39·7 years."

Sir G. Lewis on Irish Emigration. (*See supra, p.* 23.)

"The operation of a system of relief in facilitating the transition of cottier farmers into labourers ought at the same time to be assisted by *colonization*, and this on as large a scale as the means of the country would permit. The redundancy of the Irish population is so great, that no one measure can in a short time be expected to produce even an approximation to the great desideratum, the maintenance of the peasantry out of wages. An extensive emigration managed by Government, and in combination with agents in Canada and the United States, would at any rate assist in bringing about this consummation. If Ireland (as it was once remarked to me) could be stretched out like a piece of india-rubber, the peasantry would be as tranquil and contented as that of England. But as this is impossible, we must strive to do what is possible. As we cannot make more land to the inhabitants, we must make fewer inhabitants to the land."—*Sir G. C. Lewis on Irish Disturbances, p. 332.*

The Effect of Emigration on Population in Ireland.
(See supra, p. 19.)

Though 500,000 persons have emigrated since 1860 the actual decrease in the population has been only 216,444, showing that the natural increase by births over deaths has filled up nearly one half of the vacancies created by emigration during the same period.

Population.	Deaths.	Births.	
5,788,415	2,831,783	2,956,632	1861
5,784,527	2,828,357	2,956,170	1862
5,739,569	2,801,963	2,937,606	1863
5,675,306	2,765.501	2,909,803	1864
5,641,086	2,745,753	2,895,333	1865
5,571,971	2,696,722	2,875.249	1866

IMPORTATIONS OF WHEAT AND FLOUR.   *(See supra, p. 32.)*

               Quarters in the Year.
Before 1846 (average of 7 years)   .   127,958
In 1860   1,383,609
In 1861   1,412,809
In 1862 .   .   .   .   .   2,112.715

IMPORTATIONS OF INDIAN CORN AND MEAL.

               Quarters in the Year.
Before 1846 (average of 7 years)   .   11,007
In 1860   1,317,514
In 1861   1,970,988
In 1862   1,773,255

Twenty-fifth General Report, 1865. (*See supra, p.* 3.)

Return showing Amounts of Money remitted by Settlers in North America to their Friends in the United Kingdom from 1848 (the first Year in which we have any Information) to 1864, both inclusive.

Year.	Amount.
	£.
1848	460,000
1849	540,000
1850	957,000
1851	990,000
1852	1,404,000
1853	1,439,000
1854	1,730,000
1855	873,000
1856	951,000
1857	593,165
1858	472,610
1859*	575,378
1860†	576,932
1861‡	426,285
1862§	381,901
1863¶	412,053
1864**	416,605

* During this year the sum of 45,798*l*. was also remitted from Australia.
† Do. do. 66,713*l*. do. do.
‡ Do. do. 78,095*l*. do. do.
§ Do. do. 81,123*l*. do. do.
¶ Do. do. 48,058*l*. do. do.
** Do. do. 44,631*l*. do. do.

Note.—In addition to the above amounts for 1863, 44,123*l*. were remitted from America and Australia, but the sum from each place cannot be specified.

S. Walcott.

Government Emigration Board,
8, Park Street, Westminster, April 1865.

Condition of the Irish People in 1834.

(*See supra, pp.* 3 & 9.)

"The Commissioners appointed in 1834 for inquiring into the condition of the poorer classes in Ireland—a Commission comprising amongst it members Archbishop Whately, Archbishop Murray, and the Right Hon. More O'Ferrall—at the commencement of their Third Report, published in 1836, state their opinion as to the condition in which the labouring classes of the Irish people were at that time. They say:—

"It appears that in Great Britain the agricultural families constitute little more than one-fourth, while in Ireland they constitute two-thirds of the whole population; that there were in Great Britain in 1831; 1,055,982 agricultural labourers; In Ireland, 1,131,715: although the cultivated land of Great Britain amounts to about 34,250,000 acres, and that of Ireland only to about 14,000,000. We thus find that there are in Ireland about five agricultural labourers for every two that there are for the same quantity of land in Great Britain. It further appears that the agricultural produce of Great Britain is more than four times that of Ireland; that agricultural wages of Ireland vary from 6d to 1s a-day; that the average of the country in general is about 8½d; and that the earnings of the labourers come on an average of the whole class to from 2s to 2s 6d a-week or thereabouts for the year round. . . . A great portion of them (agricultural labourers) are insufficiently provided at any time with the commonest necessaries of life. Their habitations are wretched hovels; several of the family sleep together on straw, or on the bare ground, sometimes with a blanket, sometimes with not even so much to cover them. Their food commonly consists of dry potatoes; and with these they are at times so scantily supplied as so be obliged to stint themselves to one spare meal in the day. . . They sometimes get a herring or a little milk, but they never get meat except at Christmas, Easter, and Shrovetide."—(P. 3.)

That the condition of the labouring classes in Ireland had not improved up to the famine, is shown by the Report of the Land Occupation Commissioners in 1845. They say:—

"In adverting to the condition of the different classes of occupiers in Ireland, we perceive with deep regret the state of the cottiers and labourers in most parts of the country from want of certain employment. It would be impossible to describe adequately the privations which they and their families almost habitually and patiently endure. It will be seen in the evidence that in many districts their only food is the potato, their only beverage water; that their cabins are seldom a protection against the weather; that a bed or a blanket is a rare luxury; and that nearly in all, their pig and their manure heap constitute their only property."

"Such being the condition of a large proportion of the people of Ireland from 1834 till 1845 when the population was at its highest amount, it is perfectly clear that a *mere increase* of population was no proof of prosperity; and if so, it is idle to argue that a *mere decrease* of the population is necessarily an evidence of decline."—*W. N. Neilson Hancock, LL.D., Supposed Progressive Decline, &c.*

Comparison of Profits on Large and Small Farms.
(See *supra*, p. 11, note.)

"This I take to be the true reason why large cultivation is generally most advantageous as a mere investment for profit. Land occupied by a large farmer is not, in one sense of the word, farmed so highly. There is not nearly so much labour expended on it. This is not on account of any economy arising from combination of labour, but because, by employing less, a greater return is obtained in proportion to the outlay."—*Mill's Political Economy, p.* 186.

Spade versus Plough. (See *supra*, p. 11, note.)

"Again, the subsoiling by spade labour may cost from 10s 8d per acre, as performed by Mr. Wilson, to £7 or £8, or even £12 per acre, as described by M. Barber, by trenching."—*Dig. Dev. Com. Summary, p.* 82.

"The cost of ordinary subsoiling with the plough may be taken at about £1 10s per acre."—*Ibid. p.* 83.

"The ordinary spade subsoiling and trenching, which consists in moving the soil with the spade to two spits deep, must always be a most costly operation."

Ibid. p. 84.

Pay of the English Soldier. (*See supra, p.* 30.)

The following extract gives a very fair estimate of the military as compared with the civil labour market in England and Scotland.

"Let us now shortly examine the state of the facts with regard to the actual terms we offer. We engage to give every recruit 7s 7d a week, and certain prospective advantages of good conduct pay and pension, with lodging, fuel, light, and medical attendance. I purposely exclude from this estimate certain articles of clothing which we have to give soldiers gratis, and certain articles of food which we supply to him on peculiar advantageous terms, as the sum which he must still expend on food and clothing, notwithstanding these advantages is equal to that which food and clothing would probably cost him in civil life." . . . .

"We buy the man out and out for the period of his service. We require him to give up in a great measure his ordinary civil rights, place him under a severe discipline, force him to serve, even in time of peace, two-thirds of his time abroad in climates which are often of great severity, forbid him to marry, and expose him to risks and discomforts to which no walk in civil life affords any parallel. It cannot be said that this bargain is to us a hard one. *Nay, is it not evident that relatively to the present enhanced price, even of unskilled civil labour, it is a most advantageous one for the employer?*"

Extract from "*Our Military Forces and Reserves,*" by *Major Millar Bannatyne*, p. 10.

Emigration from the Scotch Highlands. (*See supra*, p. 21.)

The following conclusions arrived at by the Duke of Argyll and Sir John McNeill with respect to the Emigration from the Highlands of Scotland, are very apposite to the topics considered in the foregoing chapter :—

"I will now shortly restate to the Society the facts and conclusions which can, I think, be satisfactorily established in regard to the past and present economic condition of the Highlands :—

1. That before the end of the last of the civil wars, the condition of the population was one of extreme poverty and frequent destitution.

2. That on the close of those wars, and the establishment of a settled Government, there was, during half a century, a rapid increase of population.

3. That this increase was out of all proportion to the means of subsistence.

4. That the introduction of potato cultivation increased the evil of a rapid increase in population, without any corresponding increase in skill or industry.

5. That the emigration of the Highlanders arose as a necessity out of this condition of things, and was in itself the first step towards improvement.

6. That the introduction of sheep farming was a pure gain, not tending to diminish the area of tillage where tillage is desirable, and turning to use for the first time a large part of the whole area of the country, which was formerly absolute waste.

7. That for the old bad cultivation of small crofters there has been substituted for the most part a middle class of tenantry, thriving, holding under lease, and exhibiting all the conditions of agricultural prosperity.

8. That the displacement of population by the introduction of great capitalists holding farms of very large value, has not taken place in the Highland counties to an extent nearly equal to that in which it has taken place in some of the richest counties of Scotland.

9. That the process which has been going on in the Highland counties, of a diminution in the population of the rural districts, is the same process which has long ago been accomplished in the other counties of Scotland and in England.

10. That in their case it was also deplored under the same economic fallacies—fallacies which are now applied only to the Highlands because the process is not yet completed.

11. That the prosperity of the Highlands will only be complete when the process shall have been completed also.

12. That no part of Scotland, considering the late period at which improvement begun, has advanced so rapidly, or given within an equal space of time, so large and so solid an addition to the general wealth of the country."

Extract from the Duke of Argyle's Pamphlet on the Condition of the Highlands of Scotland, p. 534.

"Any one acquainted with the county of Argyll will at once perceive that this progressive diminution in the proportion of paupers to population corresponds closely with the diminution in the proportion of the population depending for subsistence on the produce of small crofts, and that the proportion of paupers increases as we recede from the districts in which the old crofting system has been superseded, and the system of the more advanced parts of the country has been established."

Extract from Mem. by Sir John McNeill, K.C.B., President of the Poor Law Board in Scotland.

Note as to the Reduction in the number of Persons of different Religions and Races in Ireland, from 1834 *till* 1861. (See *p*. 33).

A religious census of Ireland was taken in 1834 by the Commissioners of Public Instruction, and, when compared with the religious census of 1861, it exhibits a very great reduction in the population of Ireland.

Population of all Ireland.
In 1834 . . . 7,954,100
In 1861 . . . 5,798,967

This shows a decrease of 2,155,133, or of 27 per cent.

The greatest part of this total reduction took place amongst Roman Catholics, who may be taken to represent the Celtic element of the Irish population.

Roman Catholics in Ireland.
In 1834 . . . 6,436,060
In 1861 . . . 4,505,165

Decrease . 1,930,795

The members of the Established Church—the element mainly of English origin—were:

In 1834 . . . 853,160
In 1861 . . . 693,357

Showing a decrease of 159,803, or about 19 per cent.

The Presbyterians—the element chiefly of Lowland Scotch extraction—were:—

In 1834 . . . 643,058
In 1861 . . . 523,291

Showing a reduction of 119,797, or about 19 per cent.

It has been supposed from these figures that there has been something unfair in the way in which the Celtic population has been dealt with.

But if we take the largest Presbyterian agricultural population, that of the diocese of Derry (which includes the greater part of the county of Londonderry, the barony of Innishowen, and a few parishes in Donegal, three baronies and two parishes in Tyrone, and one parish in Antrim), we get the following result:—

Presbyterians in Diocese of Derry.
In 1834 118,339
In 1861 79,287

Decrease . 39,052, or at the rate of about 33 per cent.

Again, if we take the agricultural population belonging to the Established Church in the south of Ireland, in the diocese of Ferns (which includes the whole country of Wexford except three parishes, part of Wicklow, and one parish in Carlow), we get the following result :—

Members of the Established Church
in the Diocese of Ferns.
In 1834 24,672
In 1861 14,383

Showing a decrease in 1861, 10,289, or 42 per cent.

If we take the Roman Catholic population in the diocese of Tuam, the largest diocese in Connaught (which includes a large part of Galway, part of Mayo, and one parish in Roscommon), we get :—

Roman Catholics in Diocese of Tuam.
In 1834 467,870
In 1861 302,367

Showing a decrease of 165,603, or 35 per cent.

In the same way, if we take the Roman Catholics in the diocese of Ardfert and Aghador (which includes all Kerry except two parishes, and part of Cork), we get :—

Roman Catholics in Ardfert (Kerry).
In 1834 227,131
In 1861 215,028

Showing a decrease of 82,103, or at the rate of 28 per cent.

It appears, therefore, that there has been about the same decrease of agricultural population from 1834 to 1861, in Derry, in Wexford, in Galway, and in Kerry; the same among the original Celts, the Scotch settlers, and the English settlers; the same in the diocese which includes the estates of the London Companies; the Protestant landlords of Wexford, the county of Kerry, with its large resident proprietors, many of them Roman Catholics, and in Galway.

The Presbyterian and Protestant emigration commenced earlier, and took place to a large extent before the famine, because they were then better educated than the Roman Catholics. When a generation of Roman Catholics grew up, who had been educated in the National Schools, commenced in 1830, they followed the example of the Presbyterians and the members of the Established Church. The famine accelerated this movement, but it would have taken place before the present time if the famine had never occurred.

W. N. HANCOCK, LL.D.

Reclamation of Waste Land in Ireland.

As to the Cultivation of Waste Land in Ireland, and its effect on Emigration. (See supra, p. 27.)

In 1841 the land of Ireland was thus distributed:—

Arable	13,464,000
Plantations	374,482
Water	630,825
Uncultivated	6,295,735

The 6,295,735 acres of uncultivated land were frequently referred to in the evidence before the Land Occupation Commissioners, and in their report.

In consequence of the extensive drainage works carried on to give relief at the time of the famine, and in consequence of the number of mountain and bog roads, made at that time under the public works and under private proprietors for the purpose of giving employment, a great deal of land was brought within the limits of profitable cultivation between 1841 and 1851. It was accordingly reported by the Census Commissioners in 1851, that the arable land of Ireland had increased from 13,464,300 acres in 1841, to 14,802,581 in 1851, showing an increase of 1,338,281 acres. The waste land had diminished from 6,295,735 acres in 1841, to 5,023,984 acres in 1851, showing a decrease of 1,271,751 acres. There was also a diminution of about 70,000 acres of plantation, converted into arable land.

Sir Richard Griffith reported in 1844, that 1,425,000 acres were improvable for cultivation, and 2,330,000 were improvable for pasture, making a total of 3,755,000 acres improvable.

As the drainage and making of roads consequent on the famine were all executed after 1844, it follows that the greater part of the 1,271,751 acres reclaimed between 1841 and 1851, were reclaimed between 1844 and 1851, and yet this period of the most rapid reclamation of waste land in Ireland that probably ever took place, was followed by the largest emigration, showing how little the improvement of waste land in Ireland, the greater part of which, according to Sir Richard Griffith, is improvable only for pasture, (and which when improved has in fact been principally devoted to pasture) can be relied on as an important means of checking emigration, when it arises from comparatively low wages and inadequate means of living in Ireland.

Since 1851 the reclamation of waste land seems to have gone

on at a slower rate ; the best and most profitable land having been first cultivated, and the inferior soils being exposed by facility of intercourse and free trade to an increased competition with foreign soils.

From 1851 to 1862 the waste lands have been ascertained by the Registrar-General, and appears to have been reduced from 5,209,492 acres in 1851, to 4,507,733 in 1862, showing a decrease of 701,759 acres in waste since 1851.

If these be added to the 1,271,751 acres reclaimed between 1841 and 1851 (and mostly since 1844), it follows that of the 3,755,000 acres reported by Sir R. Griffith, to have been improvable at the commencement of 1845, almost 1,973,510 acres, or more than one-half have been reclaimed since 1844.

Thus, instead of the 3,755,000 acres, reported by Sir R. Griffith improvable in 1844, there would appear to be a little less than half that quantity (and that, of course, the most unprofitable half) now available for improvement.

As an increase of pasturage in Ireland, as well as an alleged neglect of cultivating improvable waste land, is often urged as a cause of the emigration, it is important to notice that the true explanation of pasture having increased so largely in Ireland, without any material diminution of the land under tillage, is to be found in the fact that nearly 2,000,000 acres have, as before shown, been reclaimed at that time.

W. N. HANCOCK, LL.D.

The Emancipation of the Dorsetshire Labourer.

In connection with the subject of Irish emigration it may not be out of place to consider an incident which has lately met with a good deal of attention from those who interest themselves in the condition of the Dorsetshire labourer.

I give it as described in the "Times" of April 2nd, 1867.

" Distressed at their unsatisfactory condition, Mr. Girdlestone saw that their wages could only be improved by the force of competition. So he announced in our columns his willingness to act as a sort of agent for introducing the labourers of his district to masters elsewhere who would give them more liberal pay. He at once received numerous applications from Lancashire, Yorkshire, Lincolnshire, Kent, and even from Ireland, and the result has been that within six months he has sent out of his parish and neighbourhood as many as fifty labourers, of whom only one has as yet returned, of these sixteen are married men with families, and the remainder single men. The married men, instead of 7s. a week, are in no case earning less than 12s. a week, in addition to a house and garden. In fact, they have doubled their wages. Nor is this the most important result. Of course, the rate of wages about Halberton has risen at the least by 1s., and in some places by 2s. a week. The process, having been once thus started, must, of course, go further. Those who have migrated will continue to send back accounts of their prosperity; and if the farmers want to keep the young men of Halberton in their service, they will have to pay them as high wages as they can gain elsewhere."—*Times, April* 2, 1867.

"Of course, this is not in all respects an agreeable task to undertake. The farmers in such neighbourhoods as these are not the most enlightened of their class, and will scarcely appreciate a change of which the only effect immediately visible is that they are compelled to pay higher wages to all their labourers."—*Ib.*

"But we have no doubt that, in time, even the farmers themselves will come to acknowledge that Mr. Girdlestone is doing them the greatest possible service. No one will benefit more than they from an improvement in the condition of their labourers. We believe that, in many cases, they will even pay less. What the farmer has hitherto refused to pay in wages he has had to pay in rates, and the poor-rate will assuredly be diminished as the rate of wages increases. In one way or another, a labourer and his family must receive enough to live upon. A half-starving man has neither the will nor the power to work, and there can be no doubt that the proverbial sleepiness and sloth of agricultural work are in a great degree due to sheer lack of vital force. If the farmer has to double the labourer's wages, he may be sure that he will double the work which he gets out of him. In some cases we dare say almost everything else on the farm has been improved by intercourse with other districts. The labourer may be improved in the same way, and with equally beneficial results, not only to himself, but to every one concerned."—*Ib.*

Now, what more has Mr. Girdlestone done than to stimulate the very process which is now taking place of its own accord in Ireland?

Instead of deploring the desire of the Irish farmer's son "to go forth and seek his fortune," we ought to rejoice at the exhibition of so much enterprize. One of the most pernicious weaknesses of the Irish character was an unwillingness to allow the junior members of the family to leave home. "Sub-letting exists from a mistaken wish to keep the family together until they are too old to go to a trade."—*Dig. Dev. Com.* p. 134. This evidence is repeated up and down the whole volume.

CHAPTER II.

In my previous observations I confined myself to the general question as to whether or not, in her present circumstances, and making due allowance for the individual suffering incident to all periods of transition, emigration had been a calamity or a blessing to Ireland; and I endeavoured to show, not only that emigration had on the whole been productive of advantage to both classes affected by it —viz., those who went and those who stayed at home—but that, whether beneficial or otherwise to the empire at large, it was a necessity of our own immediate situation.

I now propose to examine the specific charge directed against the landed proprietors of Ireland —viz., that the legalized injustice of their proceedings has been the principal and active occasion of emigration.

Many eminent persons say that such is the case. "The landlords are the cause of the emigration," is the naked and unqualified statement which has been put forward in Parliament. "More than a million persons have fallen victims to their injustice," is a common assertion, and various instances of wholesale evictions are referred to in illustration of the statement. Now, what these gentlemen say I am sure they believe, and the vehemence of the commentary which accompanies their statements is only natural to men of a generous and patriotic temper; but accusations involving a large class of our fellow-countrymen in so hateful a responsibility cannot be lightly accepted, and I therefore propose to examine their validity by such tests as can be conveniently introduced into a hasty controversy like the present.

Indeed, if we believe so much, there is a great deal more we must believe. We must believe that all those general incentives to emigration which I have already enumerated, and which have told with such effect upon England, upon Scotland, and upon Germany, have had no influence in Ireland, although the peculiar circumstances of Ireland were so well calculated to intensify their operation. We must believe that the emigration from Ireland has been entirely confined to the rural population of the country, and confined not only to the rural population, but to less than one-half of the rural population—viz., the occupiers of land. We must believe that the wages of labour have doubled in 15 years —not in consequence of the emigration of the farm-servant as distinguished from the tenant-farmer, but from some other cause which has yet to be explained; and, finally, we must believe that the individuals of that class to which alone it is alleged emigration has been confined—viz., the occupiers of land—have one and all vacated their mud cabins and strips of blighted potato ground, not because they found they could no longer feed their pig or grow oats with advantage on an acre of land,—not because they heard that wages were 4s a day in New York* and that farms could be got for nothing in the Western States,—not because their friends besought them to cross the Atlantic, and sent millions of money to pay their passage,— but solely and entirely in consequence of their having been driven from their homes by the wanton cruelty of their landlords and the injustice of Parliament,—a series of assumptions incompatible with ascertained facts.

Before, however, addressing myself to the details of the question opened up by the foregoing consi-

* FARM WAGES IN THE UNITED STATES —The February official report on agriculture contains an elaborate compilation of the statistics of the wages of farm labour throughout the country. An average rate of wages for white labour, without board is made $28 (=£5. 16s 8d) per month; $15. 50c (= £3. 4s 7d) per month with board. The average rate of freedmen's labour is $16; (=£3. 6s 8d); with board furnished, $9. 75c. (=£2. 0s 7½d). The highest rate for States is in California, which is about $45. (=£9. 7s 6d). Massachusetts pays the next highest, $38. (=£7. 15s 4d). The average rate for the Eastern States is $33. 30c. (=£6. 18s 9d): in the middle States $30. 7c. (=£6. 5s 3½d): in the Western States, $28. 90c. (=£6. 0s 5d); in the Southern States for freedmen, $16. (=£3. 6s 8d). The increase in the price of labour since 1860, is about 50 per cent.; since 1835, upon Carey's estimate 70 per cent.

derations, there is one important misconception against which I wish to guard myself. In conducting this inquiry, I have no intention of discussing whether the landlords of Ireland, as a class, are good men or bad men, kind or cruel. In all probability they are as selfish, as interested, and as unscrupulous as any other collection of human beings possessing the same amount of education and intelligence. But the supposed moral attributes of a particular class, or trade, or profession cannot come within the cognizance of the politician. His only safe rule will be to take it for granted that every class, and every individual in every class, will pursue his own advantage with unflinching pertinacity; and, having meted out as justly as the clumsiness of human legislation may admit, the boundaries which are to circumscribe the respective rights of each, he must be content to accept as economically legitimate whatever does not overpass them. In all ages there have been unrelenting creditors who have insisted on their pound of flesh, but would it not be unreasonable on that account to stigmatize the recovery of debt as injustice? Unhappily, legal obligations can seldom be rendered co-extensive with moral responsibilities, and an attempt to correct an exceptional hardship in one direction, too frequently leads to the infliction of greater injuries in another.

Still less do I propose to notice any particular accusations of cruelty or injustice which may be alleged against individual proprietors. In the first place, they are necessarily derived from *ex parte* statements, and their merits cannot be readily investigated;* and, in the next, their

* It is not often, that an opportunity occurs of subjecting these charges to the test of an impartial inquiry, but whenever an investigation is set on foot they hardly sustain strict scrutiny, a fact especially recorded in the summary of the evidence taken before the Devon Commission.

"Many of the witnesses appeared to be impressed with the idea that the power of ejectment is frequently used by landlords from caprice to strengthen their political party, or to persecute their religious opponents; and some cases were brought before the commission as instances of that power having been so used. *But upon investigation of these cases few of them appear to justify such imputations. In general either the allegations were altogether unfounded, or mainly based upon hear-say—or it appeared that the ejectment was brought in consequence of the tenant having incurred a heavy arrear of rent, and being unwilling, or unable, to discharge it.* In many estates, a small sum of money was given to those who resigned their land; and the extent to which the increased holdings were brought, was generally but small, barely sufficient for those who remained."

"There is no question that the condition of the property, as well as of the occupiers, in most of these cases, required a change, as their previous state was for the most part very miserable."—*Digest Devon Commission, Summary, p.* 830.

And again:

"There were frequent charges made against agents of oppressive conduct, which in general *when investigated*, appeared merely to have consisted in compelling the payment of an arrear of rent, or *preventing a ruinous subdivision of the farms.*"

Digest Devon Commission, Summary, p. 1027.

Evidence of Christopher Galwey, Esq., agent to Lord Kenmare.

"My reply to the statement made by Mr. Barry as to the dis-

assistance in guiding us to an opinion on questions involving such an enormous range of observation must obviously be infinitesimal. Two of the very instances adduced during a recent debate in Parliament, prove the truth of this observation. For the first is the case of a landlord who turns his tenants out at midnight in winter, without previous notice, and the other tells us of a would-be purchaser of an Irish estate who was only prevented from evicting a number of cottiers by being himself hanged for murder before he had concluded his bargain. Now, as by law every tenant must receive at the least eight or nine months' notice before he can be forced to surrender possession of his holding, the first case proves nothing against the laws regulating the relation of landlord and tenant, while in the second story the hero, not having been an Irish proprietor at all, can scarcely

possession of tenants on the Earl of Kenmare's estates, in the village of Hospital, in the county of Limerick, is as follows:— In the year 1810 the lease of a small farm, comprising twenty-three acres, bordering on the village of Hospital, expired. A number of very poor people, inhabiting the most miserable description of hovels, resided on the skirts of the land; their hovels formed one side of the village of Hospital. I purchased, on the part of the Earl of Kenmare, these holdings from these poor people, at a valuation; and though I cannot now state the precise sum paid to each, the sum total distributed amongst them was £400. They were all perfectly satisfied, and quietly gave up possession. I moreover offered to each of them a free passage to America, with provisions during the voyage, an offer which they all refused to accept."

Digest Devon Commission, p. 466.

be paraded as a type of the class. That many acts of harshness and cruelty have been perpetrated in Ireland, more particularly during the time of the famine, I have no doubt. But, it is to be remembered that the famine year was an exceptional period; a sudden storm had broken out of a clear sky; the ship lay a wreck on her beam-ends. It was such a scene as reveals the mingled baseness and heroism of human nature, and doubtless, in the extremity of peril which threatened the landlords, their wives, and their children, many a man enforced his legal rights with distressing severity. That this was not the general practice is clearly stated by Judge Longfield in his evidence before Mr. Maguire's committee.

In answer to a question as to whether or not a bad feeling had arisen from many proprietors in different parts of Ireland having taken steps, at the time of the famine, to consolidate their farms, he replies, "I do not think that had much to do with it; the tenants were voluntarily giving up their lands in great quantities then;" and a little further on he states that "cases of forcible eviction for the proposed consolidation were *very few*."* Now Judge Longfield's testimony on such

---

* The same opinion was educed by the Devon Commission.
"Much evidence of a most contradictory character was given upon the consolidation of small farms into large. Many statements were made of cases in which such consolidation had been effected; but these statements were, in general, met by

a point is conclusive. He was the first and
most important witness summoned before Mr.
Maguire's committee. His professional position,
his experience, the peculiar nature of his duties,
his well-known calmness and impartiality, and
above all his manifest sympathy with the cause of
the tenant, invest his evidence on matters of fact
with an authority that cannot be gainsaid. And it
stands to reason that matters should have fallen out
as Judge Longfield has described. What inducements had the poor people to stay? Their staff of
life had withered in their hands and could not be
replaced. A plough could hardly have turned in

counter statements, denying the general truth of the accusa-
tion, or alleging great exaggeration in it. It seems to be hardly
the province of a digest, such as this, to enter into the question
of the veracity of the witnesses in each particular instance of
alleged oppressive consolidation, as these instances only
affected the characters of particular individuals, and not the
general question as relating to the country at large. It may
suffice, that it appears that, in some cases, tenants have been
ejected for the purpose of consolidating farms; but that there
are *few* estates upon which evictions for this purpose have occurred, though on some of those few estates many tenants
have been ejected.

"*It appears, too, that in general, where such evictions have occurred, the ejected tenants owed considerable arrears of rent,
which, in most cases, were remitted*, and that some allowance in
money or value was made to them. The farms, too, from which
they were removed, seem to have usually been below the minimum size capable of affording a maintenance or profitable and
constant employment to an average family."

Digest Devon Commission, Summary, p. 451.

their potato gardens,* they had neither seed, nor horses, nor even food, to carry them through the winter. No difference of tenure would have saved them. Had they owned the fee, it would have been all the same.† Their only chance of life was to get away—some to the poor-house,‡ others to America.§ As for the landlord, his position was every whit as bad. It was not a question of rent,

---

* "The effects of sub-division are very bad; first the land is cut into such small patches that a plough and horses in many cases will hardly turn in the field."—*Dig. Devon Commission*, p. 426. *Evidence of John Hancock, Esq., (an Ulster Agent).*

† "To grant to the occupiers the fee of their holdings, freed from every rent and tax, would not cure our vital distemper. This is undeniable, when we find that the day labouring population in many districts, are almost wholly without employment, and that the entire produce of the holdings of nearly one-half of the occupiers of land throughout Ireland would be inadequate to the proper sustenance of the families residing upon them, supposing that no charge for rent or taxes existed."

Dig. Dev. Com. Summary, p. 757.

‡ As many as 3,000,000 persons were at one time in receipt of public relief.

§ The poverty stricken condition of the small tenantry of Ireland at this period cannot be depicted in truer or more graphic terms than those adopted by Mr. Fishbourne, himself a tenant farmer.

"The small tenantry are generally without any capital, except what is barely sufficient to get in the crop and keep a cow. Many of them are in a deplorable condition, being overwhelmed with debts to loan funds, usurers, and mealmen, owing to the damage to their potatoes for the last three years. In several instances their stock and furniture have been sold, under warrants from loan banks, &c; that I know of my own knowledge."—*Digest Devon Commission*, p. 199, *evidence of Jos. Fishbourne, Farmer.*

but of existence. His lands lay around him a poisonous waste of vegetable decay, while 25s. in the pound of poor-rate was daily eating up the fee-simple of his estate.* Self-interest, duty, common sense, all dictated the same course,—the enlargement of boundaries, the redistribution of farms, and the introduction of a scientific agriculture, at whatever cost of sentiment or of individual suffering.† Even so, the struggle too frequently proved unsuccessful, and the subsequent obliteration of nearly an entire third of the landlords of Ireland, while it associates them so conspicuously with the misfortunes of their tenants, may be accepted in atonement of whatever share they may have had in conniving at those remoter causes which aggravated the general calamity.

* One landlord alone spent £13,000 in assisting those who had flocked into the poor-house to emigrate.—*See Answers to Queries, p.* 292.

† The difficulties arising out of this situation of affairs is admirably described in the summary prefixed to the digest of the Evidence given before the Devon Commission.— *See Appendix*, p. 145.

That as a general rule the inevitable changes were effected in a humane manner is sufficiently exemplified in the subjoined evidence, taken at random from a mass of similar statements.

Andrew Durham, Esq., Land Proprietor.

" Has there been any considerable consolidation of farms in your neighbourhood?—The tendency to consolidate is increasing, and encouraged by most landlords. It is generally effected by purchase, and not attended by agrarian disturbances. The consequences are greater productiveness, more tillage, and increased employment of agricultural labour. Rents are paid in the same proportion."— *Dig. Dev. Com. p.* 456.

On turning to the statistics which bear upon this question, the argument I have thus roughly sketched

Mr. John McCorten, Linen Manufacturer, Bleacher and Land Agent.

" Have you known many instances of ejectment without compensation, in order to effect such a consolidation ?—No, I do not think it is ever done. It would be looked upon as a very tyrannical measure ; and consolidation is very rarely attempted, unless where it can be done without injury to any party."

" What becomes generally of the out-going tenants in such cases ; do they emigrate, or do they locate themselves elsewhere ?—Some emigrate, and others locate themselves elsewhere. In some cases they become labourers, or go to some other employment."—*Ibid. p.* 417.

Lieutenant-General Sir Richard Bourke, Bart., Land Proprietor and Magistrate.

" Has there been any consolidation of farms in the district with which you are acquainted ?—Very considerable within these twenty-five years. I should say, in general, that the consolidation has been advantageous to the property and to the occupier left upon the land, as he has been placed in a more comfortable position ; and in the cases of those who have been removed, where the removal has been managed with humanity and discretion, I am not aware that they have been the sufferers. I have myself removed persons whom I have sent to New South Wales, and I am sure they are much better off than they were in Ireland. I began very early. Some farms of mine came out of lease between 1818 and 1827 ; and in many, where there was a population which I thought it not to the advantage of the landlord or the occupier to remain upon the land, I had to remove a great many of those, and I hope I removed them without any great hardship or oppression ; and their farms have been since in a very good condition, with only one tenant upon each farm.

" To what size did you raise the farms ?—From twenty to thirty acres in some cases ; in other cases, from fifty to sixty.

will be enforced in a still more striking manner. If it is true, as is asserted, that the emigration has

"Have you found that those farms have been subdivided?—No; I have looked very close after them to prevent it, but it requires a great deal of supervision on the part of the landlord and agent.

"You assisted them to emigrate?—Yes; and in other cases, where there were mountains attached to the farms, I gave them a part of the mountain, and they have been acting since as labourers to farmers on the estate. In other cases, I gave them sums of money to go away; but in no case did I ever turn a man out with harshness.

"What system did you adopt with respect to those who emigrated?—I paid their passage, and gave them a small sum of money in hand, and gave them a recommendation to some friend there. That has been done since I came home from Australia—since the year 1838.

"Has the course adopted by you been the course generally followed out in the district?—I believe, in many cases, it may have been adopted, and in others it may not. Hence arose the complaints."—*Dig. Dev. Com. p.* 465.

James Galwey, Esq., Land Agent.

"When I became agent to one of the properties, there was a good number of people put out at a particular place, where it was necessary they should be got rid of. *They had not paid rent for years,* and they got £3, and some of them £4 or £5, up to £7, and they went away."—*Ibid. p.* 466.

"I have always given them a year's notice. I have said, 'I will not give you notice to quit, but the next year you must go.' It has been because they have been complained of as bad characters. The last year I was obliged to put out five tenants of Lord Cremorne's—two were bad characters, and the other three were put out because they were complained of by the rest of the tenants, who were respectable. I told them they must go, and I gave £8 to each of the five families to enable them to emigrate, and they went away quietly, and gave up without any trouble."

Dig. Dev. Com. p. 467.

been principally confined to a class which cultivates the soil—the only class, in fact, which can

Robert O'Brien, Esq., Agent, Tenant, and Land Proprietor.

" Has the consolidation of farms taken place; to what extent has it been carried; with what objects and by what means has it been accomplished, and with what consequences?—The system of consolidation is not carried on to any great extent in this district, and indeed bears no relative proportion to the subdivision of land, which is going on in spite of every effort of the landlords. However, here and there may be cases of clearing, and the desire to effect it exists, no doubt, in the minds of many who are deterred by unwillingness to enter into such a contest; others by humanity, knowing the wretched condition that the people so turned out would be in. The desire to effect it arises from the neglected state of the houses and land of such tenants; the frequent failure of their means to pay the rent, from bad tilling; the irregularity of their dealings and carelessness in fulfilling their engagements; the frequent disputes with landlords for cutting timber, burning land, wasting or selling turbary, dividing land amongst their families, letting strangers build cabins on their farms. The operation of the law, as it stands at present, frequently leads to a landlord turning out tenants, from whom, in the first instance, he would have been satisfied to recover his rent, which proceeds from the necessity of bringing an ejectment on the title where tenants-at-will are in arrear of rent, a course attended with considerable delay, and the tenant so evicted has no right to redeem."—*Dig. Dev. Com. p.* 466.

Captain Thomas Bolton, Land Agent to Lord Stanley.

" What is the more general size of the farms?—Under twenty acres decidedly.

" Have you had the management of the estate for any length of time?—Since the year 1832.

" In that time have you had occasion to make much alteration in the holdings?—I have altered in some cases the size of the farms, and in some cases I have removed tenants in order to do so.

be directly affected by the tyranny and injustice of the landed proprietor—it must necessarily follow

"Have you had occasion to remove many tenants?—Yes, when I first came; from one property.

" What class were they?—The very small pauperized class of tenantry living near the bog, in the county of Limerick. They were removed, and the land set in large holdings.

" What system did you pursue in removing these people? —I distrained them. They were very badly off, and in a miserable state; their mode of living was by stealing turf and selling it in Tipperary. They nominally had paid rent for the land, but they were greatly in arrear, and I gave them money to emigrate, and they went to America without any trouble. From about eighty acres of land there were 290 men, women, and children sent away.

" Were those proceedings carried on without any disturbance?—Yes, it excited no ill-will.

" Have the tenants you put in the farms continued there till this time?—Yes, they are there now.

" Can you recollect the largest size of the holdings of any of those you removed?—I should think in one case as far as eight or nine acres; no holding was over ten, and many of them two, or three, or one."—*Dig. Dev. Com. p.* 467.

William Hamilton, Esq., Land Agent.

" When landlords have removed excessive population, they have generally offered the alternative of emigration on very favourable terms. This has been sometimes accepted, but more generally refused. Compensation is then given, either by money or free occupation for a certain time, or both, the tenant carrying away crops, materials of houses, &c. Where the arrangements are made with firmness, but at the same time judiciously and humanely, the majority of the persons affected acquiesce in their necessity, and are often benefited by them."
Dig. Dev. Com. p. 467.

Rev. Robert Sargeant, Land Agent.

" Was it usual in general to make an allowance to assist

that the number of emigrants must bear a very close proportion to the number of persons who them in providing for themselves?—Undoubtedly, it was always. I never knew an instance in which they were not allowed something, either by arrears of rent or in some other mode."—*Dig. Dev. Com. p.* 469.

E. L. Swan, Esq., Agent to Lord De Vesci.

"Has there been any consolidation of farms upon the property with which you are connected?—Yes, and subletting in some instances has been carried on to a ruinous extent, contrary to his lordship's wishes, by tenants holding under old leases, who, taking advantage of the well-known benevolence of his lordship, and the consequent high value set upon being found on the land at the expiration of the lease, have realized large profit rents by subdividing their farms; to prevent which, when a case of the kind comes to my knowledge, I cause the intruder to be noticed, that he will have no claim on his lordship at the fall of the lease; and to consolidate such farms, his lordship either sends the occupier to America, or provides him with the means of procuring another residence."

Dig. Dev. Com. p. 469.

William Hamilton, Esq., Land Agent.

"It is a change, however, to be made with much care and tenderness, and with every possible attention to the feelings of the persons to be removed, but which, when accomplished, is attended with beneficial effects, upon production, employment of labour, and security of rent."—*Dig. Dev. Com. p.* 470.

Robert D'Arcy, Esq., Land Agent to the Marquess of Clanricarde.

"When those farms in partnership fall out of lease, we send the surveyor, Mr. Cooper, whom we pay by the year for regulating Lord Clanricarde's estate, he surveys the land, and we find there is generally double or treble the people upon the townland than can live upon it; and the direction he has got is, to lay it out in fifteen or twenty acres; and then the great

have been so ruthlessly dealt with. Now the reductions of the holdings in Ireland between 1841

difficulty arises, when that is done, ' What is to be done with the tenants?' * * * "About a mile from the town there were about twelve persons to be disposed of. I saw the impossibility of satisfying them, and I proposed that they should cast lots for the land. They agreed to cast lots, upon condition that each man going out was to get £20, his lordship paying half, and the tenant who got the land paying the other. That was settled, and they got their money, and a good many went to America. * * * The whole of the expense of those tenants for those two years was £551. 13s 3d.' "

John Duke, Esq., M.D.

" Has the consolidation of farms been carried on to any extent in this district? * * *—There has been an anxiety, on the part of the landlords, latterly to do so. They are doing it, where they can do it peaceably, to the satisfaction of the outgoing tenant."

D. H. Kelly, Esq., Land Proprietor, Magistrate, and D.L.

" Has there been any consolidation of farms in the district? I am doing it in every way I can. I am getting the tenants wherever I can to buy adjoining land when it is vacant; but if you refer to consolidation by the ejectment of whole villages, in order to make large farms, there is nothing of the sort; but where there is a beggarman, and he is inclined to go away, or one man is inclined to buy of another, I have made both into one holding, and have always assisted the party by lending him money, and in every way I could."

" To what size have you thought it desirable to bring the farms?—If I could I should not like to have any thing under twenty acres; but I am content with ten, and put up with six."—*Dig. Dev. Com. p.* 471.

Captain K. Lloyd, Land Proprietor, Agent, and Magistrate.

" Has there been any consolidation of farms, and to what

and the present date is, of course, the measure of
the limits within which the consolidation of farms

extent, in the district?—Yes, it is very generally practised
now.

"To what extent, and with what objects?—To introduce
a better class of tenantry, and also to benefit the proprietor
who finds, if he can increase the size of his farm, it benefits the
land.

"To what sized farms has it gone?—I think they vary
from fifteen to twenty acres and thirty acres—that seems to
be the favourite size, I think, for persons removed above the
mere peasant.

"Do you mean to say, in many instances, large numbers
of people have been dispossessed with a view to increasing the
size of farms?—No, by no means; but I say that practice is
generally introduced, and is recognized throughout the country,
and where it can be done without oppression, it is generally
practised; and the persons going out have been generally
assisted to go to America, or otherwise provide for themselves;
it only anticipates the day when they must go—for it is manifest that sooner or later they must go; the longer you keep
them the worse is their condition."—*Dig. Dev. Com. p.* 472.

Lord George Hill, Land Proprietor.

"The estate was mapped and surveyed at very considerable
expense, and the farms remodelled, so that each tenant has his
land together in one place (with few exceptions), instead of
being as formerly in several detached places. This was effected
with much difficulty, the people themselves having the greatest
antipathy to any change. In doing this, each man's case was
attentively considered, so that no injury or loss was incurred
by any. In consequence of this new state of affairs the tenants
were obliged to shift their houses, which was easily accomplished, as the custom of the country is, on those occasions, to
hire a fiddler, who, taking up his position upon the intended
site, scrapes away whilst the neighbours are busy bringing
stones from all quarters, and when a sufficient quantity has
been collected, the evening is finished by a dance."—*Ib. p.* 455.

has been effected and evictions have been possible. But it so happens that the total number of holdings in Ireland containing 15 acres and upwards has increased enormously since 1841. In fact there are now nearly twice as many small farmers—using the term in what in England would be thought its most modest acceptation—as there were before the famine. This will, undoubtedly, be considered an extraordinary statement, but it is, nevertheless, the fact, that holdings of between 15 and 30 acres have increased by 61,000, or 78 per cent. within the last 20 years, and holdings above 30 acres by 109,000, or 224 per cent., during the same period, while those between 5 and 15 acres have decreased by less than half those amounts;*

---

* TABLE showing the increase of Holdings in Ireland between fifteen and thirty acres from 1841 to 1861.

	Leinster.	Munster.	Ulster.	Connaught.	Ireland.
1841	20,688	27,611	25,219	5,824	79,342
1861	24,226	26,805	57,660	32,560	141,251
Increase.	3,538	— 806	32,441	26,736	61,909

Leinster	3,538	being an increase of 17·1 per cent.
Munster	— 806	a decrease of 2·9 ,,
Ulster	32,441	an increase of 128·6 ,,
Connaught	26,736	,, 459·1 ,,
	62,715 — 806		
	806		
Ireland	61,909	,, 78· ,,

the emigration, so far as it has extended to the occupying class at all, having been chiefly confined to the poor people who attempted to get a living out of bits of land ranging from half-an-acre to five or six acres,* and whose destiny, no custom, or law of tenant-right, however liberal, could have materially affected.† No doubt, the diminution of the holdings in this last category has been enormous, but even among these, as compared with the area of land under tillage in Ireland, the reduction has not been so startling as it might have first appeared: the proportion amounting, in

TABLE showing the increase of Holdings in Ireland above Thirty acres from 1841 to 1861.

	Leinster.	Munster.	Ulster.	Connaught.	Ireland.
1841	17,943	16,665	9,655	4,362	48,635
1861	39,384	55,833	39,464	23,152	157,833
Increase	21,441	39,168	29,799	18,800	109,208

Leinster	21,441,	being an increase of	119.5 per cent.
Munster	39,168	,,	235·
Ulster	29,809	,,	308·7
Connaught	18,790	,,	430·8
	109,208	,,	224·6

* The reduction in the number of holdings between half an acre and six acres, as compared with the reduction in the number of holdings between six and fifteen acres, is as
$$314 + x \text{ to } 76 - x.$$

† This is sufficiently established by the fact of something like 100,000 holdings of this description having disappeared in Ulster alone.

the case of tenements under five acres, to one per annum on every area of 400 acres; and in the case of holdings under 10 acres to one per annum on every area of 1,600 acres.* Of course, the process has neither been so gradual nor so uniform as this calculation would imply, the principal rush having taken place immediately after the potato failure, and from those districts most exposed to its effects; the devastation among the small tenements of Ulster being as tremendous as in any other part of Ireland. Allowing, however, for all subsidiary corrections, it is very evident that so far from the landlords being responsible for the entire emigration, they held no relation, good or bad, with perhaps three-fourths of those who went, even though you counted as emigrants every man, woman, and child that may have quitted—whether of their own free will or on compulsion—the agricultural tenancies that have been extinguished.†

* It is curious to contrast the view Mr. Mill seems to take of the extinction of very small tenancies, with the language of those who hold up the landlords of Ireland to obloquy for having promoted within very moderate limits, and as a general rule, by the most legitimate and humane means the very improvement he desiderates.

"The principal change in the situation consists in the great diminution, *holding out a hope of the entire extinction,* of cottier tenure. The enormous decrease in the number of small holdings, and increase in those of a medium size, attested by the statistical returns, sufficiently proves the general fact, and all testimonies show that the tendency still continues."

Mill's Polit. Economy, p. 413, Vol. I.

† It has been objected that inasmuch as Ireland is an agri-

But it is well known that vast numbers of the cottier tenantry, instead of emigrating, were converted into labourers, and either found employment in the neighbourhood of their birthplace or removed into adjoining towns,* or came over to England,† while hundreds of others were placed in possession of some of the 160,000 farms which, as I have already stated, have been reconstructed since the famine year;‡ thereby reducing still

cultural country, the landlords are responsible for the condition of the whole population, whether immediately connected with the land or not. Such a doctrine is scarcely reasonable;—the general condition of a people must depend upon their industry, enterprise, intelligence, and forethought. Though a landlord may do something to inculcate the foregoing qualities, his best efforts too frequently produce disheartening results even amongst those with whom he is immediately connected; but as I shall have occasion to show, the almost universal practice of granting leases for a long term of years, deprived most of the landlords of all control over their tenantry; it is unjust therefore to hold them solely responsible for the unhealthy social system which came to exist on their own estates: to credit them with the misfortunes of the non-agricultural population would be absurd.

* During the last twenty years the Catholic population of Belfast, Derry, and the manufacturing towns of Ulster, has increased nearly one-third. The influx, of course, having proceeded from the southern and western parts of the island.

† Among a number of Irish navvies, working in London, whom I have questioned, I never found one who had either held land, or been forced to leave his country against his will. Nearly all used the same expression in accounting for their departure from home, "it was the potato failure drove us away." All pretty nearly named 6d a-day as the rate of wages they were receiving in their native place, and none now are getting less than 4s a-day in England.

‡ For every two holdings which have disappeared from the

further the number of the land-occupying class who have taken part in emigration, and who probably with their families have never amounted to one-fourth of the entire number.*

This moderate share taken by the tenantry in the emigration from Ireland has greatly decreased during the last ten or twelve years. Between 1853 and 1862 the number of farms in the country actually increased under the alleged exterminating policy of the landlords, and if within the last four years there has been a slight diminution, it is to be accounted for by the three successive wet seasons, which signalized the period during which the decrease has taken place. Even so it is probable that for the last twelve or thirteen

category of those below 5 acres or below 15 acres, a new one has been added to the class of farms of 15 acres and upwards.

* I am happy to find that exactly the same proportion as that noted above has been arrived at by a writer in the Home and Foreign Review, with whose calculations I was unacquainted at the time I published my own conclusions.

"These figures seem to prove very clearly that the largest proportion of those whose emigration can be even indirectly traced to their having, *either voluntarily or under compulsion*, given up their land in Ireland is, roughly speaking, *as one to four*. But if we leave statistics aside for the moment, and found our observations on the personal experience of those well acquainted with the emigration movement, we shall find that the great majority of emigrants who leave Ireland for America, or for the manufacturing districts of England or Scotland, consists of unmarried men and women—the junior members of small farmers' and cottiers' families, who are unable to find remunerative employment at home, and set out to seek it in other countries."

H. & F. Review, Ap. 1864, p. 343.

years no more than three or four per cent. of the total number of emigrants have been holders of land.*

Such a conclusion is, of course, quite contrary to the popular belief, but it is, nevertheless, a fact within the cognizance of every one who is acquainted with the subject. Judge Longfield states it over and over again. He is asked if he knows

* "There is one point in connection with the emigration movement which should be noticed, in order to dispel a very erroneous impression which the tone of certain journals has done much to create, viz. that there is a feeling of despair amongst the agricultural class in Ireland, and that the farmers have given up, or are giving up, their land, to go to America. Speaking from trustworthy information derived from various parts of Ireland, we must deny this to be the case; and we very much doubt if in the whole of Ireland twenty instances could be found where the tenant of either a large or a small farm, who has paid his last half-year's rent and is able to pay the next, has voluntarily resigned his land in order to emigrate.

"Statistics clearly show that, however the number of inhabitants may have diminished in Ireland within the last seventeen years, the agricultural population is still much in excess of the agricultural population of either England or Scotland;† and bearing this in mind, we cannot avoid the painful conclusion that, if the people of Ireland be destined to remain as exclusively as now dependent on the land for their support, there is no reasonable expectation of any rapid decrease, much less of a cessation, of the emigration."‡

Home and Foreign Review, Ap. 1864, *p.* 344.

† Irish Emigration considered, by M. J. Barry, Esq., Barrister-at-Law, pp. 9—11.

‡ The average annual preponderance of births over deaths in Ireland is about 60,000; so that, in the absence of any other disturbing causes, a yearly emigration to nearly that extent would not have the effect of making the population less than it now is.

that a great deal of emigration from Ireland has been going on. " Yes," he replies, " but I do not think that the emigration is much caused by the landlord and tenant question." Again he is asked if good tenants have not been driven away from the country by the supposed insecurity of the tenure. He answers, " In some instances an active man *may* have been prevented from investing his capital in Ireland on that account, but I do not think that class form a large proportion of the emigrants as yet," and a little further on he calculates the emigrants who belong to the tenant-farmer class as amounting to about four out of every 100 persons who quit Ireland, the great bulk of the exodus being composed of small tradesmen, artizans, and labourers.

Happily, the case admits of even closer proof. In the denunciatory addresses to which I have referred, the tenant of Ulster is justly indicated as occupying an exceptionally good position, and many have declared they would be satisfied if the tenantry of the south could obtain, under an Act of Parliament, one-tenth of the security accorded by custom to the tenantry of Ulster. If, therefore, the oppression and legalized injustice which is supposed to desolate the homesteads of the south, is absent from the north, it would be natural to imagine that the extinction of tenancies in Ulster would have been *infinitesimal;* but as a matter of fact the havoc amongst the small farmers of Ulster during the first few years succeeding the potato failure was as portentous as in any other province in Ireland, for whereas in Leinster only 44,514, in Munster 85,929, in Connaught 78,958 holdings between one and fifteen acres disappeared, in Ulster as many as 95,429 have been obliterated.* If we restrict the comparison to holdings between one and *five* acres, Ulster's sinister pre-eminence over Leinster and Munster is still maintained, nearly twice as many holdings of this description having been extinguished in Ulster as in Munster, and almost three times as many as in Leinster, the numbers being in Leinster 27,007, in Munster 44,956, in Ulster 74,650, and Connaught 81,786.

It has been urged that the foregoing figures prove nothing, inasmuch as Ulster contains a farming population largely in excess of that of Munster and Connaught, and nearly twice as numerous as that of Leinster, and that we must ignore the fact of nearly 100,000 small holdings having disappeared in Ulster, on the ground that they formed a smaller percentage on the total number of farms in that Province than did those which have suc-

* Reduction of Holdings between 1 and 15 acres, from 1841 to 1861:

	1841.	1861.	Decrease.
Leinster	96,149	53,363	42,786
Munster	119,610	35,695	83,915
Ulster	201,820	110,511	91,309
Connaught	145,656	69,831	75,825

For the particulars of the entire period from 1841 to 1865, see Appendix.

cumbed to a similar fate in Munster, Leinster and Connaught, to the total number of farms in their respective Provinces.

If this latter statement were correct, it would not be a valid objection. Every one is aware that the agriculture of the North has always been in a sounder state than that of the South and West,* and in a subsequent chapter I hope to account for that circumstance. But as it happens even the *proportionate* obliteration of the very small holdings in Ulster, viz : of those between 1 and 5 acres has been 19 per cent greater than what it was in Leinster, within $4\frac{3}{4}$ per cent of what it was in Munster, only $8\frac{1}{2}$ per cent below what it was in Connaught,

* Throughout the whole of this discussion I have carefully abstained from drawing any invidious distinction between the people of the North and South of Ireland, nor do I now wish to do more than hint at a consideration, which, in drawing a comparison between Ulster and Munster, it would be as undesirable to omit altogether, as it would be to press unduly, viz. :—that a more indefatigable spirit of continuous and persistent industry seems to pervade the inhabitants of the North that can, with perfect impartiality, be attributed to those of the South. This circumstance, I imagine, will hardly be disputed, though it may fairly be argued, that when controlled and disciplined by necessity, the labourer of the South will work perhaps harder and quite as willingly as any one in the world.

What he seems to lack is a spontaneous inclination to unremitting and dogged exertion (which is certainly a characteristic of the Ulster population), perhaps to be accounted for by the natural liveliness of his disposition, and even the superiority of some of his intellectual faculties. Nor should the influence of the unhappy past be left out of consideration, in any estimate of the national character.

and almost identical with the general average for the kingdom. It is true, if we ascend to the next class of farms, viz: those between 5 and 15 acres, or if we take the farms of all sizes which have been extinguished in the four provinces during the last five and twenty years, Ulster—as might have been expected—will show a more favourable percentage, the proportionate decrease being 14·2 per cent in Ulster, against 15·1 per cent in Leinster, 29·9 per cent in Munster, and 22·6 per cent in Connaught; but when it is remembered that the absolute number of extinguished farms represented by these percentages is 33·628 in Ulster, as compared with 20·347 in Leinster, 35·144 in Connaught, and 48·900 in Munster, it will be admitted that even from this point of view the share borne by the prosperous tenantry of Ulster* in the general

---

* In accounting for the stability of the small Ulster tenant, I must not forget to mention a fact which undoubtedly exercised a very perceptible influence on his destiny, viz.: the prosperity of the sewed-muslin trade, which, though now in abeyance, was maintained for several years subsequent to the potato failure. In almost every farmer's cottage, the daughters of the house busied themselves with this industry. A girl of sixteen could earn from tenpence to a shilling a day,—and the united exertions of the female members of the family amounted to a considerable sum at the end of the week. This circumstance, together with the assistance which a large proportion of the smaller farmers (particularly in Armagh and Antrim) derived from hand-loom weaving, enabled many to hold their ground who otherwise would have been swept away, while the subsequent extension of the flax cultivation (which, in some respects, is very suitable to small farms, and was greatly stimulated by the prosperity of the linen trade) still further invigorated their prosperity.

calamity sufficiently shows with what impartial severity every part of Ireland was visited, and how unfair it is to attribute solely to the oppression of the landlords of the south a disaster which wrought an enormous though perhaps not an equal amount of ruin in those districts where their malign influence is acknowledged not to prevail.*

But the measure of the Irish landlord's responsibility is not allowed to be limited by the decrease of agricultural holdings; nay, though it appears from the census returns that during a period of ten successive years, ending in 1861, the number of farms in Ireland actually increased, we are still told that because a considerable portion of the population is leaving the country, its departure cannot possibly be occasioned by any other cause than the consolidating policy of the landlords. Let us then continue the application of the test made use of in the preceding paragraph. If emigration is only occasioned by landlord oppression, Ulster ought to have enjoyed a comparative immunity from the general depletion. But what is the fact? Although immediately after the famine the emigration from the south was, for obvious reasons, in excess—though not very largely—of that from the north, the first

	Holdings in 1841.	Holdings in 1861.	Decrease.	Decrease per cent.
* Leinster	134,780	116,973	17,807	13·2
Munster	163,886	118,333	45,553	27·8
Ulster	236,697	207,635	29,059	12·2
Connaught	155,842	125,543	30,299	19·4

wave of emigration that ever left the shores of Ireland proceeded from Ulster,* and during the last fourteen years Ulster's contribution to the general emigration has been greater than that of either Connaught or Leinster, and in the ratio of twenty-three to twenty-seven as compared with the average of the three provinces.

But the greater density of the population of Ulster may be again suggested in mitigation of this comparison. Such a consideration hardly alters the result. The ratio of emigration from Ulster to the population of that province has been as great as the ratio of emigration to population from Leinster and Connaught, though less than that from Munster in the proportion of 1 to 2.†

Parliament and unjust landlords we are told are depopulating the south: what occult agencies are effecting a similar operation in the north?

* See Appendix, p. 85.

† $\text{Ratio of Emigrants from Leinster 1851 to 1865} \over \text{To Population of Leinster in 1861}$ = $308,609 \over 1,457,635$ = 21.1 per cent.

$\text{Ratio of Emigrants from Connaught 1851 to 1865} \over \text{To Population of Connaught in 1861}$ = $197,892 \over 913,135$ = 21.4

$\text{Ratio of Emigrants from Ulster 1851 to 1865} \over \text{To Population of Ulster in 1861}$ = $436,354 \over 1,914,236$ = 22.8

$\text{Ratio of Emigrants from Munster 1851 to 1865} \over \text{To Population of Munster in 1861}$ = $626,958 \over 1,513,558$ = 41.4

There is yet another method at our disposal of testing the justice of these accusations.

By a recent Statute, it has been enacted that no eviction shall take place in Ireland without the intervention of the Sheriff, who is bound to register every operation of the kind. Unluckily this improvement in the law did not occur until March, 1865. Consequently, although we have Sheriff's lists of evictions for some years back, they are more or less imperfect until we come to the returns for the past year, which have been kept in accordance with the Act of Parliament in all the counties of Ireland except four. Of the evictions in these four counties we can arrive at a sufficiently correct estimate by an independent process.

By a previous Act of Parliament every landlord, before proceeding to evict a tenant, was compelled to give notice of his intentions to the relieving officer of the Union, who kept a return of all such notifications: these returns extend over the last six years, and have been presented to Parliament. Of course they do not give us the exact number of actual evictions, because it frequently happens, when the landlord has resorted to this procedure for the recovery of his rent, that the tenant pays up at the last moment, and no eviction takes place, though the notice to the Relieving Officer remains uncancelled. During the first three years of the series great neglect occurred in making up the lists, and even for the last year no information is supplied from a considerable number of the electoral divisions. Luckily, however, the returns of the relieving officers from the four counties, for which the Sheriffs made no returns, happen to be perfect, and more than supply the links necessary to complete the list of evictions for the whole of Ireland during the past year, as will be seen on reference to the opposite table. With the exception of those for Dublin, and a few other places, no distinction has been made between the urban and the agricultural evictions, though for the purposes of the present argument such an analysis would have been desirable. On the other hand the return of evictions during a single year is not altogether a safe guide to an average over a longer period. I therefore propose to convert the figures with which we are furnished for 1865, into a round number, and to take the general rate of rural evictions in Ireland at about 1,500 per annum, which is probably considerably in excess of the truth. (*See* Table).

TABLE showing the Sheriffs' return of evictions actually executed in the year 1865.

	Actual return of Evictions executed by Sheriffs.		Actual return of Evictions executed by Sheriffs.	
	In Counties.	In Counties of Cities & Counties of Towns.	In Counties.	In Counties of Cities & Counties of Towns.
Carlow	11			
Dublin	15			
Dublin, City of		42		
Kildare	20			
Kilkenny	56			
Kilkenny, City of		3		
King's Co.	25			
Longford	55			
Louth	*23			
Drogheda, Co. of the town of		5		
Meath	27			
Queen's Co.	30			
Westmeath	15			
Wexford	54			
Wicklow	14			
LEINSTER			345	50
Clare	19			
Cork	71			
Cork, City of		14		
Limerick	*66			
Limerick, City of				
Kerry	25			
Tipperary†	36			
Waterford	22			
Waterford, City of		5		
MUNSTER			239	19
Antrim	11			
Armagh	92			
Cavan	36			
Donegal	100			
Down	29			
Fermanagh	25			
Londonderry	36			
Monaghan	25			
Tyrone	*130			
ULSTER			484	
Galway	48			
Leitrim	47			
Mayo	72			
Roscommon	*79			
Sligo	20			
CONNAUGHT			266	
IRELAND			‡1334	69

* In these instances the Sheriffs' returns were imperfect, and the figures have been supplied by assuming that the number of evictions executed equalled the entire notices served on the Relieving Officers.

† This is given in the returns as the 'County of Clonmel,' and it is presumed that Tipperary was meant.

‡ It will be seen that this total includes all the Urban evictions, with the exception of those for Dublin and four other towns.

TABLE showing the proportion of persons affected by evictions to the average number of Emigrants, 1865.

	Arable Acres.	Population in 1861.	Holdings in 1861.	Yearly average number of Emigrants, 1860 to 1855.	Evictions, 1865.	Individuals affected.	Per-centage of Persons affected to Emigrants.	Per-centage of Evictions to Holdings in 1861.	
Ulster	4,057,563	1,914,236	216,905	21,313	484	2,420	11·4	0·22	or 1 in 448 Holdings.
Leinster	4,079,130	1,457,635	131,420	14,774	395	1,975	13·3	0·30	or 1 in 332 Holdings.
Munster	4,538,054	1,513,558	128,158	37,330	258	1,290	3·5	0·20	or 1 in 496 Holdings.
Connaught	2,790,078	913,135	133,562	11,492	266	1,330	11·5	0·20	or 1 in 502 Holdings.
Not distributed				7,078					
Ireland	15,464,825	5,798,967*	610,745	91,987	1,403	7,015	7·0	0·22	or 1 in 437 Holdings.

N.B.—This table includes both the Metropolitan and Urban evictions, for which, of course, the landed proprietors of Ireland are not responsible; a very considerable deduction ought to be made from the above figures on that account.

* Including 403 seamen and others at sea on census night.

The total emigration from Ireland has averaged during the same interval about 90,000 a year.* If therefore this emigration has been so swollen by evictions, the annual average of such evictions ought to be proportionate to that emigration; but the average of evictions during the same period, as compared with the number of emigrants, has been at the rate of about two to every 100. That is to say, among every 100 persons who have left Ireland during the last six years about ten persons, if we include the family of each indi-

* Table showing the emigration from Ireland and its provinces from 1860 to 1865, both years inclusive.

	Ireland.	Leinster.	Munster.	Ulster.	Connaught.
1860	76,756	13,366	27,428	27,790	8,172
1861	58,427	8,576	22,404	21,323	6,124
1862	65,179	11,368	33,452	14,115	6,244
1863	110,202	15,020	54,870	22,497	17,815
1864	106,161	19,790	48,397	19,853	18,121
1865	92,728	20,524	37,426	22,301	12,477
	509,458	88,644	223,977	127,879	68,953
Not stated	42,472				
Total 6 years	551,930				
Yearly average	91,988				

vidual dealt with, have done so under the compulsion of a landlord. In other words, and to display the case still more explicitly in relation to the whole subject, during the only period for which we have trustworthy statistics, evictions have been effected (supposing the responsibility for them be distributed over the entire landlord class, which is the theory insisted on) at the rate of one, once in every five years, on each estate; or, to put the case geographically, at the rate of one a year over every area of 10,000 acres of occupied land. It is further to be remarked that evictions have been fewest in Munster, the Province from whence the largest emigration has taken place.*

Not only, however, do we know the number of evictions during the last ten years, but we also know what proportion of these evictions was necessitated by the non-payment of rent. It is true the returns which give this information again confound the urban with the rural districts, but it may fairly be supposed that the same proportions prevailed in either category; and if that be taken for granted, it would appear that of the total number of evictions which the landlords have effected in Ireland two-thirds were for non-payment of rent.

* It is also to be noted, with respect to the foregoing table, that not only have the number of evictions in Ulster been absolutely greater than those in the other provinces, but that the percentage of evictions to holdings was higher in Ulster than in two out of the other three provinces.

When, therefore, it is considered how many are the other contingencies,—such as the infraction of covenants, intolerably bad cultivation, subletting and illegal squatting, which not only entitle but render it incumbent on a landlord, from time to time, to free his estates of an undesirable tenant; and the extraordinary number of tenants on each estate, which of course must multiply the chances of collision, it is impossible not to come to the conclusion that the annual rate of evictions for other causes than that of non-payment of rent, whether taken with reference to the number of occupiers, or to the extent of the area occupied, —in the one case amounting to 0·08 per cent per annum, in the other to one eviction per annum to every 30,000 acres, proves conclusively that the relations of the landlords of Ireland with their tenantry, are by no means on that uncomfortable footing which is alleged, and that to describe Ireland as " *a land of evictions*" is to adopt an expression calculated to convey a false impression.*

But it is now objected that though the list of evic-

---

* Perhaps no better proof can be given of the general ignorance prevailing throughout Ireland on the subject of evictions than the avidity with which the returns for the *notices of ejectment*, commonly called Lord Belmore's returns, were seized upon by almost every newspaper in Ireland, as the basis on which to calculate the number of persons " *annually driven forth to perish* " by their cruel landlords.

Taking it for granted that a notice of ejectment and an eviction were identical circumstances, the total number of

tions may not witness so conclusively as might be desired to the tale of oppression, that a record of

notices were immediately multiplied by five and the product, amounting to 100,000 per annum, was gravely submitted to the public as the figure which represented the exact number of victims to landlord oppression. The slightest acquaintance with agricultural affairs would render such mistakes impossible, and the bona fides with which they are committed only shows how little qualified to offer an opinion are many of those who profess to instruct the conscience of the nation.

From a Correspondent of the Daily News, Jan. 1867.

"The eviction returns of Dr. Hancock are employed, but these have been superseded by the more recent returns of Lord Belmore, which show that within the last six years more than 40,000 occupiers, amounting with their families to 200,000 persons, have been evicted. But it should be remembered that these returns are to the utmost degree imperfect: for no evictions could have been included in them, but such as were registered and authorized by the Courts of Law, and it is a well-known fact that *ten-fold more* (*i.e.* 2,000,000) are dispossessed— *ten-fold* more evictions (*i.e.* 400,000) are effected by a mere "notice to quit" of which there is no public register and can be no returns, than by process of ejectment, of which returns might be procured. Hence these returns must be most imperfect and cannot form a just formation for any reliable conclusion."

From a Correspondent of the Freeman's Journal, Jan. 1867.

"In view of the social charges since 1828-38, assuming that there were only two defendants—an average obviously too low —in each of Lord Belmore's ejectments, the 35,463 cases represent 70,926 holdings and at the usual Irish rate of 5 persons to each family, these indicate 709,260 human beings actually or liable to have been dispossessed in the six years in question!"

The true relation which a service of ejectment and an eviction bear to one another, as well as the kind of occasion on which

evictions is, after all, but an incomplete indication of what is going on, and that it is the fear of eviction which uproots the people, before the landlords have occasion to put in motion the machinery of the law. The difficulty of disproving so indefinite a charge is obvious. The fact that more than a decade has passed without diminishing by a single tenancy, the number of farms in Ireland,* is not likely to make much impression on those who

this step is taken, is sufficiently recorded in the subjoined extracts from the Digest of the Devon Commission.

"A very small proportion of the ejectments brought are carried out to the eviction of the tenants, the action being generally compromised on the payment of the rent arrear."

Dig. Dev. Com. p. 830.

"It likewise appears that the ejectment process is rarely carried to extremities, as compared with the numerous cases in which the first steps are taken, for the purpose of enforcing payment of rent; but that the service of the ejectment process in the great majority of instances, produces the desired settlement of the rent, without coming to a decree."—*Ibid. p.* 805.

Philip Reade, Esq. land proprietor.

"What is the usual mode of recovering rent against defaulting tenantry?—Distraining.

"Is that increasing?—It is diminishing. I perfectly remember when no tenant paid his rent without being distrained, no matter how rich he was, otherwise *it would not have been handsome conduct towards his neighbours.* I perfectly recollect that."—*Ibid. p.* 807.

	1851.	1862.	Increase in 11 years.
* Total Holdings	608,066	609,385	1,319

have started this new theory. Still less would the inference that no landlord can have an interest in dispossessing a good tenant who pays his rent. I therefore recur to more positive data. Fortunately for the cause of truth, it is the practice of the Custom House authorities in their register of the persons embarking for foreign countries carefully to note their previous occupations. Now, it appears from these returns, which extend as far back as the year 1854, that the total number of the farming class who have quitted the United Kingdom during the last 13 years, amounted to 86,388 persons, that is to say, to about 4 per cent. of the total emigration.* Even supposing, therefore, that no English or Scotch farmer were included in the category, the total number of occupiers leaving the ports of Britain would only form eight per cent of the emigration from Ireland alone; but I have been favoured by the kindness of the Emigration Commissioners with an analysis of the nationality of the agriculturists who emigrated during the years 1865 and 1866, from which it appears that the Irish element was very little in excess of the British, and that the total number of Irish occupiers who sailed from any part of the United Kingdom was exactly $2\frac{1}{2}$ per cent of the Irish emigration during the same period.†

* See Appendix, p. 86.
† Return showing the number of Irish Farmers who have

In fact, turn the matter as you will,—apply what test you please,—start from whatever point you emigrated during the years 1865 and 1866, as far as can be ascertained from the Passenger Lists furnished by the Custom House authorities.

Year.	Port of Departure.	United States.	British North America.	Australasia.	All other Places.	Total.
1865	Liverpool	1,674	176	93	4	1,947
	London	7	..	106	..	113
	Plymouth	..	..	17	..	17
	Glasgow	211	32	..	..	243
	Cork	14	..	..	..	14
	Londonderry	169	142	..	..	311
	All other Ports	..	38	..	1	39
	Total	2,075	388	216	5	2,684
1866	Liverpool	1,847	122	55	37	2,061
	London	..	..	48	20	68
	Plymouth	..	..	23	..	23
	Glasgow	111	2	..	..	113
	Cork	4	..	..	..	4
	Londonderry	157	85	..	..	242
	All other Ports	..	..	3	..	3
	Total	2,119	209	129	57	2,514

Government Emigration Board,
  8, Park Street, Westminster,
    15th February, 1867.

Ratio of Irish occupiers to Irish Emigrants in 1865 $= \dfrac{101,497}{2684} = 2.6$ p. c.

                "   1866 $= \dfrac{100,602}{2514} = 2\cdot 5$ p. c.

The number of emigrants in 1866 is deduced from the average of the last five years.

choose,—all the evidence converges to the same conclusion, and establishes beyond a doubt that out of every 100 persons who cross the Atlantic, not more than two or three are induced to do so by any difficulties which may have arisen out of their relations with their landlords.*

After this I trust we shall hear no more of the landlords of Ireland annually driving hundreds and thousands of victims into exile. And when it is further observed that the number of emigrants who are classed as gentlemen, professional men, merchants, &c. almost equal the number of those who are entered as farmers,† perhaps the possibility will be admitted that the same economic laws and inevitable casualties which have influenced the destiny of the one class may have also operated on the other, without their having become the special victims of landlord oppression.

* See Appendix, p. 88.

† Total number of Farmers who have emigrated from the United Kingdom in 1864 7245
Total number whom the Commissioners have classed as Gentlemen, Professional Men, Merchants, &c. . 5842

APPENDIX.

Emigration of Protestants from Ireland. (*See* p. 72.)

It appears that there was a continual emigration of Protestants from Ireland to America throughout the last century, at which time persecution by the Catholics could not have occurred. The emigrations appear to have almost constantly taken place from the northern ports: thus seven ships, leaving Belfast for America with 1000 passengers, in 1728, are mentioned in Boulter's Letters, vol. i. p. 288. The number of emigrants who left Ireland in 1771, 1772, and 1773, is stated in Newenham's Inquiry into the Population of Ireland, p. 59: the ports from which the ships sailed were Belfast, Newry, Derry, Larne, and Portrush. Arthur Young gives the following more detailed account of this subject:—

"The spirit of emigrating in Ireland appears to be confined to two circumstances, the Presbyterian religion and the linen manufacture. I heard of very few emigrants, except among manufacturers of that persuasion. The Catholics never went, they seem not only tied to the country, but almost to the parish in which their ancestors lived."—*Tour in Ireland*, part ii. p. 30.

"It is well known that in the counties of Fermanagh, Tyrone, and Donegal, extensive confiscation took place, and a large number of farmers (Protestants) were in possession of from fifty to one hundred and fifty acres, some fee simple, more than 2s 6d an acre, which they inherited from their predecessors. In the lapse of years their families increased, and having received favourable accounts from persons who had emigrated some half-dozen years previously, farmers who had three, four and five sons or daughters approaching to maturity, considered it prudent to sell their lands, emigrate, and purchase double or treble the quantity in a new country; 'Because,' said they, 'if we split our farms and apportion to each child a share, it will be *but a few acres each*, and they and theirs will become poor.'"

Sir G. C. Lewis on Irish Disturbances, p. 457.

"In a certain sense, it may be said with truth, that the emigration of the Protestants has been owing to the pressure of the Catholics. The Catholics having multiplied rapidly, and being destitute of the means of subsistence, have increased the difficulty of obtaining employment, have lowered the rate of wages, and raised the rent of land by their competition. The Protestants, unwilling to submit to the degradation, and unable to resist the tendency to sink, preferred emigration to impoverishment, and left the country while they had still the means of defraying the expenses of their passage and outfit."

Ibid. p. 458.

RETURN of the EMIGRATION from the United Kingdom to all parts of the World, during the years from 1854 to 1866, both inclusive; showing the TRADE, OCCUPATION or PROFESSION of the ADULTS, so far as can be ascertained from the Passenger Lists furnished by the Custom House Authorities.

Occupation.	United States.	British North America.	Australasia	All other Places.	Total.
ADULT MALES.					
Agricultural Labourers, Gardeners, Carters, &c.	5,208	2,098	33,315	1,562	42,183
Bakers, Confectioners,&c.	3,554	310	1,247	72	5,183
Blacksmiths and Farriers	1,568	456	2,132	195	4,351
Bookbinders and Stationers	160	39	128	18	345
Boot and Shoe Makers	3,613	783	1,410	156	5,962
Braziers, Tinsmiths, Whitesmiths, &c.	1,580	122	297	46	2,045
Brick and Tile Makers, Potters, &c.	233	39	347	19	638
Bricklayers, Masons, Plasterers, Slaters, &c.	9,331	756	5,058	400	15,545
Builders	339	20	289	16	664
Butchers, Poulterers, &c.	1,182	139	985	34	2,340
Cabinet Makers and Upholsterers	314	86	431	56	887
Carpenters and Joiners	14,778	2,115	8,602	646	26,141
Carvers and Gilders	302	43	61	8	414
Clerks	5,571	1,582	3,043	912	11,108
Clock & Watch Makers	615	156	172	20	963
Coach Makers and Trimmers	72	25	136	28	261
Coal Miners	1,083	187	605	4	1,879
Coopers	1,183	157	240	30	1,610
Cutlers	343	11	66	1	421
Domestic Servants	1,592	387	1,189	207	3,375
Dyers	164	37	66	3	270
Engine Drivers, Stokers, &c.	32	7	15	9	63
Engineers	1,565	292	1,103	286	3,246
Engravers	261	14	78	10	363
Farmers	58,526	9,427	17,653	782	86,388
Gentlemen, Professional Men, Merchants, &c.	13,578	3,745	12,191	3,431	33,125
Jewellers and Silversmiths	347	29	135	17	528
Labourers, General	333,215	27,068	95,228	2,643	458,154
Locksmiths, Gunsmiths, &c.	85	7	41	6	139
Millers, Malsters, &c.	886	229	466	18	1,599
Millwrights	104	39	134	28	305
Miners and Quarrymen	22,470	3,437	11,259	996	38,162
Carried forward					

Occupation.	United States.	British North America.	Australasia	All other Places.	Total.
ADULT MALES—*contd*. Brought forward .					
Painters, Paperhangers, Plumbers, and Glaziers	4,042	250	1,140	130	5,562
Pensioners . . .	152	305	175	16	648
Printers . . .	899	133	558	54	1,644
Rope Makers . .	57	18	63	2	140
Saddlers and Harness Makers . . .	341	57	248	47	693
Sail Makers . . .	48	15	60	3	126
Sawyers . . .	176	121	755	45	1,097
Seamen . . .	2,568	495	1,154	71	4,288
Shipwrights . .	149	38	192	53	432
Shopkeepers, Shopmen, Warehousemen, &c.	6,142	676	5,509	232	12,109
Smiths, General . .	4,491	331	1,107	146	6,075
Spinners and Weavers .	6,266	1,131	921	7	8,325
Sugar Bakers, Boilers, &c.	500	56	246	12	814
Surveyors . . .	54	16	160	9	239
Tailors . . .	10,163	1,483	964	99	12,709
Tallow Chandlers and Soap Makers . .	35	6	26	2	69
Tanners and Curriers .	338	38	165	18	559
Turners . . .	193	40	99	11	343
Wheelwrights . .	283	112	595	53	1,043
Woolcombers and Sorters	60	34	199	10	303
Trades and Professions not before specified .	23,000	2,428	5,703	444	31,575
Not distinguished . .	97,296	11,093	38,065	10,459	156,913
ADULT FEMALES.					
Domestic and Farm Servants, Nurses, &c. .	62,651	5,535	65,279	2,013	135,478
Gentlewomen and Governesses . . .	1,370	484	977	472	3,303
Milliners, Dress Makers, Needlewomen . .	4,619	259	1,302	118	6,289
Married Women . .	149,613	19,851	72,060	8,600	250,124
Shopwomen . .	20	4	109	3	134
Trades and Professions not before specified .	737	247	277	9	1,270
Not distinguished . .	252,417	23,699	45,693	3,305	325,114
CHILDREN.					
*Male Children . .	105,975	19,622	46,746	4,519	176,862
*Female ditto . .	99,474	17,629	44,921	4,234	166,258
Infants . . .	50,574	7,277	16,179	1,093	72,123
Not distinguished . .	94,505	47,459	7,627	28,865	178,556
Grand Total .	1,463,333	214,784	556,945	77,812	2,312,874

* Previous to 1856 the Adult Age for the purposes of the Passengers' Act was 14; since that date, by the Act of 1855, it was fixed at 12.

GOVERNMENT EMIGRATION BOARD, *February* 1867.

TABLE showing the OCCUPATIONS, SEX, and GENERAL DESTINATION of the EMIGRANTS in 1864.

Occupation.	United States.	British North America.	Australasia.	All other Places.	Total.
ADULT MALES.					
Agricultural Labourers, Gardeners, Carters, &c.	344	61	1,779	29	2,213
Bakers	229	12	50	1	292
Blacksmiths and Farriers	48	13	180	10	251
Bookbinders & Stationers	14	3	10	3	30
Boot and Shoe Makers	218	19	111	3	351
Braziers, Tinsmiths, Whitesmiths, &c.	175	6	11	2	194
Brick and Tile Makers, Potters, &c.	41	1	17	—	59
Bricklayers, Masons, Plasterers, Slaters, &c.	803	17	226	3	1,049
Builders	50	—	18	—	68
Butchers, Poulterers, &c.	93	8	42	3	146
Cabinet Makers and Upholsterers	32	—	36	2	70
Carpenters and Joiners	761	92	466	18	1,337
Carvers and Gilders	19	4	2	—	25
Clerks	331	79	189	185	784
Clock and Watch Makers	61	4	10	4	79
Coach Makers & Trimmers	7	—	5	—	12
Coal Miners	26	4	16	—	46
Coopers	90	6	21	3	120
Cutlers	45	1	1	—	47
Domestic Servants	259	20	86	34	399
Dyers	9	5	4	—	18
Engravers	28	1	2	—	31
Engineers	77	14	79	42	212
Farmers	5,213	932	925	175	7,245
Gentlemen, Professional Men, Merchants, &c.	2,555	665	1,676	946	5,842
Jewellers and Silversmiths	36	2	9	7	54
Labourers, General	45,210	2,699	9,930	158	57,997
Locksmiths, Gunsmiths, &c.	6	1	3	4	14
Millers, Malsters, &c.	65	5	29	2	101
Millwrights	4	—	14	1	19
Miners and Quarrymen	2,539	203	454	70	3,266
Painters, Paperhangers, Plumbers, and Glaziers	238	22	72	5	337
Pensioners	8	16	14	7	45
Printers	90	14	32	2	138
Rope Makers	4	—	8	—	12
Saddlers & Harness Makers	41	2	18	—	61
Sail Makers	6	—	4	—	10

Occupation.	United States.	British North America.	Australasia	All other Places.	Total.
ADULT MALES—*continued*.					
Sawyers	6	7	29	—	42
Seamen	232	51	78	18	379
Shipwrights	12	—	11	3	26
Shopkeepers	400	45	305	47	797
Smiths, General	685	10	64	4	768
Spinners and Weavers	763	332	61	1	1,157
Sugar Bakers, Boilers, &c.	2	—	28	1	31
Surveyors	5	1	9	2	17
Tailors	1,473	19	49	6	1,547
Tallow Chandlers and Soap Makers	1	—	1	—	2
Tanners and Curriers	61	2	10	1	74
Turners	10	—	7	1	18
Wheelwrights	33	2	39	—	74
Woolcombers and Sorters	—	—	1	—	1
Other Mechanics not before specified	2,028	202	85	74	2,389
Not distinguished	3,073	463	1,606	2,720	7,862

Appendix to 25th Report of the Emigration Commissioners, p. 56.

CHAPTER III

Having shown that the " exterminating policy " of the Irish landlords has resulted in the existence at the census of 1861, of a greater number of holdings of all sizes in Ireland than there were in 1851, and of 160,000 more tenant farmers of fifteen acres and upwards than there were twenty years ago, (and on referring to the evidence given before Mr. Maguire's Committee it will be seen that, in the unanimous opinion of Judge Longfield, of Mr. Dillon, of Mr. M'Carthy Downing, of the Catholic Bishop of Cloyne, and of Mr. Curling,* fifteen acres are the smallest area which can be cultivated with advantage, or over which those gentlemen would themselves be willing to extend the protection of a lease,) I would have passed to the third point in our inquiry, had it not been objected that I have mistaken the nature of the accusations directed against the landlord class in Ireland, who, I am informed, have been so ruthlessly gibbeted, not exactly on

---

* By fifteen acres, 15 Irish acres=24 statute acres were probably meant by these gentlemen. I should not myself have drawn so hard a line or passed so sweeping a condemnation on farms of this size.

account of their own acts, but as representatives of those bygone generations to whose vicious mismanagement of their estates the present misfortunes of the country are to be attributed. That such is not the issue raised in the various manifestoes which I have undertaken to consider, will be at once apparent on referring to them; but, as it may be useful to ascertain what have been some of the historical sources of Ireland's *economic* difficulties,* I will endeavour to discriminate between the share in them attributable to the former owners of the soil and that which is due to other causes.

The writer who thus proposes to antedate our responsibilities seems satisfied he has arrived at the fountain-head of Ireland's calamities when he points his finger at the Irish proprietory of former days; nor does he dream of inquiring whether the landlord of 70 or 80 years ago may not himself have been a creature of circumstance, involved in the complexities of a system of which he was as much the victim as his tenants. And here again I eliminate from the discussion all reference to the supposed personal characteristics of the class. The popular conception of the Irish country gentleman of former days is principally derived from works of fiction and caricature, and is probably as correct as is usual with information gathered from such

* Though intimately connected with her economical career, I do not profess in this treatise to enter upon the consideration of Ireland's *political* and *social* difficulties.

sources. In many respects it stands in favourable juxtaposition with the picture drawn of his English cotemporary by Macaulay, though the noxious influences which emanated from the policy pursued by England towards the Catholics of Ireland must have been as demoralizing to him as it was to every other member of the dominant community. But with any estimate of his individual vices or virtues we are not now concerned. Of one thing alone can we be certain—that in dealing with his property he pursued his own advantage with more or less intelligence, and in doing so exercised a right not only legitimate in itself, but which has been universally recognized as the mainspring of human progress. But it is objected that the practical results of his proceedings have been over-population, rack-rents, and an exodus of 2,000,000 souls. The question is, have these phenomena followed in such direct sequence as is alleged, or have other influences, independent of the landlord's agency, vitiated a system which otherwise would not have been unhealthy? Now, of the three evils he is supposed to have occasioned, the two last are the direct consequences of the first. A rack-rent is the product of competition, and both competition and emigration are the results of over-population. The true measure, therefore, of the responsibility of the Irish landlord is the share he has had in disturbing the equilibrium which ought to have been maintained between the increase of population and the development of the country's industrial resources.

But, first, had space permitted, I should have wished to exhibit, as I have already done with regard to emigration, the true nature and origin of the rack-renting system, which is invariably described as the offspring of landlord rapacity. As a matter of fact, it does not appear that the Irish landlords of former days dealt harshly with their tenantry. Even Mr. Butt admits that during the whole of the 18th century there were scarcely any evictions, and that long leases were almost universal;* while Judge Longfield states that so late as 1835 there was very little land in the southern and western counties not on lease, and that "*most of the leases were all in the tenants' favour.*" Nor is it alleged that the landlords themselves exacted exorbitant rents; the principal complaint against them is that they leased their lands to middlemen, and that sometimes they were separated from the actual occupiers of the soil by a dozen derivative tenures. From this fact it is evident that the rents they charged must have been comparatively moderate. But long leases at moderate rates are hardly a

---

* In earlier days tenancies at will seem to have been preferred by the tenants to a lease. "Irish landlords," says Spenser, "do not use to set out their lands in farm, or for terms of years, but only from year to year, and some during pleasure; *neither indeed will the Irish husbandman otherwise take his land than so long as he lists himself.*"

criminal arrangement. It is true the increasing pressure of a teeming population, and the natural instinct which, Judge Longfield tells us, is inherent in every Irish tenant—to turn himself into a landlord if he gets the chance—resulted in a state of things replete with mischief. But for the development of this unexpected phase in the Irish land system, the proprietor is by no means responsible to the degree which is supposed. Up to nearly the close of the last century the great proportion of the country was in pasture, and the population was less than half of what it amounted to in 1841. The holdings were of considerable size,* and when a

---

* Both the soil and climate of Ireland are peculiarly adapted to pasturage, and consequently to large farms, but there was a peculiar reason why, during the earlier half of the last century, the holdings were necessarily of a considerable size.

Amongst the many infamous statutes known as the Penal Laws, was one which precluded Catholics from purchasing lands, from holding a lease of more than thirty-one years, or from deriving from the permanent occupation of land any profit in excess of one-third of the rent; consequently the proprietors of estates had no option—as Mr. Thornton very justly remarks—than to let their lands to the few capitalists who could legally occupy them. I have placed in an appendix Mr. Thornton's admirable description of the circumstances under which Ireland continued to remain a grass country until the close of the last century. (See Appendix, p. 147.)

" The Protestant landlords also suffered indirectly from the operation of the same penal laws; for in letting these estates, they were to a great degree confined in the selection of their tenants, to those who alone could enjoy any permanent tenure under them, and were exclusively entitled to the election franchise. Many landlords parted with the whole or a great portion

farm was let the landlord never dreamt of its being converted into tillage, and no provisions against subdivision were introduced. But as population multiplied the situation changed, and the enormous rise in the price of grain and provisions on the breaking out of the French war made it the interest of the tenant to subdivide his land as minutely as he could.* He accordingly introduced an Irish edition of what is known as 'la petite culture.'

It is true most of the later leases contained clauses against subletting, but an unexpected legal subtlety rendered them practically inoperative, and when attempts were made to stop an innovation, which in no way benefited the landlord, most proprietors found, after going to great

---

of their property for long terms, and thus avoided all immediate contact with the inferior occupiers, so that all the duties of a landlord were left for performance to a middleman. The latter, on the other hand, in the favourable position in which the laws had indirectly placed him as regarded the proprietor, *dictated very frequently his own terms to the landlord;* and restrictive covenants against subletting or subdividing were seldom inserted."—*Digest Devon Commission, Summary, p.* 1109.

* "The introduction of the 40*s* franchise and its extension to the Catholic population also acted as an inducement both to the proprietors and to the middlemen to subdivide and to sublet. The war with France raised considerably the profits of the occupier, who was thus enabled to pay a large rent to the mesne lessee. These causes produced throughout the country a class of intermediate proprietors, known by the name of middlemen, whose decline after the cessation of the war, and the fall of prices in 1815, brought with it much of the evils we have witnessed of late years."—*Ibid.*

expense that they were completely powerless.* The practice consequently spread, and an obnoxious class of middlemen, as they were termed, relet the greater proportion of the soil of Ireland at rack-rents to their teeming countrymen.† But though the ma-

* " Many of the witnesses, however, seemed to be impressed with the idea, that even with the assistance of the subletting Acts, there is frequently much expense and difficulty in preventing subletting in the case of leasehold farms ; and this opinion has tended to prevent the grant of leases."—*Dig. Dev. Com. Summary, p.* 418.

† " The high prices of agricultural produce during the late continental war, and the consequently increased value of land, appear to have much increased subletting, by enabling the large farmers, without personal trouble, to derive from their leaseholds considerable incomes in the form of profit rents."
Ibid. p. 418.

" Lord George Hill records, among other facts relating to rundale, that one person held his farm in forty-two different patches, and at last gave it up in despair of finding it ; and that a field of half an acre was held by twenty-two different persons."

" The evidence proves clearly that these malpractices have produced the results which might naturally be expected, and that sub-tenants, the tenants of lands much subdivided, and of farms held in rundale, are in general excessively poor, and their lands much exhausted."—*Ibid. p.* 419.

" It will be observed that several of the covenants above mentioned have for their object the prevention of the subdivision of farms, which is alleged to be so common and so injurious an effect of leases."

" But none of these covenants provide against the possibility of the farm, upon the death of the occupier, becoming subdivided, either by the provisions of his will, or by the operation of the statute of distributions, although it appears that these are the causes most frequently operating to produce subdivision."—*Ibid. p.* 237.

jority of middlemen became constituted in this manner, there is no doubt that sometimes they were

"This tendency to sublet even discourages the building of cottages."—*Dig. Dev. Com. p.* 49.

"Some proprietors felt disposed to build cottages for them, (the cottiers on their estate) with small allotments, held direct from themselves; but the chief difficulty in this case is, to secure that the original evil may not thus be increased by still further increasing the glut of the labour market, which would be the effect, unless the farmer can be restrained from still bringing in additional people for the mere profit he may derive in letting to them a house or garden; this tendency has long been felt, and is likely to continue the chief difficulty in the management of property."—*Ibid. p.* 130.

The following is a fair example of the history of most Irish estates.

"This estate has been for ages in the family.

"Between the years 1777 and 1787, James Lord Caher let great portions of it on sixty-one years' leases. Lessees were conditioned in all cases not to sublet, and in most cases to build a good house on the farm.

"It is almost needless to state that there is scarcely an instance of a house being built by the lessee of the slightest value; and every lessee has sublet generally to a great extent.

"These farms at the time they were let were all in grass, with scarcely any inhabitants on them, and the lessee held the whole farm.

"There was no use in the head landlord attempting by law to have the clauses in the lease observed, as no jury would find a verdict against a tenant, for the probability was that some of the jurors were in the same state as the defendants as regarded subletting."—*Dig. Dev. Com. p.* 437.

"Subletting was barred in all these leases; but the landlord never could have found a jury to put the clause in force. The late Lord Glengall endeavoured to break some of these leases thirty years ago, which were proved to have been forgeries by connivance of the agent, after the decease of the late lord's predecessor; but, though Judges charged in favour of the land-

placed in possession of land by the owners, with the express intention they should sublet, and it is with lord, and the Superior Courts gave verdicts also in his favour, still the county juries never would agree, and the landlord failed.

"Timber and slates are given to them by the landlord, consequently the estate is now, on these new farms, varying from twenty to fifty acres, studded with slate houses."

Dig. Dev. Com. p. 437.

"Between the years 1780 and 1787, James Lord Caher let immense tracts of land in large farms to single individuals. They have now enjoyed them for sixty-one years, and the leases are about expiring—some have expired. Those farms have been sublet in the most astonishing manner, and except upon one or two of those great farms, varying from 1,000 acres to 100, I do not think there are above two or three lessees now in possession of any part of those lands which were let to them by James Lord Caher.

"They are entirely new people brought in?—Entirely a new population. The lands were altogether in grass in those years. They were great grazing farms. In the high times during the war, those lessees sublet their lands *ad infinitum*, and became middlemen; and when the peace came prices fell, and the middlemen became totally ruined.

"What course has your lordship taken upon them?—I will take the first case which presents itself to me in the statement, Kilcoran, 161. That is 281 acres Irish, and the rent formerly paid was 13s 10d an Irish acre.

"What the sub-rents were you do not know?—No. The lease was for sixty-one years, let in 1782. It was completely deluged with paupers, and the lessee himself did not hold above sixteen acres. One house, inhabited by a most notorious ruffian, was thrown down and the man turned out. The land was squared as much as possible into from fifteen to twenty acre farms to residents, the rest of the people still remaining on the lands in their houses . . . . . .

"Are they numerous?—Very numerous, I should say. The land is remarkably good, generally speaking, and worth from about 30s to 35s an Irish acre.

"As what they had been in the habit of paying?—I cannot

this method of procedure adopted by a few that the entire class have been credited. But though exactly answer that question for this very simple reason—the lessee, the middleman, being in abject poverty from idleness, took fines, so that it is impossible to tell."
Rt. Hon. the Earl of Glengall, Dig. Dev. Com. p. 278.

Evidence of Wm. Hamilton, Esq. Agent.

" Did any of these old leases contain the non-letting clauses?—Yes; but they were inoperative.

" Do you know of any cases in which an attempt was made to oblige the tenants to act under them?—No; because the law was, that any permission or toleration of a breach by the landlord, did away with the covenant altogether until the recent act; then, as in most instances, partial consents were given, or breaches overlooked; it became a matter quite hopeless on the part of the landlord to enforce the covenant when the evils of subletting became apparent."—*Digest, Dev. Com. p.* 281.

Evidence of Mr. Ed. Byne, Farmer.

" Do the landlords permit the sale?—They are very seldom consulted; they would not be satisfied generally. In Lord Carrick's leases there was a covenant against subletting, still the tenants broke through that, and the trustees could not prevent them doing so."—*Ibid. p.* 345.

William Ford, Esq. Sessional Solicitor for County Meath, Land Agent and Town Clerk to the Corporation of city of Dublin.

" What do you conceive to be a power which could be fairly given to prevent too minute subdivisions?—If I were going to make a law to regulate the tenure of land, I certainly would make it part of that law to prevent the too minute subdivision of it, because I would coerce by the law the parties to send their families to earn their bread at different trades. That would create manufacture, and put them in other callings, and they have now other countries to go to, which would lead to emigration. Without compulsion they would learn trades and business, and go abroad of their own accord, and perhaps return to the hive enriched."—*Ibid p.* 424.

the experiment turned out unsuccessfully, there was nothing at the time to warn the proprietor against

Richard White, Esq. Land Proprietor.

" What clauses are there in your leases in reference to subletting or subdividing the lands? In some of my leases since the year 1832, there are clauses against subletting, but I am sorry to say I have not put them in force. In fact I think it a dangerous thing in Ireland to do it.

" What then is likely to be the consequence?—That is one of the most difficult questions. I am perfectly convinced, if there could be an end, generally speaking, to subletting, it would be one of the greatest blessings that could occur to the country; and in order to do that—I am speaking now from experience—if landlords could only give sufficient land, not too much nor too little, to a man, it would be the best thing they could do. If a landlord gives a large farm, there is no doubt, as soon as a son marries and the daughter-in-law is brought in, the son gets a part, and the second and third son the same, so that it is cut up into small bits, and when it comes into the landlord's hands it is over-populated. He goes upon the sweeping system, and he is held up as a cruel man; but a landlord cannot help doing it. If there was a law passed of a strict nature to prevent subletting, it would be a great advantage to the country. The tenants would be obliged to send some of their children out into the world, and to provide for them in some other way—a thing seldom dreamt of."

Dig. Dev. Com. p. 424.

John Hancock, Esq. Agent to Lord Lurgan (Ulster).

"Is there much subletting or subdivision of farms?—Yes, subdivision prevails to a great extent. Every tenant, if permitted, would divide his farm, in equal shares, amongst all his sons. . . . . . .

" *On leases,* as soon as a son marries, he builds a room, or a 'bay,' as it is called, to his father's house, and gets a share of his father's land. The linen manufacture offers the strongest inducement to subdivision, because a very small portion of ground, in addition to the looms, will support a family.

it, and it can be easily conceived that many a landlord, speaking neither the language, nor

The effects of subdivision are very bad; first, the land is cut into such small patches, that a plough and horses, in many cases, will hardly turn in the field; and a large quantity of ground is lost in fences; habits of slovenliness and idleness is increased; and, as I have already stated, *the most subdivided leases are the worst paid, although cheap,* and the places are in the worst condition. I oppose subdivision all I can, but there is no duty connected with the management of property more difficult to be performed. . . . . The sons have been brought up ignorant of any other occupation. . . . . . . What are they to do? . . . . . . Subletting also prevails to a very large extent. The high prices that weavers will give for houses and small gardens offer great temptations to the farmer."—*Dig. Dev. p.* 425.

Evidence of J. V. Stuart, Esq. Land Proprietor, and Magistrate.

"In answer to that question I should state a practice which exists only in this country, and in a very remote part of it, and it is this, that they have gone on subdividing so far that instead of its being called a 'cow's grass' *it is gone down to the 'cow's foot,' which is one-fourth of a cow's grass—nay, they have gone so low as a 'cow's toe,' which is one-eighth of a cow's grass.*

"To what extent is the subletting or subdividing of farms carried out, and is it permitted by the landlords?—Subletting or subdividing existed formerly to a great extent, and it is still universal where the landlord or agent is not most vigilant; it is generally to provide for tenants' children, but often to exact income from cottiers. Its effects are certain, and generally proximate pauperism; generally it is against the landlord's consent, and is prevented by limiting the quantity of fuel. Ejectment is an example, and watchfulness on the part of the bailiff when it can be secured.

"What are the effects of subletting on the accumulation and introduction of capital, and also on population?—It puts an absolute stop to the accumulation of capital, in the same proportion that consolidation assists its accumulation; and, if carried to any extent, the ground ultimately produces little

professing the same religion as his tenants, might consider it not only a very convenient, but a very

more than food for the rapidly accumulating population to be fed out of it. When subdivided with tenants' sons it encourages improvident and early marriages (already too general), and consequently a fall in the condition of the farmer; and, when sublet for the sake of income to cottiers, a most exacting rent is enforced with rigorous punctuality in the shape of money and labour utterly disproportioned to the value received, and leading the farmer rather to depend upon this income than upon his own industry, and is therefore a great discouragement to agricultural improvement.

"I conceive the evil at this moment is, that if a man comes into a farm held under me, he subdivides it, and before I can take any proceedings against him, the evil has grown up, and I should have to increase the evil by driving the man out."

Dig. Dev. Com. p. 428.

Evidence of H. L. Prentice, Esq. Agent to Lord Caledon. (Armagh and Tyrone.)

"Has subdividing or subletting been carried on to any extent in other districts?—Yes, to an alarming extent.

"How minutely have you known farms to be subdivided? —I have known ten families on a farm of six Irish acres.

"Was that a case where land was held under a determinable lease or at will?—There was a lease of it.

"Do you find that a man holding by lease even in perpetuity disposes him to divide?—Yes, it does."—*Ibid. p. 428.*

Evidence of James Johnson, Esq., Land Proprietor.

"It is not carried to a great extent in Donegal, but it does exist, I am sorry to say; and although every means are taken by both proprietors and agents to prevent it, they find it almost impossible to put a stop to it.

"Do you find that subdividing farms takes place to a greater extent on those estates than where the proprietor is resident? —Yes, it must do so; and even with a resident proprietor it is very difficult to prevent a father giving his children portions of his farm"—*Dig. Devon Com. p. 429.*

popular alternative to give a long lease at a low rent to some person less alien to the peasants in

Evidence of Mr. John M'Carten, Linen Manufacturer and Agent.

"Has subletting been carried on to any great extent in your neighbourhood?—I may say it has, though the landlords are every day watching it, and do all they can without quarrelling with the people: there is a great desire for it on the part of the tenants.

"Have you ever known any legal measures taken by landlords to stop it or counteract it?—I am not aware that any legal steps have been taken, under a lease, to enforce the covenants against the tenant for subletting; but on some estates, leases are refused in consequence of it and in order to check it; and I have known other cases where a reduction of rent, actually contemplated, was refused to the tenant because he had subdivided the land contrary to the landlord's wishes."— *Digest, Dev. Com. p.* 432.

Evidence of J. E. Taylor, Esq., Landholder, Agent and Magistrate.

"The only reason I can assign for it is, that there are some old leases, and on the old leases and cheap farms there is more subletting than on the recent set farms.

"Then, in point of fact, those 309 subdivided farms have been held principally under old leases?—Yes; and they are the cheapest, and most unimproved, and the hardest to get the rent from."—*Ibid. p.* 432.

Andrew Orr, Esq., Land Proprietor and Farmer.

"With regard to the subletting and subdividing of farms, to what extent has it been carried out, and what are its effects?—This is a ruinous measure to both landlord and tenant, and almost impossible to prevent. The people are apt to contract early marriages. A farmer's son brings home a wife, and then, after some time, the barn is fitted up for the newly married couple: the farmer then finds he cannot do without the barn, and a new house has to be erected for his son, and then he prevails on his father to give him part of the

race and religion than himself, upon the understanding that he might relet it in smaller areas.*

land. The landlord of course sets his face against the measure; but still the evil proceeds, until all are driven to beggary and ejected. That, so far as I perceive, is what generally happens."
Digest, Dev. Com. p. 432.

Evidence of Richard Mayne, Esq., Agent and Magistrate.

"Does the subletting or subdividing of farms still continue?—Oh, yes.

"Is it permitted by the landlords?—They cannot stop it.

"What means do they take to attempt to stop it?—They cannot take any; they try as well as they can, by turning out the tenant; but if you dispossess a man and his family, it creates such a sensation that people cannot do it; it is impossible to do it."—*Ibid. p.* 432.

Evidence of Edward Spoule, Esq., Linen Bleacher and Land Proprietor.

"Is the subletting or subdividing of farms carried on to any extent?—It is too much so; and it is injurious to the landlord as well as the tenantry themselves; it is destructive to the accumulation of capital, and lowers the farming population, so as to render them subject to greater privations than day labourers. It is done in two ways—one to provide for children marrying, by dividing the tenement, and another to procure some money, by the sale of a portion of the farm, to enable a struggling farmer to clear of a debt. In both cases the evils are permanent and the benefits slight."—*Ibid. p.* 432.

Evidence of William C. Collis, Esq., Land Proprietor and Magistrate.

"Subletting . . . . . . exists from a mistaken wish to keep the family together, and have the benefit of their labour until they are too old to go to a trade, and have formed such habits

---

* *Charles King O'Hara, Landed Proprietor and Chairman of Board of Guardians.*

" When a tenant has proved himself to be industrious and

If the event proved unfortunate, it was not because the tenant was a middleman, but because he dealt as are only fitted for tilling the land, then the extreme difficulty of getting other farms reduces the parent to the necessity (I will call it) of dividing his farm. . . . Landlords cannot well prevent this, except by most rigid and unpopular means, though they see and understand the evil. And I have here to remark, that this difficulty of obtaining farms arises chiefly from the odium that is attached to a landlord, under any circumstances, for dispossessing a tenant."—*Dig. Dev. Com. p.* 434.

John P. Molony, Esq., Land Proprietor.

"Does the subletting or subdividing of farms still continue?—Yes, indeed it does.

"Is it permitted by the landlords?—Not where they can prevent it; but it is generally done without being brought under the eye of the landlord, and sometimes in consequence of a man having a large farm—as his children marry off he gives them a portion of it. If he has eight or ten acres he will give one son four or five, and another three, and in that way."

Ibid. p. 434.

---

trustworthy, and has acquired capital, the landlord is by no means averse to place under his management improveable land, with a promise of a lease when improved; reserving to himself a controlling power over the subletting and management of the sub-tenants. *Such middlemen are necessary, and, under proper control, become salutary links in the chain connecting the lord of the soil with the humblest occupier thereof;* they co-operate with the landlord in maintaining peace and good order, being equally interested therein, and become a check to general combination, so likely to prevail where the landlord, unsupported, has to contend singly with one uniform mass of small tenants combined for a common object and interest: they afford a support and protection to the landlord, of which, latterly, he stands much in need. I do not think that you can act upon any one decided principle; you must bring all into practice. You will find some middlemen very well intentioned, and improving, and valuable members of society; and on the other hand they may be otherwise."—*Dig. Devon Com.* p. 417.

with his comrades and co-religionists more unmercifully than might have been expected.*

Evidence of Thomas Ware, Esq., Land Proprietor, Vice-chairman of Board of Guardians, and Magistrate.

" What steps do they take to prevent it ?—They are generally obliged to yield to it, the remedy afforded by law is so difficult of attaining. . . . . . At the time that the Subletting Act was in force in this country, my father and I jointly let a small lot of ground to a Roman Catholic clergyman ; there was as strong a clause inserted in the lease against subletting as the skill of the legal man could devise. . . . . . He gave a part of the ground to his brother, and a part to his sister. His sister got a license, and opened a public-house upon the premises. I did not like this getting on. My immediate tenant retained in his own hand one small field, containing probably an acre or an acre and a half of land. I brought an ejectment against him for a breach of covenant in subletting. I had a record in court upon it, and it was with extreme difficulty that I was able to sustain the case, though I proved that the county rate was paid in three separate payments—one by the brother, one by the sister, and a third portion for the small field he kept as a colourable possession in his own hand. I succeeded in getting a verdict, but it was afterwards set aside, and an order for a new trial came down—and all this arising from the impossibility on my part to prove that those lettings had taken place by written agreement. It was set up by him, 'I put in my brother as my steward or caretaker, and lent my sister

---

* " It appears that as one means of abolishing the class of middlemen, proprietors in many cases on the expiration of a lease, set the land to the occupying tenants, letting to the middleman that part only of the farm which he retained in his own hands. And to avoid the operation of this system many middlemen have sought to remove the competitors for a renewal, and have ejected all their sub-tenants previous to the lapse of their own interest. This has not unfrequently caused much suffering and outrage."—*Ibid.* p. 1029.

Whether even the middleman is deserving of all the abuse which is heaped upon him may be a the use of the house ;' but finally I succeeded."—*Digest, Dev. Com. p.* 433.

Evidence of M. Mahony, Esq.

" I will give you an instance of it (subdivision):—One portion is called Ballycarberry, forming three ploughlands. The occupying tenants some years ago divided the land into little divisions among themselves. They calculated each division as the grass of four cows. There was one man of the name of Crahan, now living on one of those lots with four cows—he had four in family; he got them all married, and the fortune he gave was a cow's grass to each; and of course, the sons came to reside upon the land. There are four families. The last of all was a daughter. He had but one cow's grass remaining. He married that daughter to my cow boy, and he got the remaining cow's grass, or he was to have one on the father-in-law's death."—*Ibid. p.* 434.

Evidence of J. Butler, Esq., Land Proprietor.

" As soon as a man has a son or daughter grown up, the first thing he does is to give them a bit of land."—*Ibid. p.* 435.

Evidence of R. T. Saunders, Esq., Land Proprietor.

" I have some leases ready, but the tenants will not accept them. . . . . With respect to subletting, a tenant-at-will cannot subdivide his farm so easily as a tenant by lease, and such never takes place on a well-regulated estate; but a tenant by lease most frequently subdivides by his last will and testament amongst his children, thereby leaving all not sufficient land to support their families, and in a short time none can pay their rent, consequently the landlord loses his rent and they lose their farms."—*Ibid. p.* 284.

Evidence of Captain Thomas Bolton, land agent to Lord Stanley.

" With respect to the subletting or subdividing of farms, does it still continue?—Yes, it does, very much, and I have much difficulty in checking it. There is more difficulty in that than any thing else. That is my reason for not granting

question. To drive a hard bargain is a failing not confined to that class of persons; and it has leases. You have no control over them with a lease. You may put stringent clauses, but presently you find a barn or stable occupied; and you find a field with a tenant, and he says, 'This man is a labourer or a servant of mine.'

"Have you attempted to enforce any of those clauses?—Yes, several times; and succeeded once on a farm of fourteen acres of ground, at an expense of £220. It was twice referred to the upper courts, and two trials at the assizes. I had enough of it, but I succeeded. The rent was about 22s an acre, upon fourteen acres of ground.

"Explain in what manner these enormous costs were incurred?—Points were raised by the defendant's lawyer with regard to the proceeding. There was a new trial, and points reserved a second time, and it went up to Dublin a second time. The tenant sold his interest in the farm; he was a drunken blackguard sort of a fellow, and I was aware before it actually took place, that it was intended to be done. I formally told him before a number of persons, that he ought not to do so, and cautioned the purchaser, who gave him £150. for his interest in the land; that I should proceed upon the lease, and if he persuaded the other man to dispose of it, I would turn him out. This was openly done, but still the purchaser gave him £150. for his interest in the land. I had to prove the subletting; and there were some difficulties I had to encounter, that I cannot call to mind."—*Digest, Dev. Com. p.* 436.

Evidence of Robert O'Brien, Esq., Land Proprietor, Tenant, and Agent.

"The subletting of land has long been a grievance, and those landlords who first broke through the system of letting their lands to middlemen were at that time hailed as benefactors to their country; but now the rule has become so general, and the class of middlemen so nearly passed away, that the evils of it are nearly forgotten, and the occupiers are now getting up a cry against the landlords as if they were unkind and hard taskmasters, forgetting that in nine cases out of ten

always seemed to me that the moral responsibility of accepting a competition rent is pretty much

their existence on the land was without the consent of the landlord; that they have much greater indulgences from him than they had while under the middleman; and that they always looked forward with anxiety to be brought into direct communication with their landlord . . . . . The great value of land during the war, induced many who were of a respectable farming class to sublet the lands and set up to be gentlemen; and one frequently meets with people who say their father had £100, £200, &c., a year out of such and such lands."—*Digest, Dev. Com. p.* 435.

W. J. Fennell, Esq., Landholder and Magistrate.

"Can you give us any instances of that subdivision?— Yes, I can. A tenant of my own held a few years ago thirty-six Irish acres of land himself, under a lease directed to himself, not under the restriction of the Subletting Act. He had a lease for lives prior to that. After a bit he got one of his sons married, and gave him one-third of the farm, and planted him on it. A little after he got a second son married, and planted him on it, and gave him one-third. One of those men not being industrious, and matters going wrong, could not pay his rent for his third, and to relieve himself out of the difficulty he gives half of his third to a fourth party, getting some money for it."—*Ibid. p.* 440.

"Were you before this division took place aware of it, and did you try to remonstrate with this person?—I did, and his reply was what else could he do with his sons? And now the stranger is not paying anything, or paying badly, and he looks to me to get the man out for him.

"Is the lease still in existence?—Yes, there are three lives in existence still. I wish to state another instance about the division of land, and the way they deal with the land. About sixteen years ago a tenant died in this place. He left me executor to his will, and guardian to his two infant daughters. He had but ten acres of land. . . . . An allowance of 5s an acre had been made for some time, and up to this time.

the same as that of profiting by the market rate of wages. If the first is frequently exorbitant, the

Still I think he was paying the value. His will was, that on the eldest girl attaining the age of nineteen, she was to get married; and upon her getting married, either to give half the ground to her other sister, or secure her in £50. On her attaining the age of nineteen, in one month afterwards she did get married, and her husband passed notes for the £50 to the other girl, instead of dividing the land, which £50 must still go out of my land, or I must have another tenant on it; I could instance hundreds of cases of that kind ...... I may notice one more particularly—a case of that kind. Another man died, leaving two sons. He had only nine acres of land. He divided this ground between them by will. One was married. The unmarried man he bound in his will to give £30 to his sister on marriage, having only four acres and a half of land. He did secure her in it, and has been three years in paying it. He has discharged it, but I believe he is beggared by it. He is pauperised. He had to sell his only cow and mule he had for the use of his farm, to provide the £30 for his sister."

Digest, Dev. Com. p. 441.

Francis E. Curry, Esq., Agent to the Duke of Devonshire.

"Does the subletting or subdivision of farms still continue?—It is a thing I endeavour to check by every means in my power. There is scarcely any subletting except under old leases unexpired, where it cannot be prevented; but the subdivision of land is more difficult to prevent, and it is done sometimes contrary to covenant and the known rules of the estate; but I endeavour to check it as much as possible by timely cautioning and watchfulness more than by any other means. In some instances I have been obliged to have recourse to stronger measures. I think there is a greater tendency to subdivide among the smaller tenants than the large ones.

"What measures have you taken to prevent the subletting or subdivision?—In some instances where I have found subdivision to exist, and being unable to check it otherwise, I have been obliged to give the parties notice to quit...... In a few

latter is as often inadequate, and inadequate wages are as fatal to efficiency as a rack rent is to produc-cases ejectments have been brought on account of it. I endeavour to prevent it as much by watchfulness as anything else. It is not practised to any great extent; the parties I have the most difficulty in watching are the small holders."
Dig. Dev. Com. p. 412.

Evidence of Thomas Butler, Esq., Agent and Farmer.

" Does the subletting or subdividing still continue ? — Whenever the tenants are allowed they will subdivide to a quarter of an acre a piece.

" Upon the property which you manage is that permitted ? —They are bound by leases not to subdivide, but they will do it in spite of you."—*Ibid. p.* 413.

Evidence of John D. Balfe, Esq., Farmer.

"The tenant having a lease, the covenants of which can only be broken by the fact of subletting, do you see any practical difficulty in the landlord preventing it ?—I think, as the law is at present, it is difficult, but it might be remedied."
Ibid. p. 413.

Evidence of Edward Elliot, Esq., Land Proprietor.

"The people would, I have no doubt, be most anxious still to divide; they would divide down to a rood at this moment if their families required it."—*Ibid. p.* 413.

Evidence of Thomas Barnes, Esq., Landholder, Agent, and Magistrate.

" To what extent is the subletting or subdividing of farms carried on ?—It is not carried on to any extent ; the landlords are doing all they can to prevent it: they seem to be doing every thing they can, and nothing is more troublesome.

" What means do you resort to to prevent it ?—We insert strong covenants against it, and we threaten legal proceedings; but we have never taken any."—*Ibid. p.* 413.

Evidence of John Nunn, Esq., Land Proprietor.

" Is there any covenant about subletting or subdividing ? —I have known even in old leases a clause to that effect put

tion; though each be the result of voluntary adjustment, it is the same abject misery and absence of in, but I believe it never availed, because the courts of law allowed what they termed waivers in such matters. If a landlord received rent after he knew the subletting had taken place, it was admitted as a waiver; and I believe for that very reason the landlords gave up inserting the clauses."

Dig. Dev. Com. p. 444.

Evidence of Robert D'Arcy, Esq., Farmer and Agent.

"The middlemen, we found, destroyed every thing they had to do with. They were not satisfied with the profit from farming, but they covered the land with poor tenants; and it is easy to explain to any one acquainted with the country the desire they have to subdivide. Every man who has twenty acres of land, if he has a good house, and a barn, and a cow-house and stable, the first thing he does is to put his son into the barn. The son says, 'I am not satisfied to live in that manner with you, and I will put up a chimney in the stable;' and they never stop till they cover the little farm, that was once a comfortable thing, and bring the greatest possible misery upon themselves. It is to get rid of those that we ship those people to America.

"Does the subletting or subdivision of farms still continue?—Very much; where a poor man can do it he will do it, particularly with their own families. When a family grows up they become a little unpleasant, and wish to settle themselves—the daughter must have her part, and the son must have his part.

"Is it permitted by the landlords?—No.

"What course do they adopt to prevent it?—Where there is a clause against subletting they proceed according to that clause to put them out, but latterly there has been some change in the Act in respect to that; that unless the penalty was set forth, and recited in the body of the lease, you could not enforce it. I think nothing would prevent it but a clause making it an avoidance of the lease."—*Ibid. p.* 444.

Evidence of John Duke, Esq., M.D., Leitrim.

"It is a common practice, where a man has five acres he will subdivide it with three sons."—*Dig. Dev. Com. p.* 445.

SUBDIVISION OF FARMS IN IRELAND.

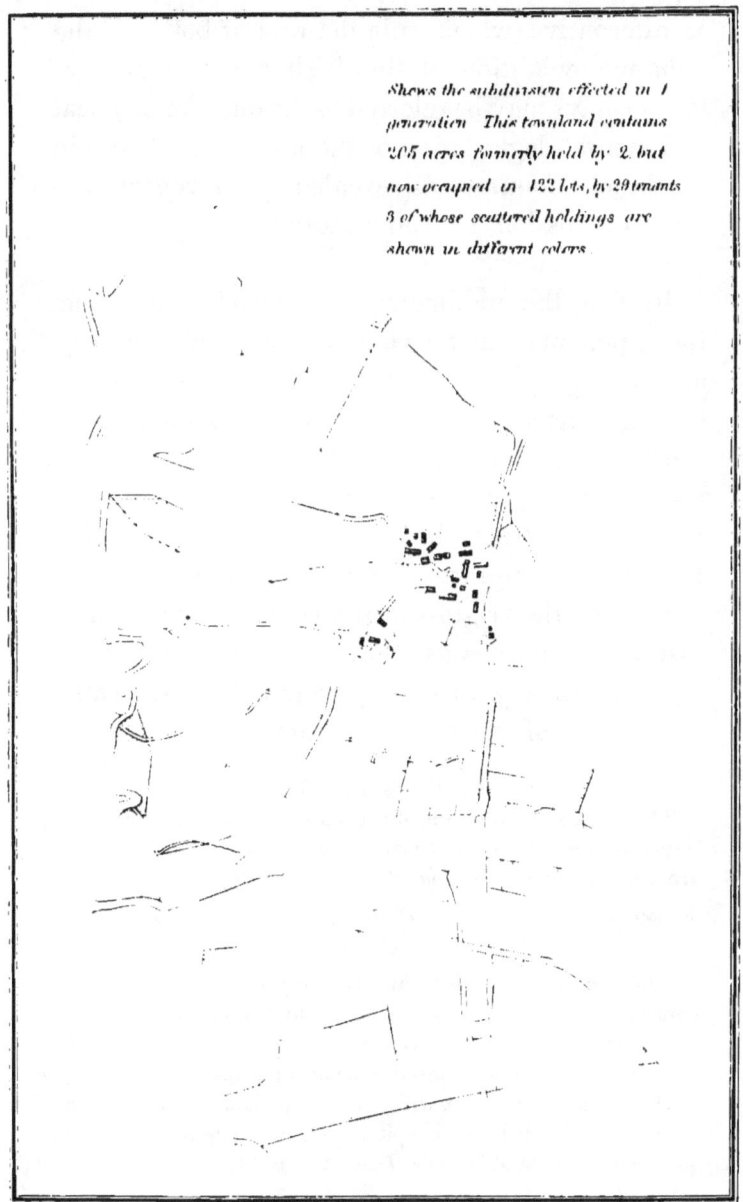

Extracted from Report of Devon Commission.

an alternative which rule the rate of both; if the unhappy condition of the Irish cottier tenant of former days may be referred to the one, the physical and mental degradation of the labouring classes in the Black Country, as revealed in the report of a late Commission, is even a more startling illustration of the other.

In fact the middlemen of Ireland were rather the exponents than the cause of the people's misery, and, though piled ten deep one above the other, on a single tenancy, they no more occasioned rack rents than the degrees on a barometer occasion the atmospheric pressure they record. Derivative tenancies, cottier allotments, potato cultivation, low wages, emigration have been the rude alleviations—not the origin—of the country's destitution; just as half-rations are the alternative for short provisions,—or any wages are preferable to starvation—a patch of ground, at a rack rent, to serfdom

Hon. W. Le Poer Trench.
"I do not see the means of preventing this subletting. . . . . Subdivisions of farms by tenants, for the purpose of alienation, are always ruinous."—*Dig. Dev. Com. p.* 286.

Evidence of Charles King O'Hara, Esq., Land Proprietor and Chairman of Board of Guardians.
"Is subletting carried out to any great extent?—It is in general practice when not prevented by the landlord: . . . . . it is practised against the consent of the landlord, who endeavours to prevent it by enforcing the penal clauses of the lease, or ousting the tenant, if at will. It is injurious to the interest of all parties, for it lessens capital, increases population, and impoverishes the land."—*Dig. Dev. Com. p.* 447.

I

and 3d. a day,— and a free farm in America to digging another man's potato garden in Connemara. Similar phenomena would have declared themselves under any system of land tenure, and in any country where the population had expanded in a degree disproportionate to its capacities for self-sustenation. If it were otherwise, every perpetuity in Ireland would be a land of Goshen,* and Ulster a paradise where rack-rents and evictions were unknown.† But it is an acknowledged fact that the low-let perpetuities of the South and West only exaggerate the worst features of the worst estates,‡ and in Ulster, though under a more

---

* "It does not appear either, as a general rule, from the evidence, that those tenants who have the longest leases, and the most beneficial interest in their farms, have brought the lands they hold to a more productive or improved state than others, not possessing such advantages or security. It is even broadly asserted by many that lands held under long leases, at nominal rents, are in a worse state than those held from year to year."—*Digest Devon Commission, Summary, p.* 16.

† "It may be assumed that the fourth class houses are generally unfit for human habitations; and yet it would appear that in the best circumstanced county in this respect (Down) 24·7 per cent., or about one-fourth, of the population live in houses of this class."—*Ibid. p.* 126.

‡ *Evidence of John Quin, Esq., Land Proprietor.*

"What, in your opinion, is the length of lease which is most calculated to encourage agricultural improvements?— The better the lease the better the improvements. At the same time I do not think that those who have long leases, and pay nominal rents, exert themselves in a way beneficial to the country or to themselves."—*Ibid. p.* 284.

subtle guise, rack-rents and the middleman are as rampant as they used to be in Connaught.

Evidence of Chas. King O'Hara, Land Proprietor.

" In this district, long leases have proved injurious to the condition of the tenants and improvement of the land. The tenant having secured a long term, procrastinates, gets into lazy habits, neglects his business, alienates portions of his farm, to meet his rent or engagements, or provide for his family; goes on con-acring and impoverishing until his land is exhausted and himself a pauper, or his land is covered with paupers—himself the greatest. Four marked cases now present themselves on my property, in proof of the bad effect of long leases. First by the termination of a lease made in 1773, to one tenant, of eighty acres, at 9s per acre; the original tenant sold his interest to the present occupier, who is in the worse condition, and no improvement whatever is made; the land is con-acred to exhaustion, and three sub-tenants on it. I know this myself. The second is a farm, leased in the year 1772 to one tenant (by whose death it terminated), of seventy-eight acres, at 5s per acre. The tenant had only sixteen acres in his possession at his death, having sublet the remainder. I believe there about fifteen families on it. The third case is 368 acres, leased in 1784 to one tenant, of excellent land in the best condition at 10s. per acre for 256 acres of upland, with 112 acres of bottom and bog not charged for. The farm is now occupied by the four sons of the lessee, holding in common; they have no division, and all the buildings, walls, fences, and drains are decayed or destroyed, and land lying unfenced and exhausted, covered with weeds; and I will venture to say, that if now surveyed, I shall not be able to find the number of acres of upland that was leased to them. They have let some of the lower part go back to bog. The term of the original lease was for three lives. The fourth case is 208 acres, leased in the year 1784 to one tenant, at 5s per acre: the lessee apportioned it among his three sons; they among six; and it now has twenty-four families on it. Each of these farms should have made the fortune of the tenant, had he been possessed of common industry. I could state several similar

This last statement requires explanation. In Ulster it is the custom for the incoming tenant to pay instances; but these have occurred within the last few weeks. There was one case of a farm, about the same size, leased by my father to one tenant. The lease lasted for many years. I found the son on it with thirty tenants, and himself the poorest man of the whole. The tenants admitted that they had been in the habit of contributing to his support. That was from drink."—*Dig. Dev. Com. p.* 286.

Evidence of Thomas Bradford, Farmer.

"What lease should a person have to remunerate him for that draining?—He should have a lease for sixty-one years at least.

"Taking, generally, large and small farms, do you see much greater improvements where there are leases than where there are tenants-at-will?—I cannot say that I do. I know a farm which is upon lease for 999 years, and there is not such a badly managed estate round the country.

"Are the lessees of that farm under that long lease subletting?—Yes, they are subletting every day.

"Are they holding any land themselves?—Yes, but they are the most wretched people I see. Upon the townland which I have spoken of, there are many families, who are neighbours of those parties, who are paying £3 or £4 an acre for their land, and they are much more snug and comfortable, and that is their character throughout the neighbourhood.

"Have those neighbours any leases who are paying £3. or £4. an acre?—Some of them have, and some of them have not."—*Ibid. p.* 279.

Evidence of Lieut. Col. Wm. Blacker, Land Proprietor.

"I passed one farm that I happened to know something of, which I know is held for ever at 3*d.* an acre, and it is in a worse condition than farms adjoining, held by an ordinary lease, at 25*s.* or 26*s.*

"Is it in possession of the lessee, or is it sublet?—It is, I believe, in the possession of the lessee, but I am not quite certain."—*Ibid. p.* 260.

the outgoing tenant a sum of money — nominally, for his improvements, really—for an indeterminate value called his "goodwill." If the worth of the improvement corresponded with the amount of the payment, the arrangement would be unobjectionable. But it seldom does. An incoming tenant will give openly, or surreptitiously, £5, £10, or £20 an acre for land let at high rent, in a bad

Evidence of Richard Longfield, Esq. Land Proprietor.

"How is it principally let—on lease or at will?—Generally on lease; but I think there is a degree of objection now and dislike to letting on lease that formerly did not exist. Many of the farms let on very old leases are in a very bad state."—*Dig. Dev. Com.* p. 274.

"Have you, in point of fact, observed that those who have very long leases among the farmers are not the most improving?—Decidedly. Nor do I believe it to be to the advantage of the landlord or tenant that the land should be at a very low rent."—*Ibid.* p. 275.

Evidence of Roudly Miller, Esq., Agent.

"On the estate let in perpetuity in this neighbourhood, the tenants generally are the poorest in this barony, and have subdivided their farms to a great extent, and cultivate them very badly.

"In that case you mean where the tenant occupies himself the land he holds in perpetuity?—The tenant of lands in perpetuity pays 2s. 6d. the Irish acre; he subdivides the lands away, and holds a small portion himself, it may be in a farm of fifty acres, he may have eight or ten tenants, he keeps a small portion himself, just as much as will give him a vote in the county.

"What is their condition?—They are very poor, generally."—*p.* 267.

condition, and without improvements, the figure generally increasing in an inverse ratio to the size of the farm and the poverty of the district, the largest tenant prices prevailing in Donegal,* and the most moderate in Down, while the payment is almost invariably made with money borrowed at a high rate of interest.† This interest is, of course,

* *Lord George Hill (Donegal).*

"The good-will or tenant-right of a farm is generally very high, often amounting to *forty or fifty years' purchase*, land being the thing most coveted, as indeed, it has been the only means of subsistence, employment being uncertain, and as till of late no support being provided for the poor and helpless every penny was carefully put by with a view of purchasing land. This took all their little capital, and very often left them in debt to some money lender, who had made up the required sum at an enormous rate of interest; by this means nothing was left them for the purchase of the cattle and seed."—*Digest, Devon Commission, p.* 299.

† The following remarks on the unrestricted sale of what is called the good-will as distinguished from fair compensation for improvements is well worthy of attention.

"It is even questionable whether this growing practice of tenant-right, which would at the first view appear to be a valuable assumption on the part of the tenant, be so in reality; as it gives to him, without any exertion on his own part, an apparent property or security, by means of which he is enabled to incur future incumbrance in order to avoid present inconvenience—a practice which frequently terminates in the utter destitution of his family and in the sale of his farm, when the debts thus created at usurious interest amount to what its sale would produce."—*Ibid. p.* 5, 24.

"The effect on the purchaser of the tenant-right to a farm is also highly injurious. He is generally a person who has managed to accumulate a small portion of funds, but not sufficient to pay off the whole amount of the purchase-

a second or rack rent paid to the lender of the purchase money, and the recipient who walks off with it is neither more nor less than a bastard middleman* who takes a fine in lieu of an annual money. He, therefore, is obliged not only to part with the whole of that capital which would be requisite to establish him in his new enterprise, but he must, at the very commencement encumber himself with a debt which requires a considerable time to liquidate.

"The equitable and legal rights of a proprietor in his land, as well as the equitable rights of a tenant to a fair return for his judiciously-invested labour and capital, are alike outraged by the existing practice in Ireland."

Digest of Evidence, Devon Commission, p. 5.

Evidence of Thos. Eyre, Esq. Farmer and Miller.

"What do you think of the effect of the tenant-right generally?—I always thought it injurious; but am not competent to judge, perhaps. I had been always living in England till 1826. I always thought it an injury to the tenant, rather than a benefit.

"In what manner do you consider it injurious to the tenant?—The incoming tenant impoverishes himself by purchasing this land. He has to go and borrow money to buy the land, in the first instance; and after he gets it, he gets credit where he should not do it at home. The shopkeepers say, "Oh, he has a farm, and we may trust him."—*Ibid. p.* 306.

* Here is a case where the lender actually becomes the Landholder.

Evidence of R. W. Codd, Roman Catholic Clergyman.

"By whom is the stamp and interest paid?—By the tenant.

"Do you know the usual rate of interest?—I have been inquiring, and I have been told it is not less than twelve per cent., generally speaking; sometimes this money costs them 10 per cent., when they give them the land in pledge. *The use of the land is granted as the interest for the money borrowed."*

Ibid. p. 208.

payment for a non-existing value. As a consequence, the new tenant commences his enterprise burdened with debt and destitute of capital. Hence low farming, inadequate profits, uneducated children, and too frequently, the ruin and emigration of the Ulster tenant, in spite of indulgent landlords and a secure tenure.

Evidence of John Forsyth, Esq., Agent.

"Supposing a man obliged to borrow money to purchase the tenant-right, and having to pay interest, and finding a difficulty in paying the interest and the rent, which is he most likely to complain of, the interest or the rent?—We do not hear much about the interest; but they frequently pay the interest where they do not pay the rent. I think they get the money very frequently from people in their own rank, who are associating with them."—*Dig. Dev. Com. p.* 292.

"That a portion of the borrower's farm is occasionally transferred to the lender as a security for the repayment of the debt, and that the use of the land is received instead of interest."—*Ibid. Summary, p.* 195.

"That the interest paid by the needy man to local usurers frequently ranges from 25 to 100 per cent."—*Ibid. Sum. p.* 195.

Charles A. Walker, Esq., Land Proprietor and Deputy Lieutenant.

"In the poorer parts of the country there are unfortunately some of those curses to society, usurers, who charge exorbitant interest to the distressed tenants, and have been the means of more injury to farmers and estates than any other cause.

"The usual way in which the interest is paid by the borrower is, he gives up to the lender the best field on his farm for three years or more, for the usurer to repay himself by the produce of it. The usurer takes wheat crop after wheat crop until the land can produce no more. The next loan is repaid in a similar manner with another field, and both tenant and land are ruined. I know miles in extent in this district which have been so treated."—*Ibid. p.* 207.

It is amusing to observe that the same persons who are anxious to mitigate the effects of competition by imposing on the owner of the land a rent fixed by Act of Parliament, always contend that the person in whose favour this beneficial interest is to be created should have the right to dispose of it to the highest bidder:* that is to say, though I am to be precluded from receiving the market value of my land,—my tenant is to be allowed to do so, by extracting a fine from whoever may be induced to make the most extravagant offer for his goodwill. It is hardly perhaps to be expected that the advocates of such measures should condescend to show how far their proposals are compatible with justice, and the narrowest interpretations of the rights of property, but at least they ought to prove them conducive to the agricultural prosperity of the country, and consonant with public policy.

* *The Church Temporalities and Landlord and Tenant Questions.—Drogheda, March 11th.—*" At a very full meeting of the Drogheda Board of Guardians—Patrick Matthew, Esq., J.P., in the chair—the following resolutions, in connexion with the above questions, were unanimously adopted:—"That we petition the Legislature to pass such a law of landlord and tenant as will give a fixity of tenure of from 61 to 100 years, according to the relative number of reclaimed acres of land in each holding, fixing rents by adding one-fourth or one-third to the present Poor Law valuation, making that sum the rent. No compensation save for permanent improvements made within fifteen years prior to the expiration of term; *also, giving a right to tenant or occupier to sell the good-will of the holding,* if anything should occur to oblige him to take such a course."
Northern Whig.

But as the result of such an arrangement would be to fill the majority of the farms in Ireland, in the course of a few years, with tenants paying a double rent, *i.e.* the Parliamentary rent to their landlords, and the interest on the fine squeezed out of them by the lucky individual to whom Parliament had attributed a share in the original owner's proprietory rights, it is difficult to see what could be the advantage of the change. It may indeed be urged that the vice in the system would only blaze into life on a change of tenancy:—but changes of tenancy are continually taking place:—not only by the surrender of farms, but on the death of every occupant. His sons succeed:—they all consider they have an equal claim to the holding:—if permitted they subdivide it;*—if not

---

* " Or, if the parents' improvidence do not reach to this extent, it gives them an erroneous feeling that at their death a fund will exist, without any previous accumulation of their own, from which their children can be all provided for. Accordingly, the death of a father generally leaves the son who succeeds to the farm encumbered to an irretrievable extent by charges for the provision of other members of the family; and this frequently upon a holding in a most unproductive or half-cultivated condition. He is obliged to sell off his stock, and is utterly unable to make those exertions which his position requires, and perhaps even incapable of fulfilling the arrangements required by his father's will. A minute subdivision of the small farm is then made amongst the members of the family, thereby laying the foundation for perhaps five or six pauper families on an extent of surface barely sufficient for the comfortable maintenance of *one* family."

Dig. Dev. Com. Summary, p. 4.

the eldest has to pay the others their share of the father's beneficial interest; and the competition price is their standard of valuation.* Consequently the permanent tenant finds himself in the same position as if he had bought the farm from a stranger:—that is to say, destitute of capital and probably in debt:—while the brothers walk off with a sum of money which if the rent is as fair as the theory of the arrangement pre-supposes, can represent no real value,† and to which therefore they have much less right than the landlord,

* *Evidence of Robert Smith, Esq. Clerk of the Peace.*

"In my opinion, such is the anxiety of the majority of the lower class of farmers, in the districts wherein I am best acquainted, that they would purchase the outgoing tenant's interest, disregarding all covenants."

Dig. Dev. Com. Summary, p. 295.

Evidence of John Hancock, Esq., Agent.

"The number of competitors have a still greater effect. The demand, in general, regulates the price."—*Ibid. p.* 295.

Evidence of John Andrews, Farmer and Agent.

"I think land, being sold at a high price by the outgoing tenant, takes away capital that ought to be left with the incoming tenant, for there is such eagerness to get land, that a man will give all he has got in the land, and leave himself without capital."—*Ibid. p.* 295.

† *Evidence of Mr. John Wilkin, Farmer.*

"With regard to the purchase of land, I may say, generally, that so much is not given for the land now; but where there is an anxiety to provide a place for a man's family to set down upon, in many cases the money is borrowed, and not repaid till it is sold again, so that it is a fictitious value."—*Ibid. p.* 305.

Evidence of Mr. Robert Macrea, Farmer.

"In the case of a farm that has been improved by the tenant, does it sell proportionably higher than one that has not

whom it has been the intention of Parliament to debar from such exactions. Now, it is not pretended that the imposition of rack rents is at all a general practice with proprietors. The high value of the goodwill on many estates is the index of the landlord's moderation, and his virtues are put up to auction in the same lot with his land.* The rents of Ireland are comparatively low,† and fines, which is the worst form of rent, are never taken: to transfer therefore the power of exaction created by competition from the landlord, against whose interest it is to enforce it, and to hand it over to the tenant, who would never fail to do so, would hardly be a change for the better; yet so little is this question understood

been improved?—No, I do not think it does; and I think small farms sell higher infinitely than many large ones."
Dig. Dev. Com. Summary, p. 308.

* *Evidence of Mr. Alex. Kinmouth, Farmer.*

" Is the value of it (goodwill) increasing or decreasing? Increasing on our estate.

" How do you account for that increase?—They have found out that Colonel Close is a good landlord."—*Ibid. p.* 294.

Evidence of Henry Leslie Prentice, Esq., Agent to Lord Caledon.

" They would go unknown to me or to any agent, and give an additional sum to get what is called 'the good-will' of it.

" Generally speaking, over the country, what is the amount of the sale of the tenant-right per acre by the year's rent?— It depends very much upon the landlord under whom the farm may be held. If he is a good landlord, and a man of character in the country, the price will be higher; if he is an inferior landlord, the price will be comparatively low."—*Ibid. p.* 171.

† This I believe is generally admitted, though there are flagrant exceptions; even a rent that is absolutely low, may be beyond the means of an indigent or unskilful tenant.

that you will hear the same person who would vehemently denounce a landlord for insisting on a rack rent, detail with complacency the enormous sums of money which this or that person has obtained for his tenant right, from some ill-advised successor to his farm, whom he has skinned by the process, and left stranded for life on the barren acres :* Yet it is in the prosperity of this latter individual, on whose solvency the proper cultivation of the land will depend, rather than in that of the outgoing tenant, that both the landlord and the community is interested.

From the foregoing considerations it is apparent that competition is an irrepressible force :† that if stifled in one direction, it will burst out in another;

---

* " It is, in the great majority of cases, not a reimbursement for outlay incurred, or improvements effected on the land, but a mere life insurance or purchase of immunity from outrage. Hence, the practice is more accurately and significantly termed, ' selling the good-will.'

" And *it is not uncommon for a tenant without a lease to sell the bare privilege of occupancy or possession of his farm without any visible sign of improvement having been made by him, at from ten to sixteen, up to twenty and even forty years' purchase of the rent.*"

Evidence of John Andrews, Esq., Farmer and Agent.

"The tenant-right is more valuable than any compensation for improvement could be, though we have not many sales of farms, except by ill-doing tenants, who work the land till they have nearly exhausted it, and then sell it, and get a good deal of money upon it; and I have seen parties get a good deal of money by such sales who would be fairly liable to an action for dilapidations."

† The subject is resumed in the following conclusions in the Summary of the Evidence given before the Devon Commission :

that a system of compulsory rents would only lead to its manifestation, in a more objectionable form; and that as a matter of policy, it is better that those alone should have the opportunity of taking advantage of it, who are the least likely to abuse their power.*

" That small holdings, in consequence of the greater competition, command a higher price than large.

" That the tenant-right confuses the rights of landlord and tenant, and is an undue interference with the interest of the proprietor.

" That the amount paid for the purchase of tenant-right injures the incoming tenant, by diminishing his capital.

" That debts are contracted upon the security of the tenant-right.

" That the children of farmers are provided f r by charges upon the tenant-right.

" That the incoming tenant is frequently compelled to borrow funds for the purchase of the tenant-right at usurious interest.

" That the existence of the tenant-right renders more difficult reclamation of waste lands by capitalists.

" That in most parts of Ireland the practice exists of selling the possession of farms held even from year to year.

" That the price of tenant-right frequently amounts to £10, £12, £20, or £25 per acre, and that sometimes as much as forty years' purchase of the rent is paid for it.

" That many proprietors have attempted to regulate and restrict its price.

" That such restrictions are frequently evaded.

" That the tenant is able to obtain a high rate of purchase for his good-will where he has effected no improvements, or has even deteriorated his farm.

" That even if the price of tenant-right be at all affected by the improvements made on a farm (a fact doubted by some witnesses), it is not so influenced in proportion to the value of the improvements."—*Dig. Devon Com. p.* 290.

* " It may be observed, that if an Irish landlord resist the temptation of a high offer, and lets his land at what he considers a

Wherever you go the same deleterious influence signalizes its presence by analogous, if not by identical effects. In the South and West the poison has infiltrated the system itself, breeding monstrous excrescences in the shape of the middleman and the rack-rented cottier. In the North it has manifested its presence by a parasitical growth of inflated tenant-right prices,* as effectually fatal to the healthy expansion of our agricultural industry. The original cause of the disease is everywhere the same. The disproportion of the opportunities of employment to population has resulted in universal pressure and universal competition,—competition in the labour market, already modified by emigration; competition in the land market—only to be relieved by the application to more profitable occupations of so much of the productive energies of the nation, as may be in excess of the requirements of a perfect agriculture.

fair rent, he often creates a set of intermediate tenants, who make a profit rent, by subletting the ground to persons who live in the extreme of misery."

Sir G. C. Lewis on Irish Disturbances, p. 313.

* I wish it to be distinctly understood, that I apply this phrase only to those cases where the price paid by the incoming tenant represents *no* real value.

The Rev. John O'Sullivan, P.P.

"The premiums paid for these holdings to one another is incredible. I have known a man to pay £35 for a plot of land for which he paid only £2. 5s a year without any lease. Mr. Hickson has been telling me of a man who gave £45 to another, who held land at a very high rent; . . . . . a man on the other side of the bridge paid £50 for the grass of three cows. . . . . There are only ten years to run of the term, and

But, it may be objected that even though emigration, rack rents—and their natural result—low farming, are equally rife under every description of tenure, and cannot therefore wholly be set down to the pernicious influence of the owners of landed property, yet, some human agency must be accountable for the perennial desolation of a lovely and fertile island, watered by the fairest streams, caressed by a clement atmosphere, held in the embraces of a sea whose affluence fills the noblest harbours of the world, and inhabited by a race— valiant, generous, tender—gifted beyond measure with the power of physical endurance, and graced with the liveliest intelligence.

It is to the discovery of this enigma that I now address myself, and in its solution it is possible we may find an answer to the famous question originally put to the Kilkenny Parliament, and lately repeated with considerable point by Mr. Bright,— " How is it that the King is none the richer for Ireland?"

he has taken it in defiance of Mr. Hickson; .... but, notwithstanding, he is going to lay out £250 upon it. I hold some land from Lord Lansdowne. He gives me the glebe, and there was a field adjoining the lawn before the house I was anxious to get, but I should not think of getting it without the full consent of the proprietor. I could not drain my lawn without draining his field. I sent to him to know what he would let me have it for. He was under ejectment at the time, and he wanted £20 for it, though it was not worth 5s. I thought I should get it for £3 or £4. I could have got it from Mr. Hickson without paying anything for it; but, of course, I could not think of that."—*Digest, Dev. Com. p.* 309.

Of course, any perfect retrospect of the economic career of Ireland would necessarily involve a review of her political and religious history, but so large a treatment of the subject would not be adapted to the present cursory discussion. I am only anxious to point out, in a very few sentences, what those influences have been which have as effectually stunted the development of our material prosperity as penal laws and religious intolerance have vitiated our social atmosphere. I allude to the commercial jealousies of Great Britain.

It has been rather the custom of late to represent the landed interest of Great Britain as the sole inventors and patentees of protection. The experience of Ireland does not confirm this theory. During the course of the last 250 years we have successively tasted the tender mercies of every interest in turn—whether landed, trading, or commercial—and have little reason to pronounce one less selfish than another. From Queen Elizabeth's reign until within a few years of the Union the various commercial confraternities of Great Britain never for a moment relaxed their relentless grip on the trades of Ireland. One by one, each of our nascent industries was either strangled in its birth, or handed over, gagged and bound, to the jealous custody of the rival interest in England, until at last every fountain of wealth was hermetically sealed, and even the traditions of commercial enterprise have perished through desuetude.

The owners of England's pastures opened the campaign. As early as the commencement of the 16th century the beeves of Roscommon, Tipperary, and Queen's County undersold the produce of the English grass counties in their own market.* By an Act of the 20th of Elizabeth Irish cattle were declared a "nuisance," and their importation was prohibited. Forbidden to send our beasts alive across the Channel, we killed them at home, and began to supply the sister country with cured provisions. A second Act of Parliament imposed prohibitory duties on salted meats. The hides of the animals still remained, but the same influence soon put a stop to the importation of leather. Our cattle trade abolished, we tried sheep farming. The sheep breeders of England immediately took alarm, and Irish wool was declared contraband by a Parliament of Charles II. Headed in this direction we tried to work up the raw material at home, but this created the greatest outcry of all. Every maker of fustian, flannel, and broadcloth in the country rose up in arms, and by an Act of William III. the woollen industry of Ireland was extinguished, and 20,000 manufacturers left the island. The easiness of the Irish labour market and the cheapness of provisions still giving us an advantage, even though we had

* See Appendix, p. 147.

to import our materials, we next made a dash at the silk business; but the silk manufacturer proved as pitiless as the woolstaplers. The cotton manufacturer, the sugar refiner, the soap and candle maker (who especially dreaded the abundance of our kelp), and any other trade or interest that thought it worth its while to petition was received by Parliament with the same partial cordiality,* until the most searching scrutiny failed to detect a single vent through which it was possible for the hated industry of Ireland to respire. But, although excluded from the markets of Britain, a hundred harbours gave her access to the universal sea. Alas! a rival commerce on her own element was still less welcome to England, and as early as the reign of Charles II. the Levant, the ports of Europe, and the oceans beyond the Cape were forbidden to the flag of Ireland. The colonial trade alone was in any manner open,—if that could be called an open trade which for a long time precluded all exports whatever, and excluded from direct importation to Ireland such important articles as sugar, cotton, and tobacco. What has been the

* An amusing instance of the feeling that Ireland was to be sacrificed to England is mentioned by the author of the Commercial Restraints of Ireland, p. 125. In 1698 two petitions were presented to the English House of Commons from the fishermen of Folkstone and Aldborough, stating that they were injured "by the Irish catching herrings at Waterford and Wexford, and sending them to the Straits, and thereby forestalling and ruining petitioners' markets."

consequence of such a system, pursued with relentless pertinacity for 250 years? This: that, debarred from every other trade and industry, the entire nation flung itself back upon "*the land*" with as fatal an impulse as when a river whose current is suddenly impeded rolls back and drowns the valley it once fertilized.*

For a long time, however, the limits of their own island proved sufficient for the three or four millions which then inhabited it. The cheapness of provisions in Ireland used to be the bugbear of the English manufacturer. But each successive century found the nation more straitened within its borders. At last a choice had to be made between the sacrifice of domestic happiness or of physical comfort; the natural liveliness of their affections, combined with a buoyant temperament, led the

---

* In 1836, the Royal Commissioners for inquiring into the Condition of the Poor in Ireland, reported

" That they could not estimate the number of persons in Ireland *out of work and in distress during the thirty weeks of the year* at less than 585,000, nor the persons dependent on them at less than 1,800,000, making 2,385,000."

" The estimate of these Commissioners received a singular but sad corroboration nine years afterwards, in the fact I have already noticed, of 3,000,000 of persons being in receipt of rations under the relief arrangements at one period during the height of the famine in 1847. It receives a further corroboration in the reduction of the population by two millions and a-half by emigration. It was the extraordinary productiveness of the potato before 1846, which enabled those 2,385,000 persons to exist, with only half work, even in the wretched condition they did."—*Dr. Hancock's Alleged Decline, &c.*

people to accept the latter alternative.* The mildness of the climate, the cheapness of the fuel, and above all, the suitableness of the potato to what is technically called " *la petite culture* " contributed to turn the scale, and early marriages continued to remain a characteristic of the Irish peasantry.† Even had the landlords interfered, their remonstrances would have been in vain, and, the downward impulse once communicated, acquired a continually accelerated momentum, for the simple reason that each succeeding generation was accustomed from infancy to a lower standard

---

* A. Young, enumerating the causes favourable to the growth of population in Ireland, says:—" Marriage is certainly more general in Ireland than in England: I scarce ever found an unmarried farmer or cottar; but it is seen more in other classes which, with us, do not marry at all; such as servants; the generality of footmen and maids in gentlemen's families are married, a circumstance we very rarely see in England. Another point of importance is their children not being burdensome. In all the inquiries I made into the state of the poor, I found their happiness and ease generally relative to the number of their children, and nothing considered as such a misfortune as having none."—Part ii. p. 61.

† The following Table, quoted by Mr. Mill, sufficiently illustrates the rapid rate of increase of population which at one time prevailed in Ireland:—

	per cent.		per cent.
Ireland	2·45	Bavaria	1·08
Hungary	2·40	Netherlands	0·94
Spain	1·66	Naples	0·83
England	1.65	France	0·63
Rhenish Prussia	1·33	Sweden	0·58
Austria	1·30	Lombardy	0·45

Mill's Polit. Econ. Vol. I., p. 360.

of comfort than that which had satisfied their fathers.* Extraneous circumstances, such as the

---

* Mr. Thornton, in his Plea for a peasant proprietory, quotes the following passage from McCulloch, and, I think, every one acquainted with Ireland will acknowledge the truth of Mr. McCulloch's observations :—

"The strong predilection entertained by the great bulk of the children engaged in agriculture for the pursuits of their fathers has been remarked by every one in any degree familiar with rural affairs. Children at liberty to divide their father's estate, possess the greatest facilities for gratifying their natural inclination. They have the power of continuing in the line of life in which they have been educated, and which must in consequence be endeared to them by all those early associations which exert so strong an influence over future conduct. Moreover, the possession of a piece of ground gives a feeling of independence to a small capitalist or a poor man, that he cannot otherwise experience." A possession of this sort may fail to render him comfortable, "but it gives him a security against want; it furnishes him with a cottage, and unless it be unusually small it will enable him to raise such a supply of potatoes as will go far to support himself and his family. In no way, therefore, can a poor man be so independent. The possession of a piece of ground renders him in some measure his own master. *It exempts him from the necessity of severe labour and unremitting application.*" From these considerations Mr. McCulloch concludes that the children of small landowners will choose "to reside on the little properties they have obtained from their ancestors, and that the process of division and subdivision will continue until the whole land has been parcelled out into patches, and filled with an agricultural population equally destitute of the means and the desire of rising in the world."—*McCulloch's Edition of the Wealth of Nations, Vol.* iv. pp. 462.

"This reasoning," observes Mr. Thornton, "must be acknowledged to possess great force." It is an exact description of what has actually occurred.

rise of prices during the French wars, stimulated the popular tendency to self expansion, until by a logical sequence of events the spectacle was presented of a nation doubling its population every fifty years, yet entirely dependent for its support upon an agricultural area which had been found barely sufficient for its needs when it was a third less numerous; under such conditions, high rents, low wages, and all the other indications of destitution would be as inevitable as famine prices in a beleaguered city.

But I may be told this frantic clinging of the Irish to the land is natural to their genius, and not a result of commercial restrictions. History supplies the perfect refutation of such a theory: Though the hostile tariff of England comprehended almost every article produced in Ireland, one single exception was permitted. From the reign of William III. the linen trade of Ireland has been free; as a consequence, at this day Irish linens are exported in enormous quantities to every quarter of the globe, and their annual value nearly equals half the rental of the island.

Many attempts were made by the rival interest in England to deprive us of this boon, and in 1785 a petition—signed by 117,000 persons—was presented* by Manchester, praying for the prohibition of Irish linens, but justice and reason for once prevailed, and the one surviving industry of Ireland

* Wade's Chronology, Vol. I. p. 539.

was spared. How has it repaid the clemency of the British Parliament? By dowering the crown of England with as fair a cluster of flourishing towns and loyal centres of industry as are to be found in any portion of the Empire. Would you see what Ireland might have been—go to Derry, to Belfast, to Lisburn, and by the exceptional prosperity which has been developed, not only within a hundred towns and villages, but for miles and miles around them, you may measure the extent of the injury we have sustained.* Would you ascertain how the numerical strength of a nation may be multiplied, while the status of each individual that comprises it is improved,—go to Belfast, where (within a single generation) the population has quadrupled, and the wages of labour have more than doubled.†

* "The injury we endured by the suppression of our trade may be best measured by the expansion which immediately followed its liberation. In 1780 the duties on the exportation of woollen manufactures from Ireland were removed. In three years the export of our woollen stuffs increased from 8000 yards to 538,000 yards of old draperies, from 494 yards to 40,000 yards, of new draperies. Again, with regard to the cotton manufacture; in 1783 130,000 yards of cotton goods were imported into Ireland within six months from Chester alone. In 1784, after the removal of the prohibition, only 18,000 yards were exported from that port during the same period."

† Extract from a letter from a Belfast Merchant.

"I think you may fairly assume that the present rate of wages earned by mill workers is about 50 per cent in excess of that paid to them thirty or forty years since. *Mechanics*

How powerfully the development of manufactures in the North of Ireland has contributed to the relief of the agricultural classes of Ulster, by giving the tenant-farmer an opportunity of apprenticeing some of his sons to business instead of subdividing among them his diminutive holding, by enabling the cottier tenant to supplement his

and artizans are receiving from 50 to 70 per cent. more wages than were paid twenty to thirty years since. *I am paying my permanent farm labourers 11s per week* when I do not provide them with a home. I should say that day labourers in Belfast, such as porters in warehouses, may be all put down as receiving fully 50 per cent in excess of what they used to get."

"The enclosed statement, which Mr. Henderson has furnished at my request, shews pretty clearly the progressive advance of wages paid to the last-named class.

"The following is a statement of the rates of wages which appear to have been paid by us to *ordinary labourers* at the periods undernoted. We give separately the wages paid to men hired by the week, and to men hired by the day. The wages paid to carters and head porters was somewhat higher.

	By the Week.	By the Day.
1828	8/"	1/6 to 1/8
1832	8/" to 9/"	1/6 to 1/8
1840	9/"	1/8
1847	9/" to 10/"	1/8 to 2/"

This was the famine year, and wages fluctuated more than usual.

| 1857 | 10/" | 2/" |
| 1867 | 12/" | 2/6 |

It will be seen that the rise in 40 years is about 50 per cent."

Belfast, 19th July, 1867

I have given in an Appendix a few facts connected with the improvement which has taken place in Belfast and its neighbourhood during the last 30 or 40 years.—*See Appendix, p. 149*

agricultural earnings with hand-loom weaving, and by a general alleviation of the pressure upon the land, I need not describe. These and many other considerations of the sort are too patent to need suggestion. It will be sufficient for me to record my profound conviction—a conviction which, perhaps, may be shared by some of my readers—that had Ireland only been allowed to develope the other innumerable resources at her command, as she has developed the single industry in which she was permitted to embark, the equilibrium between the land and the population dependent upon the land would never have been disturbed, nor would the relations between landlord and tenant have become a subject of anxiety.

I will not pursue this portion of the inquiry further. Feeling convinced that our best chance of dealing with the difficulties of Ireland is to arrive at a correct appreciation of their origin, I have done my best to detail the facts which prove that it is unjust to refer them wholly or to any extraordinary degree to the influence of the owners of landed property in Ireland, while I have indicated a succession of circumstances amply sufficient to account for them. If my language has betrayed too warm a sympathy with the class of which I am a member, the groundlessness of the accusations with which it has been assailed must plead my excuse. No such instinctive partiality has extended to the disposition of my facts or the array of my arguments. If I seem to have suppressed all cognizance of the instances of harshness and mismanagement laid to the charge of individual landlords by men of the highest honour, it is not because I do not acknowledge and deplore their existence, but because they are so manifestly exceptional as to have produced an inappreciable effect on the current of events we are considering. In dealing with the economic interests of a great country, it is on the essential forces which are producing specific results, rather than on the capricious accidents of the situation, that we must fix our attention.

If, on consideration, it should be found that the responsibilities of the landed proprietors for the ills of Ireland have been grossly exaggerated, I have sufficient faith in the generosity of their accusers to believe that they will rejoice rather than regret to discover that so numerous and important a section of their fellow-countrymen neither are nor have been unworthy of their esteem; and my conviction gathers strength from the fact that our conclusions on such a point cannot materially affect any pending controversy between the landlords and their tenantry. If an alteration is to be made in the tenure of land in Ireland, that alteration must be founded on abstract principles of justice, and the requirements of present policy. Many eminent statesmen view with regret the relative position of the Catholic and Protestant clergy of Ireland. But whenever the time arrives for effecting an improvement, the change will be made—not because a century ago Irish Bishops were sometimes lax and individual clergymen inefficient, but because it has been always required by justice and is now recommended by expediency. By a parity of reasoning it would be as great an outrage to visit with penal legislation the recent purchaser of a property in the Encumbered Estates Court because fifty years ago the grandfather of the former proprietor created 40s freeholders (a tenure of which Mr. Butt, I observe, speaks almost with approval) and took the best rent, as it would be to load the woollen manufacturers of Lancashire with the responsibility of Ireland's misfortunes because the particular industry in which they are interested owes more than any other its present prosperity to the cruel policy towards Ireland inaugurated by their predecessors.*

---

* It is a great satisfaction to me to find that the following observations by Mr. Cobden which have been published since the foregoing chapter was written, bear out the view of the subject I have taken.

"But whatever were the causes of early degradation of Ireland, there can be no doubt that England has, during the last two centuries, by discouraging the commerce of Ireland,—thus striking at the very root of civilization—rendered herself responsible for much of the barbarisms that afflicts it.

"However much the conduct of England towards the sister-island, in this particular, may have been dwelt upon for party-purposes, it is so bad as scarcely to admit of exaggeration.

"The first restrictions put upon the Irish trade were in the reign of Charles II.; and from that time, down to the era when the united volunteers of Ireland stepped forward to rescue their country from its oppressors, (the only incident, by the way, in the Chronicles of Ireland, deserving the name of a really national effort) our policy was directed, incessantly to the destruction of the foreign trade with that country. Every attempt at manufacturing industry, with one exception, was likewise mercilessly nipped in the bud. Her natural capabilities might, for example, have led the people to the making of glass: it was enacted, that no glass should be allowed to be exported from Ireland, and its importation, except from England, was also prohibited. Her soil calculated for the pasturing of sheep would have yielded wool equal to the best English qualities; an absolute prohibition was laid on its exportation; and King William, in addressing the British Parliament, declared 'that he would do everything in his power to discourage the woollen manufactures of Ireland.' Down to the year 1779 we find that the export of woollen goods from that island remained wholly interdicted.

"Not only was her commerce with the different parts of Europe fettered by the imposition of restrictions upon every valuable product that could interfere with the prosperity of England; not only was all trade with Asia and the East of Europe excluded by the charters which were granted to the companies of London; but her ports were actually sealed against the trade of the American Colonies.

"Although Ireland presented to the ships of North America the nearest and noblest havens in Europe, and appeared to be the natural landing-place for the products of the New World, her people were deprived of all benefit,—nay, they were actually made to suffer loss and inconvenience from their favoured position; laws were passed prohibiting the importation of American commodities into Ireland, without first landing them in some part of England and Wales, whilst the exports of Irish products to the Colonies excepting through some British port was also interdicted.

"If we add to this that a law was enacted, preventing beef or live cattle from being exported to England, some idea may be formed of the commercial policy of this country towards Ireland,—a policy savouring more of the mean and sordid tyranny of the individual huckster over his poorer rival, than of any nobler oppression that is wont to characterize the acts of victorious nations."

* * * * *

" There are those who think the Irish genius is unsuited to that eager and persevering pursuit of business which distinguishes the English people; and they argue that, but for this, the natives of a region in all respects so favourable to commerce must have triumphed over the obstacles that clogged their industry."

"There is, we believe, one cause existing less connected with the injustice of England, and to which we are about to allude why Ireland is below us and other Protestant nations in the scale of cizilization; yet if we look to the prosperity of her staple manufacture, the only industry that was tolerated by the Government of this country,—it warrants the presumption that, under similar favouring circumstances, her woollens, or indeed her cottons might equally with her linens, have survived a competition with the fabrics of Great Britain."

Cobden's Polit. Writings, Vol. I. p. 53.

" The two great objects for which the patriots contended were, legislative independence *and commercial freedom.*"

" With regard to the latter object, it was not merely the mistaken or prejudiced policy of a party, but the pure selfishness and jealousy of the English nation, which denied this object to Ireland: it was a mixture of ignorance and selfishness not less prejudicial to British than to Irish prosperity. But I am only now concerned in showing that such was the spirit and disposition of the English towards the Irish people; and that by its operation those feelings of animosity and alienation were so deeply rooted in the latter country, that no subsequent concessions, no change of policy, however liberal and complete, have been able to extirpate them. In proof of this part of the case I must produce the testimony of Mr. Huskisson. " Recollecting," he says, "that for centuries it has been a settled maxim of public policy, in all great states having dependencies, to make the interests of those dependencies subservient to the interests, or the supposed interests, of the parent state. There is, perhaps, no country where the consequences of persevering in such a system can be so forcibly illustrated as in our own. In the first place, let us look at Ireland till the year 1782. The many other causes which contributed to keep that fertile island in a state of misery and depression, I shall pass by on the present occasion; but is it not a well-known fact, that, till the year 1780, the agriculture, the internal industry, the manufactures, the commerce, the navigation of Ireland, were all held in the most rigid subserviency to the supposed interests of Great Britain?" In 1778, a partial relaxation of this exclusive system was proposed in the English Parliament: "and what was the reception these proposals met with in the House of Commons, and on the part of the trading and manufacturing interests of the country? The opponents of these limited concessions, enumerating the boons already conferred on Ireland, declared that to grant more would be fatal to the commerce and manufactures of England. . . . Our merchants and manufacturers, our shipowners, our country gentlemen, all took the alarm—all were to be ruined, if we granted the proposed participations to a country almost without debt, and paying the same taxes with ourselves. Resting on these and other grounds, petitions poured in from all quarters. The merchants of Glasgow prayed 'that neither the present nor any future advantage should be granted to Ireland, which might in the least degree operate to the disadvantage of Great Britain.' . . . *The language of Manchester was still more decided in reprobating the proposed concession.* Liverpool, also, did not hesitate to predict, that by the adoption of the proposals that town and port would be speedily reduced to their original insignificance. In 1779, a more limited concession to Ireland was proposed in the British House of Commons, but this measure was negatived on a division. Towards the close of that year, the events of the war in North America, and the state of things in Ireland, produced a different feeling in the British Parliament. State necessity, acting under a sense of political danger, yielded without grace, that which good sense and good feeling had before recommended in vain."

Greville's Policy of England towards Ireland.

"At the same time that a wide and impassable line was drawn by the law between the two religions in Ireland, and the one persuasion was made a privileged, the other an inferior class, the *whole* of Ireland was treated as a province or colony, whose interest was to be sacrificed to those of the mother-country. Hence arose the restrictions on Irish commerce,—on the exportation of corn, cattle, and woollen goods,—avowedly for the benefit of England. A system of government administered in this spirit, and in a country where a people were already in a state of great rudeness and disorder, necessarily led to the degradation and demoralizing of the bulk of the population."

Local Disturbances of Ireland and the Church Questions, by Sir G. C. Lewis, p. 47.

APPENDIX.

The Difficulties of an Irish Landlord's Situation.

The following extract from the Summary prefixed to the Digest of Evidence taken before the Devon Commission, describes very clearly the difficulties with which an Irish landlord has to contend when dealing with a property which has been subdivided and over-populated during the continuance of a long lease.

"It is quite evident that if the gross produce derived from a limited holding amount to £8, and that it be occupied by a family of five persons, in a district where there is little or no assistance for them in the way of profitable or casual labour, we find a most difficult and embarrassing situation to be presented, both as regards the land proprietor and the tenant; and yet this is by no means an exaggerated or uncommon case. The most moderate calculation of a year's maintenance for such a family would amount to £24, to pay which, together with the rent, the taxes, and the seeding of his farm, there is only the value of the gross produce, £8.

"Thus the gross produce would amount to only one-third of the sum requisite to support the family, without allowing for either rent, seed, or taxes. The seed and taxes must, however, come as a charge prior to maintenance—they are inevitable. The landlord then looks for his rent. His just claim is not the point which the debtor or the public considers when he seeks for its liquidation. The broad fact of a rich man pressing a wretchedly poor man for a payment of money is the point that arrests attention; it matters little whether the rate of rent be in fact low; any claim, however moderate, made by the landlord, appears exorbitant, not from its disproportionate amount as a rent, but from the utter destitution and inability of the tenant to meet it, however small it may be! Goods are distrained, or legal proceedings instituted, and the landlord at once acquires the character of an oppressive rack-renter. Inattentive management permits the subdivision of farms to increase: the £8 worth of gross produce must now provide for two or three families. This needy class of tenants increases in number and destitution, and the landlord's character for oppression increases in a like proportion, although his land may be let much below the rate that well-circumstanced tenants could pay with ease; and although his list of arrears may prove that a considerable portion of that rate has not been levied!

"The evil grows to an extent that threatens the annihilation of the landlord's income; a clearance of the tenants, or consolidation of farms, is resorted to, and forms the climax of tyrannical landlordism, from which a sacrifice equal to the fee value of his estate could not cleanse him. Nor would his granting their holdings to such tenants free of rent, materially mend their case; as although it might raise the annual means of support for a family from £3 to £4, or from £6 to £8, it must be recollected that from £15 to £24 would be required to supply them even with the necessaries of life.

"Numerous witnesses have proved the extreme tendency that there is amongst the tenants to subdivide their lands below the quantity that will maintain the occupiers in comfort. They concur in describing the unremitting vigilance required to prevent a rapid recurrence of this evil, even after the estate has gone through the distressing ordeal of correction."

Digest Devon Commission, Summary, p. 8.

"*The Pastures of Ireland.*" (pp. 94 and 130.)

" From the earliest times then, until late in the last century, Ireland was almost entirely a grazing country."
p. 193.

*   *   *   *

"Its level surface, overspread with the most luxuriant herbage, presented a wide field over which the cattle of the first settlers might freely range and multiply at an exceedingly rapid rate. Their owners became proportionably wealthy."—pp. 196 and 197.

*   *   *   *

"The pastoral occupation of the primitive Irish was not laid aside as soon as they had divided their new country amongst them, and had stationed themselves on particular spots; but continued to be practised by their descendants for many generations. The principal obstacle to change was probably at first the nature of the climate which, Mela says, was as unsuitable for grain as it was favourable to the growth of grass (Pomp. Mela, de Situ Orbis, lib. iii. cap. 6); and this was, perhaps, the sole reason why, as late as the twelfth century, the people could still be represented as despising husbandry, and as not having laid aside their ancient pastoral mode of life. Even in the beginning of the 16th century the Book of Ballymote is said to have been purchased for 140 milch cows. More than a hundred years later, we find the poet Spenser lamenting that "all men fell to pasturage, and none to husbandry;" and recommending that an ordinance should be made to compel every one who kept 20 kine, to keep one plough going likewise."
pp. 180 and 190.

*   *   *   *

" In the long period of anarchy which succeeded to the conquest by Henry the Second, the incessant warfare between the English Colonists and the natives, acted as an effectual bar to agriculture, for both parties thought it wiser to keep their property in the shape of flocks and herds, which could easily be removed to a place of refuge, than in corn stacks, or standing crops, which must have been left to the mercy of a successful invader."—p. 191.

* * * *

" In the year 1762, the Irish Parliament granted high bounties on the inland carriage of grain; and in 1783 and 1784, granted further bounties on its exportation, and prohibited its importation from abroad; and the rise of price which took place in consequence, was further promoted by the demand for foreign corn in Great Britain, after the commencement of the war with France, and by the abolition in 1806 of all restrictions on the corn trade between this country and Ireland. Inducements were thus given to landholders to substitute tillage for pasturage, and as the tracts held by single graziers were in general much too extensive to be cultivated by the actual tenants, they were divided into farms of more convenient size, and let to such persons as were willing to undertake them. There was not, however, capital enough in the island to meet the requirements of this revolution in husbandry, and most of the new race of farmers were so poor, that they could not pay their labourers in any other way than by assigning to them pieces of ground to build cabins upon, and to cultivate for their own subsistence. Together with the farmers, therefore, a considerable body of cottars sprang up, and in this manner the bulk of the peasantry were converted into occupiers of land."—*Thornton's Plea for Peasant Proprietors,* pp. 190 and 191.

PROGRESS OF BELFAST.

The following statement will give an idea of the progress of Belfast during the last half century.

Population of Belfast in 1811 . . . 27,000
,, ,, 1865 . . . 150,000

New Erections.

In 1856	. 176	In 1862	.	840
,, 1857	. 251	,, 1863	.	1455
,, 1858	. 409	,, 1864	.	1505
,, 1859	. 378	,, 1865	.	1037
,, 1860	. 225	,, 1866 (6 mos.)		953
,, 1861	. 730	—		—

Griffiths' Valuation—In 1861	.	.	£253,900
,, ,, ,, 1862	.	.	278,892
,, ,, ,, 1863	.	.	297,551
,, ,, ,, 1864	.	.	311,041
,, ,, ,, 1865	.	.	333,894

Tonnage entering the Harbour.

Tons under.
In 1818 . . . 506,953 Revenue, £23,911
,, 1865 . . . 1,111,581 ,, 52,282

Expenditure on quays and dock accommodation, £716,000, giving an extent of tidal and floating dock room of 92 acres, besides 34 acres of water storage for timber.

One of our floating docks is 450 feet long, 60 feet width of entrance, and 15 feet depth of water on sill at high water neap tides.

Water Supply.

£150,000 are being expended by the Water Commissioners, giving an estimated daily supply of 6,000,000 gallons of water.

Iron Ship Building.

Three screw steamers are being constructed, each 3000 tons burthen; and wages paid in one establishment (whose owners, Messrs. Harland and Wolff, have been appointed constructors for the Admiralty up to 5000 tons), range from £1000 to £1200 weekly.

Machine Making and Engineering Establishments.

Turning out work yearly value for £550,000; of this £320,000 is for Ireland; £70,000 for England and Scotland; and £110,000 is for Europe, Asia, Africa, and America.

Spinning and Weaving by Power in Ireland.

Total cost, £3,514,416; and of this there is, within a radius of ten miles from Belfast, £2,476,920.

Deposits.

Our three local Banks have at their command, in deposits and other resources, upwards of £8,000,000 sterling; and the value of the exports from this harbour last year amounted to £11,755,170.

CHAPTER IV.

Though my previous observations have been received with great indulgence, particular passages have naturally provoked a good deal of criticism.

As no one can hope to escape all error in reviewing the economical condition of a great country, it is probable that some of this criticism may be just. In so large a survey, taken from a single point of view, the perspective is apt to be out of drawing, nor can a sketch in which the objects are foreshortened lay claim to the accuracy of a geometrical plan. On the other hand, it is possible that some of the exceptions taken to my views may be occasioned by the objector's attention having been attracted to some point whose importance has become unduly magnified by its proximity to himself, though hardly affecting the general contour of the landscape.

Having, however, done the best I can to give a faithful picture of the general situation as it presents itself to my own contemplation, I must be content to allow the conflict of opinion which never fails to arise out of the discussion of an Irish question, to evolve whatever further amount of truth can be extracted from the subject.

To one point only will I recur.

Of the several observations I have made, none seem to have elicited such lively comment as those referring to the disproportion still existing in Ireland between the numbers dependent on agriculture and the proportion necessary for the perfect cultivation of the soil. As this is a vital point in the discussion, I may be permitted to adduce one or two further proofs of the correctness of my previous suggestions.

My method of calculation was a simple one. Having ascertained the number of hands employed in the cultivation of specified areas in those parts of England and Scotland where agriculture is best understood, I applied a similar scale to the occupied area of Ireland, and on its appearing that there were still about 300,000 more persons engaged in agriculture in Ireland than are found necessary to a very high rate of production in Great Britain I argued, not, as it has been absurdly stated, that this surplusage of agricultural industry should of necessity remove from the country, but that the application of a considerable portion of it to other employments would tend to reduce competition, and to increase both the profits of the farmer and the wages of the labourer. But as the analogy I drew was necessarily imperfect, I purposely went on the supposition that the whole of the 15,000,000 of acres in Ireland was cultivated as tillage land. But, in reality, little more than a third of this area (or 5,700,000 acres) is cropped, the remaining nine millions and a-half being under cattle, and consequently, requiring only one-eighth of the amount of labour necessary on a corresponding expanse of tillage.*

If, therefore, I had desired to push the argument to an extreme length, I might have brought out a more startling result. But being perfectly aware of the fallacy involved in too close a comparison between countries so differently circumstanced as the sister kingdoms, I contented myself with an approximation, as unfavourable to my case as possible, but which, nevertheless, was sufficient to prove that the disproportion of agricultural labour in Ireland to the area under cultivation, and to the amount of capital invested in the pursuits of husbandry,—originally deplored by Archbishop Murray, Mr. More O'Farrell, and Archbishop Whately,—still existed. As, however, it may be useful to elucidate this point to the fullest extent, I now subjoin a comparative table of the proportion of cultivators to the extent of land under tillage and pasture, in Belgium, Flanders, England, Ireland, as well as in the four provinces, and in some of the counties of the latter kingdom, together with the amount of produce obtained from corresponding areas in each locality.

* *Evidence of John Quinn, Esq.*

" Upon the plains of Roscommon one man has 4000 sheep, and only two herds attending the flock."—*Dig. Dev. Com.* p. 73.

Table, showing the proportion of Male Cultivators to the land under cultivation in England, Belgium, East and West Flanders, Ireland, as well as in the Provinces and some of the Counties of the latter kingdom. The ratio of persons employed on pasture lands to those employed on tillage is taken as 1 to 8 for corresponding areas.

	No. of Acres under Tillage.	No. of Acres under Pasturage.	Male Cultivators Employed on Tillage.	Male Cultivators Employed on Pasturage	Proportion of Cultivators to Acres.	
					Tillage.	Pasturage.
Ireland*	5,931,296	9,533,529	985,265	197,689	1 to 6	1 to 48
England and Wales .	14,234,183	17,766,817	1,229,117	191,947	1 to 11½	1 to 92
Belgium	3,795,042	781,245	676,478	17,118	1 to 5⅝	1 to 45
Leinster	1,665,098	2,414,032	211,709	38,335	1 to 7¾	1 to 63
Munster	1,482,180	3,055,874	253,364	61,788	1 to 5¾	1 to 47
Ulster	1,965,197	2,092,366	339,705	44,415	1 to 5¾	1 to 47
Connaught . . .	818,821	1,971,257	177,618	53,020	1 to 4½	1 to 37
Flanders, East & West†	972,087		244,549		1 to 4	
Cork County . .	507,499	909,465	84,582	18,908	1 to 6	1 to 48
Kerry County . .	162,826	573,065	34,643	15,194	1 to 4¾	1 to 38
Antrim County . .	263,361	354,487	36,912	5,898	1 to 7¼	1 to 58
Down County . .	338,797	186,361	47,717	3,278	1 to 7	1 to 56

* See Appendix, pp. 206, 207, 208.
† The Belgian Statistical Returns do not distinguish between Tillage and Pasture in Flanders.

From the foregoing statistics it would appear that the same amount of labour which is found sufficient in England to cultivate 11½ acres in a highly efficient manner is employed in Ireland in the less perfect cultivation of 6 acres. In other words, whereas in Ireland it takes four men to raise 15 tons of grain off 24 acres, in England only two men are required to raise 16 tons off 23 acres.*

Now, whatever allowance it may be desirable to make for the diversity of conditions under which husbandry is prosecuted in the two countries, or with however light a touch the comparison is applied, it is evident that if the area under cultivation in Ireland were treated with the same skill, energy and intelligence as is employed on the soil of England, a far larger amount of produce might be obtained with a far fewer number of hands. But it is urged that it is unfair to argue that because great economy of labour is practicable on the large farms of England,† a similar rule can be applied to the small subdivisions of Ireland. If this were indeed the case, it would be

---

* Thanks to the value of our potato and flax crops this disadvantageous proportion in the acreable result of our cereal cropping is not maintained on a comparison of the money-value of the total produce of the two kingdoms taken in globo.—*See Appendix.*

"D'après les chiffres recueillis par M. Ducpetiaux 1,000 agriculteurs nourriraient 4167 personnes dans le Flandre orientale, 3,861 dans la Grande-Bretagne, et 1,511 en Irlande. Ces nombres, ou le voit, sont encore plus favorables à l'agriculture flamande que ceux indiqués ici."

De Laveleye's Econ. Rurale, p. 57.

† The average size of farms in England is below what is generally supposed;—more than two-thirds of the farms in England are under 100 acres in extent.—*See Morton's Handbook of Labour, p. 11.*

an admission very damaging to the advocates of the small farm system; but though in some respects there may be a saving of labour, over extensive areas, as compared with very diminished ones, the necessary difference will be found far less than is supposed;—within certain limits, economy of labour, though not of buildings or of machinery,* is as practicable on reasonably small farms as on large. If a proof were wanting, we need only again refer to the table, when we shall see that the tillage lands of Ulster and Leinster, the two provinces from which the largest rate of produce per acre is obtained, are cultivated by a fewer number of hands than are crowded into the husbandry of

---

* "The large farmer has some advantage in the article of buildings."—*Mill's Political Economy*, p. 180.

"It has been suggested that machines and horses should be held in common by small farmers, but the practical execution of such arrangements are very difficult. In an uncertain climate like that of Ireland, it may be of the most vital importance to take advantage of the few days of fine weather which after weeks of expectation may afford a transient opportunity of reaping a crop already compromised, or of ploughing a field still saturated with moisture at the end of April. All the co-proprietors of the plough horses and machines would require the use of them simultaneously."—*Ibid.* p. 180.

"Some soils, however, are unsuitable for spade husbandry; as, for instance, heavy wet lands liable to inundation; stony, gravelly, or shallow soils, more especially if incumbent on chalk. *Manual labour is also inapplicable where the climate is precarious, and it is necessary to be expeditious in tilling the land, and in sowing and harrowing for a crop. On these accounts, spade husbandry cannot be universally resorted to* with advantage either to the agriculturist or the community."
Macdonald's Estate Management, p. 261.

Munster and Connaught; and that in Down and Antrim, the two Irish counties in which agriculture is supposed to be most advanced, and the average size of the farms smaller than elsewhere,* the proportion of cultivators to the acre is considerably less than it is in Cork and Kerry. In fact, the density of the agricultural population over the several areas referred to appears to be in an inverse ratio to the rate of their agricultural produce; and no matter how the calculation is conducted, or what districts are brought into comparison, whether England with Ireland, Ulster with Connaught, or Down with Cork, the same conclusion is evolved, viz.: that in those districts which are worst cultivated, a far larger number of persons are engaged in agriculture than are necessary to obtain the same results as are arrived at in those districts which are better cultivated.†

But it is urged that if only the Belgian system could be introduced into Ireland, our present agricultural population would be anything but in excess of the requirements of the country's husbandry.

I shall show, by and bye, how inapplicable to the present circumstances of Ireland is the Belgian system of agriculture, if by Belgian cultivation

---

* This is a common statement, but I doubt the accuracy of the latter part of it. If due allowance is made for the land under pasture, it would probably appear that the *tillage* farms of the best parts of Ulster are larger than the average of those in many parts of the south and west, though exceptional areas in the south and west may contain farms of larger size than are usual in Ulster.

† See Appendix, pp. 206—209.

is intended the minute garden husbandry of East Flanders; but even admitting such a change of system not only to be possible, but proximate, a further reference to our table will show that at all events in many parts of Ireland, if not in all, the proportion of the agricultural population to the area it occupies is almost as dense as it is in Belgium. If, therefore, the Belgian system is to be introduced, and our tenant-farmers are to take to growing tobacco, hops, onions, colza, and carrots, on patches of three or four acres, in the expectation of making a fortune, emigration cannot be accused of having deprived them of the opportunity.

But in Belgium it is only by dint of the most unremitting industry, and a traditional skill,* which

---

* " L'accroissement de la population développa nécessairement les forces productives du pays, et l'on est étonné de voir à quelle époque reculée remontent les procédés les plus perfectionnés de la culture. Un grand nombre des villages actuels sont désignés dans les chartes les plus anciennes ; même les noms de beaucoup d'entre eux se rapportent aux croyances religieuses de l'époque païenne."—*De Laveleye, Economie Rur.* p. 12.

" Ce qui lui permet de subsister avec un salaire aussi insuffisant, c'est le travail sans relâche de tous les membres de la famille. La journée finie, et souvent la nuit au clair de lune, le père cultive le petit champ, d'une dizaine d'ares, qu'il loue autour de sa chaumière. Depuis que la vapeur a brisé l'antique symbole de l'industrie domestique, le rouet, *la mère et les filles font de la dentelle,* travail délicat et gracieux, mais trop peu rétribué, et surtout trop incertain, comme tous les travaux qui répondent aux besoins du luxe et aux fantaisies de la mode. Les fils que les occupations des champs ne réclament pas encore élèvent des lapins pour le marché de Londres.

has been the growth of centuries, by a vast expenditure of capital, and by the application of enormous quantities of manure, that the agricultural class, whose rate of increase is slow,* and whose redundant members a flourishing manufacturing industry is ready to absorb, has been able, under peculiar advantages of climate, situation, and markets, to maintain an existence at all times considerably straitened, and daily becoming more difficult under the pressure of increasing competition. In Ireland these fostering conditions are as yet completely wanting, and years may elapse before they are created. How can we be justified then, in the expectation of so remote a contingency, in tethering down to the soil by artificial means, an agricultural population far in excess of the requirements and the system of husbandry best adapted to the present circumstances of the country, in the expectation of the ultimate introduction of a system of 'petite culture,' which, even

Leurs humbles mains mettent à profit la moindre touffe d'herbe oubliée dans les taillis ou le long des chemins, diminuent le gêne de la maison paternelle et donnent lieu à un mouvement d'exportation qui n'est pas à dédaigner, tant il est vrai qu'en agriculture il n'est rien qui n'ait de l'importance. Il s'exporte par Ostende seulement, 1,250,000 lapins par an, d'une valeur de plus de 1,500,000 francs. La peau est conservée dans le pays pour la fabrication des chapeaux."—*De Laveleye, Économie Rurale, p.* 70.

* The population of Flanders has actually diminished since 1846, in East Flanders by 16,000, and in West Flanders by 18,000. In all the other provinces of Belgium the population has increased.

then, would hardly afford adequate employment to our existing numbers.

But I turn from any calculations of my own to evidence of a more unexceptionable character. Five witnesses besides myself were examined last year before Mr. Maguire's Land Tenure Committee. No one will pretend that the sympathies of those gentlemen were unduly enlisted on the landlord's side. Some of them were members of the National Association, and their bias—so far as their minds were susceptible of bias—was clearly in favour of the tenant.

All were asked the same question. What is the smallest area which a tenant can cultivate with advantage, or over which you would extend the protection of a lease? How did each reply? Judge Longfield says (Q. 401):—

"To grant a 21 years' lease to the occupier of five or ten acres would generally be no use." "He himself would not grant one." "No improvement on so small an area would pay."

Mr. Dillon says (Q. 1,859):—

"He would not grant a lease to a man who held a very small or bad farm." (Q. 2, 108—"Twenty acres of good land at a fair rent was the holding on which he could live with comfort."

Mr. M'Carthy Downing doubles the desirable *minimum*. He is asked what he considers a small holding. He replies (Q. 2,562):—

"From 15 to 20 acres."

Again he is asked (Q. 2,563):—

"Do you consider so small a holding is good either for the country, the tenant, or the landlord?"

He answers:—

"If I had land without any population on it, I would rather

not have so small a holding as that, though, if the tenants were there, I would not remove them; but from my experience, a tenant paying £25. per annum is as good a tenant as a larger one." (Q. 2,564)—"That would be a man holding 40 or 50 acres."—"Yes."

Even the Catholic Bishop of Cloyne, when pressed to name the *minimum* area on which a farmer could live, admits that " small farms, with any amount of industry, must be precarious," and that a tenant to be comfortable ought to have " 20 acres or *upwards;*" while Mr. Curling declares " that he would not be disposed to give a lease even to an industrious and punctual tenant, unless his farm were over 15 acres in extent."* Now, what is the necessary deduction from this evidence produced by Mr. Maguire himself on behalf of the tenant? If reason and not passion is to guide us, it must be conceded that a greater amount of intelligent energy than necessary is dissipated in the cultivation of land. At all events, if the champions of the tenant's cause are themselves found condemning small holdings and 15-acre leaseholds as unprofitable and "*precarious,*" and if it is shown that the extinction of farms in Ireland has been hitherto almost entirely confined to that category, may not the landlords be absolved from the charge of undue consolidation?

* The following opinion of Mr. Mill is well worthy of consideration in connection with this subject:—

"That each peasant should have a patch of land, even in full property, if it is not sufficient to support him in comfort, is a

Let us now examine the agricultural system of Belgium, to which reference is often made. Fortunately, in the work of M. De Laveleye, we possess a text book on the subject of European celebrity.

According to popular belief Belgium is cultivated by a peasant proprietary twice as numerous in proportion to the area they occupy as the agricultural population of Ireland, living in peculiarly easy circumstances, and affording unmistakeable evidence of the advantages of *la petite culture*. The real facts are these:—That, making a proportionate deduction for the population employed on the pasture lands of both countries, the total population dependent on tillage in Ireland is probably almost as dense as that of Belgium. That the greater portion of Belgium is cultivated, not by small proprietors, but by tenants (and almost entirely so wherever *la petite culture* is carried to

system with all the disadvantages, and scarcely any of the benefits, of small properties; since he must either live in indigence on the produce of his land, or depend as habitually as if he had no landed possessions, on the wages of hired labour; which, besides, if all the holdings surrounding him are of similar dimensions, he has little prospect of finding.

"The benefits of peasant properties are conditional on their not being too much subdivided; that is, on their not being required to maintain too many persons, in proportion to the produce that can be raised from them by those persons. The question resolves itself, like most questions respecting the condition of the labouring classes, into one of population. Are small properties a stimulus to undue multiplication, or a check to it?"—*Mill's Political Economy, p.* 346.

excess.)* That the competition for land is intense, and rack-rents universal.† That from 1830 to 1846

---

* "En Flandre la plus grande partie du sol est exploité par des locataires."—*Economie Rurale, p.* 72.

"Dans la Flandre orientale 166,311 h. étaient cultivés par des locataires, soit 75 p. c. et 52,673 par les propriétaires ; dans la Flandre occidentale, 229,970, par les locataires, soit 85 per c. et 40,831 h. par les propriétaires. Le recensement officiel constate que dans cette dernière province la terre tend à échapper complètement aux mains qui la cultivent."—*Eco. Rur.* 72.

"On a remarqué en Belgique un rapport constant entre l'étendue des exploitations et le nombre des propriétaires qui font eux-mêmes valoir leurs biens. Ainsi dans les provinces de Namur et du Luxembourg, les trois quarts des cultivateurs sont propriétaires de la totalité ou de la plus grande partie des biens qu'ils exploitent, et c'est aussi dans cette région qu'on rencontre le plus de fermes au dessus de 20 hectares et le moins d'occupations inférieures à 1 hectare, tandis que dans les Flandres, où les cultures sont extrêmement petites, les quatre cinquièmes du sol sont mis en valeur par des locataires."

Eco. Rur. 246.

Taking the whole kingdom, the proportion of holdings cultivated by tenants to those cultivated by the proprietor is as 65·78 to 34·22.

† "D'autre part, dans un pays aussi peuplé que la Belgique le nombre des fils de fermiers qui cherchent à se placer est toujours plus grand que celui des exploitations vacantes ; il en résulte que, n'entrevoyant d'autre carrière ouverte devant eux que celle du cultivateur, et incapables de calculer les profits probables d'une entreprise agricole, ils enchérissent à l'envi l'un sur l'autre, jusqu'à ce qu'il ne leur reste pour prix de leur rude labeur qu'un minime salaire et un intérêt insuffisant de leur capital engagé."—*Eco. Rur.* 234.

"La petite propriété combinée avec la location dans un pays très peuplé, comme cela se voit toujours, place le cultivateur dans *la pire des situations.* Appliqué à des populations

rents have risen 25 per cent, and between 1846 and 1860 40 per cent.,* though the price of grain has only risen 5 per cent. That leases are rarely granted for a term exceeding nine years, and frequently for only three or five years.† That the average profits of the farmer are scarcely more than three per cent., instead of from 7 to 10 per

qui n'auraient pas pour les travaux des champs un goût instinctif très prononcé, ce système produirait le découragement, et pourrait avoir pour la production et le travail agricoles les plus fâcheuses conséquences."—*Eco. Rur.* 238.

" Or, dans les circonstances actuelles, cette multitude d'hommes rassemblés sur un espace relativement restreint amène la concurrence des bras qui s'offrent au rabais, et par conséquent la portion de la richesse produite qui reste entre les mains des classes laborieuses ne suffit pas à la satisfaction de leurs besoins."—*Eco. Rur.* 242.

* " Ce qui frappe surtout en Belgique quand on étudie les faits réunis dans les publications officielles, c'est la hausse constante et rapide des fermages. Depuis 1830 jusqu'en 1846, ils s'élèvent de 30 per cent.; c'est à dire de près de 2 per cent. par an et depuis 1846 l'augmentation, loin de se ralentir, s'est plutôt accélérée."—*Eco. Rur.* 231.

"En effet, d'après les statistiques officielles, le prix de location par hectare a été porté, de 1830 à 1846, dans la Flandre occidentale, de 60 à 73 francs, soit une hausse de 21 pour 100, et dans la Flandre orientale de 71 à 93 francs, soit une hausse de 30 pour 100. Depuis 1846 jusqu'en 1860, l'augmentation, loin de se ralentir, s'est plutôt accélérée, surtout dans la première de ces deux provinces : on a constaté qu'elle a été en moyenne de 40 pour 100 en trente ans, tandis que, pendant la même période, le prix des céréales ne s'est élevé que de 5 pour 100."
Eco. Rur. 72.

† "Mais de nos jours il a complètement disparu pour faire place au bail de neuf ans, terme qui est généralement en usage." (See also Appendix, p. 209.) *Eco. Rur.* 126.

cent., as in England.* That the condition of the agricultural population is worse where the subdivision of farms is greatest, and best where the farms are largest.† That the Belgian labourer is

* "Malheureusement la condition des hommes laborieux qui ont amené l'Agriculture à un si haut dégré de perfection n'est point en rapport avec la masse des produits qu'ils récollent. *L'ouvrier Agricole des Flandres est peut-être celui de tous les ouvriers européens qui travaillant le plus est le plus mal nourri.* Le petit fermier ne vit guère mieux, et si l'on y regardait de près on se convaincrait que, loin de tirer du capital engagé dans son exploitation, les 10 p. c. qui est nécessaires en Angleterre, il n'en obtient pas 3 p. c. en sus de salaire qu'il mérite par son travail personnel."—*Eco. Rur.* 69.

† "Dans les districts où domine relativement la grande culture, le sort des cultivateurs locataires est sans doute plus heureux que dans la région de la petite culture."
Eco. Rur. 232.

"On nous pardonnera sans doute d'avoir insisté sur ce fait particulier, car il met nettement en relief le contraste que présentent les Flandres, où la production agricole, la plus riche qu'on puisse voir, ne laisse aux mains de ceux qui travaillent la terre que juste de quoi vivre, et d'autre part, l'Ardenne, où ceux qui font valoir le sol jouissent d'une certaine aisance relative, malgré l'infériorité de la production et des procédés agricoles."—*Eco. Rur.* 215.

"De tous ces faits on serait tenté de conclure que si la petite propriété offre d'excellents résultats et pour la culture et pour le cultivateur, quand celui qui exploite la terre la possède, dans le cas contraire la grande propriété assure une meilleure condition au fermier."—*Eco. Rur.* 238.

"Nulle part, (*i.e. in the East of Belgium, where the farms are largest*), je n'ai vu ni la propreté ni les soins, ni l'aisance apparente des chaumières flamandes. Mais nulle part non plus des indices de l'extrême misère qu'on rencontre trop souvent dans les Flandres."—*Eco. Rur.* 214.

"Et néanmoins dans cette contrée ingrate, dont l'homme n'a

supposed to be the most industrious and the worst paid of any labourer in Europe, that the farmer is scarcely better off than the labourer ;* and that in Flanders population is not merely at a standstill, but diminishing.

It may be objected that, however little advantageous to the agricultural classes themselves, *la petite culture* of Belgium turns out a greater amount of gross produce than any other method of cultivation known in Europe. This is probably the case, if we omit all reference to cost, and, under suitable circumstances, it is (at all events, for the

pas même appris à faire valoir toutes les forces productives, les populations rurales jouissent d'une aisance beaucoup plus grande que dans les belles campagnes des Flandres si admirablement cultivées. D'ailleurs le fermier jouit ici d'une large aisance rustique ; il vit beaucoup mieux que le fermier flamand."—*Eco. Rur.* 193.

* " Il nous reste à faire connaître la condition du simple ouvrier rural. Elle ne se présente pas, il faut bien le dire, sous des couleurs plus favorables que celle des locataires. Le salaire moyen était porté pour 1846 à 1 fr. 13 c. par jour. Depuis cette époque, il s'est relevé, et on pourrait le porter pour 1860 à 1 fr. 40 c. S'il approche, dans certaines parties du pays, de 2 fr., dans d'autres districts il tombe même au dessous de 1 fr."—*Eco. Rur.* 210.

" La statistique officielle constate elle-même que la population rurale de la Belgique est l'une des plus mal nourries du continent."—*Eco. Rur.* 240.

" Dans la région flamande, de beaucoup la mieux cultivée, l'ouvrier de la campagne gagne moins que dans la région wallonne, où se sont surtout fixés l'industrie et les exploitations minières.

" La ligne de partage entre les hauts et les bas salaires suivrait à peu près les limites qui séparent les Flamands des Wallons."

Eco. Rur. 239, 240.

landlord) a most profitable system.* But the provinces of Belgium where *la petite culture* prevails are thickly studded with populous towns and innumerable villages,† and the land around them is

* "Sans doute nous avons vu en Flandre que, malgré de telles circonstances, la petite culture associée à la petite propriété peut donner un produit brut énorme; mais là aussi nous avons été frappés du triste contraste que présentaient ces magnifiques récoltes et l'existence misérable de ceux qui les font naître. Ainsi un grand nombre de petits propriétaires sans aucun intérêt direct dans la culture, superposés à la classe plus nombreuse encore de ceux qui exploitent la terre, et élevant sans cesse la rente aussi haut que peut la porter une concurrence excessive, voilà le fâcheux revers qu'offre l'organization agricole de la Belgique, surtout dans ses parties les plus riches."—*Eco. Rur.* 234.

"Il n'en est pas de même quand le sol est partagé entre un grand nombre de propriétaires qui ne cultivent pas eux-mêmes les terres qui leur appartiennent. Dans ce cas, le produit brut peut encore être très élevé; mais la condition de ceux qui le créent n'est point ce que les sentiments d'équité feraient désirer qu'elle fût. Tous ces petits propriétaires n'ont qu'un but, élever le fermage aussi haut que le permet la concurrence des locataires."—*Eco. Rur.* 233.

† "La population rurale ne forme ici (in East Flanders) que le tiers de la population totale."—*Eco. Rur.* 56.

The intimate dependence of the Agriculture of Belgium on the long-established manufacturing industries of that country is brought out in strong relief by M. Laveleye.

"Les progrès de l'agriculture, qui suivirent le développement de l'industrie de la laine. Cette marche parallèle du travail agricole et du travail industriel semble remonter très haut."—
Eco. Rur. 11.

"Les terres communes de la tribu ayant été partagées entre les chefs de famille, la part de chaque cultivateur semble avoir compris une étendue à peu près équivalente à celle des petites fermes actuelles qui entretiennent un cheval. Dans la plupart

devoted to an extensive system of market-garden-

de ces menses soumises au seigneur, les femmes filaient la laine et le lin, les hommes fabriquaient des étoffes de drap et de toile qui s'exportaient dans toutes les contrées du nord et principalement en Angleterre. Les relations commerciales, s'étendant jusqu'au fond du pays, y firent pénétrer quelques lumières et quelque richesse. Cette prospérité, dérivée de deux sources différentes, s'accrut rapidement. Les hameaux situés aux lieux où les navires pouvaient aborder avec facilité se peuplèrent et s'agrandirent. C'est ainsi que l'industrie enrichissait les campagnes, tandis que le commerce créait les villes."—*Eco. Rur.* p. 12.

" La Flandre était alors pour l'Angleterre ce que ce dernier pays est aujourd'hui pour le continent (1): *une nation chez qui l'accumulation de la richesse produite par l'industrie et le commerce fait faire à l'agriculture des progrès incessants.*"

Eco. Rur. p. 13, 14.

" Il suffit de visiter les riantes demeures groupées au milieu des prairies qui bordent le Jaër, de voir l'ordre et la propreté qui y règnent, pour juger jusqu'à quel point un travail de main-d'œuvre intimement associé au travail des champs peut transformer un canton pauvre et isolé."

" Le village flamand est formé non de l'agglomération des fermes, mais de la réunion des industries que réclament les besoins de la nombreuse population dispersée dans les campagnes. Quelques-unes de ces communes comptent de six à huit mille habitants."—*Eco. Rur.* p. 75.

" Quand, pour se soustraire aux exactions des seigneurs et pour répondre plus facilement aux demandes d'une exportation croissante, les tisserands vinrent se grouper autour marchands et constituer les gildes de la laine à l'abri des murailles, alors même l'industrie ne déserta point les campagnes, où l'on continua d'associer aux soins d'une culture déjà très variée *la fabrication du drap et de la toile.*"

" Aux yeux des chroniqueurs anglais du XIIe et du XIIIe siècle *tout cultivateur de ce pays est un homme qui sait faire du drap et manier les armes.*"— *Eco. Rur.* p. 13.

" Lorsque les communes de Gand et de Bruges, d'Ypres et

ing,* only practicable in such localities. The facilities for obtaining manure are exceptional, and high

de Courtrai, enrichies par l'exportation des étoffes, arrivèrent à compter deux ou trois fois plus d'habitants qu'elles n'en ont aujourd'hui, il fallut arracher à un sol rebelle les subsistances nécessaires à une population à la fois si dense et si aisée."
Eco. Rur. p. 6.

"Les progrès de cette culture sont dus à trois causes principales : l'aptitude et le goût très prononcé des habitants pour les travaux des champs, *l'association intime de l'agriculture et de l'industrie*, enfin la liberté et l'indépendance dont ont joui les populations."—*Eco. Rur.* p. 19.

* "La culture, ainsi poussée jusqu'au point *où elle devient du jardinage*, exige, on le comprend sans peine, un capital d'exploitation relativement considérable."—*Eco. Rur.*

The way in which garden cultivation is promoted by the neighbourhood of a large town, and the consequent facilities for obtaining manure, cannot be better illustrated than by the subjoined statement of a gentleman who resides in Bedfordshire.

"I enclose you a set of questions I sent to my steward, with his answers."

Questions.	Answer.
About how many acres in all, under garden cultivation?	4000 acres, at a rough guess.
What is the largest held by one occupier?	300 acres.
What is the smallest held by one occupier?	10 acres.†
Highest rent?	£7, including rates.
Average rent?	£4.

---

† "I know some of my own tenants, whose rent my "steward himself receives, who hold three or four acres; but "I fancy he does not consider them gardens, unless they grow "cucumbers and onion seed."

manuring at a cost of from £10. to £18. to the

Any leases, and for how many years?	Not any that I know of.
Any covenants?—and what?	None.
Largest value per acre for any one crop?	£50 to £60.†
Average do.?	£20 some years, but not the last five or six years.‡
Largest quantity of manure per acre you ever knew applied to an acre?	60 loads.
What is the average of owners of the small lot to occupiers?	Not 1 owner in 20 tenants.

"Every fresh Railway opens out a new field for the supply, and what is still more disadvantageous, creates a fresh demand for manure, thereby decreasing, or tending to lessen, the price of the produce, and increasing (or tending to increase), the price of manure. Without London manure, the whole system is impossible."

It will be observed, that in this case, "la petite culture" is entirely dependent upon the manure brought down by rail, that proximity to a railway station on a line communicating with a large town, is almost as advantageous as proximity to the town itself, and that the extension of railways, and of the advantages they confer, has a tendency to diminish the profits of this system of agriculture in particular localities, and to

---

† At present perhaps £60 may be the largest; but not very long ago, I have heard of £120 worth of onion seed per acre.

‡ The causes of the falling off in the value of garden produce are—
1. The potato disease.
2. The greatly increased area now under cultivation for this particular produce.
3. The great increase in the number of railways radiating from the metropolis.

acre,* stolen crops,† together with the cultivation of diffuse them over a larger area. It is to be noted, that as many as seven lines of railway and two canals radiate from Ghent, which is the central point of la petite culture in Belgium.

"Toutes les villes sont reliées au réseau ferré, et il est tel chef-lieu de province, comme Gand, par exemple, où viennent aboutir sept voies différentes."—*Eco. Rur.* 260.

"Aux environs d'Anvers, la terre très maigre; *mais le voisinage de cette grande cité commerciale a permis de communiquer au sol une extrême fertilité et de lui appliquer à peu les procédés de la culture maraîchère.* Près de Malines, on rencontre des prairies magnifiques arrosées par les eaux de la Senne et de la Dyle, et des terres cultivées comme celles des Flandres; elles se vendent à des prix encore plus élevés, c'est à dire au delà de 5,000 francs l'hectare."—*Eco. Rur.* 142.

"La terre arable ordinaire vaut donc de 4 à 6,000 fr. l'hectare; mais aussitôt qu'elle est à proximité des centres industriels où on peut la louer en parcelles *pour les ménages d'ouvriers,* elle atterent une valeur de 8, à 10,000 fr. l'hectare."

Eco. Rur. 157.

* "Les inscriptions tumulaires de l'époque Romaine attestent même qu'alors déjà les habitants des rives de l'Escant allaient chercher en Angleterre de la marne pour amander leurs terres, preuve certaine d'une culture avancée."—*Eco. Rur.* 11.

"Aussi peut-on porter à une moyenne de 80 à 100 francs par hectare la somme qu'il consacre à l'achat des engrais que livre le commerce et des tourteaux nécessaires à la consommation de ses étables."—*Eco. Rur.* 44.

"Se procurer des engrais, telle est la grande préoccupation du cultivateur. Il n'essaie pas de se dérober à cette coûteuse nécessité, car il n'ignore point qu'autrement il perdrait le loyer qu'il doit payer et la valeur des labours qu'il a exécutés."

Eco. Rur. 43.

"Les récoltes d'hiver reçoivent d'ordinaire au moment des

† "Les cultures dérobées comprennent le navet et les pergule, qu'on met après le colza,—le lin, le seigle et les pommes de

plants used in the adjacent manufactories,* are the keystones of Belgian agriculture. In a great number

semailles de vingt à trente voitures de fumier d'étable par hectare, valant de 100 à 150 francs, et au printemps de 150 à 300 hectolitres de purin, estimés de 60 à 75 francs."—*Eco. Rur.* 44.

"De nous jours, l'agriculteur flamand a voué aussi une sorte de culte à l'auxiliaire indispensable de ses travaux, à l'engrais qu'il appelle dans énergique langage le *dieu de l'agriculture*. L'engrais joue dans l'économie rurale de la Flandre un rôle prédominant."—*Eco. Rur.* 44.

---

de terre précoces,—la carotte, qu'on sème au printemps dans les récoltes sur pied et qu'on sarcle avec soin après que la moisson est faite,—le trèfle incarnat et le seigle à couper, qui, après avoir occupé la terre pendant l'hiver, la laisse libre pour les semailles d'avril,—le chou cavalier, qui continue à se développer, même pendant la saison froide, et dont la tige énorme, haute de six pieds, donne en abondance des feuilles excellentes pour les vaches laitières. Les cultivateurs attachent une grande importance à ces récoltes."—*Eco. Rurale, p.* 47.

* "La culture de la betterave à sucre y a surtout beaucoup contribué en donnant à l'art agricole une impulsion comparable à celle qu'imprima le colza vers la fin du siècle dernier."
Eco. Rurale, p. 155.

"Le tabac est cultivé en grand dans certains cantons notamment aux environs de Commines et de Wervicq, où il acquiert une odeur pénétrante appréciée jusque sur l'autre bord de l'Atlantique. Le produit en est beaucoup plus grand qu'en France, même dans les meilleurs départements."
Eco. Rurale, p. 87.

"De même que le houblon remplace ici la vigne, ainsi la chicorée tient lieu de café, et la betterave de canne à sucre."
Eco. Rurale, p. 90.

"Ce n'est donc qu'en cultivant du lin ou du colza, du tabac ou de la chicorée, que le fermier parvient à satisfaire aux engagements qu'il a contractés envers le propriétaire."
Eco. Rurale, p. 39.

"Le lin jouait jadis dans l'économie du pays, quoiqu'en des

of instances where the plots of land are very diminutive the farm is only auxiliary to its occupier's trade, just as the little holdings in Antrim or Down are auxiliary to the hand-loom weaving of Ulster.*

conditions plus humbles, le même rôle que la soie dans celle de l'Italie. Il était pour le cultivateur une source de produits à la fois agricoles et industriels, car tout le travail qu'exigeait la confection des célèbres toiles de Flandre se faisait aux champs."
Eco. Rurale, p. 86.

"Cependant le rouissage, le teillage et le tissage distribuent encore parmi les populations rurales une somme de salaires très importante."—*Eco. Rurale, p.* 86.

"Dans ses moments perdus, l'ouvrier retourne à la bêche ce coin de terre qu'il s'estime heureux d'avoir obtenu même aux conditions les plus dures."—*Eco. Rurale, p.* 52.

"Les exploitations inférieures à 1 hectare se rencontrent tout aussi fréquemment ici que dans les Flandres mêmes. C'est que non seulement les ouvriers agricoles, *mais même la plupart des travailleurs employés dans les mines ou dans l'industrie veulent avoir leur lopin de terre* pour y récolter une grande partie des aliments nécessaires à la consommation de leur ménage."
Eco. Rurale, p. 161.

* Infinitesimal sub-divisions are rendered possible in Switzerland by exactly analogous circumstances.

"Besides these, however, there is a more numerous body of smaller proprietors, whose territorial possessions consist only of a field or two, altogether not larger than an ordinary garden, and much too small for the maintenance of the family to which they belong. Here there may seem to be an instance of excessive subdivision. *But the owners of these patches of land are almost invariably manufacturers rather than husbandmen: they constitute indeed the bulk of the manufacturing population of a country which has but two superiors in manufacturing importance.* Most of the cotton and silk goods of Switzerland are produced in the rural districts of Zurich, Basle, St. Gall, Appenzel, and Argovia; and even of those famous Swiss watches so much admired for their delicacy and

And, lastly, both in respect of climate, in the forcing power of the sun, (without which stolen crops

beauty, as many come from chálets among the mountains of Neuchatel as from the workshops of Geneva.

"This affords a clue to the true explanation of the minute partition which has taken place.

"But although retaining the name and all the privileges of peasants, they gain their living principally as manufacturers."

Thornton's Peasant Proprietors, pp. 87 *and* 88.

"In most parts of the country, particularly in the baronies of Oneilland, Armagh, and Lower Orior, the condition of the peasantry is better than in any of the inland counties with which I am acquainted."—*Edward Tickell, Esq., Assistant Barrister, Dev. Com. Digest, p.* 370.

"Are they weavers in those districts which you speak of as being better?—There is a great number of weavers in those districts. I never saw a more comfortable-looking set of £10. freeholders than appeared before me at the registry, from those portions of the county; they were holding farms from about twelve to twenty English acres of very good land; great numbers of them had orchards on their farms, and they had the appearance of a set of English yeomen."

Edward Tickell, Esq., Assistant Barrister, Digest, p. 371.

John Lindsay, Esq., Magistrate and Chairman, Board of Guardians.

"The small tenantry formerly kept three or four looms going in their houses; and there might be some sons, or what they call dieters, coming in, and they employed them to weave; but the weaving fell, and that reduced their circumstances. The small tenantry of eight or ten acres, would eat all that grew upon their farms, and earn their rent by their trade."

* * * * *

"An occupier of three acres, with a trade or occasional occupation as a labourer, I consider (next to those having above twenty-five acres) as most likely to do well."

Richard C. Brown Clayton, Esq., (land proprietor), Digest, p. 413.

are very precarious), and in variety of plants for which a ready sale can be obtained, Belgium has advantages in which parts of Great Britain and nearly all Ireland are deficient. To expect, therefore, that because holdings of three, four or five acres can be cultivated with advantage around a cluster of large Belgian towns,* and amid the densest population in Europe, of which the agricultural class forms less than one half, a similar system can be introduced into Ireland, with its rainy, sunless climate,† its sparse

---

* East and West Flanders together comprise a smaller area than the County of Cork, and contain the following towns:— Grammont, 8,500; Eecloo, 8,500; Menin, 9,000; Renaix, 11,000; Lockeren, 17,000; Ostende, 16,000; Bruges, 48,000; Thorout, 8,000; Poperinghe, 10,500; Ypres, 16,500; Courtray, 22,000; Ghent, 108,900; Alost, 18,000; Dendermonde, 8,500; St. Nicolas, 21,000; the urban population of Flanders being little short of 400,000,—nearly three times as large as the urban population of the County of Cork; which in addition to its city of 80,000 inhabitants, can only boast of two towns with a population of 9000, another two with a population of 6000, and three or four with a population of 3000. In connection with our present argument, I might very fairly include in the urban population of Flanders, the adjacent town of Antwerp, with its 100,000 inhabitants.

† "Belgium seems to possess a perfect climate for promoting rapid vegetation: plenty of moisture and a hot sun."

"Bien que la quantité de pluie qui tombe ne soit pas très considérable, 800 millimètres par an; mais il pleut très souvent (un jour sur deux)."—*Eco. Rurale,* p. 10.

"There are countries where oats will ripen, but not wheat, such as the North of Scotland; others where wheat can be grown, but from excess of moisture and want of sunshine affords but a precarious crop; as in parts of Ireland."

Mill's Polit. Econ. p. 127.

As the excessive wetness of the Irish climate may not be

urban population, its restricted markets, and its limited manufactures,* seems as unreasonable as to argue that because it pays Mr. Early Pease, of Brompton, to employ a press of hands and £50. of manure per acre in raising asparagus for Covent-

thoroughly understood, I subjoin a table of the rainfall observed at Dublin during the last eight years, from which it will be seen that, on an average, seven inches of rain fell in that locality during the months of harvest. But Dublin is on the east coast, and the rainfall of Dublin is no more a guide to the climate of Kerry, Galway, Limerick, Mayo, or Donegal, than the climate of London and Edinburgh is to that of Cornwall or the Hebrides. In 1861 rain fell even in the least rainy part of Ireland on 218 days, and in 1863 on 221 days.

Inches of Rain which fell in July, August, and September, as registered at Ordnance Survey Office, Phœnix Park.

Year.	Inches of Rain	Dry Years. Below average.	Wet Years. Above average.
1855	6·5	·6	—
1856	7·6	—	·5
1857	4·7	2·4	—
1858	7·2	—	·1
1859	4·9	2·2	—
1860	8·8	—	1·7
1861	11·0	—	3·9
1862	6·7	·4	—

* Here again M. de Laveleye, speaking of the rise in the value of land, which he says has nearly doubled in thirty years, enlarges on the intimate connection between the agricultural and the manufacturing prosperity of Belgium :—

" D'innombrables usines de toute espèce, disséminées dans toute la contrée, favorisent ainsi l'essor du travail et l'accroissement de la population : elles multiplient les sources de prospérité

garden market,* a similar expenditure and a similar method of cultivation should be adopted in the valleys of Wales and the straths of the Highlands.

The chief lesson which we may learn from Flemish husbandry is this,—that a very high rate of production is compatible with low wages, rackrents, and exceptionally short leases; and that diminutive tenancies, under certain favourable conditions, may be profitable to the proprietor while they are disadvantageous to the tenant.†

The example of Belgium is salutary, therefore, so far as it implies thrift, industry, skill, and great attention to manuring, but of questionable authority with respect to its short tenures and minute

et tendent à donner au sol une valeur que n'aurait pu créer seul le progrès agricole, quelque réel qu'il ait été d'ailleurs."
De Laveleye's Eco. Rurale, p. 158.

* "S'il fallait estimer tout l'avoir réalisable d'un fermier, il faudrait le porter au moins à 700 francs, et à 1,000 francs par hectare pour une ferme très bien garnie."—*Eco. Rurale*, p. 49.

† Even if we take the average size of Belgian farms for our standard, we shall see that consolidation in Ireland has not enlarged our holdings to any unreasonable degree; the mean size in Belgium varying from 7½ acres to 11 acres; whereas in Ireland two-fifths of the acreage under tillage is subdivided into holdings averaging less than ten acres in extent, and of the total number of farms, more than half are less than 15 acres, and of the remainder, two-fifths are below 30 acres.

"Aussi l'étendue moyenne de chaque exploitation, que M. de Lavergne porte pour l'Angleterre à 60 hectares, tombe t-elle en Belgique à 4½ hectares, si on compte tout le domaine productif, et même à 3 hectares si on défalque les bois et les terres incultes: c'est là réellement de la petite culture."
Eco. Rur. 213.

subdivisions* and I maintain the correctness of my original proposition,—that if a certain proportion of

---

* M. de Laveleye is evidently of opinion, that unless where the land is cultivated by the owner, the minute subdivision of the soil under a system of petite culture, and the intense competition it engenders, is productive of great misery to the agricultural class. In this view I cordially agree.

"A la vérité, il parait que, dans certâines provinces françaises, notamment en Alsace et en Lorraine, on se plaint de l'excès de la division du sol, qui empêche un assolement rationnel de s'établir, et qui arrête l'extension des cultures fourragères."—*Eco. Rur.* 53.

"Ce n'est pas à dire que la subdivision des exploitations soit un idéal à proposer aux sociétés modernes, car elle exige de l'homme un redoublement de travail et d'efforts peu compatible avec le développement de ses facultés intellectuelles; mais au sein de l'organisation actuelle, et en Flandre, on peut affirmer qu'elle n'a eu jusqu'à ce jour que des résultats avantageux, au moins pour la production et pour la rente."

Eco. Rur. 55.

The pleasure M. de Laveleye evidently takes in describing those parts of the kingdom, which though less productive are not cultivated under the pressure of such intense competition, is very remarkable.

Speaking of the Eastern District of Belgium, he says:—

"On ne rencontre que rarement ici les tempéraments lymphatiques, dus à une alimentation exclusivement végétale. Le paysan a le teint animé et chaud, la chair ferme, l'œil vif et la jambe nerveuse; il est toujours bien vêtu et bien chaussé, et s'il élève un porc, ce n'est pas pour le vendre afin de payer sa rente, mais pour en manger le lard avec ses pommes de terre. La main-d'œuvre se paie cher: on n'obtient guère un journalier à moins de 1 franc 75 cent. ou 2 francs, et encore à ce prix ne pourrait-on réunir un grand nombre d'ouvriers. En même temps que le salaire est élevé, les denrées sont à bon compte; il y a donc double avantage pour celui qui doit vendre son travail et acheter sa nourriture. Avec son doux climat,

the tenants of Ireland who are struggling to make a living off their seven or eight acre holdings could be enabled to apply their energies to more promising

ses gracieuses collines et ses beaux rochers, la zone du Bas-Luxembourg est sans contredit l'une de celles qu'on visitera en Belgique avec le plus de plaisir. La Semoy, dans ses capricieux et innombrables méandres, l'arrose tout entière et baigne les murs des pittoresques petites villes de Chiny et de Bouillon. Le sol, sans être trop morcelé, est divisé entre un nombre considérable de parts, presque toutes exploitées directement par les propriétaires. Chacun pour ainsi dire cultive son propre champ et peut s'asseoir à l'ombre de son noyer. Il en résulte pour tous une sorte d'aisance rustique qui dérive non de la possession de grands capitaux, mais de l'abondance de toutes les denrées. Une réelle égalité règne dans les conditions sociales : nul n'est assez riche pour attendre à l'opulence et à l'oisiveté, nul non plus n'est assez pauvre pour connaître les extrémités de la misère. C'est ainsi que dans ce pays agreste, où les beautés de la nature s'unissent pour former de charmants paysages, à celles qui trahissent la culture et les soins de l'homme, une population honnête et laborieuse peut subsister et même augmenter son bien-être en perfectionnant ses procédés agricoles, sans renoncer à une division du travail et de la propriété qui favorise une équitable répartition des produits. Aussi conseillerions-nous au voyageur agronome qui voudrait connaître les diverses régions rurales de la Belgique de terminer ses excursions par la visite de cet heureux district, afin que, sous l'empire de la dernière impression, il conserve un plus agréable souvenir de sa tournée."

Eco. Rur. 213.

" Les habitants de ce district, n'ayant à exécuter aucun des rudes travaux qu'exige ailleurs la culture de la terre, mènent une vie facile assez semblable à celle des tribus pastorales. Ils jouissent d'une certaine aisance, parce que la concurrence n'a pas encore surélevé les fermages, et ils sont vêtus avec plus de soin et de propreté que dans les cantons voisins."

Eco. Rur. 180.

pursuits, and so increase the size of the farms occupied by the remainder, it would be for the benefit of both.

I will conclude this short reconsideration of the subject by quoting a passage from Judge Longfield's address to the Statistical Society of Dublin:—" Mere agriculture, even in *its most improved state*, will not afford sufficient employment to the population of Ireland, unless it is very considerably reduced."* When, in a previous chapter, I expressed a far less sweeping opinion, I was unaware of this strong corroboration of its correctness.†

* " But mere agriculture, even in its most improved state, will not afford sufficient employment to the population of Ireland unless it is reduced very considerably; and in order to keep the people in comfort, or indeed to keep them in the country, it is necessary to find some means of preventing them from being entirely dependent upon that one branch of industry for their support."—*Judge Longfield's Speech to the Statistical Society*, 1865.

† "The population of Ireland, in fact, reduced though it be, is still far beyond what the country can support as a mere grazing district of England. It may not, perhaps, be strictly true that, if the present number of inhabitants are to be maintained at home, it can only be either on the old vicious system of cottierism, or as small proprietors growing their own food. The lands which will remain under tillage would, no doubt, if sufficient security for outlay were given, admit of a more extensive employment of labourers by the small capitalist farmers; and this, in the opinion of some competent judges, might enable the country to support the present number of its population in actual existence. But no one will pretend that this resource is sufficient to maintain them in any condition in which it is fit that the great body of the peasantry of a country should exist. Accordingly the emigration, which for a time had fallen off, has, under the addi-

I now come to the third point in our inquiry—viz., whether it is fair to refer the evictions in Ireland to the injustice of the landlords rather than to the neglect of their legitimate obligations on the part of the tenants. What has been already said almost answers this question, while the fact that two-thirds of the registered ejectments are for non-payment of rent speaks for itself. But as it is the fashion to talk of the act of eviction as if it were a crime, I would ask your readers to analyze the nature of the operation.

First, let us define the respective rights of landlord and tenant. A landlord is an owner of land; that is to say, he has either bought it himself, or inherited it from those who have bought it. In either case, the land he possesses represents a specific amount of capital, accumulated either by his own industry or by that of his forefathers, for which he is content to receive interest at a rate seldom exceeding $2\frac{1}{2}$ or 3 per cent. I may here observe that considerable prominence has been given of late to

---

tional stimulus of bad seasons, revived in all its strength. It is calculated that within the year 1864 not less than 100,000 emigrants left the Irish shores. *As far as regards the emigrants themselves and their posterity, or the general interests of the human race*, it would be folly to regret this result. The children of the immigrant Irish receive the education of Americans, and enter, more rapidly and completely than would have been possible in the country of their descent, into the benefits of a higher state of civilization."

Mill's Polit. Econ. p. 415, Vol. I.

the fact that in the time of Elizabeth, Cromwell, and William, extensive confiscations of property took place in Ireland, and it has been more than hinted that such a circumstance might justify the repetition of an analogous process. But, however strongly this argument may appeal to the conscience of the small minority who are able to trace their present proprietorship to an historical source, it will hardly commend itself to those whose possessions represent the mercantile industry of some distant ancestor, improved by centuries of hereditary thrift, or the proceeds of their own exertions invested in land on the faith of a Parliamentary title. Whether vague suggestions,—which (as far as they mean anything) would imply the uprooting of the whole of the population of Ulster, and the transference of nearly all the landed property of Ireland, from those whose legal title to it is indisputable to a thousand competitors whose claims would rest on distinctions of race* and religion,—are calculated to attract capital to the country or promote a feeling of security, it is needless to inquire.

* On a map of Ireland, executed in Queen Elizabeth's reign, which has been discovered by Mr. Froude, at Vienna, the possessions of the contemporary chieftains are delineated. Occupying a prominent place in the centre of the island, is a rich district described as the country of the O'Sheridans. As a native representative of what appears to have been, at all events at one time, an opulent house, I might be tempted to urge the expulsion of its present alien owners from the rich heritage of my ancestors.

Such barren speculations cannot alter the fact that at present the owner of landed property in Ireland holds it in exactly the same sense, and under the same conditions, as the owner of property in England.* He can sell his interest in it, he can let it,

* "Men are ever ready enough to believe that their misfortunes are caused by others rather than by themselves; and the long-cherished belief in the existence of a grievance is always hard to dispel. The Irish tenantry have been taught to believe that their position as to their legal rights is far worse than that of the tenant class in England; that the law which in England protects, in Ireland oppresses, the tenant; that while in England he is safe from capricious eviction, in Ireland he is daily liable to it; that whilst the Irish landlord is a rack-renting tyrant, his English brother is a mild, humane, disinterested, easy-going man, satisfied with a very moderate rent for his land, and ever burning with anxiety to build barns, byres, and dwelling-houses, at his own expense, and solely for the benefit of his much-loved tenant. Now no one, knowing the two countries, requires to be told that these representations are at least very highly coloured. It is well known that, though the landlord in England may build the farmhouses and offices in the first instance, and may sometimes (according to the custom of the district where his property lies) aid in keeping them in repair, while in Ireland the landlord has hitherto usually left these things to be done by the tenant, yet the English proprietor receives an ample equivalent in the much higher rent that his farms produce than that at which land of the same intrinsic value is generally let in Ireland. Nothing can be more fallacious than the idea that the power of evicting an improving tenant in Ireland is greater than it is in England, or that the English tenant class are in practice perfectly free from the capricious exercise of it by their landlords. A very cursory reference to the evidence taken before the Agricultural Customs Committee of the House of Commons in 1848 will suffice to show that tenants' grievances are not peculiar to Ireland."

Home and Foreign Review, April 1864.

he can cultivate it himself, as he may please, so long as he does not infringe existing contracts or the laws of his country.

A tenant, on the other hand, is a person who does not possess land, but who hires the use of it. He embarks his capital in another man's field, much in the same way as a trader embarks his merchandise in another man's ship. Experience teaches him that by expending a certain amount of labour and capital in the cultivation of the soil he is able within a limited period to get back from it not only the original capital he had expended, but also a profitable rate of interest upon that capital.* What rate that interest may reach will depend on his own skill and discretion, just as the trader's profits will depend on the judgment with which he sorts his cargo or selects his port. In either case, the amount of hire paid for the use of the ship or for the use of

---

The writer of the foregoing passage is by no means inclined to side with the landlord; any one who reads the article will see that his opinion is that of an impartial witness.

* "Thus, then, the inherent qualities of the soil are the distinct property of the landlord."

"The labour and capital which a tenant may employ to call those qualities into activity, are the equally distinct property of the tenant. And various are the previous considerations upon commencing a tenancy which must enter into any equitable calculation, having for its object the apportionment of the produce between these two claimants, whilst their interests are connected, or the fixing what shall be the final balance due to either when they separate."

Dig. Dev. Com. Summary, p. 6.

the land will be determined by competition, and will affect the balance of gain or loss on both transactions. If ships are few and land is scarce, freight and rent will rise, and the rise of each will in a great measure be regulated by the disproportion of ships to goods and of farmers to farms. But the rate of freight or the amount of rent are not the only circumstances which will affect the profits of either speculator. In the case of the trader, all will depend on his goods being landed at the port he intended, whilst the most promising expectations of the agriculturist may be ruined unless he retain possession of the land he occupies for a definite period. A clear understanding, therefore, ought to exist in both cases between the parties interested, as to the course of the ship and the duration of the tenancy. The shipowner may want to send his vessel to one port and the trader his goods to another, just as the proprietor of an estate may wish to let his land for one term and the tenant to hire it for another. The definitive arrangement will depend upon the respective necessities of the contracting parties and the balance of competition. On the previous supposition that ships are few and land scarce, the advantage of the bargain will remain with the owner of the ship and the possessor of the field—the one consenting to call at the desired port, unforeseen contingencies permitting, the other agreeing to let his land on such conditions as may be most suitable to his ulterior views.

Both arrangements may be thought by the impartial observer unfavourable to the two interests affected by it—the one to commerce, the other to agriculture—but inasmuch as each was a voluntary contract between persons who must be supposed capable of managing their own affairs, any legislative interference to amend the bargain might occasion greater mischief. For instance, a law requiring the ship to call at certain ports, or the landlord to let his land for what he might consider a longer term than was desirable, would be a grievance to both shipowner and landowner; they would probably protect themselves either by refusing to carry the goods and to let the field, or by raising the rate of their freight and rent. This result would suit neither merchant nor farmer. Parliament might again intervene, and not only lay down the plan of the voyage and the duration of the tenure, but might impose a specified scale of freights and rents, and declare the shipowner incapable of freighting his own ship, and the landlord of tilling his own land. But so violent an interference with the rights of property would be unjust, impracticable, and obviously productive of greater evils than those it was intended to remedy.

If the foregoing illustration be apposite, it follows that the tenant's interest in the farm he hires is quite as limited in its character as the trader's interest in the ship he charters. The voyage concluded, the lease expired, both ship and field revert to their respective owners.

It is hardly reasonable to deny the analogy on the ground that the ship is a manufactured article, but the earth is the gift of God. The land I have bought is probably itself as much a manufactured article as the ship: and the iron or wood of which the ship is built is as much the gift of God as the land: the labour or enterprise by which the land has been rendered valuable is as clearly represented by the money I gave for it, as the industry and ingenuity exercised on its construction is represented by the price the owner has paid for the ship. It is true the country of which my estate is part belongs to the nation, and consequently my property in that estate is over-ridden by the imperial rights of the commonwealth. But this fact cannot invest the individual who may happen to hire my land, *when once his tenancy is terminated either by lapse of time or by the violation of his contract*, with any peculiar rights in excess of those which may be inherent in the community at large.

Of course, in the case of land, the desirable duration of a tenant's occupancy may vary with circumstances, from one year to a hundred; it might equally suit him to take, and me to let, a corner of my park for a single crop, or a bit of pasture for a few months grazing, or a tract of heather under a reclamation lease of sixty years. But if the principle of the arrangement is to be defined it may be stated as an axiom that, unless otherwise provided for by special agreement, a tenant's *equitable* claim to the occupation of his farm extends to such a period as shall enable him to put back into his pocket the capital he has expended on its improvement, together with a fair amount of interest upon that capital;* for it is evident, first, that were the profits of agricultural enterprise to be artificially hoisted to a rate of

---

* It is sometimes objected that land having been made valuable by the exertions of the former generations of tenants, the additional fertility thus created ought to devolve like an apostolic succession on the actual occupants. But if the persons referred to conducted their business properly, they have been already remunerated by their annual surplus of profit. The increased value permanently acquired by the land through their exertions, was a subsidiary accident which they neither intended, nor could prevent. It was in expectation of such a result the land was let to them. In pursuit of their own interests they happened to disengage the latent virtues of the soil, which were the property of the former owner, and which, after they had been developed, the subsequent purchaser of the estate acquired.

For a tenant, therefore, to claim a share in the increased value of the land in addition to his fair profits, would be as unreasonable as for the labourer to claim a share in the tenant's profits in addition to his own wages, on the plea that those profits resulted from the increased fertility communicated to the land by his manual toil. The argument is as cogent in the one case as in the other. Moreover, as a matter of fact, though the labour of former tenants may frequently have improved the land, the operations of the actual tenant have as often deteriorated it: and virgin soil that was worth a great deal before a spade had touched it, may become completely exhausted by bad cultivation.

interest beyond the amount appropriate to such investments, the consequent stimulus to competition would immediately reduce them to their normal level; and, secondly, that to endow the present chance occupiers of farms with an indefeasible tenure would be tantamount to the imposition of a disability on the rest of the non-occupying population to hold land. The tenant's claim to occupation being necessarily, then, of a terminable character, he has no right to complain if his landlord finds its advisable, *on the expiration of his term*, to confer on another advantages similar to those he has hitherto enjoyed. Many considerations indispose both parties to change their relationship. Ancient associations, habits of friendly intercourse, the fellowship which unites old customers, may preserve the bond for generations; but when once it becomes the imperative interest of either to cancel it, the endeavour of any third party, such as the State, to force the maintenance of a connexion, which in its very nature is one of voluntary obligation, will tend to precipitate the rupture.

It is admitted by the witnesses on the other side that an industrious tenant is seldom, if ever, turned off an estate in Ireland; but it is a mistake to imagine that non-payment of rent is the only circumstance which can justify evictions. Any one acquainted with the management of land is aware that an idle or unskilful farmer, even though he pay his rent, may do his landlord's property more harm than an industrious tenant who is occasionally in arrear. Few things are more liable to deterioration than land, and the value of a field may be as completely annihilated* for a certain number of years as that of a house off which you take the roof. One of the landlord's most important duties is that of insuring the consummate cultivation of his estate, and to hold him up to obloquy because he makes a point of weeding his property of men whose want of energy or skill, or capital, renders them incapable of doing their duty by their farms, and replacing them by more suitable tenants, is hardly reasonable.

Again, the failure of the potatoes, the repeal of the Corn Laws, and the application of steam and machinery to husbandry have converted a primitive art into a complicated science.† If the Irish

---

* I quote the subjoined statement for the sake of the picturesque way in which the annihilation of the fertile properties of the soil is described:—

James Carnegie, Esq., Land Agent.

"In reference to the consolidation of farms, I may state that in 1823 I found a ploughland on an estate within three miles of Macroom, in the possession of a number of miserable cottiers; seeing that the property could not be improved by them, and *that they had dragged the life and soul out of the ground*, I recommended the landlord to take it away from them, and to give each of them his house, and from five to six acres of ground, during his life at a nominal rent. This was done, and the land taken up and improved, and let in larger farms to solvent tenants."—*Dig. Dev. Com. p. 463.*

† "The number of persons fitted to direct and superintend any industrial enterprise, or even to execute any process which cannot be reduced almost to an affair of memory and routine,

agriculturist is to hold his own with the foreign producer, it can only be by high farming, a large expenditure of capital, and great economy of labour—conditions of industry almost incompatible with the maintenance of unreasonably small farms. There has consequently arisen a desire on the part of both landlord and occupier to increase existing holdings, and when such a feeling prevails in the minds of the two parties chiefly interested, the tendency will not be arrested by legislation.

Fifteen years' experience in the management of property in Ireland has convinced me that the farmer of 20 acres at a fair rent makes a larger profit, educates his children better, accumulates more capital, and is more contented than the holder of eight or nine acres at the same rent, and that, at least, up to 30 or 40 acres, the advantage continues in an ascending ratio. Many advocates of the small farm* system would carry it higher, and almost every tenant on my estate is probably of their opinion. I am by no means disposed to

is always far short of the demand; as is evident from the enormous difference between the salaries paid to such persons, and the wages of ordinary labour. The deficiency of practical good sense, which renders the majority of the labouring class such bad calculators—which makes, for instance, their domestic economy so improvident, lax, and irregular—must disqualify them for any but a low grade of intelligent labour, and render their industry far less productive than with equal energy it otherwise might be."—*Mill's Polit. Econ.* p. 134.

* I have placed in the General Appendix a few observations on the respective merits of small and large farms.—*See General Appendix*, p. 833.

consider the English system of large farms applicable to Ireland;* on the contrary, I believe we shall eventually settle down to an average size of farm, as exceptionally suitable as is the guage of our railways; but if a landlord wishes to furnish his estate with farm buildings of his own erection,† and to better the position of his industrious tenants, by rendering the size of their farms proportionate to

* " There is, we are sorry to say, a growing disposition in (English) Land Agents to abolish small farms altogether. The sizes that farms ought to be, however, are not to be arbitrarily determined. The whole question depends on circumstances, comprehending the qualifications of tenantry, the nature of the soil and climate, also the best system of farming which is possible in the circumstances. Not only are small farms profitable in a national point of view, but they serve as steps in the ladder by which men of small means and industrious habits may raise themselves in the social scale; and such men succeed wonderfully by dint of hard labour and rigid economy."—*Macdonald's Estate Management*, p. 251.

† " With this constant and irresistible tendency to subdivide land, it often happens that the landlord, at the expiration of a lease, finds thirty or forty tenants, and as many mud cabins, instead of the one tenant to whom the farm was originally let. What is a landlord under these circumstances to do? Either he must surrender to the evil, which will inevitably go on increasing; or he must set about clearing his estate, in order to consolidate the holdings."

" If an Irish landlord wishes to improve his property, he finds that he cannot venture to lay out capital upon it, without increasing the size of the holdings. He cannot erect farmbuildings on plots of a few acres; the construction and repair of farm-buildings by the landlord implies the existence of large farms, and a respectable tenantry. A landlord has no hold on a cottier tenantry: they are not responsible persons, nor can they be trusted with valuable property."—*Sir G. C. Lewis on Irish Disturbances*, p. 320.

their capital and energies, no law should impede his action, even though the operation involve the occasional conversion of a struggling tenant into a well-paid labourer or prosperous emigrant.* Far from

---

* I subjoin some evidence from the Devon Commission on the respective prospects of the large and small farmer, *i.e.* the man of five or six acres, and the occupier of 25 or 30 acres.

"The best opinion, however, appears to be, that the condition of those large farmers, who adopt the improvements in agriculture suggested by the progress of science, is advancing; but that those who neglect those improvements are stationary, or declining in circumstances."

"It must be observed, that many witnesses apply the term of large farmers to the occupiers of twenty, thirty, or forty acres."

"The opinion, that the condition of the small farmers is in general very wretched, is supported by a great weight of evidence. It appears that in most parts of Ireland their sole food was the potato, accompanied with milk, salt, or salt herrings when procurable. Many witnesses asserted that the condition of this class was even lower than that of the labourers; but it must be remembered that the occupiers of two, three, or four acres, are frequently included under the title of "small farmers."—*Dig. Dev. Com. p.* 364.

"It appears that where agricultural knowledge is diffused amongst this class, their condition is improving; that the progress of temperance has been very useful, but that in general they are gradually sinking into deeper misery. The subdivision of farms, which seems to be frequently practised in defiance of the proprietors, is one powerful cause of this degradation."

Dig. Dev. Com. p. 364.

Thomas Davison, Esq., Agent.

"As to the condition of the farming population, is it improving or otherwise?—The condition of this class, speaking of large farmers, is always superior to the small tenantry. The large farmer must necessarily have a capital to carry on his

considering the latter alternative a hardship, I have invariably counselled emigration to any healthy business—his plans to ensure success must be carried on upon system; hence, the superior tillage generally upon the larger as compared with the smaller farms. The small tenantry are generally without capital. When a bad year arises, the whole produce of the farm barely suffices for the maintenance of the family; how then, or from what other source, is rent to be met or provided for?"—*Dig. Dev. Com. p.* 369.

Rev. James Porter, Presbyterian Minister.

" With respect to the condition of the farming population, do you consider the large farmers improving or otherwise?—When I speak of large farmers, you will perceive I mean persons possessing fifty acres; our largest farms are thirty-five acres on the average. Those are better off at present than the very small tenants; and my reasons for saying so are these, that they have more substance, and more capital in their hands."

" With respect to the smaller tenantry, what should you say?—They are miserably off; those are the persons I have described as falling into the hands of usurers, as to meal."

" What is the average size of the farms of those persons? —Three acres, some of them, and some would hold still less."
Dig. Dev. Com. p. 372.

James Sinclair, Esq., Land Proprietor.

" With respect to the condition of the farming population, do you consider that the condition of the larger farmers is improving, or the reverse?—I should be inclined to think they are very much improved."

" With respect to the means of the smaller class of tenantry, do you think they are improving or stationary?—I think that the very small tenantry have not improved. I think any man who can sell a good deal of produce off his land is in a better state than he used to be."—*Dig. Dev. Com.* p. 380.

Mr. Robert M'Crea, Farmer.

" With respect to the condition of the farming population,

single young man among my tenants in whom I was specially interested, and whose embarrassments at home compromised his future. In doing so I recommended the course I myself should have adopted under similar circumstances, and in no instance has the step been regretted. At this moment several of the most prosperous farmers on

are the large farmers, in your opinion, getting better in the world?—There is an appearance of more comfort with them. There is a taste for a better style of living and appearing in public, but I fear that their circumstances are not better by any means. There is more industry and a closer attention to business, which have enabled them so far to keep up former appearances. Increasing education gives them a taste for a better style of living, but their circumstances are by no means better."

"Are the small tenantry getting better in their means?— I think that the very small tenantry are not; they are if any thing worse, and but a little better off than the labourers upon their farms."—*Dig. Dev. Com.* p. 380.

David Wilson, Esq., Land Proprietor.

" With respect to the condition of the farming population, do you consider that the large farmers are improving in their circumstances?—The condition of graziers and large farmers, I should say, is decidedly improved. * * * * The small tenantry are to a very little extent improved—in many instances not at all so."—*Dig. Dev. Com.* p. 381.

Mr. Benjamin Cox, Farmer.

"With respect to the condition of the farming population, are the larger class of farmers getting better in the world?— Of this class there are few in the district; their condition is rather comfortable."

" Are the small tenantry getting better off?—For the most part their condition is very low, and not getting better."

Dig. Dev. Com. p. 381.

my estate are men who went out in their youth to Australia and to America, and have returned in the prime of life with an ample supply of capital, to renew with myself on a still more permanent basis the connexion which had subsisted for many generations between our respective ancestors.

It may be justly urged—and I have sufficiently explained myself on this subject in a previous publication—that the moral character of an act of eviction will greatly depend on the complete termination of the tenant's legitimate interest in his farm; but my argument presupposes this essential condition; and when it is remembered that according to Judge Longfield's dictum " no improvement on a small farm will pay," and that the deterioration of the land, if justly estimated, would be found to outweigh, in most cases of eviction, the counter-claim of the tenant for compensation, it is improbable that many instances have occurred in which this condition has not been fulfilled.*

* " But there is no small portion of the land of Ireland in the hands of tenants to whom a promise of compensation for bonâ fide improvements would be useless. They have neither skill, capital, or energy to undertake such tasks. Their only hope is to live, that is, to sustain life upon the land, and divide it among their children. That a farmer ought to possess some capital, and be able to pay some rent, is a proposition that has never entered into his head, and he is never ashamed to tell his landlord that he is not worth a single penny, never supposing that the natural inference is, that he is unfit to be a farmer."—*Judge Longfield's Add. to the Stat. Society.*

Therefore, while I heartily admit that a heavy obligation rests upon the landlord to exercise such extreme rights with great moderation, and with a charity far in excess of his legal responsibilities, in the face of the foregoing considerations, I cannot believe it would be either just or wise to curtail them.

In fact, the transition which is affecting the agricultural world of Ireland resembles the revolution which overturned the manufacturing system of England on the introduction of the power-loom. In each case an improvement of method threw a large proportion of the population of either country out of their accustomed groove, and great suffering and discontent ensued; but, for Parliament or public opinion to compel the agricultural interest of Ireland to maintain an unprofitable or exploded system of husbandry, for the purpose of preventing emigration, would be as unreasonable as an edict to preclude the mill-owner of Manchester from adopting such mechanical improvements as economize manual labour, or from working half-time during a cotton famine.

That a moral duty rests on the promoters of every industry, whether commercial or agricultural, to mitigate the distress incident to those periods of transition which periodically disturb all branches of employment cannot be too strongly insisted upon; but there can be no such essential difference in the relations between a landlord and his tenants, and an employer of wages and his workmen, *on the expiration of their respective contracts*, as should render such obligations more imperative on the one than on the other. Indeed, if a distinction were to be drawn, it would tell rather in the landlord's favour, inasmuch as the wealth accruing to him from the exertions of his tenants chiefly represents a low rate of interest on capital already accumulated without their co-operation; whereas, in the case of the manufacturer, a great portion of his capital, and of its rapidly increasing profits, has been created by the toil of those whom he finds it convenient to dismiss at a week's notice.

But, whatever the nature of the moral duties of landlord or master, under such circumstances, it is clear they cannot become the subject of legal enactment; and if any proof were needed of the ripeness of the working classes for a large extension of the franchise, it might be found in the economical sagacity and keen moral sense which have enabled them to distinguish the limits within which Parliament can be justly required to arbitrate in such matters between themselves and their employers.

I now turn to the two concluding points in our inquiry, viz.—1st, the extent to which the present discontent is to be attributed to laws affecting the tenure of land; and 2nd, the degree to which any change in those laws would modify that discontent. I have no disposition to deny the existence of a certain amount of disaffection in the minds of a large section of the Irish race;* but, in the first place, in defining its extent I think we may safely be guided by the statements of the Catholic Prelates of Ireland, who have authoritatively pronounced it to

* "The total number of persons arrested up to the end of November, 1866, was 752. Of these, 314 were tradesmen, artisans, and millworkers. Many of these might be shopkeepers, but as they were entered merely as "tailor" and "shoemaker," they were classified among the tradesmen. There were 52 shopkeepers, 25 publicans, 45 clerks and commercial assistants, 30 shop assistants and shopkeepers' sons, only 35 farmers and 20 farmers' sons (three of whom were students); the remainder consisted of national schoolmasters, persons who had been in the American army, labourers, &c. (An Hon. Member—"How many national schoolmasters?") Not less than 29 (a laugh), and I am sorry for it. (Hear.) But I repeat that, of the 752 arrested up to November, under the Lord-Lieutenant's warrant, only 35 were persons in the occupation of land. (Hear.) That is sufficient to show the House the particular class of persons who are engaged in this conspiracy, and the House will learn with satisfaction that the most important and numerous class of persons of these districts, who are in possession of almost all the wealth and industry of the country, have abstained from taking any part in this movement."—*Extract from the Report of Lord Naas' Speech on the Continuance of Suspension Habeas Corpus Act, February* 21, 1867.

In opening the Queen's County Assizes Chief-Justice Monahan alluded to the same subject, remarking in conclusion:—

"*No respectable farmer* has taken any party in this conspiracy. It is confined exclusively to foreign emissaries, idlers, and the worthless characters about the towns; and it is needless to observe how utterly unable they have been and always must be, to resist the constituted authorities."—*March* 13.

be confined to the least respectable portion of the community; and, in the next, we must entirely dissociate it from the more subtle feeling of uneasiness which is said to pervade the minds of the tenant farmers of the south and west. What I see reason to dispute, is that the hostility manifested towards the Government of England by the Irish in America, in the great manufacturing towns of England and of Scotland, and by the non-occupying population of Ireland itself, has been occasioned by laws affecting the tenure of land, or is likely to be modified by any change in them.

Fixity of tenure would not have materially impeded the exodus after the potato famine, nor have affected the action of the landlords, in so far as they may have contributed to it; for even that fantastic desideratum—as advocated by Mr. Butt—presupposes good husbandry and the payment of rent; two conditions of which the great majority of the small occupiers who either left of their own accord or were evicted during these last five-and-twenty years were from the circumstances of the case incapable; so, even admitting that much of the ill-feeling of which Fenianism is the exponent is to be traced to the resentment of those who emigrated, it is clear that so long as the landlord is to be left with any control or proprietorship at all over his land neither his conduct nor their opinion of it would have been materially modified. The same observation holds good even in a greater degree with respect to any law which might have regulated compensation, as the improvements on a cottier tenancy would have seldom been of an appreciable amount.* As a matter of fact, I believe that few of the actual occupiers of land are tainted with Fenianism. Scarcely any farmers have been implicated in that conspiracy, though, perhaps, some of their relatives (in other words, persons with a much more modified interest in land than themselves) may have been entrapped. The tenant of a piece of land, even under the alleged disadvantageous conditions of his existence, has much more to lose than to gain by the overthrow of the existing order of things. The adult male population of Ireland is about 1,900,000. Of these 441,000 are the occupants of farms.†

---

* The same view has been taken by the writer of the Review I have already quoted.

"Now the best friends of the Irish tenant must allow that there are fewer of the small land-holders who (in the sense that any tenant-right bill could recognise) have hitherto been improving tenants than there are of the reverse. Any legislation, therefore, that merely gave the tenant a property in his *bona fide* improvements could be a boon, at the present moment only to the minority of the tenant class. The larger number of the cottiers and small farmers, not having made any improvements, would be unaffected by the protecting law, and would be as liable as ever to unrecompensed eviction."

Home and Foreign Review, April, 1864, *p.* 353.

† It has been the habit of some authorities first to talk of the 600,000 tenant farmers of Ireland, and then having multiplied

In the event of a revolution the non-agricultural majority could alone hope to benefit by it. As political disturbances are unfavourable to the development of manufactures and the importation of capital, the population of Ireland would become more dependent upon the land than they are at present. It is true the landlord's rent would be at the disposal of the community; but, as it is but a fourth of the produce, its confiscation would only make room for about 100,000 new occupiers, without improving the condition of the present ones. But there will remain above a million of more or less necessitous persons to be accommodated, among whom, therefore, large sections of the present holdings would have to be divided, and filibustering patriots from America* might prove as exacting as

that figure by five to describe the total of the occupying population as amounting to 3,000,000, *i.e.* to a third more than its real amount.

The error has arisen from mistaking detached holdings occupied by the same individual, for distinct tenancies inhabited by different farmers. As there are 680,000 agricultural labourers in Ireland, most of them with families, it is evident such a calculation would prove the rural population to exceed the total population of the island. Had I adopted this version of the case, it would indeed have brought out an extravagant disproportion between the amount of labour absorbed in the cultivation of land in Ireland, as compared with other countries.

* A tenant in the South of Ireland lately received a letter from America, warning him at his peril to break up some pasture, as the writer intended on his arrival to appropriate the farm, of which it formed a part, himself. Were an American-

Cromwell's troopers. But, though the farming classes of Ireland regard Fenianism with hostility and terror, it cannot be denied that in many districts they are restless and dissatisfied with their own position. The degree of this discontent is dependent upon different circumstances. Nowhere in Great Britain does there exist a more orderly or contented body of men than the tenantry of Ulster; and I believe that, so far from regarding what are called "the tenant-right agitators" with favour, they rather shrink from the risk of reducing the gracious customs which are now voluntarily maintained between them and their landlords into the definite and inelastic phraseology of the most liberal Tenants' Compensation Bill which could be devised.*

Irish invasion ever to take place, the traditional claim which might be set up by the sons of a former generation of emigrants to portions of existing holdings might prove very embarrassing to their present occupants.

* *Evidence of John Hancock, Esq., Agent.*

"Although tenant right exists, as I will hereafter explain, it exists by custom and not by law; and many landlords and others deem it injurious, and are opposed to it. The tenants therefore, naturally look upon it as uncertain in amount. *They also fear the introduction of any law on the subject,*" &c. &c.

Dig. Dev. Com. p. 261.

No one will dispute the authority of the above witness on such a subject. Most Ulster landlords would be only too glad to refer all their disputes with their tenantry to a Court of Equity. The Ulster tenant is quite aware that an equitable arbitration would generally give him less than he now gets from his landlord's liberality.

In the south and west, matters are, I fear, very different; but even there great diversity of sentiment exists; the aspirations of the peasantry being apt to take a local colouring, varying with the influences which have been brought to bear upon them,—differing on different estates and in different counties, in some districts their utmost pretensions being most reasonable, while in others they are such as no legislation could satisfy; nor, unhappily, does it always follow that those tenants are the most contented who are treated with the greatest indulgence. But, though embodied in a hundred different modes of expression, the disquietude of the Irish occupier may be referred to three distinct conditions of thought:—First, a fear of any change in his position acting on a mind possessed with a blind, unreasoning hankering after a bit of land; the traditional failing of a people to whom for centuries land has been the only means of support. and which leaves them the moment they are surrounded by other associations. Secondly, a vague jealousy springing from his incapacity to understand the laws which regulate investments of capital in civilized countries, which makes the tenant grudge any expenditure on his farm that will be of ulterior benefit to his landlord, though it might in the meantime repay himself, capital and interest, twentyfold. And thirdly, the legitimate anxiety of a thoughtful man, whose prospects are kept in perpetual hazard by his landlord's unwillingness or inability to grant an appropriate lease. Of these three separate causes of discord between the landlords and their tenants, I believe the two first to be by far the most prolific of ill-feeling, and at the same time the most difficult to remove.

In a subsequent chapter I purpose to consider the various plans which have been proposed for the amelioration of this condition of affairs.

APPENDIX.

Number of Cultivators in Ireland.

Table showing the Male Population employed in the Cultivation of Land in Ireland. Census 1861.

	Ireland.	Leinster.	Munster.	Ulster.	Connaught.	County Cork.	County Kerry.	County Antrim.	County Down.
Farmers	413,309	70,235	89,096	171,530	82,448	28,472	14,805	19,536	21,506
Graziers	182	136	13	19	14	1		4	6
Herds and Drovers	26,607	7,703	8,647	5,339	4,918	3,006	1,167	404	500
Ploughmen	52,791	19,580	14,818	15,498	2,895	4,498	888	2,187	3,817
Labourers, agricultural	374,425	81,322	120,346	97,452	75,305	36,438	19,186	10,972	13,158
* ditto, unclassed agricultural	315,640	71,068	85,232	94,282	65,058	31,076	13,791	9,819	12,008
Total	1,182,954	250,044	318,152	384,120	230,638	103,491	49,837	42,922	50,995

* (See next page.)

* As the authority by which these persons are entered under the head of Agricultural Labourers, may be questioned, I subjoin a memorandum on the point by Mr. Donnelly the Registrar-General of Ireland, to whose admirable official Statistics, unrivalled probably in their accuracy, extent, and the universal confidence they command, I in common with every one else have been so much indebted.

"Almost the entire number of persons classified in the Census as 'labourers' may be considered as Agricultural Labourers.—Some of them were no doubt employed in towns and cities, at the date of the Census:—the number of whom may be approximately ascertained from the numbers in the Occupation Tables for the following towns given as labourers in the Census, under the head "unclassified," viz. :—

Drogheda	566
Dublin	12,686
Kilkenny	669
Cork	6,954
Limerick	2,145
Waterford	1,140
Belfast	5,250
Galway	983
	30,393

The number of labourers under the head of "Unclassified," in 1861, was	346,816
From which deduct as being employed in towns—*not on* agricultural labour, as per preceding statement	30,393

This will leave the foregoing number (346,816), who may be considered as having been employed as farming labourers, and servants . . 316,423

To which, if there be added those actually returned on the Census Papers, as farm labourers and servants . . 374,425

There will thus be a general total of agricultural labourers of . . . 690,848

CORRESPONDING TABLE FOR ENGLAND AND WALES,

Census 1861.

Farmers and Graziers	226,957
Sons, grandsons, nephews, and brothers of farmers living on the farm	92,721
Agricultural labourers	914,301
Farm servants—indoor	158,401
Herds and Shepherds	25,569
Drovers	3,125
Total .	1,421,064

There were also 300,000 labourers entered in the English Census as unclassified,—but this number would amount to a very small per centage on the total population of England and Wales, and I am informed by the Registrar General of England, that no appreciable proportion of them can be included in the cultivating population of Britain.

Table showing the Number of Male Cultivators employed in Belgium and Flanders. (*see p.* 162.)

	Belgium.	E. and W. Flanders.
Propriétaires cultivateurs, et fermiers, economes, et directeurs de rurales . .	300,473	111,824
Bergers, nourrisseurs, pâtres .	4,811	736
Journaliers et ouvriers agricoles, domestiques, etc.	388,342	127,131
	693,626	239,691

Length of Belgian Leases.

"Les baux ne se contractent généralement que pour un terme de trois années, et l'on trouve encore un très-grand nombre de propriétaires qui louent pour trois, six, et neuf ans."—*Report : Belgian Census,* 1856.

CHAPTER V.

Those various plans which have been proposed for the settlement of what is called 'the Irish land question' may be grouped under four distinct methods of procedure, which I shall consider in turn.

First in order comes the scheme, (advocated by Mr. Bright,) of enabling the peasantry of Ireland to buy up, with money advanced by Government, the estates of British noblemen happening to be owners of property in both countries, at a price 10 per cent. in excess of their value. Now, it would ill become an Irishman to allude to such a proposal in any terms but those of respect and gratitude; and I hail the proposition as a genuine proof of the author's goodwill towards us. Nor do I dissent from Mr. Bright in regretting that so much of the land in Ireland should be possessed by those whose permanent home is never likely to be in that country, although the selection of names by which his well meant suggestion was disfigured happened to be unfortunate. Had he contented himself with expressing a hope that it might be found convenient to some of the gentlemen circumstanced as he described, to allow their Irish property to descend in the line of their second sons,* I should have cordially agreed with him, especially as the fact of estates being now in the course of sale at the rate of £1,000,000 a year in the Landed Estates Court renders his offer of a premium unnecessary.†

With regard to the eventual result of Mr. Bright's scheme on the happiness of the people I do not feel so certain. In the first place, the practical difficulties in the way of its execution would be enormous:—unless land is let much lower than Mr. Bright would probably care to admit, there are not many tenants who could afford to pay, in addition to their usual obligations, 5 or 6 per cent. for a number of years on whatever sum the fee simple of their holdings might be worth; and, in the next —until the operation was completed, Government would find itself charged with the responsibilities of a land agency of a most onerous character, over property scattered in innumerable small subdivisions up and down the country. Occasions would arise when the increased rent would cease to be forthcoming, and, as trustees for the tax-payer, the State would have to proceed against the defaulting

* When the above was written, I did not know that Mr. O'Connell had made a similar suggestion.

" I would give him readily the choice of bestowing his Irish estate upon his second son."—*D. O'Connell, Esq., M.P., Dig. Dev. Com. p. 1093.*

† The amount of property which has passed through the Landed Estates Court has been between £25,000,000 and £30,000,000, representing an income of at least £2,000,000.

tenant with inflexible rigour,—to resume possession of his holding,—probably much deteriorated by necessitous husbandry,—and either to confiscate the paid-up portion of the purchase-money, which would be considered a gross injustice by the person evicted, or to return it to him, which would be an equally sensible loss to the Exchequer. But, supposing the creation of these small proprietorships happily effected, is it so certain that the general condition of the country would be improved? What guarantee have we against these several infinitesimal estates acquiring the character of the already existing perpetuities?* It is the fashion to argue that the relation of landlord and tenant, as it exists in England, cannot be comprehended by the genius of the Irish people. But it is the only relation the Irish peasant does (at least so long as he remains in Ireland) thoroughly appreciate. The labourer's dream is to become a tenant; the tenant's greatest ambition is to enjoy the dignity of a landlord.† What he cannot

---

* Mr. Mill, with his usual sagacity, has detected the difficulties which might arise out of the indiscriminate conversion of the present tenantry into peasant-proprietors.

"A large proportion also of the present holdings are probably still too small to try the proprietary system under the greatest advantages; nor are the tenants always the persons one would desire to select as the first occupants of peasant-properties."—*Mill's Polit. Econ. p.* 411.

† "There is a very great desire with nearly all of them to become landlords, and sublet the land."—*Judge Longfield's Evidence, Q.* 524.

be made to realize is, that an independent labourer is a more respectable personage than a struggling farmer, and a prosperous husbandman than a rack-renting squireen.* It is true, were Mr. Bright's

---

* A very acute observer, the agent of an estate in the North of Ireland, though himself a native of the South, thus signalizes the dangers which are already becoming apparent from the minute division of property now promoted by sales in the Encumbered Estates Court.

"I have several times mentioned to you the evils likely to arise from the sales in the Landed Estates Courts. Under the original Encumbered Estates Court, properties were brought to sale in large lots, suitable only for the purses of moneyed men, and accordingly they were purchased at such a price as enabled the buyer to let the lands at fair rents to the tenants. After a time the demand for land in small lots became so great, owing to many of the farming class returning with money from the gold diggings, &c. &c., that persons having the carriage of sales, at once decided on making the 'lots to suit purchasers,' and in almost every instance the landlord class of gentry were, and still are, beaten out of the market. The large prices given by the class I have mentioned, being such as to reduce the interest on the outlay in several instances which I could mention below two per cent. . . . . The buyer is not of the standing in life to care for the comforts of those under him; his income is small—much smaller owing to the high price he gave for the lot. . . . . The reason I mention middle men is that I see daily a class of men becoming landlords, in consequence of the sale of small lots in the Landed Estates Court, who are in every respect similar to those men."

Professor Cairnes has made the same observation.

"There is, however, a partial counter-current, of which I have not seen any public notice. A class of men, not very numerous, but sufficiently so to do much mischief, have, through the Landed Estates Court, got into possession of land in Ireland,

scheme to be put in operation, it would be perfectly justifiable for the state, while in promoting these purchases with public money, to impose stringent conditions against subletting ; but such precautions would be found practically inoperative, or only to be enforced by a code of primogeniture, entail, and limited ownership, such as would keenly shock the advocates of the change.* Supposing, however, the

who, of all classes, are least likely to recognise the duties of a landlord's position. These are small traders in towns, who by dint of sheer parsimony, frequently combined with money-lending at usurious rates, have succeeded, in the course of a long life, in scraping together as much money as will enable them to buy fifty or a hundred acres of land. These people never think of turning farmers, but, proud of their position as landlords, proceed to turn it to the utmost account."—*Mill's Polit. Econ.* p. 413.

The result of the evidence given before the Devon Commission on this important subject is thus summarized in the digest.

" It seems to be the general impression of the witnesses that the estates of large proprietors are better managed than those of small ; some, however, are of the contrary opinion."—*Dig. Dev. Com.* p. 1028.

I, myself, have no doubt upon the subject. The tenantry on the larger estates in Ireland are for the most part in a better position than those on the very small estates, not that the larger proprietors are better men than their humbler neighbours, but that they can afford to be more liberal and are less tempted by their own necessities to deal hardly with defaulters.

* It is very important that this tendency inherent in the Irish peasant to quarter his children and his grandchildren, his daughters and his sons-in-law upon his farm, either by a successive series of subdivisions or by pecuniary charges under his will, should not be lost sight of, and when surprise is expressed at the alleged unwillingness on the part of the landlords to

system worked no worse in Ireland than in France, the state of agriculture in France, with so many grant leases, it must be remembered that it has been found very difficult to check this disastrous practice when once a lease has been issued. This point is clearly set forth in the following extract from the Digest of the evidence given before the Devon Commission :—

"Though from the above-mentioned causes, the practice of subletting is now much less prevalent than it formerly was, it appears that the practice of subdividing farms as a provision for the children of tenants still continues to a very great extent, notwithstanding the most active exertions of proprietors and agents.

"The evil is one difficult, or almost impossible to prevent. The parent possessed of a farm looks upon it as a means of providing for his family after his decease, and, consequently, rarely induces them to adopt any other than agricultural pursuits, or makes any other provision for them than the miserable segment of a farm, which he can carve for each out of his holding, itself perhaps below the smallest size which can give profitable occupation to a family. Each son, as he is married, is installed in his portion of the ground, and in some cases, even the sons-in-law receive as the dowries of their brides some share of the farm. In vain does the landlord or agent threaten the tenant; in vain is the erection of new houses prohibited, or the supply of turf limited. The tenant relies on the sympathy of his class to prevent ejectment, and on his own ingenuity to defeat the other impediments to his favourite mode of providing for his family.

"The fear of this subdivision, and its ruinous consequences, appear, from the testimony of many, to be the principal causes preventing the grant of leases, as the power of the landlord to resist them, though always insufficient, is considered to be much diminished where the tenant holds by lease, no matter how stringent the covenants against subdivision may be, it being stated that the difficulty of enforcing the covenants in leases is in general very great.

"It appears that subdivision is occasionally caused by the

advantages of climate and with such variety of resource, is not a re-assuring precedent.* At this

tenant selling a part of his farm, in order to raise money for some temporary purpose.

" Some strange cases are detailed in the evidence of the extent to which lands have become subdivided by the operation of the above-mentioned practices. Amongst these, the statements of Lord Glengall, Mr. Kincaid, and Mr. Williamson, seem particularly worthy of attention. The last of these mentions 387 Irish acres, of which but 167 acres are arable, held by 110 tenants."—*Dig. Dev. Com.* p. 419.

" The provision made by farmers for their daughters is stated to be in many cases very much larger than their capital warrants. It appears too that on the death of a tenant, he frequently either bequeaths his farm to be divided among his children, or disposes of it to one son, but charged with sums of money payable to the other children, often utterly out of proportion to the value of the farm. It is asserted that this practice, by subdividing the farms into portions too small for the support of the occupiers, or by depriving the tenant of the

---

* I have no personal acquaintance with the state of agriculture in France, but making every allowance for the improvement which has undoubtedly taken place of late years in French farming, (*See App.*, p. 276) it is still a considerable way behind England and Belgium, and whatever progress is being made is rather in spite than in consequence of the extreme comminution of the soil. Even Mr. Mill admits the tendency to subdivision in France has been too great, though the cultivation of the vine is so peculiarly adapted to " la petite culture." Native authors visit it with more serious reprobation.

" I know that ten years' produce per acre in France, as a whole (though not in its most improved districts) averages much less than in England."—*Mill's Polit. Econ.* p. 189.

" The inferiority of French cultivation (which, taking the country as a whole, must be allowed to be real, though much exaggerated) is probably more owing to the lower general average of industrial skill and energy in that country, than to

moment I believe there are several hundred thousand small freeholders in that country too indigent capital necessary for agricultural operations has a very injurious effect."—*Dig. Dev. Com. p.* 365.

" The incumbrances for portioning off younger children at the death of parents frequently leave the successors to the farms without capital."—*Ibid. p.* 194.

Evidence of Rev. Jas. Porter, Presbyterian Minister.

"How do the farmers in general provide for their families in the event of their death ?—In all the districts, a little farmer, when he dies, let his rent be what it may, is in the habit of dividing his substance amongst his children. He divides his farm between the two eldest, and gives something to his daughters and younger sons according to his circumstances; but they are beginning to see that these small divisions are injurious to them; and as education is blessing the country, that feeling is spreading."—*Ibid. p.* 373.

Rob. M'Crea, Farmer.

" By what means are the children usually provided for at the death of their parents?—For the most part the farm is

any special cause; and even if partly the effect of minute subdivision, it does not prove that small farming is disadvantageous, but only (what is undoubtedly the fact) that farms in France are very frequently *too* small, and, what is worse, broken up into an almost incredible number of patches or *parcelles*, most inconveniently dispersed and parted from one another."—*Ibid.* p. 18.

" Undue subdivision, and excessive smallness of holdings, are undoubtedly a prevalent evil in some countries of peasant proprietors, and particularly in parts of Germany and France."

" The governments of Bavaria and Nassau have thought it necessary to impose a legal limit to subdivision, and the Prussian Government unsuccessfully proposed the same measure to the Estates of its Rhenish Provinces."

" Wherever the small properties are divided among too many proprietors, I believe it to be true that the large properties

to contribute their penny or halfpenny a year to the taxation of the country.* An excessive pro-

given to the eldest son, and he is charged with the support or provision for the rest."—*Dig. Dev. Com. p.* 381.

John Lynch, Esq., Solicitor.

" In the case of a man having a leasehold interest dying, how is that interest arranged; do disputes frequently arise among the surviving members of the family?—It is a source of continual dispute between them, unless he settles it by deed or will. If he dies intestate they are all mixed up together. One says, 'I wish to improve this;' another says for obstinacy, 'You shall not.' One will have a pig feeding here, and the consequence is, that all improvement is impossible."

" In your opinion, is the question of a succession to a leasehold interest a very fruitful source of litigation in this country?—No question at all about it.

" Is it the habit among the people in this country, holding small leasehold interests, to make charges upon them for the females of the family?—Yes. It is a most extraordinary thing. I have often said, 'One would suppose you had Lord Kenmare's estate to dispose of.' They have a miserable

---

also are parcelled out among too many farmers, and that the cause is the same in both cases, a backward state of capital, skill, and agricultural enterprise."—*Ibid.* p. 363.

At the time Mr. Mill made this observation, he calculated that the average size of these small farms in France might be taken at 8½ acres, and a large proportion at 15 acres; at the present moment about 20 per cent. of the farms of Ireland are below 5 acres, and more than 50 per cent. only average 10 acres.

It is right I should append to the above quotations the modi-

---

* On the 1st of January, 1851, there were 7,846,000 proprietors in France, and 126,000,000 separate holdings (parcelles). It is stated by M. About that of these 7,846,000 proprietors, 3,000,000 were so indigent that they were unable to pay the Land Tax, although in 600,000 cases its amount did not come to a half-penny a year.

portion of arable land lies fallow; the gross produce per acre is much less than it is in Belgium

patch of land, and they have four or five children, and they will say, 'To A so much is given; to B so much is given; to C so much; and to D so much is given.' And it is a common practice with them, after they have got husbands for their daughters, and have got rid of their children in that way, to dispose of it to another party in the same way, who is ignorant of the previous disposition. Then between these parties, the rightful owner, in the first place, and these other parties, there is an eternal scene of litigation taking place." - *Ibid. p.* 382.

Rob. O'Brien, Esq., Agent and Land Proprietor.

"This class (small farmers) also embarrass themselves very much in giving marriage portions to their daughters, consisting often of some money, some stock, and generally a promissory-note for a part of it. . . .

"By what means are children provided for at the death of their parents?—The case of children is one of the most difficult of solution, and a constant source of controversy between landlords and tenants, as amongst the small farmers

---

fying remarks which Mr. Mill has added in his last edition to the chapter from which they are taken.

"Impressed with the conviction that, of all faults which can be committed by a scientific writer on political and social subjects, exaggeration, and assertion beyond the evidence, most require to be guarded against, I limited myself in the early editions of this work to the foregoing very moderate statements. I little knew how much stronger my language might have been without exceeding the truth, and how much the actual progress of French agriculture surpassed anything which I had at that time sufficient grounds to affirm."—*Ibid.* p. 191.

As, however, the subdivision of holdings and *parcelles* in France has considerably increased between the dates of the two editions, I do not apprehend that Mr. Mill has changed the opinion he had previously expressed on this *latter* point.

"La révolution de 93, en morcelant les biens nationaux, a fait une chose agréable au peuple et même utile pour un certain

and England ;* a large number of their Liliputian estates are grievously encumbered ; † of some the

the custom of the country being for the parents to settle off their children as they grow up, so that the youngest generally is the one to inherit the house, or rather the eldest unsettled, or perhaps the widow. . . . The general custom, where they can venture to do so, is, either to divide the land share and share alike amongst their children. . . . reserving for the old widow the house (as the son is required to build a house for himself), and an acre or so of land ; this, at the time, is generally stated to return to the son, but in course of time, it is given at her death by the widow to one of the daughters ; and as the stipulation is that the acre should be rent free, there are constant complaints and quarrels on the subject, and it generally ends by the landlord being obliged to make a new agreement, and take with each as separate tenants, or else to eject the whole to get rid of the intruders."—*Dig. Dev. Com. p.* 382.

Daniel O'Connell, Esq., M.P.

" Take what precautions the landlord will, the lessee will and must contrive to have more occupiers on the land than the landlord would wish. If you prohibit him from having addi-

---

temps. Il est bon qu'il y a beaucoup de propriétaires. Mais personne n'avait prévu l'effet désastreux que ces deux causes associées devaient produire en un demi-siècle. Le paysan, ivre de propriété, a fait pour la terre toutes les folies qu'un amant fait pour sa maîtresse. Tout le monde a voulu acheter, presque personne n'a voulu vendre. Si un hectare tombait aux mains de dix héritiers, chacun d'eux prétendait garder et cultiver ses

---

* " La répartition des cultures dans les provinces belges tient le milieu entre celle que pratique l'Angleterre et celle qui est suivie en France : elle vaut mieux que l'assolement français, on les cultures améliorantes, y compris une énorme proportion de jachères qui ne produisent rien, occupent seulement le tiers du sol."—*Eco. Rur.* 224.

† An admirable paper on the effects of the subdivision of land in France has been written by Mr. J. G. T. Sinclair, to which, I trust, he will give a wider circulation.

original purchase money has not been paid;* while Mr. Michelet has declared the position of the

tional houses, and have a clause to take down those additional houses, they will live in one house; the daughter will marry, and the son-in-law will be brought in, and the son will marry and bring in his wife."—*Dig. Dev. Com. p.* 254.

Rich. Byrne, Esq., Vice Chairman of the Board of Guardians.

" Is the charge left upon the farm for the unprovided daughters and sons, by the father, generally very disproportionate to the value of the farm?—Yes, where he makes a will, it is; but where he fortunes them out during his life, he generally gives much larger fortunes than he ought, considering the value of his land, to give. I have known an instance of a man holding four acres of ground, getting three daughters married, to each of whom he gave £20 fortune; and another man holding fourteen acres got three of his daughters married, to each of whom he gave £25 fortune: and those were both tenants holding at will." *Ibid. p.* 386.

Mr. Thomas Bradford, Farmer.

" How do the tenantry generally provide for their children

---

dix acres. Celui qui avait entre les mains un petit capital disponible, ne s'en servait pas pour améliorer sa terre, mais pour en acquérir une nouvelle. La concurrence des acheteurs a produit une telle hausse que le revenu net est tombé en plus d'un endroit au-dessous de 2 pour 100. Et plus d'un malheureux, aveuglé par la passion, empruntait à des taux usuraires de quoi payer le prix de son champ! C'était la ruine organisée; la ruine des hommes et de sol." * * *

" Changeons le point de vue. Suivez-moi en Alsace, dans une

---

* " Many of the so-called peasant proprietors of France have not completed the purchase of their property, and are more properly tenants at a fixed rent."

Thornton's Peasant Proprietors, p. 157.

The total amount of the encumbrances on land in France is not excessive; but the burden does not seem to be evenly distributed: all the evidence points to a congestion of debt on the very small properties.

small French proprietor to be so intolerable, that left at their death?—The farmer generally leaves the farm to the boys, and leaves sums of money to the girls, if he has money; and sometimes he leaves money to be paid by the sons, which the sons are never able to pay."

R. F. Saunders, Esq., Land Proprietor and Magistrate.

" Children are most frequently provided for at the death of their parents by the father ' making his fortune on his deathbed.' That is the common expression. He leaves the farm to his eldest son, and charges it with more than it is worth (without leaving any assets to pay those charges), as provision for the remainder of his family. Litigation ensues, and the farm is lost in the end. I have known many farmers who have charged a property lease with a great deal more than the farm is worth, and which never has made any thing during his lifetime. Sometimes he subdivides his farm, and during his lifetime passes bills to the husband of his daughter, and distresses himself to pay them."—*Dig. Dev. Com. p.* 588.

Thos. Davidson, Agent.

" In what manner are people generally provided for at

---

commune de deux cents feux, peuplée d'environ mille individus des deux sexes, grands et petits, tours cultivateurs. Ils possèdent, entre eux tous, cinque cents hectares en bonne terre, c'est-à-dire un demi-hectare par tête. L'hectare vaut là de quatre à cinque mille francs. Donc ces gens sont riches en comparaison de bien d'autres. En fait, rien de plus mal vêtu, mal logé, mal nourri; rien de plus misérable et de plus ignorant qu'eux. Ne les accuser pas de paresse ou d'ivrognerie, vous auriez tort; ils travaillent toute l'année et ne boivent guère que de l'eau. Mais leurs propriétés sont si bien divisées qu'ils ne sauraient avoir ni pré ni herbage, et partant ni chevaux ni bœufs."—*Le Progrès, par E. About.*

Of the present condition of the agricultural population we have an account by M. Thiers, in his speech in the French Chamber, on Saturday, the 10th of March, 1866:—"Si ceux qui m'interrompent avaient lu la multitude des ecrits que j'ai sous la main, écrits non pas signés pas des ecrivains s'occupant

the only hope of salvation for the agricultural
the death of their parents?—We prohibit them dividing the land as much as we can; but they leave them sums to be paid and some articles of furniture or cattle. Supposing a man to have four or five sons or daughters; one son is selected for the tenant, to whom he gives the farm, and very often charges him with a provision to some extent, for the younger branches of the family; and I have found sums charged upon them often more than I thought the land would bear."—*Ibid. p.* 369.

Philip Reade, Esq., Land Proprietor.

" In what way are the children of the small tenantry provided for at the death of their parents?—Their wish is to give their farms amongst their families, and when that is prevented, the son who gets the farm endeavours to pay certain portions to other members of his family, particularly to his sisters, varying in my neighbourhood from ten to a hundred pounds.

" What proportion should you say these fortunes in

---

de ces sujets au point de vue theorique, mais signés par des agriculteurs respectables, habitants de toutes les parties de la France très connus dans leur pays, ayant des situations qui les mettent au-dessus du soupçon, et qui, en outre, ont vos opinions bien plus que les miennes, entendez vous! si vous aviez la ces ecrits, vous verriez à quel point de souffrance l'agriculture est parvenue."

The motion on which this speech was made contained the following propositions:—

" L'agriculture eprouve dans ce moment des souffrances cruelles.

" Nous avions voulu donner un temoignage de sympathie aux populations agricoles si laborieuses, si modestes, et si dévoués au Gouvernement et a l'Empereur; nous avions voulu surtout que leur plaintes arrivassent jusqu'au pied du trone."

I also subjoin what M. de Laveleye has said incidentally on the subject of French agriculture:—

" En France, avec un territoire seize fois plus grand, le produit n'est que dix fois plus considérable."—*Eco. Ru.* p. 229.

" Le revenu net du domaine agricole belge était en 1846 de

interest of France lies in the repudiation of all mortgages.*

general bore to the rent of the farm?—It is incredibly large. I know an instance of a farm of thirteen acres Irish, or twenty-two acres English, paying a rent of 30s. the Irish or 18s. the statute acre, where the farmer has given to each of his family on being married, £100."

" Does not the larger provision, made by farmers at their death, for unprovided children, leave a large amount of debt upon the farm?—Yes, and it is a very great cause of litigation at the quarter sessions. It is also the cause of the bad farming of the land, and the complaints generally made throughout the kingdom; for these parties generally endeavour to get a reduction from their landlord to pay their father's debts. Those must be paid, and it is only from the landlord they can expect any indulgence; they can expect none from the other parties."—*Dig. Dev. Com. p.* 369.

That the desire to subdivide the land is still pretty rife may be seen from the following observations made upon the

---

155 millions, ce qui fait par hectare productif une moyenne de 75 francs, et de 59 francs si on prend la surface totale du pays. Pour la même époque, M. de Lavergne d'estimait la rente moyenne par hectare qu'à 30 francs pour la France, à 40 hectares pour le Royaume Uni, et à 60 francs pour l'Angleterre considérée isolement. En comparant ces chiffres, il ne faut pas oublier qu'en Belgique, on se contente, pour les immeubles, des intérêts moindre qu'en Angleterre c'est à dire que la terre s'y vend plus cher relativement au revenu qu'elle donne."—*Eco. Ru.* pp. 230-231.

" La statisque officielle de 1846 portait la production moyenne annuelle de grains de tout espèce, soit 7 hectolitres par chaque hectare de la superficie total du pays ici, à son tour, la Belgique l'emporte notablement sur l'Angleterre et plus encore sur la France, car un calcul semblable ne donne pour la première que 5 et pour la seconde que 3 hectolitres à l'hectare."—*Ibid. p.* 225.

---

* An able writer on this subject thus reviews the present

If, then, competition, generated by a very minute subdivision of landed property, has produced these

subject at a Farmers' Club, in Cork. A body of gentlemen who it appears are engaged in framing a bill to regulate the tenure of land.

"*Mr. Keller* said that no arguments could convince him of the justice of preventing a father giving a portion of his farm, if he had one, to his son. *It would be preposterous and unjust to prevent him.* He held suppose, 300 acres, and saw his boys growing up around him, and helping to cultivate the land, yet he was not to have the power to settle any of them on a part of it, even though it was of sufficient extent to admit of ten divisions.

Mr. Dill said, subletting did not include devising of interest, or the handing over of a portion from one to another. The object of the clause was to prevent a man taking a farm at say its real value from his landlord and turn the holder, constituting himself a middleman or second landlord, and subletting it to some unfortunate person at a higher rate, pocketing the difference.

Mr. Carroll said, suppose a farm of 500 acres had on it build-

---

state of agriculture in France as exemplified by the most recent statistics.

"Some curious statistics have come out in connection with the inquiry into the state of French agriculture, although the report of the commissioners has not yet been drawn up. There is a dearth of capital, of labour, and intelligence, and the division of property is asserted to be a great impediment to improvement. The agriculturists say that the population does not increase because agriculture makes no progress, and that France could not feed more people than at present. Since 1821 the French importation of corn has exceeded the exportation by more than thirty-five million hectolitres (twenty-two gallons each), and within the last twenty years the price of cattle has doubled, though the importation exceeds the exportation. These two facts show how little progress has been made, as France well cultivated would not be forced to import corn, nor

results in France, where the rural population scarcely increases, and where there exists a large manufacturing industry to absorb the surplus labour of the agricultural districts, its effect in Ireland might be yet more disastrous. Therefore, though heartily sympathizing with Mr. Bright in his desire to see a yeoman class established in Ireland, and admitting that to many individual cases the objections I have indicated would not apply, I am afraid the comprehensive scheme by which he proposes to

ings suitable to such a large holding, which if divided into five small holdings of 100 acres each, buildings should be erected on each of those sub-portions, and the large buildings originally necessary would become dilapidated and waste. If the sons and daughters of the farmer in such a case would all hold together they could farm the land in one piece. (Oh, and great laughter.)

Mr. Keller. Aye, and live together in the same garrison.

Mr. Forrest. I will ask you one question. If you, Mr. Carroll, as a merchant owned the largest establishment in this city, and that you were an old man and had two sons, would you not think it a great hardship if you were prevented giving one or both of them a share in the concern?

Mr. Carroll. I would do as I liked to be sure. (Laughter.)

Mr. Forrest. And why prevent another man doing as he likes?" *Cork Advertiser, Jan.* 1867.

---

would the price of cattle be double what it was twenty years ago if their number had increased as it should have done. The division of land is a great drawback to all draining, irrigation, and innovation, as the small holder can lay out but little money and can afford to risk none. Two-thirds of France is in small farms, and it is estimated that the proprietors work their farms with a capital of under £4 per acre, whereas more than double that sum is necessary."

attain that object, is not sufficiently promising to justify us in running the risk it would entail; nevertheless, if he can persuade the British taxpayer to agree, I should certainly offer no opposition to the experiment.*

We now come to a series of proposals of a very different complexion, proposals which involve the transfer of a large amount of proprietary rights from the landlord to the tenant. Now I do not deny the right of the state to deal in a very peremptory manner with private property of all kinds, and especially with landed property; but, in assuming this right, it must be made clear that its exercise will be of indisputable benefit to the community at large, and the individual to whose prejudice it is enforced must be compensated at the public expense

---

* The opinion of M. de Lavergne, himself an advocate of "la petite culture," and thoroughly master of this subject, may be worth considering. If it is objected that M. de Lavergne is a foreigner, I would venture to reply that he is probably better acquainted with the agricultural condition of Ireland than most Englishmen.

"Pour la petite propriété proprement dite, dont beaucoup d'excellents esprits, entre autres M. Stuart Mill dans ses nouveaux Principes d'économie politique, avaient réclamé l'introduction, elle me parait beaucoup moins désirable en présence de pareils faits. Probablement l'Irlande arrivera quelque jour à la petite propriété, c'est sa tendance naturelle; mais, pour la moment, sa population rurale est trop pauvre: elle a besoin de gagner dans la culture de quoi devenir propriétaire: il n'est pas de son intérêt d'y penser auparavant."

Essai sur l'Économie Rurale d'Angleterre, &c. p. 420, par M. L. de Lavergne. Paris, 1863.

to the full amount of the injury he sustains.* The safety of a nation may depend upon the security of an arsenal, and that of the arsenal on the conversion of a hovel into a redoubt; yet the engineer in command dare no more remove a brick from the obnoxious premises without the sanction of an Act of Parliament, and an elaborate valuation, than he dare blow up St. Paul's.

But considerations such as these, the authors of the various schemes "for dealing vigorously with the Irish landlords" deem beneath their notice.

* Even Mr. Mill, though inspired with no very indulgent feelings towards the landlords of Ireland, admits this principle.

" The claim of the landowners to the land is altogether subordinate to the general policy of the state. The principle of property gives them no right to the land, but only a right to compensation for whatever portion of their interest in the land it may be the policy of the state to deprive them of. *To that, their claim is indefeasible.* It is due to landowners, and to owners of any property whatever, recognised as such by the state, that they should not be dispossessed of it without receiving its pecuniary value, or an annual income equal to what they derived from it. This is due on the general principles on which property rests. If the land was bought with the produce of the labour and abstinence of themselves or their ancestors, compensation is due to them on that ground; even if otherwise, it is still due on the ground of prescription. *When the property is of a kind to which peculiar affections attach themselves, the compensation ought to exceed a bare pecuniary equivalent.* The legislature, which if it pleased might convert the whole body of landlords into fundholders or pensioners, might, *à fortiori,* commute the average receipts of Irish landlords into a fixed rent charge, and raise the tenants into proprietors; supposing always that the full market value of the land was tendered to the landlords, in case they preferred that to accepting the conditions proposed."—*Mill, Polit. Econ.* p. 289.

The most notable plan is one lately promulgated by Mr. Butt, a gentleman of eminence in his profession. As his plan is typical of a large series of others, it may be well to examine it. It is embodied in the form of a projected Act of Parliament, which declares that after the said Act every tenant who chooses to claim its protection shall be entitled to a lease of 63 years at a rent one-third below the full or competition value. Thus, by a single stroke of the pen, the whole of the landed property of Ireland is to be withdrawn from the control and enjoyment of those who have either purchased or inherited it, and is to remain for two entire generations at the disposal of the 540,000 persons who may happen at the time of the passing of the Act to be in the occupation of its several sub-divisions. This, too, without reference to their individual qualifications, and in the teeth of the condemnation passed by the tenants' best friends on even a 21 years' lease, if granted for a holding of less than 15 acres, within which category more than one-third of the farms of Ireland still remain.

Let us now look more narrowly into the operation of this plan, and, as every Irishman will probably judge of it as it affects himself, let me be excused for taking the same narrow view. I possess a strip of some three or four hundred acres, bordering the Lough of Belfast, peculiarly suitable for villas. I have been offered from 15*l.* to 20*l.* an acre for a portion of this land (most of which I have inherited from an ancestor who made his fortune as a merchant, and part of which I have recently purchased with the proceeds of the sale of some English property). A railway along the shore still further increases its attractions, and at a particular point there is a sandy bay which—as the site of a bathing village—may eventually become a favourite resort for the inhabitants of Belfast. For various reasons I have hitherto deferred leasing any of the land, and it is at present in the occupation of agricultural tenants, all of whom have been for many years in the enjoyment of beneficial leases, which have either expired or will shortly do so. We will suppose that Mr. Butt's Bill passes; the accidental occupants of this property become tenants for another additional term of 63 years; I am unexpectedly precluded from applying my land to its most remunerative use; and a project which would have diffused the wealth of a rich community over a large agricultural area is indefinitely postponed—unless, indeed, I choose to buy back my own property, at a price, probably, not much lower than the original value of the fee simple, from tenants who have neither legal nor equitable claims against me.* Moreover it is to be remembered that the circumstances I have detailed are not exceptional, but prevail more or less in the vicinity of every large town; that there is no district which may not, at one time or another, be affected by analogous influences, and that it is its very susceptibility of a rise in price that

* This instance is rendered the more striking by the fact that I am paying £9 an acre per annum, *i.e.*, its market price, as building ground, for part of the land for which my agricultural tenants are only paying me 30s. By Mr. Butt's Bill, both arrangements would be made equally permanent.

contributes an important element to the value of landed property, and reconciles the purchaser to the low rate of interest proximately derived from it.*

But let us regard Mr. Butt's proposal from another point of view. Probably, if asked for a justification of his measures, he would allege the right of the tenant to the enjoyment of his "improvements," and on that head perhaps my ideas are as liberal as his own. But how about the improvements which have *not* been made by the tenant, or which have been bought up by the landlord, or which though effected by the tenant have been executed under express contracts, and in consideration of reduced rents or long leases?† By what canon of justice does he expropriate these? Surely, if a tenant have an equitable claim for compensation, or to extension of occupancy in lieu of compensation, for money he imprudently risked on the prospective chance of his landlord's liberality, the landlord himself has a right to be continued in possession of that to which his equitable claim is as good, and his legal right so much better?

But it will be said, "the improvements on farms in Ireland are invariably made by the tenants." In a great number of instances this is the case. But

---

* "In such a measure, there would not have been any injustice, provided the landlords were compensated for the present value of the chances of increase which they were prospectively required to forego."—*Mill, Polit. Econ.* p. 410.

† A large proportion of the farm steadings on my own estate have been erected in accordance with the provisions of the beneficial leases, under which the farms were held.

the reverse is far more frequent than I was aware. Judge Longfield has stated that almost all the larger drainage works, and a considerable proportion even of the minor improvements, have been executed by the proprietors. We know from official returns that within 18 years more than 1,800,000*l.* of borrowed money has been sunk by them in draining and building alone. This sum is no test however of what they have expended besides out of their incomes. The Devon Commission reported that on 22 estates (many of them the largest in the country), the buildings had been erected at the sole expense of the landlord. But this statement does not imply that there were not other properties on which the same rule prevailed. Only a certain number of estates were brought under their notice. My own property for instance was not visited, neither were those of many of my neighbours. Yet in my neighbourhood great exertions have been made by the landlords, and I am informed that on numerous estates in various parts of the country sums varying from 30,000*l.* to 40,000*l.* have been expended on farmsteadings and cottages during the last 50 years.*

* Even within the knowledge of the limited number of witnesses examined by the Devon Commission five and twenty years ago, the following scale of allowances for draining and other operations, were made by the landlords. It is to be observed, that the acreage over which these arrangements extended must have been considerable.

			No. of instances.
"Allowances made by landlords to tenants,	$\frac{2}{3}$ of expense,	2
,,	,,	$\frac{1}{2}$ of expense,	21
,,	,,	$\frac{2}{3}$ of expense,	1

I myself have spent 10,000*l.* in buying up the improvements of my tenants, besides what I have sunk

			No. of instances.
Allowances made by landlords to tenants,		⅓ of expense,	2
,,	,,	¼ of expense,	1
,,	,,	£8 an acre,	1
,,	,,	£2 an acre,	4
,,	,,	£1 an acre,	1
,,	,,	2½*d.* a perch, and under,	7
,,	,,	3*d.* or 4*d.* a perch,	7
,,	,,	7*d.* a perch, and upwards,	1
,,	,,	year's rent,	1
,,	,,	2 years' rent	1
,,	,,	not precisely specified	84
Effected at landlord's expense, or tenant allowed whole cost of		. . . .	19
Money advanced to tenants at interest, or a per centage charged on landlord's outlay		. .	7

Dig. Dev. Com. p. 86.

I subjoin some individual instances:—

H. Leslie Prentiec, Esq.

"What is the arrangement entered into upon that subject? —The arrangement made by Lord Caledon is an allowance of £2 per Irish acre for all lands drained on his estate, according to the directions of the person appointed for that purpose.

"Does he charge any interest or per centage upon the sums so paid?—No, nothing whatever; he gives it as his own contribution towards a permanent improvement on his property, to all tenants holding determinable leases or at will."

Ibid. p. 98.

John Barré Beresford.

"Upon what principle does he make the allowance for draining?—He advances the money at five per cent., and all they pay him is that five per cent. But most of the work is done by themselves, so that the money is advanced to them."—*Ib.* p. 103.

in executing new ones. Many of my neighbours are doing the same, and every year our efforts in this

Fitzherbert Filgate.

" With respect to the draining, *each tenant gets* 2½*d a perch*, for each perch of the parallel drains on the Deanston system and 1*d* a perch for the main drains."—*Ib. p.* 104.

Edw. Golding.

" I offered 2½*d* for the running perch for parallel drains, 4*d* for the main drains."—*Ib. p.* 105.

D. J. O'Neil, Farmer and Physician.

" The tenant who cannot afford to drain is supplied with £50. or £100. and is required to pay at the rate of £5. per annum till it is paid, and no interest is charged."—*Ib. p.* 111.

Wm. Monsell, Land Proprietor.

" It varies from 3*d* to 5*d*, according to the nature of the subsoil."—*Ib. p.* 112.

Wm. Monsell, Land Proprietor.

"The landlords allow for cutting the drains."—*Ib. p.* 112.

Mr. James Kelly, Agriculturist to Longford Farming Society.

" Describe to us what you do upon Lord Longford's or Mr. Harman King's property?—On Lord Longford's property I get the tenants to drain the wet lands; (Lord Longford pays half the expense.) I have made drains in spring last, on two or three townlands."—*Ib. p.* 115.

Mr. Geo. Cecil Wray, Farmer.

" Mountain farms are also on many properties given to the younger sons free from rent for the first five or six years."

Ib. p. 371.

James Carnegie, Esq. Land Agent.

" In 1835, a large tract of land, containing about 3000 acres of inland and mountain, which was held by a middleman, and by him under-let to a number of miserable tenants, came into the hands of the head landlord by the expiration of the lease. I went over it all, accompanied by an excellent judge of land; we divided it into regular farms, ten of which I set to men of skill and capital, and I removed the under-tenants to the mountains,

direction are likely to extend, unless, indeed, Mr. Butt's ingenious device for proving the superior discretion of keeping our money in our pockets should suddenly put a stop to the process.

Having glanced at the probable wrong to the landlord, let us estimate the degree to which the tenant would be benefited. Leases are undoubtedly favourable to agriculture, and an advantage to the tenant. But as to the terms of tenure, there is a great diversity of opinion. Judge Longfield condemns long leases, and I quite agree with him; nor was the state of Ireland 40 years ago a very satisfactory proof of their efficiency. In Belgium three, five, and nine years are the accepted terms;* in

---

and gave them from twenty to fifty acres each, *rent free*, for seven years. The ground set, independently of those small holdings, pays considerably more rent than was paid to the middleman, and I believe there is not in this county an estate so improved within the same period of time."—*Ib. p.* 463.

"Advances had been made to as many as 2000 owners; the number of loans had been made, 4210; the largest loan made was £7000, and the smallest £100; there had been 2092 loans under £500.; and the total amount advanced since 1847 had been £1,866,000, the whole of which had been expended in the permanent improvement of land."

Lord Naas' Speech. Times, Feb. 19, 1867.

"The practice, however, of proprietors giving to their tenants some assistance in the erection of the farm house and buildings, has of late years been introduced on many estates, and appears to be extending. There are twenty-one proprietors of whom it is recorded on the evidence, that the whole cost for farm buildings is supplied by them for their tenants."

Dig. Dev. Com. Summary, p. 127.

* " Les baux ne se contractent généralement que pour un

Scotland, 13 and 19; in England, 21.* By what statistical canon does Mr. Butt arbitrarily extend

terme de trois années, et l'on trouve encore un très grand nombre de propriétaires qui, assimilant leurs terres à une maison, louent pour trois, six et neuf ans. On comprend qu'avec de pareilles conditions, il est difficile aux fermitos de faire des améliorations, dont ils ne sont pas certains de profiter."
Statistique de la Belgique, Recensement Général, p. xlix.

* *John Hancock, E. Agent, Armagh.*

"The tenure, in my opinion, best suited to this district, is that of twenty-one years, certain. It is sufficiently long to afford a man fair remuneration for capital laid out on his farm, and yet not so long but that every man expects to outlive it."
Ibid. p. 261.

"Leases for short periods are better than none. All leases should endure such a number of years as would be a multiple of the years of the rotation which best suits the soil,—the four-shift should then be 12 years, the five 15, the six 18, and so on."
Macdonald's Estate Management, p. 199.

"A tenure of from 16 to 20 or 25 years, is the best for reciprocating the interests of landlord and tenant. The latter can pay a higher rent, and can use his own money on improvement with the firm hope of reaping benefit. He reclaims, encloses, drains, manures, limes, and does all that is pleasing and remunerative."—*Ibid.* p. 202.

"The Scotch nineteen years' lease appears to insure a good improving tenantry, and a large increase of rental at the end of the term."—*Ibid.* p. 210.

"We readily admit that, whilst advocating leases of fifteen or twenty years' duration, we disapprove of the long leases granted in the last century for sixty-one years or three lives, to which must be ascribed, in a great measure, the backwardness of agriculture in a country (Scotland) possessing so many natural advantages. Such preposterously long leases encourage idleness and neglect of the most common and necessary improvements. Leases of too long duration are worse than none, both for the landlord and tenant."—*Ibid.* p. 216.

them to 63? We have already seen the fervent advocates of the leasing system deprecate the extension of leases to such small areas as 15 acres; others of even greater experience, and no less friendly to the tenant, have raised the *minimum* to 30, 40, 50 acres.* Even Mr. Bright takes a man paying 50*l.* of rent as his typical yeoman. In the face of these opinions why should any one seek to stereotype a condition of affairs confessedly detrimental to the interests of agriculture? One of the greatest benefits to Ireland has resulted from the legal machinery invented to transfer the estates of incumbered proprietors to the hands of persons with sufficient capital to improve them. Surely the same policy ought to be pursued in facilitating the transference of farms from the impoverished agriculturist to the man of energy and capital? Yet Mr. Butt, like the malevolent fairy in the tale of the "Sleeping Beauty," would curse us with the doom of rigid immobility for the greater portion of a century, without the prospect of that magic "after-glow" of renewed life and vigour which completes the story.

Again, though this is his intention, the means he adopts would lead to another result. With a fatal ingenuity, he contrives to make it the imperative interest of the landlords to get rid of their tenants, and at the same time furnishes them with ample facilities for the process. He plucks the lion's beard with one hand, and whets his fangs and talons with the other. If the landlord is precluded by law from letting his land except on disadvantageous terms, he will naturally prefer to keep it in his own hands. Bad husbandry and non-payment of rent constitute, even according to Mr. Butt, just occasions of eviction.* By the inflexible application of these principles there is no property in Ireland which would not be cleared of a large proportion of its occupants in ten years, and the immediate effect of his beneficent efforts would be universal discontent and an enormous stimulus to emigration, counterbalanced perhaps by a rapid improvement in cultivation and a brevet promotion for some hundreds of thousands of agricultural labourers at the expense of a corresponding number of tenant farmers.

With regard to the minor principle involved in Mr. Butt's plan of fixing the rent of land by a Government officer, I need not trouble my readers. A moment's reflection will show how impossible it would be for any one but those immediately inter-

---

* "The interest in the soil thus conferred upon him he should retain only so long as he proves himself a punctual and improving tenant. Non-payment of the rent should be followed by forfeiture of his interest. I propose to make the ejectment for non-payment of rent an absolute one. At present the eviction is subject to redemption by the tenant at any time within six months. This privilege I propose to abolish, and to make the eviction absolute at once.

"I propose to bind the tenant to proper cultivation of the farm, and to the maintenance of all improvements; and, in the event of his failing in either of these conditions he incurs, in like manner, the forfeiture of the interest which the statute confers upon him."—*Fixity of Tenure, by C. Isaac Butt, p.* 5.

ested to arrive at a correct estimate of what particular areas could afford to pay. At this moment there are three standards of land valuation in Ireland,—there is the competition, or tenant's rent, which is generally in excess of what his limited skill and capital would enable him to produce; there is the agent's rent, which is regulated by what his experience tells him the tenant is able to pay without embarrassment; and there is the theoretical rent, which the land ought to pay if properly cultivated.* This latter rent would

* Supposing that land which, if properly cultivated, would bear a rent of 40s per acre, and for which the tenants themselves would offer 30s at an auction, (which, for the sake of argument, we will admit their want of skill and capital would render them incompetent to pay,)—were valued by the Government officers at 20s, what would be the effect? Why that at the first devolution of the tenancy, the outgoing tenant or his representative would exact from the in-comer a fine exactly equivalent to so many years purchase of the difference between the restricted rent of 20s an acre, and the competition rent of 30s: the effect of the transaction being that the new tenant would be charged with a double rent for all time to come, and that the landlord would have been defrauded of what so far as it represents any value at all, is a portion of the fee simple of his estate. It is useless to object that the vigilance of the landlord could prevent so nefarious a transaction. The landlord in the first place is almost powerless to restrain these surreptitious arrangements, as any one who knows the north of Ireland is aware, and in the next place, he would have no particular interest in doing so. The sagacious legislation we are considering will have reduced the landlord to the position of a mere mortgagee on what was once his property. Nothing that he can do, will either enhance or diminish its value. All personal relations between his tenantry and himself would be at an end, and his functions as a proprietor would be confined to

probably far exceed even the competition rent, yet no other one could be equitably adopted in any compulsory valuation.* Judge Longfield has effectually issuing instructions to his solicitor to evict the moment his rent was a shilling in arrear. Whether the result would diminish or encourage landlords to live on their estates, I leave to the consideration of those who may be inclined to pursue the investigation further.

* Of the difficulties in the way of such subtle valuations, the subjoined extracts will give an idea.

" It seems hard to discover any sound general principle adopted by the ordinary valuators for rent; some merely 'jump at their conclusions,' others seem to imagine that a certain uniform proportion of the gross produce ought to be set apart as rent, and this proportion has been variously estimated by different witnesses as one-fifth, one fourth, one-third, and two-fifths."—*Dig. Dev. Com. p.* 705.

" The general tendency of the evidence given by professional valuators, as shown by the above analysis, goes to prove that a lamentable deficiency exists in this very important profession, and that there is no sound, uniform principle adopted by the members of that profession to regulate the practice pursued by them.

" The most general opinion amongst them appears to be, that some uniform proportion of the gross produce may be set apart for rent, when a full consideration of the subject must prove that no uniform proportion can possibly be fixed, but that every variety in the quality of the land, and in the circumstances attending its position, cultivation, and taxation, must necessarily modify the share or proportion of the gross produce which the cultivator can afford to pay to the proprietor for its use.

" Rich and well-circumstanced meadow and first qualities of pasture, for example, might be well worth a rent equal to two-thirds or more of the gross produce, while very inferior ill-circumstanced tracts are to be found that would not pay for the labour requisite to till them, and therefore could not

illustrated the impracticability and injustice of any such system, based, as it is, upon a principle in direct produce any rent; and between these two extremes it is clear that every intermediate degree is to be found."—*Ibid. p.* 708.

"It is somewhat discouraging to find by the evidence of the Ex-Professor of Political Economy, now Professor of Common Law in the Dublin University, that he is hopeless as to the power of reducing the right theory on this subject to successful practice."

"He appears to adopt Loudon's desponding opinion, that it is impossible in practice, to apply the true theory of estimating, from the value of the produce and cost of production, what may be the value of the land."

He does "not think that any man who ever lived, having all the data given to him, could, with any certainty, determine it. He would still be unable to form a judgment of the aggregate value of the produce of the land."—*Ibid. p.* 709 *et seq.*

"Several witnesses have suggested as a remedy, that some control should be exercised over the proprietor in determining the amount of rent payable to him for his land. It is, however, more than questionable whether even this interference with property would accomplish any of the good which those witnesses anticipate. What they complain of is only one out of many indications of other extensive evils; the chief of these are, first, the omission to make the numerous resources which the country offers available for the employment of the industrious classes. This causes an extravagant competition for the inadequate supply of land offered for their use as the only chance of obtaining a livelihood for their families. The second, their deplorable ignorance and incapacity in the management of the land of which they thus become possessed.—*Ibid. p.* 756.

Appendix to Address by Judge Longfield to Stat. Society.

"The following cases are fair specimens of the discrepancies which are to be found in different valuations made of the same property."

"Since I wrote the above, the estate of John Campbell Jones was offered for sale, and the following are the differences be-

antagonism to the conditions which usually regulate the relations betwixt man and man, and therefore I need not dwell upon it longer.*

tween the valuations made by a Civil Engineer, and by the Ordnance valuation of the same lots :—

KILLIEWINGAN.

Engineer	£120	0 0
Tenement valuation	57	0 0

No. 5.

Valuator	£8	10 0
Tenement valuation	2	5 0

RATHCLINE.

Valuator	£29	17 7
Tenement valuation	8	0 0

FOX AND CALF ISLAND.

Valuator	£10	0 0
Tenement valuation	3	0 0

LOT 9.

Valuator	£10	0 0
Tenement valuation	1	6 0

LOT 10.

Valuator	£8	4 3
Tenement valuation	1	4 0

In the estate of Rutledge the following are two of the valuations :—

CREGGANROE.

Valuator	£53	1 7
Tenement valuation	17	10 0

BALLYKIT.

Valuator	£226	13 7
Tenement valuation	131	12 0

Although the valuations which I have stated differ so much, I believe that they were all honestly made by careful and skilful professional valuators. I have given those examples, not as

---

* " And, first, as to fixity of tenure,—that is to say, a law that every occupying tenant, no matter what his contract may be,

Before, however, dismissing from our attention these barren schemes for fixity of tenure, compulsory being the most remarkable that could be found, but because they were the most striking cases that came before me within a few days after I made the above remarks. I believe that in those cases both the valuations which I have contrasted were intended to be fair, and were made by skilful valuators.

"It may be asked, is there no mode of valuing a farm? must the tenant make a mere guess at what he is to offer? No; the landlord and the intending tenant have means of knowing the value of the land which no other person is likely to possess and to employ. They both may know the past history of the farm, and of all the farms in the neighbourhood; what rent was paid for them, in what manner they were cultivated, and whether the tenants appeared to thrive on them, or the contrary. No man has such an interest in discovering the exact value as the person who proposes to become a tenant, and as his object is to make a profit by his occupation as farmer, it is not to be supposed that he will give more for the land than he can pay, reserving a reasonable profit to himself."

Report of Stat. Soc.

"Some of the ablest and most competent witnesses have proved that the land in Ireland is low rented in comparison with similar qualities of land in England, Scotland, Belgium, &c., although absolutely high rented in reference to the produce derived and the capabilities of the occupiers."

Dig. Dev. Com. Summary, p. 756.

In the neighbourhood of Cork, an English farmer has just taken a farm of 169 acres, valued at £180 per annum in the Government valuation, at a rent of £300 per annum.

---

shall be entitled to hold his land for ever, if he is willing to pay the rent. It is not creditable to the country that a scheme at once so impracticable and so unjust should find so many advocates. It really is not a matter concerning landlords and tenants as a class; it is simply a proposal to confiscate the property of the present landlords in favour of the present tenants."—*Address to Stat Socy by Judge Longfield.*

leases of greater or less duration, and arbitrary rents, I would ask their authors and advocates whether it is altogether wise to persist in conjuring up before the imagination of ill-educated and impulsive men delusive expectations which can never be realized, and which, if realized, would only work their ruin.* It is an easy task to persuade even the best-

---

" The present tenants converted into landlords by the fixity of tenure, would know well how to grind the future tenants that should come within their power. Oppressive grinding landlords, and dishonest insolvent tenants would then become not the exception but the rule."—*Judge Longfield's Address to the Statis. Society.*

"Nothing can be more unjust than for the law to interfere, and alter the contract so as to increase the value of the tenant's interest at the expense of the landlord. It would rob the landlords for the sole benefit of the individuals who might happen at the moment to be occupiers of land. But to the tenants of Ireland, considered as a class, of which the individuals are frequently changed, it would be of no service."—*Ibid.*

"There would be no reciprocity in fixity of tenure. Even now, when there is a lease, there is no power to prevent a tenant who does not find his holding profitable from selling his stock and emigrating. But even if there could be reciprocity, it would introduce a new inconvenience, that a man wishing to occupy some land for a short period should be unable to get it except on the terms of his taking a lease for ever."—*Ibid.*

* *Mr. Thornton* observes with respect to Mr. O'Connell's proposal to make a 21 years' lease compulsory :—

"The late Mr. O'Connell, by whom this expedient was recommended, acknowledged it to be a violent remedy ; but a more serious objection is, that it would probably have little effect upon the disease. The value of leases depends entirely on their provisions ; and the Legislature, although it might require them to be granted, could not pretend to regulate the demands for rent, or the other conditions to be imposed upon tenants."

Thornton's Peasant Proprietors, p. 214, *et seq.*

balanced minds that what appears to be for their interest, is right; but to blunt the moral perceptions of ignorant men, to put evil for good, and good for evil, to sow dissension between those who should be friends, and to inaugurate a hopeless agitation in a country whose only chance of happiness is in peace and quiet—seems to me too sinister a mission to be excused by the perverted benevolence which inspires it.*

---

* See Judge Longfield's Evidence. Q. 247. I do not think this claim for compensation has been the result of agitation at all; the clamorous men who call for fixity of tenure care comparatively little about this. I think they would rather keep the grievance they complain of.

" Even at present the hope, however delusive, of the establishment of a tenant right by law has an injurious effect. It not only diverts men's attention from more practicable means of improving the condition of the people, but it increases the desire to obtain, and to retain possession of land, no matter how incapable the possessor may be of cultivating the property. There is a hope that the temporary possession will be converted by law into a valuable estate. In some districts the agitation on the subject has fixed it like a principle not to be controverted in the peasant's mind, that the possession of land, however acquired, is a property which it is unjust to take from him without paying him ample compensation. The relation between landlord and tenant is made the constant subject of violent declamation, but the peasant hears only one side of the question. His imaginary rights are assumed as if they were too clear to require argument. And indeed this is necessary, for they will not bear argument."—*Address of Judge Longfield to Stat. Soc.*

It may not be uninstructive to subjoin the late Mr. O'Connell's opinion of fixity of tenure.

" A more absurd and unjust plan he never heard of; it did
" not do anything for the labourer of the country, it trans-

I now come to a very different group of propositions—propositions advocated by persons of gravity and authority, having for their object, not the confiscation of property, nor the curtailment of indefeasible rights; but the restoration to a more healthy condition of those relations between the owner and the occupier of land, which peculiar circumstances have invested with an abnormal character. If I cannot accept them as a resolution of our difficulties, it is not that I deny the existence of the evils they are intended to remedy, or that I fail to sympathize with the motives which have led to their suggestion.

The object proposed is the establishment of a conviction in the mind of every tenant in Ireland that if he invests his capital in the proper cultivation of his farm, either his occupation shall be sufficiently prolonged to enable him to reap the full reward of his industry, or, if abruptly terminated by the caprice of his landlord, he shall receive a corresponding recompense in money. The claim embodied in the foregoing formula is obviously founded on the principles of natural justice. When a landlord hands over his field to the husbandman, even if there be no written agreement, a tacit understanding is implied that the man who

―――――

" ferred the fee-simple from the present proprietor to the
" present occupier of large farms; it was in fact creating a
" smaller monopoly than the former one, but equally mis-
" chievous in its nature."

sows shall reap; a contrary supposition would be adverse to public policy. Consequently, a law of emblements prevails in every civilized country. But, as the ulterior considerations of the bargain are susceptible of every variety of arrangement, they have been left by the common consent of mankind to be regulated by contract, in whatever manner may suit the convenience of the parties interested. It is urged, however, that in Ireland the dependence of the population upon agriculture is so complete that competition has destroyed the tenant's freedom of action. He has been driven into a bargain so inequitable as would justify the state in substituting for the conditions he himself is eager to accept such an extension of the principle out of which has originated the law of emblements as shall secure to him the fruits of his investments,—whether in the larger operations of husbandry, or in the erection of the farm buildings they require. But it is to be observed that this plea of the helpless position of the tenant, whatever force it might have had, is no longer valid, inasmuch as the alternative of adequate wages is open to him;* that the reckless acquisition

---

* "Some reason must be given for making land an exception to the ordinary rules of commerce, and fixing the price by law, instead of letting it be arranged by mutual agreement between the buyer and the seller, the landlord and the tenant. The reason formerly assigned was that the possession of land was a question of life or death to the tenant, that he had no other resource to preserve himself and his family from starvation, and that therefore he was obliged to submit to any terms which an

of land, to which often he cannot do justice, is the result of a passion to be discouraged rather than avaricious landlord might impose. That the parties to the contract stood on such unequal ground, as to make it necessary for the law to interfere to protect the weaker party. It could not be pretended that this argument ever was applicable except to the case of small pauper tenants. It never could have had any bearing on the case of those tenants who hold the greatest part of Ireland, viz: men who have capital of two or three hundred pounds, and who are farmers, not from necessity, but from choice: because they find the occupation of a farmer more profitable, or more suitable to their taste or education, than any other employment. The introduction of poor laws, and the increased demand for labour, now put it out of any man's power to say that he is obliged to offer an exorbitant rent for a farm in order to preserve himself from destitution.

" It should always be borne in mind that it is essentially a dishonest act for a man to enter into a contract which he does not believe that he will be able to fulfil. The man who has obtained possession of a farm by promising a rent that he cannot afford to pay, has committed a dishonest act, and an act injurious to society. He has done a wrong to the landlord from whom he has obtained possession of the land under false pretences, and has done wrong to the competitors for the farm whom he has outbid. The dishonesty may be palliated by the strength of the temptation to which he has yielded, but it cannot be altogether justified, and it certainly should not be made the subject of approbation or reward. Granting even that he has no resource to keep him from the workhouse, except by promising what he cannot perform, has he any claim to a higher standard of maintenance than his neighbour, who may be actually in the poor-house on account of the sturdy honesty which prevents him from promising what he cannot afford to pay. There is no peculiar merit in the man who has got a farm under false pretences, and if he is entitled to a better support than a common pauper, merely because he is called a farmer, no matter by what means he obtained the farm, it is not easy to see why this support should be given to him not by the entire neigh-

stimulated; and that the same considerations which would justify the State in regulating the incidental conditions of occupancy, would also entitle it to fix the remuneration of labour; it is doubtful, therefore, whether any circumstances would render it advisable for Government to depart from the rule which experience has taught us to be best in the long run—viz., to leave the rights of contract between individuals as free as possible.

This conclusion acquires greater force, when we consider how objectionable are the means which even the most sagacious minds have suggested for the application of a contrary principle—such, for instance, as the extension to the tenant of a legal right, first, to make what he may call an "improvement" against the express wish of his landlord, and then to claim compensation for it. Now the very essence of the law of emblements is, that the operation for which compensation is claimed should be of indisputable advantage to the landlord's property. Ploughing, seeding, and manuring fulfil these conditions. But the best method of conducting the more complex operations of husbandry,

bourhood, but by the landlord whom he has defrauded. If land is to be set at a price not fixed by contract, the fairest means of carrying out such a measure would be for the present occupiers to give up possession, and then to divide the land among all the inhabitants equally. Undoubtedly the person who obtains possession of land by false promises ought not to gain any advantage over his more honest competitors."—*Address of Judge Longfield to Stat. Society.*

not even excluding draining,* and certainly including the erection of farm-buildings, is often a matter of dispute between high authorities; and a tenant may embark in an expenditure which, though not exactly disadvantageous to his farm, may be very detrimental to the estate of which his farm is part. Judge

* In all drainage operations, however, the great point to insure is, that they be skilfully planned and efficiently executed. The subject is a science of itself. It requires no slight amount of geological isometrical knowledge to determine exactly the system best suited to each quality and lie of soil, and to save expense as much as possible by exactly proportioning the work to the requirements of the land. Nothing can be more rash than leaving drainage operations to be planned by persons conversant, perhaps, with the general run of agricultural processes, but quite destitute of the engineering science required for the one in question. Nor can anything be more penny wise and pound foolish than, after the plans of an engineer have been obtained, to entrust their carrying out to ordinary labourers, by whom, ten to one, they will be bungled.

The farmer ought always to submit his land to the inspection of an educated and experienced draining engineer. It is of great importance, too, that the plan of operations be as general as possible. *Partial drainage frequently entails greatly increased expense and trouble, which would have been saved if the work had been originally undertaken upon a comprehensive and satisfactory scale.*—*Macdonald's Estate Management*, p. 75.

"The working drawing should be finished, the levels fixed, and the specifications made out before a spade is inserted in the ground. The advantages of this method are found frequently in a considerable saving of expense, always in the completeness and efficiency of the works, and in the facility with which the farmer is afterwards able, in the event of any of the drains going wrong, to consult his plans and lay his hand in a moment upon the channel which requires being cleaned out or cut into."—*Ibid.* p. 76.

Longfield himself tells us that "no improvement on a small farm will pay," consequently such improvements, if they are made at all, should be made at the tenant's own risk, and not at the risk of the person who objects to them.* It is urged that the quality of the intended improvement might be decided by some impartial tribunal; but should the owner of a property be convinced that a particular operation would damage rather than benefit his estate—would interfere with his own schemes of improvement, would load, for instance, with useless agricultural erections, lands he contemplated devoting to building purposes—it would be unjust to allow an assistant barrister (even though instructed by a *comitatus* of experts) to override his decision. This would be felt so keenly—that, should a tenant be found commencing an "improvement" against which his landlord had protested, he would invariably receive notice to quit. I fear, therefore, we must

* "Q. 691. You were asked this question by Mr. Cardwell, at Question No. 89, "Do you think, speaking generally, that the smaller the holding the greater the prospect of agricultural improvement?" Your reply was, "No; a small holding can scarcely be improved." Do you mean that such holdings are so highly improved already that they are incapable of further improvement?—A. No, I do not, but that many improvements require a certain space to make them pay and be available and require a certain intelligence to direct them; and it is not reasonable to suppose, that a small farmer, a poor man, will have the intelligence and the capital to improve the land; and even if he had, the improvement over a small space would not pay."

reject this principle, as both unjust and impracticable.*

---

* A tenant of my own once took advantage of my agent's illness, to run up on his farm, which happened to be near the sea, a very unsightly lodging-house. From this erection, he has derived considerable profit, and considered by itself, it has therefore added to the rental of my estate, and might be called an "improvement." When, however, the time comes for leasing the adjoining land in building lots, the first thing I shall have to do, will be to take down the structure in question,— as an ill-built whitewashed barrack in the midst of a cluster of handsome villas, would detract from the letting value of the property. If, therefore, I had been compelled to grant him compensation on the ground that his expenditure had added to the rental of the estate, I should have suffered an injustice. As it happened, though I was annoyed by what had been done, I allowed the house to stand, rather than injure my tenant, and, by this time, he has repaid himself, I hope, for his outlay; but the intelligent reader will see that, had it been possible for him to raise a legal claim for compensation against me for what he had done, I should not have shown him the same indulgence. It will be urged that abuses of this particular description will not be permitted under any bill. But such an instance exemplifies how possible it is for an improvement to add something to the rental of an estate, at the same time that it deteriorates the property. Analogous cases might arise in a hundred ways. A tenant occupying a small farm sub-divided into innumerable little fields desires to drain. His landlord might suggest that half his fences should be obliterated, and the fields squared up before such an operation is commenced. The tenant takes a different view, drains according to his own plan, and claims compensation. It is quite possible that even though badly executed, the operation has slightly improved the land; but the moment the farm passed into the hands of a really capable tenant, the preliminary alteration of the fences, originally suggested by the landlord, would take place, and all the draining would have to be done over again.

We now come to the proposal made by the late Government—a proposal dictated by an anxious desire to make as large a concession as possible to the equitable claims of the tenant, and which—with a moderation that did them honour—was accepted, I believe, by the most distinguished of the Liberal members for Ireland, as a settlement of the question. The essence of the arrangement was, to leave the right of contract perfectly free; but to substitute, where no contract existed, a presumption that, within certain limits, any improvement made by the tenant was his property. That such a declaration on the part of the law is no interference with the right of property, cannot be disputed, and it is in some such compromise, if in any, a solution of the Irish land question is to be found.

The wisdom of Parliament would, probably, have simplified the details of the measure. In my own opinion, the safeguards introduced for the protection of the landlord, only confused the principle of the bill. Instead of limiting the tenant's claim for compensation, on account of an uncovenanted improvement, to a maximum of £5 per acre, it would be better to leave him entirely unrestricted in his expenditure. Instead of declaring his

A distinguished Agriculturist in Kerry has furnished me with the following instance of over-fencing:—"On an area of 137 statute acres, there are 2,500 perches of fences. Taking each fence with a gripe at either side to be about 12 feet wide, it would follow that of the 137 acres, 13 are occupied by banks."

ownership in that improvement to be annihilated at the expiration of an arbitrary period, the law should presume it to endure as long as the beneficial effects of its operation lasted. Instead of attempting to regulate the relations of the two parties by the ambiguous provisions of a fictitious lease, it would be simpler to reverse the existing presumption of law, that whatever is affixed to the soil belongs to the landlord, and to declare instead, that any *bonâ fide* improvement, executed by a tenant, outside of a written contract, is the property of the tenant, for which, on surrendering possession of his farm, whether of his own accord or under compulsion, he shall be entitled to receive compensation from his landlord to the amount of the additional value annually accruing from it, to be assessed by arbitration, or recovered in a court of law. It may be objected that such a method of procedure involves an inequitable principle of compensation, and prejudices the interests of the landlord. That I admit. I have already stated that a tenant's *equitable* claim to compensation should be regulated by the original cost of the improvement, and the rate of interest due to such investments,* but in declaring a pre-

---

* Judge Longfield is very explicit on this point. See his Evidence:—

Q. 854. I understand the way in which you estimate improvements is to consider the value they confer upon the land?

sumption *in the absence of a contract*, the law does not pretend to lay down a canon of equity, and the change would be only unfair to the landlord to the

A. No. What the improvements cost and their present value.

Q. 855. Not the value conferred upon the land?

A. Certainly not, * * * * because every penny beyond the *natural interest* for the money really proceeds from the land itself, and not from the improvement.

See also Mr. Curling's Evidence to the same effect.

A. 3962. Fourthly, I fully agree with Lord Dufferin, that if, in the increased letting value of his holding, the tenant is given a duration of beneficial occupancy, sufficient to compensate him for his original outlay, with compound interest at 5 per cent., or proportionate pecuniary payment if evicted in the meantime; it is the utmost that he can fairly claim, and that any additional rental value incidental to such improvements may justly be considered as the contribution of the landlord in the latent capabilities of the land in the partnership which has existed between them.

The Roman law, which is the foundation of the agricultural law of Europe, declared "that when the tenants had derived profits from the improvements (*meliorationes*) sufficient to cover the principal sum, and interest of the money laid out upon them, no compensation was to be held due."—See a Parliamentary Paper on the Roman Agricultural Law, 6th July, 1853.

See also the Report of Mr. Pusey's Committee, paragraphs 10, 11 :—

Par. 10. That its amount (*i.e.* the amount of compensation) is found by valuers, who ascertain the cost of the several improvements, spread that cost over a certain number of years, within which each kind of improvement respectively is supposed to repay itself, and then deduct from that number, the time during which the tenant has enjoyed the benefit of the improvement.

Par. 11. That this system is highly beneficial, &c. &c.

same degree and in the same sense as the converse is now unfair to the tenant.

Under the existing statute, if a yearly occupier of a farm expends £500 in the erection of a house, the law *presumes* the building to belong to the owner of the soil, and he might claim possession the day after it was built. For the law to declare its value to be the property of the tenant as long as that value endures would be even a less extravagant presumption. It was never contemplated, however, that a naked presumption of this kind should regulate the ultimate arrangement; but as, in the absence of any specific agreement on the subject, it was necessary to attribute the property to some one, it was naturally assigned to the person with whose estate it had become irrevocably incorporated, in the expectation that the original presumption created by the law would be expressly confirmed, modified, or reversed by a subsequent agreement framed in accordance with the interests of the contracting parties. Unhappily, in Ireland this expectation has been frustrated. Those very persons to whom the unmitigated application of this legal presumption would be most injurious, have been too careless,—too confiding,—too dependant—to adopt the countervailing precautions which, in other countries, the prudence of mankind has rendered universal. As a consequence, the untempered presumption of the law acts occasionally in Ireland with a severity it was never intended should attach to it. Let us then change that presumption, and impose upon those who are in a better position to do so, the obligation of protecting themselves from whatever consequences its unqualified application would entail;—since the tenants will not insist upon defining their rights by specific agreements, let us make it the interest of the landlords to do so, and as it is the general practice in Ireland for the tenant to execute a considerable proportion of the improvements, let us bring the presumption of the law more into harmony with the actual practice of the country. By this means, a constant statutory bias would be brought to bear in favour of the tenant; he would obtain immunity from the consequences of his own carelessness, and he would invariably profit by the carelessness of his landlord; while, at the same time, the latter would have it in his power to correct the partiality of the law by the provisions of an equitable contract.*

* But the landlord and the tenant are not the only persons interested. The position of the mortgagee, and the remainder-man has to be considered. As the law now stands the limited owner cannot charge the succession with a sixpence on account of any improvement, however remunerative, nor can the owner in fee interpolate a new charge of prior obligation amongst those already in existence. To invest a tenant with a power denied to the landlord would be absurd. Yet under the foregoing arrangements it might happen, that an injudicious expenditure on the part of a tenant might be credited by an incompetent valuator with a beneficial character which did not belong to it; in which event the new charge against the estate to which the so-called improvement had given rise, would be in excess of the annual addition to the rental supposed to accrue from it. Some time might elapse before the discrepancy became

But if this much is conceded to the peculiar position to which subdivision, competition, and an inapparent, but from the moment it existed, the security of the mortgagee would be deteriorated to a corresponding extent. Though a hardship would be entailed upon the landlord by such a miscarriage of justice, it is a risk from which it is not necessary for the legislature to protect him, as he might have secured himself against any such contingency by a written contract. But the mortgagee and the remainder man occupy a different position; they cannot control the management of the property, and it is not desirable that their interests should be compromised by the carelessness of a proprietor, the blunders of a tenant, or the incompetence of a valuator.

Although therefore there may be no necessity to limit the tenant's claim to compensation as against the landlord, it would be necessary to provide against any injury which might accrue either to the mortgagee, or to the remainder man, out of an operation which must be, to a certain degree, of a speculative character. This, however, I do not think it would be difficult to accomplish.

That even Government officials are not infallible with regard to the results to be obtained from works of reclamation and so called agricultural improvements, the following instance strongly illustrates:—

"On vous citera un exemple plus mémorable encore, celui de la société de bienfaisance fondée en 1818 avec le concours du gouvernement hollandais. Elle acheta, 1,000 hectares dans les communes de Wortel, Merxplas et Ryckevorsel, et après avoir dépensé en quatorze ans plus de 5 millions de francs, elle ne parvint à conquérir à la culture, d'une manière définitive, que 125 hectares. En 1847, sous les auspices du gouvernement belge, une nouvelle tentative de colonisation fut faite, cette fois au moyen de petites fermes de 5 hectares, dont 1 hectare déjà fumé et emblavé, 1 hectare de prairie irriguée, et 3 hectares de bruyères. Ces petites fermes, situées dans la commune de Lommell, étaient louées à des familles de cultivateurs pour un terme de trente ans, avec des conditions, si favorables, qu'en

ordinate desire to possess land has reduced the Irish tenant, it would be advisable, both in the interest of the tenant himself and of the landlord, to accompany the foregoing alteration of the law by some subsidiary provision for the registration of every improvement on which it is intended to found a claim for compensation. The necessity for such a precaution is self-evident. Without it no Court would possess trustworthy data for estimating the nature and cost of an alleged improvement made ten or fifteen years before the inquiry into its title to compensation was instituted. Were such matters to be left to oral evidence, and to the recollection of the individuals interested, a satisfactory settlement could never be attained.* A single exemplification will suffice.

payant un léger amortissement, les fermiers demeuraient propriétaires à l'expiration du bail. Ces combinaisons semblaient parfaites, et pourtant jusqu'à présent le succès n'a point tout à fait répondu aux espérances qu'on avait conçues. D'autres sociétés qui avaient en vue non une œuvre de bienfaisance à accomplir, mais une spéculation à faire, n'ont pas été plus heureuses, à en juger du moins par les resultats acquis."

Similar miscalculations, I am told, have occasionally been made by the Board of Works in Ireland, with regard to draining operations.

* *Mr Robt. Purdon, land valuer, on Mr. Griffiths' land valuation.*

" After a lapse of time it is difficult to determine the just allowance to be made to the tenant for his share of the improvements upon the soil; for there is a great deal in the tillage and drainage of land which does not appear, and it is difficult to ascertain what has been done, without knowing the state which the land was formerly in."— *Dig. Dev. Com.* 166.

" I should think it more desirable, *if the amount to be laid*

Perhaps there is no improvement more common, more deserving of compensation, or requiring a longer term of occupancy to repay itself, than that which consists in quarrying, and in removing or burying the rocks which crop up in a shallow and stony soil; yet the very perfection of the operation destroys all internal evidence of what has been done. The tenant's claim will therefore have to rest on testimony. But long before any question of compensation comes to be raised, the author of the improvement may have died, or he may have handed over his interest in his farm to another man. The estate itself may have been sold, and a new agent and a new landlord have come upon the scene. Yet though all the parties privy to the original arrangement have disappeared, the claim itself would be as rife as ever. How is the matter to be adjudicated in the absence of competent witnesses or trustworthy data? And it is to be remembered that the difficulty of adjusting *bonâ fide* claims of this description, is the true measure of the facilities which would be afforded for establishing unsubstantial and fraudulent pretensions on venal evidence.

<small>out in improvements was determined on before the improvements took place; it is difficult to determine it afterwards. It is frequently impossible to please both parties. The tenant claims more than the landlord will allow; and it is difficult, after a lapse of years, to determine what would be a just and proper sum to allow the tenant. I state that as a general impression which occurs to me."—*Ib. p.* 166.

"If you see land worth £1. per acre, how could you say what it was worth twenty years before."—*Ib. p.* 166.</small>

Again, if tenants are to be entitled to get back from their landlord whatever they may choose to lay out on their farms, it is essential that the latter should have the means of acquainting himself with the bill which is being run up against him on various parts of his estate. No one would allow the most trustworthy steward to embark in an unlimited expenditure on his home-farm without looking occasionally at his books; still less would it be advisable to allow a numerous tenantry to incur, on behalf of their landlord, an unknown amount of responsibilities which, however insignificant in each instance, would, in the aggregate, amount to an enormous sum. In some parts of Ireland as many as 4000 or 5000 tenants are located on a single property; and it must be recollected that frequently they have become thus numerous, not through the landlord's neglect, but by the evasion of express covenants against sub-letting. Supposing each tenant to spend £10 a year in some alleged improvement,—the straightening of a fence, the repair of a gable end, the erection of a pigstye—at the end of five years the owner of such a property might find himself confronted by a claim to compensation amounting to £200,000.* With this contingency in prospect, but without any means of

* We have also to consider what would be the position of the purchaser of a property with respect to these indefinite and unrecorded liabilities. For the charges in the schedule of incumbrances a due deduction of price has been made in the purchase money, but of these other claims, *and the law expenses arising out of them*, no one could pretend to form an estimate.

ascertaining the rate at which the burden was accumulating, the landowner would be in a position of such insecurity as would compel him either to reduce his tenantry to more manageable proportions, or else to emasculate their claims by imposing a specific agreement on each tenant to execute *seriatim* every agricultural operation of which his farm was susceptible. It is argued that the very fact of warning the landlord of what was taking place on his estate would tend to discountenance a tenant's improvements. Such an objection can hardly be seriously urged. Under any circumstances an improvement hatched like a conspiracy, and exploded like a mine would probably lead to the improver being hoisted with his own petard.

Lastly, it is the interest of the tenantry, even more than that of their landlords, that the investment of capital in improvements should be effected with care and economy, and kept at a *minimum*, as the burden of compensation invariably falls on the incoming tenant. This point was very distinctly noted in the report of Mr. Pusey's Parliamentary Committee;[*] and it is evident that, if a landlord is to pay a certain sum to an outgoing tenant for his improvements, he will recoup himself, either by clapping an equivalent percentage on the rent of the new tenant, or by accepting a fine equivalent in amount to the sum he has paid

---

[*] Paragraph 9.—Report by Mr. Pusey's Committee:—"In practice, the compensation agreed to be paid by the landlord to the outgoing tenant is paid by the incoming one."

away. To stimulate an unnecessary expenditure on any estate, whether in the shape of superfluous farm buildings or other so-called improvements, is only to embarrass the community located upon it with a burden as irredeemable as a national debt. Yet no surer way to encourage such extravagance can be devised than to allow one set of men to disburse without restraint or enquiry sums of money which they expect another set of men will have to repay. The possibility of the claim being eventually disallowed would be too remote a contingency to influence their conduct, while the chance of the award being in excess of their expenditure would still further neutralize their prudence.

Stripped, however, of the complicated provisions which confused and indeed altered the original principle it professed to enunciate, the Bill of the late Government certainly contained the germ of what might prove both a politic and legitimate measure. As to any further or more intimate interference by the legislature between landlord and tenant I am not sanguine. Some persons would prefer to create by Act of Parliament a model lease, and then to render the position of any landlord who might decline to adopt it so untenable as to impose on him, if not a legal obligation, at all events an imperative necessity to bring the tenures on his estate into conformity with its provisions. Now, no one has been a stronger advocate for leases than myself. To refuse a lease to a solvent industrious tenant, is, in my opinion, little short of a crime. Not only have I never refused a lease myself, but I have done my best to persuade my tenantry to apply for them. The prosperity of agriculture depends on security of tenure, and the only proper tenure is a liberal lease. Yet I cannot conceive a measure more fraught with disaster to agriculture, more productive of discontent, more certain to inflict suffering on a large proportion of the present tenant farmers of the country, than that the Irish landlords should be driven by any such legislation as this into an indiscriminate issue of leases for a term of years.

None but persons acquainted with the management of Irish property, can have an adequate idea of the variety of instances in which it may become inexpedient to grant a lease. Very frequently, particularly in the North of Ireland, the tenantry unfortunately prefer an indefinite understanding to a specific contract.* It is doubtful whether, even

---

* M. de Laveleye has very well described the reason for their preference of an indefinite tenure. "En Angleterre, la constitution de la propriété et de la culture amène des conséquences différentes. Le grand propriétaire, jouissant d'un revenu considérable, n'est pas obligé pour vivre de pressurer sans cesse ses fermiers. Il s'établit entre la famille du *landlord* et celles des tenanciers des relations . . . . , et qui empêchent le maître de faire des conditions trop dures à ceux qui dépendent de lui. Les sentiments affectueux propres au régime patriarcal modifient et adoucissent la dure loi moderne de l'offre et de la demande. Les fermes sont généralement tenures *at will* ou *à volonté*. . . . . L'absence du contrat écrit, qui en Belgique est considérée comme la pire des conditions, est au contraire préférée

in the South, leases for anything but an unreasonable period would be considered as a boon.* Yet to force a lease on an unwilling tenant is only a degree less objectionable than to evict him for refusing to take one. In many instances, the only reason for which

par les fermiers anglais. Ces appréciations opposées indiquent seules déjà la différence des deux régimes, car la tenure *at will* serait pour le locataire aussi funeste en Belgique qu'elle est avantageuse en Angleterre. *Tandis qu'en Belgique elle provoquerait une hausse incessante du fermage, limitée maintenant par le terme habituel de neuf années, en Angleterre, elle favorise le maintien de la même rente parfois pendant plusieurs générations successives.*" Curiously enough, he illustrates his meaning by a reference to an estate in the north of Ireland.—*Eco. Rur.* p. 235.

* "Many witnesses stated that the occupiers have no wish for leases at the resent rents, and that the cost of the stamps and of the execution of leases has also much effect in removing the desire to obtain them; and many, without mentioning the cause of the disregard of leases, assert that frequently, where proprietors are ready to grant, the occupiers do not manifest any wish to receive them. In the northern counties, where the custom of tenant-right prevails, the number of witnesses who state this fact is very considerable."—*Dig. Dev. Com.* p. 225; see also *Mr. Robertson's Report*, p. 345.

The Right Honourable the Earl of Mountcashel.—" Many of them hold by lease, but a great number from year to year. On my own estate, I do not think there is a great inclination on the part of the tenants to take leases; latterly I have given a great many, but I find a great number who are quite satisfied without any. I cannot say whether that is the case upon other estates—I doubt it; and it may be here remarked, that it is a very curious thing, though I reside here, I have much larger estates in the north of Ireland, in the county of Antrim, and I have been in the habit of acting in the same way towards my northern tenants and towards my southern, and my northern tenants do not wish to take leases as far as I have found. There

a lease is desired, is to obtain a document on which money can be raised, or an extravagant charge for younger children effected.* If, therefore, some of the landed proprietors of Ireland evince a disinclination to grant leases, it is, in many instances, because bitter experience has taught them that previous leases have generally proved to be, as Judge Longfield has observed, " all in the tenant's favour"—that a certain proportion of their actual tenants are incapable of fulfilling the obligations of a contract—that security of tenure,—in other words, immunity from all sense of responsibility,—instead of stimulating the industry of the occupier, too often acts as a premium on idleness,† and that the difficulties of preventing the subdivision and subletting of leased

---

are several under-tenants whose leases were out some years ago, and I sent to my agent Mr. Joy, in the county of Antrim, and desired him to inform the tenants that I was ready to grant leases, and he wrote back to inform me that they were content to remain without leases."—*Dig. Dev. Com.* p. 257.

* *Wm. Morris Reade, Esq., land proprietor.*

" Is there any anxiety for leases on the part of the tenants at their present rents ?—As far as I can judge, they are not at all anxious but for one reason—when they come to make marriage contracts for their children, they are anxious to show they have a hold upon all of the land, but upon other occasions they are perfectly indifferent."—*Dig. Dev. Com.* p. 279.

† *Mr. Jos. Lambert, farmer.*

" What extent of tenure would induce a man to make these improvements ?—I see among the poor people having land, that those who have leases are much less inclined to make improvements than those who have not."—*Ib.* p. 191.

lands, are almost insurmountable.* The case of a solvent and improving tenant being refused a lease, is, I suspect, much rarer than is supposed.†

The consequences of forcing leases by Act of Parliament, are sufficiently obvious. Hitherto, one of the chief accusations brought against the Irish proprietor has been his indifference to the character and the solvency of his tenant, and in order to correct this indifference, it is proposed to abolish the priority of his claim on the rent, and to reduce him to the ranks of an ordinary creditor. If, therefore, under these circumstances he is precluded from letting his land, except under a thirty-one years' lease, an inexorable necessity will be imposed upon him to exclude from such a permanent arrangement those of his existing tenants who are in debt, or who are likely to fall into embarrassment during the obligatory term. Now perhaps the tenantry of no estate in Ireland is more prosperous than my own; yet my agent informs me, that unhappily, more than a third of the farmers upon my property are under heavy pecuniary obligations through the country, in addition to those incurred towards myself. At present their creditors are aware that to drive them from their

---

* "But the principal reason alleged by most of the proprietors, is the difficulty of preventing subdivision where a farm is leased."—*Ib. Summary, p.* 236.

† I do not think it can be denied, that leases are sometimes withheld from political motives; but for this abuse the ballot would be the proper remedy: though England, with her tougher moral fibre, may not need such a contrivance. I have often thought the ballot might prove advantageous in Ireland.

farms by the application of any premature pressure would only reduce to a minimum their own chances of receiving payment. My own inclination is to give them every opportunity to extricate themselves from their difficulties; and though the position of affairs is not satisfactory, nor can the ultimate destiny of many of these persons be doubtful, a reasonable amount of forbearance on my part, may save some, and greatly mitigate the hardship of their situation to the rest.

If, however, I found myself suddenly called upon by Parliament to lease away my estate for a whole generation, matters would be brought to a crisis, and in self defence I should be forced, (very much against my will,) to exclude from the intended benefits of the arrangement every single individual circumstanced as I have described. No landlord could be expected to grant a lease to a bankrupt, or to enter into a contract with a person incapable of fulfilling its obligations.*

But in addition to those of my tenants, who are actually in debt, there are a certain number who are so destitute of capital,—so unskilful,—occupiers of such small and inconvenient patches,—so near the verge of ruin,—as to be very unfit recipients of a lease. However willing I might be to

---

* "You know a very large number of occupiers of land in Ireland, holding a very limited acreage, and of course you would not give a person with 5 or 10 acres' holding a 21 years' lease, would you?—A. Generally speaking it would be no use, because a 21 years' lease has general useful covenants in it, and those men are not amenable to any covenants."

Judge Longfield's Evidence.

continue them in their present holdings until an opportunity shall occur of establishing them as labourers, or of enabling their sons to emigrate, or of converting the old people into pensioners, a very different arrangement would be necessary if Parliament held a pistol to my head, and left me no choice, but to give them 31 years' leases, or resume possession of my land. Now if these undesirable contingencies might arise on a prosperous estate in Ulster, it is scarcely necessary to indicate what would be the consequences of such anomalous interference by Parliament in the south and west of Ireland.

Take the case of the falling in of an old 61 years' lease, on which, in spite of all covenants to the contrary, a vast congeries of cottier tenants have been collecting for generations. Perhaps the size of the holdings may not average four acres a piece: a great deal of it may be held in rundale: all of it is sure to be in the worst possible condition; yet the only chance of introducing a better system,—of inducing the people to agglomerate their patches,—of making arrangements for the squaring up of fields, and the re-distribution of the area into a shape more suitable to existing circumstances,—is that the landlord should have some power of controlling the ignorant prejudices of those for whose well-being he has become suddenly responsible. Under any circumstances the task will require patience—above all--time; five, ten, fifteen years, perhaps a life-time, will be necessary if the operation is to be performed with due regard to the feelings of the people concerned. But if the landlord be peremptorily required to re-lease his land for another generation, any such benevolent reconstruction will be impossible, and the only alternative left to him, will be to re-stereotype the existing chaos, or to convert his estate into a tabula-rasa.*

In fact, the more the matter is considered the greater are the difficulties which present themselves. Unless great care is taken we shall injure rather than improve the position of our clients. As long as a numerous population is cursed with a morbid craving to possess land, so long will the owner of land be able to drive hard bargains in spite of Queen, Lords and Commons, and any exceptional legislation we may devise will be more apt effectually to embarrass the judicious management of the liberal landowner, than it will control the injustice of the oppressor, while the ultimate result of our well meant endeavours may be to transfer the management of a great portion of every estate in Ireland from the hands of the land agent into those of the solicitor.†

* "Upon some well-regulated estates, the property of intelligent and liberal landlords, who are upon the best footing with their tenants, no leases are given; but we cannot forbear to express our opinion, that as a general system it is more for the interest of both landlord and tenant that leases of a moderate length should be granted. *We feel, however, that this is one of the points which must be left to the discretion of individuals, and we cannot recommend any direct interference by the Legislature.*"
—S. Dig. Dev. 1122.

† "If, on the other hand, nothing more be meant than that an ejected tenant should be entitled to compensation for substantial improvements, the advantages of a law to that effect

There is, indeed, one further suggestion I am disposed to hazard, which might go far to diminish discontent and stimulate production amongst the agricultural class. In considering the question of tenants' improvements it appears to me that a satisfactory settlement for the past is even a greater desideratum than the most favourable arrangement for the future. The legal attainment of this object has been given up by everyone as impracticable; yet if the people of England are really disposed to be as liberal as Mr. Bright's proposal implies, I see no reason why the same principle which has been introduced by Parliament to facilitate the future improvement of Ireland might not be adopted to obliterate all misunderstanding as to the past. No later than last Session a million of money was voted to enable the owners of property in Ireland to erect farm buildings, and labourers' cottages, to drain and to reclaim. If a similar loan were granted on the same terms, or if the present loan were made accessible to those landlords who might be willing to buy up the existing improvements of their tenants, I have no doubt advantage would be taken of the opportunity. Precautions could be adopted by the Board of Works to ascertain that the improvements to be purchased were sufficient security for the sum borrowed. Though the landlord would be responsible for the debt, the interest on it would be repaid,

would probably be more than counterbalanced by the endless litigation to which it would give rise."—*Thornton's Peasant Proprietors.*

either in whole or in part by the tenant. The tenant would be benefited by receiving a lump sum, which, if judiciously invested in his farm, would return him a profit of 3, 4, or 5 per cent. in excess of the yearly instalment for the discharge of the interest. It might be even advisable for the Board of Works to make these loans conditional on the occupier's receiving a lease.

By this simple expedient it would become the landlord's interest, not only to recognise the *minimum* claims of his tenant, (which in many instances I fear would become almost inappreciable beneath the strict scrutiny of a Court of Equity,) but to deal with them in a liberal spirit; while both landlord and tenant would have an inducement to refer all matters in dispute between them to the arbitrament of a Board, in whose decision it would be the policy of each to acquiesce. A better understanding would be introduced between the two classes; even evictions would lose their most obnoxious characteristic; and, above all, a large sum of money now locked up in homesteads and farm buildings would be immediately transmuted into capital applicable to the cultivation of the soil.

It is impossible to lay too great stress on this last advantage. When people talk of *le petite culture*, and the reduplicated employment afforded by spade husbandry, they quite forget that, except in very favoured soils, low farming reduces land to a *caput mortuum*. All the labour in the world will not fertilize a sandbank; but convey to it the scourings of a great city, and a *minimum* of labour will turn it into a garden.* Let capital overflow her soil,—an analogous transformation will take place in Ireland,—and though her superficial area remain the same, the stimulus to her powers of production would be equivalent to an accession of territory sufficient to support thousands in affluence, where at present hundreds find a difficulty in extracting a bare subsistence.

But it may be asked, Is this, then, all you have to propose? Have you no comprehensive remedy to prescribe for the perennial discontent of Ireland? Can no styptic be discovered for the unprecedented emigration from her shores? I answer that such inquiries lie beyond the scope of this hasty dissertation. I have never presumed to discuss the state of Ireland at large: but many persons having expressed an opinion that Irish disaffection, and the emigration from Ireland, were occasioned by the conduct of the landlords towards their tenants, and the iniquity of the laws affecting the tenure of land, I have ventured to examine the grounds on which those opinions are founded. The result has tended

---

* "En définitive, il faut que le laboureur travaille avec énergie ; mais cela ne suffit pas, et ce n'est meme pas le point principal, car il y a bien des contrées où l'homme se tue à retourner la terre pour n'obtenir que de maigres récoltes. Ce qu'il faut avant tout, c'est apprendre à connaître, soit par la science, soit par la pratique journalière, les lois de la nature et ce que le sol réclame pour récompenser, par de riches produits, les efforts de ceux qui le cultivent."—*Écon. Rurale*, 96.

T

to show not only that no alteration of tenure would have an appreciable effect upon either, but that even the amendments I have indicated, however desirable in themselves, could have no very immediate effect on the evils we deplore. These evils are too deeply seated, too intimately interwoven with the past, to be cured by any emperical peddling in the land-laws of the country. To expect "a tenant's compensation bill" to quell Fenianism, or to prevent those who cannot get a living at home from crossing the Atlantic, would be as reasonable as to try to stifle a conflagration on the first floor by stuffing a blanket down the kitchen chimney, or to staunch the hœmorrhage from an artery by slipping the key of the house-door down your back. No nation can be made industrious, provident, skilful, by Act of Parliament. It is to time, to education, and, above all, to the development of our industrial resources, that we must look for the reinvigoration of our economical constitution.

I have now finished my ungracious task. To many I shall have appeared to take the part of the rich against the poor, of the strong against the weak, but to those who are practically acquainted with the subject it will be apparent that I have been arguing in the real interests of the latter, even more than in those of the former. If I am anxious to prevent the introduction of a vicious principle into the land-laws of Ireland, it is because I am convinced that the evil consequences of such mistaken legislation will fall again, as it has done before, on the tenant, rather than on the landlord. If I run counter to the instincts of that great Liberal party to whom Ireland owes so much, and from which it has still so much to expect, it is because I know its confidence has been abused. My only object has been to establish truth and to advocate justice. The doctrine that Ireland is to be saved by the sacrifice of the rights of property is a violation of both,—and its application would only aggravate our existing difficulties.

ANSWERS TO QUERIES,

AS TO THE RATE OF WAGES, SUPPLY OF LABOUR, AND CONVERSION OF ARABLE INTO PASTURE, &c.

As some diversity of opinion seemed to exist as to the real rate of agricultural wages in Ireland, as well as to other matters of fact connected with our enquiry, I ventured to distribute through different parts of the country, a series of questions on the points with respect to which it was desirable to obtain information. Most of these queries were forwarded through the obliging intervention of an eminent Judge, of an officer of the Board of Works, and of different Government Inspectors. The answers emanate from gentlemen with whom I have no personal acquaintance, but who were considered by those who kindly distributed my questions the best authorities on the subject, comprising Agents, County Surveyors, Inspectors of Public Works, and Land Surveyors.

Rate of Wages.

The first query related to the rate of agricultural wages: subjoined are the answers I received.

1. One shilling and fourpence a day.—Co. Antrim.
2. Seven shillings per week.—Co. Carlow.
3. The rate of wages in this district is from one shilling to one shilling and sixpence per day.—Co. Cork.
4. Seven shillings to eight shillings; best men, ten shillings.—Co. Cork.
5. One shilling per day, throughout the year, wet and dry, with some perquisites.—Co. Cork.

6. One shilling and sixpence per day on an average. In the winter months labour can be had for from one shilling to one shilling and threepence per day, but in the spring it rises to two shillings.—Co. Galway.

7. The rate of wages varies according to the season, but I give to my best men one shilling per day in all seasons.—Co. Galway.

8. Seven shillings a week.—Co. Kildare.

9. One shilling and twopence a day for constant labourers.—Co. Kildare.

10. The average rate of wages for good labourers is seven shillings per week in winter, and nine shillings in summer; and skilled labourers, such as quarrymen, two shillings over.—Co. Kerry.

11. One shilling and threepence per day for labourers; four shillings per day for carpenters and masons.—Co. Kerry.

12. One shilling—in some few cases, fourteen pence.—Co. Mayo.

13. At the rate of seven shillings and eight shillings per week.—Co. Meath.

14. In Kerry, one shilling and fourpence, average one shilling and twopence; in King's Co., one shilling and fivepence, average one shilling and threepence; in Monaghan, one shilling and fourpence, average one shilling and twopence—for winter and summer all round.—Co. Monaghan.

15. One shilling per day.—Co. Roscommon.

16. The present rate of wages in this district, for agricultural labourers, averages one shilling and twopence per day. I pay in money, to my best men, seven shillings weekly; they are constantly employed at one work or another on the farm, gardens, or demesne.—Co. Tipperary.

17. One shilling and twopence per day for best men.—Co. Waterford.

18. Permanent wages for labourers, one shilling a day; occasional labourers, or those depending on the market, from one shilling and twopence to one shilling and sixpence per day.—Co. Waterford.

19. Seven shillings a week, and a house.—Co. Wexford.

20. I think one shilling per day is the standard rate for ordinary men constantly employed, one shilling and twopence to best

men. One shilling and sixpence is paid to casual labourers, and farmers often add diet.

21. At present, nine shillings per week, or one shilling and sixpence per day.

22. Eight shillings a week.—Co. Tipperary.

23. To the ordinary labourers of my own staff I pay, throughout the year, one shilling per diem.—Co. Limerick.

24. Eleven shillings a week.—Co. Down (within five miles of Belfast).

Of the foregoing twenty-four instances of the rate of wages paid to agricultural labourers in various parts of Ireland, ten state it to be from 1s to 1s 2d, 1s 3d, and 1s 6d per day; ten state it to be from 1s 2d to 1s 4d, 1s 6d, 1s 8d, and 2s per day; one states it to be from 1s 3d per day; two state it to be from 1s 4d per day; one states it to be from 1s 6d per day.

Rate of Wages for Unskillled Labour, employed on Railways, Quarries, Timber Felling, Draining, &c.

1. One shilling and sixpence a day.—Co. Antrim.
2. Nine shillings per week.—Co. Carlow.
3. About one shilling and sixpence per day.—Co. Cork.
4. Cutting drains 4 feet deep, ninepence per 16½ feet.—Co. Cork.
5. From one shilling and sixpence to one shilling and eightpence per day.—Co. Cork.
6. One shilling and threepence per day.—Co. Galway.
7. From a shilling to one shilling and sixpence.—Co. Galway.
8. About ten shillings per week.—Co. Kildare.
9. I pay the same wages as for agricultural operations, but generally do drainage, &c. by task, when men in summer can earn one shilling and sixpence per day.—Co. Kildare.
10. One shilling and sixpence per day.—Co. Kerry.
11. Seven shillings to nine shillings per week, or one shilling and two pence to one shilling and sixpence per day.—Co. Kerry.
12. The railway contractor pays nine shillings per week. I do not think the wages differ in other respects.—Co. Mayo.
13. This work is generally done by task.—Co. Meath.

14. Same as to agricultural purposes. Quarrymen, if good may command twopence per diem higher.—Co. Monaghan.

15. Variable according to circumstances—from one shilling to two shillings per day.—Co. Roscommon.

16. I believe that nine shillings to twelve shillings per week may be set down in answer to this query. Drainage is executed very much by task at so much per week, and for this a class, not so good as the first, earn eight to ten shillings per week. I can't say what wages men felling timber receive; there are not any extensive woods in this district. I have heard that one shilling and sixpence per day has been paid to men occasionally so employed, and I would pay at that rate.—Co. Tipperary.

17. Men employed in this neighbourhood at draining, quarrying, and felling timber earn about one shilling and sixpence per day.—Co. Waterford.

18. The work referred to in this query is mostly done by ordinary labourers. No railway work has been carried on here.—Co. Waterford.

19. Eight shillings to eleven shillings a week.—Co. Wexford.

20. Of this class of works there are none doing in my neighbourhood, except some drainages. These are usually performed by task, or piece work, and I find that at the prices generally sanctioned by the Board of Public Works, a healthy, willing man can earn one shilling and sixpence or more, on an average, per day.—Co. Limerick.

21. Ten shillings a week to labourers employed at railway cuttings. Two shillings and sixpence a day to quarrymen. Draining is generally done by contract. Nine shillings a week to men felling timber.

22. One shilling and eightpence per day.

23. Nine shillings per week, when the work is not let by task or the job.

Rate of Agricultural Wages at Harvest Time.

1. One and eightpence a day for extra hands.—Co. Antrim.
2. From two to three shillings per day.—Co. Carlow.
3. My own staff do most of my work, getting diet during harvest.—Co. Cork.

4. Extra labourers in harvest time commonly get from one and sixpence to two and sixpence per day.—Co. Cork.

5. Twelve shillings per week.—Co. Cork.

6. It averages about one and sixpence, but under some circumstances rises to two shillings.—Co. Galway.

7. As I give constant employment my wages vary but slightly, but farmers give as high as two shillings a day, frequently with feeding.—Co. Galway.

8. Constant labourers wages are raised from one and twopence to one and sixpence a day during harvest. Farmers who do not keep constant labourers pay two shillings, and sometimes two and fourpence a day for a few days in harvest.—Co. Kildare.

9. Average 18s per week.—Co. Kildare.

10. Two shillings per day with diet, is about the average.—Co. Kerry.

11. One and ninepence to two shillings per day.—Co. Kerry.

12. Generally one shilling and sixpence per day, and at times one and eightpence.—Co. Mayo.

13. From one and eightpence to two and sixpence per day.—Co. Meath.

14. Personally, or for my employers, I do not make much difference between harvest and other times, but small farmers pay as high as two shillings per diem, and even two and sixpence and give diet besides, in the extreme middle of harvest.—Co. Monaghan.

15. One and sixpence per day.—Co. Roscommon.

16. The rate of wages in harvest for men varied from 2s 6d to 3s 6d per day, and for women 1s 6d to 2s per day. I paid 2s 6d to men and 1s 8d to 2s to women for a short period last autumn.—Co. Tipperary.

17. From 1s 8d to 2s 6d with diet.—Co. Waterford.

18. Reapers get from 1s 6d to 2s 6d a day, binders (women) half the wages of the men; mowers, 3s to 4s a day, or an average of 3s per acre; binders, after the mowers, from 1s to 1s 6d a day.—Co. Waterford.

19. Two to 3s a day and diet.—Co. Wexford.

20. To mowers for cutting either hay or grain crops, from 3s to 3s 6d per day, sometimes diet added. To common labourers from 1s 6d to 2s, with diet.—Co. Limerick.

21. Twelve shillings a week for any additional labourers I am obliged to take in during harvest time.

22. Men mostly mow the corn in this locality at per day, average 3s 4d, cutting three roods of fair growing corn. When the men reap, 2s 4d per day ; when the above men are dieted for reaping, 1s 8s per day. Mowing, with diet, 2s 6d per day.

23. Last harvest the wages varied from 1s 6d to 2s 6d per day, the farmers adding diet.—Co. Tipperary.

Supply of Labour.

The next query related to a very important point, viz: the supply of labour. Although the answers I received indicate some difference of opinion, it is very evident that when proper wages are given, an ample supply of labour can be obtained in most localities, even in summer :—in winter there appears to be a redundancy of labour, and no difficulty anywhere, or at any time, where a permanent engagement is offered.

1. There is a difficulty in procuring labourers at the above rate of wages *unless for a permanent engagement*, which the time of year does not affect.—Co. Antrim.

2. I do not find much difficulty in procuring labourers generally, keeping my own staff, but men are more easily had in winter than in spring and harvest.—Co. Cork.

3. As a general rule there is not any difficulty in getting labourers.—Co. Cork.

4. Not for ordinary work, but for drainage it is dearer than in Scotland.—Co. Cork.

5. *In winter the supply of labourers is abundant.* There is no difficulty except during the seed sowing time in spring, haymaking and harvest, but plenty of men can be had during those times by giving an advance of wages.—Co. Carlow.

6. There is great difficulty in procuring labourers during the spring and summer months, *but not in the winter.*—Co. Galway.

7. The difficulty is increased and increasing, more especially

in the spring and summer months, when the younger class of labourers go to England.—Co. Galway.

8. Great difficulty in procuring able bodied men, both in summer and winter.—Co. Kildare.

9. No difficulty at any season except for turf cutting in May, and for a few weeks in harvest; generally speaking there is plenty of employment and men always to be got when required. —Co. Kildare.

10. There is no difficulty in procuring labourers, but not so great in the winter as in the summer. The wages are higher in spring than at any other period.—Co. Kerry.

11. I find it impossible to procure labourers for public work from the 10th March to the 1st June, except at advanced wages. *From 1st November to March there are enough to be had*, except in some thinly peopled districts.—Co. Kerry.

12. There is generally difficulty in procuring labourers in country parts. The difficulty is greater in summer than winter. —Co. Mayo.

13. *There is no difficulty during the winter season.* In summer there is a scarcity of labourers.—Co. Meath.

14. I have never found any difficulty in procuring labourers, though the farmers sometimes complain in all three districts. Wages are much higher to those who only give casual employment in spring and harvest than in mid winter or summer. The cheapest time is mid winter.—Co. Monaghan.

15. Some difficulty in spring and harvest.—Co. Roscommon.

16. Residing near the town of Nenagh I have not any difficulty in procuring labourers, they are not however as good a class of men as those regularly employed. *In winter many are not employed more than four days in the week.* In spring, summer, and autumn all are engaged at good wages. In the rural districts the farmers in some places complain that they cannot get labourers from there not being cottages. This in summer and harvest is much increased, and they are obliged to resort to the towns for male and female labour.—Co. Tipperary.

17. No great difficulty, less in winter than in summer. *At times there is a want of employment for able-bodied labourers.*— Co. Waterford.

18. No difficulty in procuring labourers except at harvest time.—Co. Waterford.

19. There is great difficulty in summer, none in winter.— Co. Wexford.

20. I having a regular staff of my own, and but little land now in tillage, do not experience much difficulty in procuring labourers. Any, however, that does exist, is much more felt in summer than in winter, *the farmers giving very little employment during the latter season.*—Co. Limerick.

21. Yes, out of the neighbourhood of towns and villages it is difficult to get labourers, particularly females ; and the difficulty is materially greater in summer than in winter.

22. Labourers can be procured at the above rate any season of the year, difficulty only in harvest.

23. Yes, considerable difficulty, not so great in winter as in summer.—Co. Tipperary.

(See also Mr. Robertson's observations on this point, *passim.*)

Allowances to Labourers.

As a low rate of wages is often compensated by allowances, I requested information on this head.

Subjoined are the answers I received :—

1. Men in charge of horses or cattle have free cottages on the farm.—Co. Carlow.

2. Men getting 7*s*, get house free and a ton of coals.—Co. Cork.

3. I give land for about half an acre of potato garden, for the manure they collect, turn out the manure, and plough the land free of any charge ; cottages free of rent, and help to draw fuel. —Co. Cork.

4. In some cases labourers get houses rent free, in addition to wages of 1*s* 2*d* a day or so. Working farmers frequently charge for houses, and sometimes pay a portion of the wages by giving their labourers some ground for potatoes, and pasture for a few sheep.—Co. Cork.

5. In a few cases my labourers hold a few acres of land, the rent of which is earned work.—Co. Galway.

6. In most cases in this district where resident proprietors employ labourers residing on their property, the rate of wages is lower, and allowances are made in the shape of lands, fuel, and rent-free cottages.—Co. Galway.

7. None.—Co. Kildare.

8. No, not in my own case, but the farmers pay in kind—part in money and rest in food; thus the wife and children at home are not half fed. Some charge double price for a hovel and rood of land; thus the labourer is defrauded.—Co. Kildare.

9. None.—Co. Kerry.

10. Many farmers pay part wages by cabins and gardens rent free, or rented at a charge allowed in account for labour. These rents always excessive in the value.—Co. Kerry.

11. Very seldom.—Co. Mayo.

12. A house, with an allowance of fuel, potatoes, milk, and butter.—Co. Meath.

13. None in any case.—Co. Monaghan.

14. Not generally. In many instances the farmer gives the use of a cottage and small garden to each of his labourers, at a nominal rent.—Co. Roscommon.

15. Several of my men have slated cottages which I built for them. I also give some fuel (turf), and to some of the most deserving a small quantity of ground, tilled and manured, in which they plant potatoes: this is along with my own tillage, for the cottages have not any land attached, merely yards with each.—Co. Tipperary.

16. There are some (but not a great many now) labourers employed by the tenant farmers who bring them about 3s a week, and give them a home and from a quarter to half an acre of land, rent free.

17. The men I employ get 1s 2d per day, with a cottage and a quarter of an acre of land, rent free.—Co. Waterford.

18. Not as a general rule, but farm labourers in the country houses and cottages at a moderate rent with a small garden. —Co. Waterford.

19. Sometimes a cottage is given.—Co. Wexford.

20. Free cottages and small gardens accompany the 1s per day from landlords I act for; when more land is given, a rent is generally deducted from the 1s per day.

21. None; save occasionally gratuities in the shape of fuel, etc., where circumstances indicate worthiness or necessity, occasioned by illness or such visitation.—Co. Limerick.

22. Yes; rent-free cottages, and in many instances small pieces of land for kitchen gardens.

23. None.—Co. Tipperary.

The Classes which have contributed to Emigration.

The next question I asked was as to whether Emigration was taking place, and of what classes it was composed.

1. There has, chiefly among the small farming class.—Co. Antrim.

2. Very great, consisting of miners, small landholders and their families, labourers and household servants, male and female, young, strong and healthy, and some few tradesmen.—Co. Carlow.

3. Some has, principally the sons and daughters, female farmers and labourers.—Co. Cork.

4. Considerable emigration goes on in this district, mostly farmer's sons and daughters and labourers.—Co. Cork.

5. Yes, labourers, artizans and farmer's sons. I receive rents in 41 parishes, and do not know of an occupier of over five acres of land emigrating for the last five years.—Co. Cork.

6. There has been considerable; the class of persons emigrating are the younger members of families, those who from youth, education, skill, and respectability, are most likely to succeed as emigrants; there are few cases where aged people emigrate.—Co. Galway.

7. There has been a steady and considerable emigration for the last few years, and chiefly amongst the most able-bodied men and women.—Co. Galway.

8. Extensive emigration of our best class of labourers.—Co. Kildare.

9. Very little, hardly ever a whole family, generally the sons or daughters of small farmers.—Co. Kildare.

10. There has been an enormous emigration within the last

fifteen years from this district, chiefly consisting of what I term *potato-tenants*. They were for the most part sent out in the first instance at the landlord's expense, when on the point of starvation, and now annually send home considerable sums of money to their friends, to induce them to join them in America.—Co. Kerry.

11. The emigration is up to the full proportion from Kerry as from the rest of Munster. The emigrants are nearly all of the labouring class, who have been sent for from America.—Co. Kerry.

12. Emigration has been considerable, chiefly of the junior members of families and the best of the labouring classes.—Co. Mayo.

13. The emigration has chiefly been of the labouring class, and a few small tenant farmers.—Co. Meath.

14. From this estate an enormous emigration took place in 1850 and 51, all of the poorest class of persons, very small farmers, and the wives and children of those who died in the famine. All these emigrated entirely at the expense of the landlord; but no evictions took place to enforce or encourage it.—Co. Kerry.

15. Yes; principally the class of servants and labourers.—Co. Roscommon.

16. The emigration from this neighbourhood has been great; very much confined to the young, strong, healthy, males and females of the farming class; in many instances entire families have gone.—Co. Tipperary.

17. There has been a moderate emigration, consisting chiefly of the labouring class, and some of the sons and daughters of the small farmers.—Co. Waterford.

18. Yes, very great, consisting of labourers and the younger sons and daughters of small farmers.—Co. Waterford.

19. Great numbers have emigrated of the most respectable and enterprising of the farming class, nearly all Protestants.—Co. Wexford.

20. Indeed, there has—very extensive emigration—a good deal composed of the small farmer class, but chiefly and in by far the greater proportion, the offspring of labourers and small tradesmen, who have had little or no land.—Co. Limerick.

21. There has been, of the labouring class and of the small farmers.

22. Chiefly of the labouring class.

23. There has been considerable emigration of the labouring class, and the sons and daughters of farmers.—Co. Tipperary.

Have the younger sons of a small Farmer any other alternative but Emigration, if their father's farm is already too small to be subdivided ?

1. It is not desirable to further subdivide the holdings, which are already so small, and as parents seldom put their sons to trades, no resource remains but emigration.—Co. Antrim.

2. None except enlisting in the army, or getting into the constabulary.—Co. Carlow.

3. In many cases I do not think that the younger sons of farmers had any other resource but emigration.—Co. Cork.

4. Not much.—Co. Cork.

5. Certainly not.—Co. Cork.

6. There are no manufactories or means of obtaining employment but that in connection with agricultural operations, and this leads to the subdivision of farms among the younger sons of farmers.—Co. Galway.

7. None whatever.—Co. Galway.

8. There is employment if they wished to avail themselves of it, but they generally prefer emigration.—Co. Roscommon.

9. No other resource was open to the younger sons of the farmers, who were not of themselves latterly anxious to subdivide their holdings, independent of the wish on the part of their landlords that they should not do so. A small sum enabled the young men to emigrate, and it was difficult, even on the payment of a large sum for the "good will" of a farm, to get one.—Co. Tipperary.

10. None. Except the ordinary trades in the neighbourhood, which afford only a limited field.—Co. Waterford.

11. If all the young men who left this neighbourhood for America or Australia for the last few years had learned to be carpenters or masons, they would have found employment.

Many are now going into the constabulary who would have emigrated had the pay not been increased.—Co. Kildare.

12. Scarcely any. A few with interest got railway appointments, but really a well educated lad finds it very difficult to get any appointment.—Co. Kildare.

13. None. Except to live at home as servant boy, and very few wish to do that.—Co. Kerry.

14. In this country the subdivision of holdings is scarce; but here are large tracts of mountain bog highly capable of improvement by drainage, &c. which would absorb much of the extra population. Yet emigration must still make room to a considerable extent.—Co. Mayo.

15. I endeavour in every way I can to discourage the subdivision of farms, and have succeeded in consolidating them to a very considerable extent. Under these circumstances the younger sons, who used to marry and subdivide, have now no other resource except emigration to America, emigration to England, which goes on to a large extent, to the northern districts, or to become "servant boys" to the farmers, for which there is a large and increasing demand.—Co. Monaghan.

16. A further subdivision of land is not at all desirable. The younger sons of farmers have scarcely any resource save emigration, there being but little trade and no manufactures in this locality.—Co. Waterford.

17. None that I know of.—Co. Wexford.

18. I consider it very undesirable to encourage further subdivision of land in this country, and though, as a rule, since subdividing has become so restricted, the younger sons of farmers have been greatly thrown on emigration, yet those who have saved money are to a considerable extent able to settle at home, by buying up small (often assumed) interests in farms which have fallen into arrear. This is very generally done through the medium of marriage, by which the outgoing party gets the fortune—the incoming either the husband or wife with the land—the outgoing people sometimes emigrate, sometimes embark in small and generally unprosperous shopkeeping in the next town.—Co. Limerick.

19. No.

20. I think they had, as tradesmen are becoming scarce, as

none of the young people have been bound to trades in my knowledge this last seven or eight years.

21. The younger sons of strong farmers emigrated because they saw no chance of getting farms, and those of small farmers did so because they did not wish to become casual labourers. Labourers emigrated because they could get better wages abroad than at home.—Co. Tipperary.

Has the Emigration been voluntary, or is it to be attributed to eviction, or to any pressure on the part of the landlord?

1. Almost in every instance the emigration has been voluntary and not attributed to eviction.—Co. Antrim.

2. Unquestionably, the greater part of the emigration has taken place without eviction or other interference of landlords.—Co. Carlow.

3. Evictions have very little to do with emigration. The majority of emigrants are farmers' sons and daughters and labourers and their families.—Co. Cork.

4. Not amongst occupiers of land.—Co. Cork.

5. The instances are rare, but I have known comfortable farmers dispose of and abandon their holdings to join relatives in Australia, &c. &c.—Co. Galway.

6. No.—Co. Galway.

7. The emigrants go of their own accord and without any pressure. I have been agent over properties in this county for 30 years and never knew a tenant emigrate from coercion.—Co. Kildare.

8. No. My experience is that no man will consent to surrender land, however small his holding, in order to emigrate, unless he and his family are on the point of starvation. In 1849 and 1850 they were on the point of starvation, and when the landlord offered them emigration free, they went in vast numbers.—Co. Kerry.

9. I am sure the great bulk of the emigrants have gone away from lands *not* evicted, and without even the knowledge of the landlords, and certainly without any pressure put upon them, and only in a very few cases have tenants been "bought out"

by the landlord at their own request mostly, or on being refused leave to subdivide.—Co. Kerry.

10. There are several instances of emigration perfectly voluntary.—Co. Mayo.

11. I have known many in the counties of Limerick and Clare, and also in my own district, who have emigrated of their own free will without any pressure put upon them by their landlords.—Co. Meath.

12. On this estate 3,500 (in round numbers) were emigrated at the landlord's expense, without a single case of eviction, or moral pressure to go. There were at that time (in 1849) 10,400 persons receiving relief in the Union, and about 3000 off this estate alone. I offered free emigration to any port they pleased in America to as many as chose to accept it, and give up their little plots of ground if they had any, to all who were in the unions *chargeable to the estate*, and I could scarcely meet my engagement, so fearful was the pressure upon me to avail themselves of my offer. They rushed out of the country as rats out of a den where certain starvation attended them, and at the rate of 200 per week I sent them out, insisting in every case that they should be admitted by the Guardians as paupers into the poor house as a test of poverty to qualify for this charity of emigration. They nearly swamped the house rushing in, but as fast as they did I sent them off at 200 heads per week. At last the plethora was relieved, and the Union of —— breathed freely. It cost the landlord £13,000; but the passage to America was cheap at that time; not one vessel was lost in which our emigrants went out.

13. Emigration in this part of the country is not confined to any particular locality, nor am I aware of the interference of any landlord having caused emigration.—Co. Roscommon.

14. Within the last few years I have known several cases of tenants emigrating of their own free will without any wish of the landlords that they should do so. In former years, 1848 to 1852, landlords encouraged emigration and afforded facilities to the smaller class of tenants to do so; it was then of advantage to both parties, as well as to the tenantry on the same estate, whose farms were enlarged thereby.—Co. Tipperary.

15. I know of no instances where the moral pressure referred to has been exercised to induce emigration, and I know many instances on areas where no evictions have taken place and in which emigration has nevertheless prevailed to a great extent.—Co. Waterford.

16. Most of the emigration from this district, except that which immediately followed the potato famine, has been of an entirely voluntary character.—Co. Waterford.

17. In almost every case the emigration was voluntary.—Co. Wexford.

18. I can furnish a tolerably long and perfectly authentic list of parties who have emigrated of their own accord.—Co. Limerick.

19. Numerous instances of emigration have taken place where evictions had nothing to do with them; but possibly where landlords would not allow subdivision, or sons or daughters, or nephews or nieces, to marry and bring wives or husbands to live in the houses of fathers and mothers, and then quarrel and seek to divide houses or lands, may have influenced many to emigrate.

20. A great many have emigrated on account of the name of high wages being in America.—Co. Tipperary.

21. Some portion of the emigration immediately after 1847, was certainly caused by small holders finding out that they could not get on when the potato crop became so uncertain.—Co. Cork.

22. The famine years of 1846, 1847, and 1848, proved the great uncertainty of the potato crop, and therefore vastly stimulated emigration.—Co. Galway.

23. I believe very few holders of land surrendered their farms in consequence of their inadequacy to support them when the potato was gone, because I believe very few surrendered their land until they were starving, and when they were starving they could not have had the means to pay for their passage to America. I believe that from 1846 to 1850, the chief proportion of emigrants consisted of the sons and daughters of small holders. Each family perhaps sending out one member, who soon sent for his or her brothers and sisters, and eventually, perhaps for the old people. I cannot

believe that many actual holders of land emigrated at all to America, for they would not think of going until all their own means were expended, and a very few landlords were sufficiently liberal to emigrate their potato-tenants when they became paupers. The general desire to emigrate, no doubt arose from the impression upon the minds of the people, that the potato being gone, the land was no longer able to support them. I speak above of the county *generally.* In this neighbood the landlord paid for the free emigration of about 3000 persons off his estate, most of whom had left their land, and gone into poor-houses, pressed by actual starvation, their small plots not being able to support them, unless through the means of the potato.

24. I am quite certain the failure of the potato was the cause. I know of many, very many cases in this County, Mayo, where the dividing and subdividing before the famine reduced the holdings to about $3\frac{1}{2}$ statute acres of arable land, when as a matter of course when the potato went, all went.—Co. Mayo.

25. The emigration was occasioned by the small holders discerning they could not exist on their plots of land without the assistance of the potato.—Co. Monaghan.

26. The failure of the potato. Besides they had encouragement from friends and hope of better wages by emigration.—Co. Roscommon.

27. I have no hesitation in giving my opinion that "the loss of the potato" occasioned the first great emigration, and in which the landlords aided the small tenants. But of late years a different cause produced the emigration of a better class.—Co. Tipperary.

28. Small tenants on poor land, especially found themselves without the means of either paying rent or supporting themselves.—Co. Waterford.

Arable v. Pasture.

The next question referred to a point which has been the subject of a good deal of angry controversy, viz: the circumstances which occasionally lead to the conversion of arable land into pasture.

Among the various other accusations with which Irish proprietors have been assailed, has been that of driving their tenantry from their estates, in order to lay down the vacated farms in grass, and it has been broadly asserted that they were gradually converting the island into one large cattle farm. I do not myself reside in a district suitable for pasture, and therefore I am not so competent to deal with this question as those who live in the great Pasture Counties, but, in the first place, there are statistics, which prove that this excessive conversion of Tillage into Pasture has not taken place at all; while, in the next, the subjoined replies on the subject from persons residing in different parts of Ireland, and not in communication with one another, show in a most decisive manner, that the recent tendency to change from crops to grass, which has been exhibited during the last three or four years, is not to be attributed to any direct or indirect interference on the part of the landlord, but to the natural inclination of the tenant to apply his land to the most remunerative uses.

In 1849, the total number of acres under crops in Ireland amounted to 5,543,748; while in 1866 they were 5,519,678, showing a decrease in 27 years of exactly 24,070 acres.*

---

* An attempt has been made to show that in 1841 there were 7,000,000 of acres under cultivation in Ireland, and that the estimated value of the crops amounted to £50,000,000; this absurd delusion has been already dealt with by Dr. Hancock, whose observations on the subject I subjoin.

"It has been alleged in the House of Commons -

"That the agricultural returns showed that in the year 1841, the number of acres under cultivation was 7,000,000, while in 1862 it was only 5,781,000."

During the whole of the last decade, so far from there being an inclination to lay down tillage land in grass, the

---

From this statement it would naturally be supposed that there was some system of collecting agricultural returns in 1841 similar to that by which the number quoted in 1862 was obtained; but such is not the fact. The collection of the agricultural statistics of Ireland was commenced in 1847, and hence I have commenced my tables with that year.

Again, it might be supposed that this information was obtained by the Census Commissioners in 1841; but no such returns were obtained by the Census Commissioners in 1841.

The Census Commissioners in 1841 obtained information of the number of cattle, and size of farms, and the total extent of *arable land*, as distinguished from waste, but no information as to number of *acres under crops*. The alleged number of 7,000,000 acres under crops in 1841 was not ascertained by official returns, and as a private estimate it is, to my mind, incredible.

From 1841 there was no extensive change in the way land was held or cropped up to 1846, so that it is safe to assume that there were as many acres under crop in 1846 as in 1841. Now, it was ascertained by careful investigation, in the collection of agricultural statistics, that there were 5,238,575 acres under crops of all kinds in 1847. Any person who had any general acquaintance with the country in 1846 and 1847, knows that 1,761,425 acres of land did not go out of cultivation in the spring of 1847.

The estimated acreage for flax may be assumed to be pretty accurate, as also may be the acreage added for turnips and hay, for, as live stock was much less numerous in 1841 than in 1849, and as potatoes were in 1841 largely grown and very productive, the acreage under hay and turnips would be much less in 1841 than in 1849.

If the corrections referred to be introduced into Mr. M'Culloch's estimate, and assuming that Mr. M'Culloch's estimate in 1846 is the authority for the estimate under discussion, the estimate of 7,000,000 acres under crops in 1841 is reduced to 5,587,141 acres, a less number than has been

tendency has been all in the opposite direction, and in 1860 there were actually 400,000 more acres under crops than there were in 1850. Since then, however, circum-

ascertained to have been under crops in any year since 1850, with the exception of 1854; and less, to the extent of 382,698 acres, than the maximum of 5,970,139 acres under crops in 1860. Thus the worthlessness of the argument for progressive decline, founded on the decrease of land under crops, is rendered manifest.

An allegation has been made that the crops in 1841 were of the estimated value of £50,000,000. This is to be rejected as unworthy of serious consideration. There were no official returns of produce in 1841; and when the private estimates of acreage seem to be so erroneous, private estimates of produce must be still less to be relied on.

It appears from a general view of all the Tables of acreage under crops, that in the year 1860 there were devoted to the growth of cereals, flax, potatoes, turnips, and other green crops, nearly as many acres as in 1849, and nearly 300,000 acres more than in 1847; to the growth of hay and clover, upwards of 400,000 acres more than in 1847 or 1849. There were in pasturage in 1860, probably upwards of 1,200,000 acres more than in 1847.

Thus, while pasturage has increased, it is not by subtraction from the total quantity of land formerly devoted to the growth of crops, but by the reclamation of land which in 1841 was considered as improvable waste.

In 1841 there were in Ireland 13,464,301 acres of arable land, whilst in 1860 the arable land of Ireland had increased to 15,400,000 acres, showing an addition of nearly 2,000,000 productive acres.

The population have not been changed from agricultural labourers into cattle-herds, as alleged by some, but extended cattle farming has been added to the previous amount of cultivation of cereals, potatoes, turnips, and flax. So far, therefore, as the industry of man is concerned, there has been no decrease in the cultivation of the soil.

W. N. Hancock, LL.D., Alleged Decline of Irish Prosperity.

stances have again led the farmer to recur to pasture ; an inclination to be referred, first to the enormous losses they sustained on their cereal crops through a succession of three extraordinarily wet seasons, and which have been estimated by Dr. Hancock as amounting to several millions ;* and, secondly, to the enhanced prices, both of wool and stock, which have prevailed during the last three or four years.†

The rise in the price of labour may also have had something, though very little, to do with it, but if the Irish farmer can only grow grain to a profit on condition that his labourers are as miserably paid as in former days,‡ he had better give up the attempt.

There is one point, however, connected with this subject, which has not escaped the acute observation of Dr. Neilson Hancock, it is well worthy of consideration, viz :— that the increase of our green crops has not been commensurate with the increase of our sheep and cattle, implying a very rude and unsatisfactory style of farming,

---

* It thus appears that the annual losses of farmers on the four chief products of oats, wheat, potatoes, and cattle, may be estimated as follows :—From July, 1860, to July, 1861, at £4,544,147 ; from July, 1861, to July, 1862, at £10,360,049 ; from July, 1862, to July, 1863, at £12,109,750. The loss in cattle was consequent on a hay famine.

† Total value of live stock in 1863 £30,050,671
      „   „   1866 £35,178,040

               Increase in 3 years £5,127,369

‡ "The evidence already given to Parliament shows that the average wages of a labouring man in Ireland (and the great mass of the poor are labourers), is worth scarcely *three pence a day.* Three pence a day for such as obtain employment, whilst in a family where one or two persons are employed, there may be four, perhaps six, others, dependent on these two for their support."—*Dig. Dev. Com.*

which he is disposed to attribute to the discouragement to high farming, entailed by the absence of leases.

I now subjoin the answers I received to my queries as to whether the conversion of arable into pasture, wherever such conversion was taking place, was to be attributed to the direct or indirect influence of the landlord, or to the prospect of profit afforded by the rise in the price of stock.*

Conversion of Arable into Pasture.

1. In no way to be attributed to landlord influence.—Co. Antrim.

2. Certainly not to the former. I do not know of any case in which a landlord interfered either directly or indirectly: the tenants do so of their own accord.—Co. Carlow.

3. I don't think it is to be attributed to the direct or indirect influence of the landlord. It is produced by the natural inclination of the occupier of the land acting in the way which he thinks most to his advantage.—Co. Cork.

4. The natural inclination of the tenant.—Co. Cork.

5. I don't think it is influenced by the landlord, the tenant thinks it more his interest to do so.—Co. Cork.

6. One circumstance that led largely to the conversion of arable into tillage land in this district was the famine of 1846 to 1848, and the subsequent insecurity of rent which threw into the landlord's hands an extent of land that he could only deal with in pasture. This was a corn growing country before the repeal of the Corn Laws—and the exports of corn from Galway was

---

* *Increase of Stock since 1860.*

	1860.	1866.	Increase.
Pigs	1,271,072	1,493,523	222,451
Sheep	3,542,080	4,270,027	728,947

The hay famine of 1859 led to a great decrease in the number of cattle, from which, during the last three years, we have been rapidly recovering:—

	1863.	1866.	Increase.
Cattle	3,144,231	3,742,932	597,701

very large—no corn is now exported, it will not pay to grow it for export, and as the price of stock has increased the natural inclination of the tenants is to convert the land as far as possible into pasture.—Co. Galway.

7. It is attributable chiefly to the difficulty of getting labourers—a landlord has nothing to do with it, besides the Irish tenant has not capital to stock land and must till it. The Irish tenant has to take his capital *out* of the farm in place of putting *it into* it.—Co. Kildare.

8. Owing to the high price of stock.—Co. Kildare.

9. The tenant is led of his own inclination.—Co. Kerry.

10. It is to be attributed to the influence of the landlord in preventing congestion to the labouring class for fear of pauperism, but mainly to the natural inclination of the tenant as living in accordance with what he considers his interest, which is produced by the scarcity of labourers preventing profitable tillage—and from the high price of butter and cattle for the last ten or twelve years. The butter produce of this country is worth three times the government valuation, £277,000= £831,000.—Co. Kerry.

11. Not from any influence of the landlord, but from the low price of corn and high price of sheep and cattle.—Co. Mayo.

12. The landlords have not used any influence directly or indirectly on very many estates, of which I have a personal knowledge.—Co. Meath.

13. Entirely to the natural inclination of the tenant in the counties alluded to, partly from the high price of stock and wool as compared with corn, and partly from the increase in the rate of wages, and in harvest, the difficulty on an emergency of procuring sufficient hands.—Co. Monaghan.

14. It is done at the free will of the tenant.—Co. Roscommon.

15. I do not think that either directly or indirectly the " landlord" influence gave any impetus to that tendency, or that the land was thrown into grazing from any advice or suggestion expressed by the landlords: it was unlikely they would so interfere with their tenants: for if matters turned out contrary to the interest of the latter in the way of making money: give the opportunity of saying, " You advised it so," the natural interest of the tenant to manage his land as he considered

it would pay him best, was, I think, the cause of the large proportion of the land being converted into pasture, another cause was, the land being given up to, or taken up by the landlords, who in many cases held it for a short time, unimproved, then let it to a class of farmers who had realized some money by grazing and who did not break it up, either to clear it or manure it.—Co. Tipperary.

16. To the high price of stock, particularly where the tenant gets any assistance from the landlord, to do so either by an allowance, for manure, or grass seeds, or for the purchase of stock.—Co. Waterford.

17. Where this tendency has shown itself, it has been solely in accordance with the tenant's own wish and interests — Co. Waterford.

18. Entirely owing to the natural inclinations of the tenantry, and the growing experience of its advantages : I do not believe the landlords have exercised any influence in this respect..—Co. Limerick.

19. The landlord's influence has nothing to do with it— none is exercised—the tenant studies his own interests; he wishes to avoid employing labourers and take advantage of the prices for live stock.

20. To the natural inclinations of the tenant acting in accordance with what he considers his interest.

21. Inclination of the tenant to make the most he can of his lands.—Co. Tipperary.

22. It is principally to be attributed to the high price of stock.—Co. Carlow.

23. To high prices.—Co. Cork.

24. The increased value of stock, wool, and butter, and *the uncertainty of corn growing in wet seasons* are the chief causes for the increase of pasture, but the advance in the price of labour has something to do with it also.—Co. Cork.

25. Chiefly on account of the high price of stock : two ewes will make as much as a statute acre of oats, and with one twentieth the cost. An acre of land that will only support two ewes will produce only about fourteen cwt. of oats, which at 1s per stone, £5. 12s, two ewes will yield £5. 10s in lambs and wool. I have tried them on the same land.—Co. Cork.

26. High prices.—Co. Galway.

27. The price of stock, as compared with agricultural produce has had some influence.—Co. Galway.

28. Increased pasturage is certainly to be attributed to the rise in stock, butter, and wool more than to anything else.—Co. Kerry.

29. The increase in the price of stock.—Co. Kerry.

30. The price of stock, and in addition to the dearness of labour, which from the actual increase in wages and disinclination for honest work is enhanced nearly 100 per cent.—Co. Mayo.

31. Certainly to the causes named, combined with discouragement from bad harvests, and what is called "scarcity of labour." *But this is only called so by those who recollect when labour was a drug in the market.*—Co. Monaghan.

32. Prices always affect the course farmers pursue in the management of their farms.—Co. Roscommon.

33. The advance in price of stock, butter, and wool, coupled with the low prices at which corn (especially wheat, though not generally a heavy crop) of all kinds, ranged for the last few years, and the natural inclination of every man to turn to the mode by which he could realize most profit from land, were the chief causes of the change from agriculture to pasture, coupled with the advanced price of labour.—Co. Tipperary.

34. Partly owing to the rise in the price of stock and butter in this locality.—Co. Waterford.

35. The rise in the price of stock, butter, and wool no doubt has weighed with the farmer in converting arable into pasture in conjunction with the uncertainty of profitable tillage.—Co. Waterford.

36. The bad seasons and the high price of stock.

37. These circumstances have certainly been great incentives to the adoption of the change referred to.

38. Mainly the high prices attainable, and the non-employment of labourers were great inducements.—Co. Tipperary.

Whether the existing proportion between the areas under crops and under cattle in Ireland, viz., 5,600,000 acres of tillage to 10,000,000 acres of pasture be the best, is a question which

I do not feel in a position to discuss. It is equally a matter beyond the competence of Parliament to determine. But the very fact of that proportion having been so long maintained, would seem to prove it very suitable to the climate, the soil, and the agricultural exigencies of the country.

Of course it is very evident that a greater number of persons can be provided with employment on tillage than on pasture, but if this argument is of any weight, it is as applicable to the 17,000,000 acres of pasture in England and Wales, as it is to the 10,000,000 acres of pasture in Ireland; at all events, in considering the present situation of Ireland, we must accept such conditions as we find established, and found our conclusions on a basis of fact, and not on speculative contingencies which may never occur.

That a large extent of pasture is an essential element in a prosperous system of agriculture, is well noted by M. de Laveleye in the following observations:—

"Pour l'entretien du bétail, l'Angleterre a l'avantage énorme d'avoir la moitié de son territoire en prairies naturelles, qui n'occupent en Flandre que la sixième partie du sol."

Eco. Rur. p. 93.

"Il faut cependant remarquer que l'infériorité de la Belgique sous ce rapport provient surtout du peu d'étendue relative des prairies naturelles, auxquelles son sol ne se prête guère. Elles n'occupent que le cinquième de la surface productive, au lieu de la moitié, comme dans les îles Britanniques; or c'est là un avantage énorme pour celles-ci, car cette grande proportion de bons herbages favorise l'entretien d'un nombreux bétail et par suite facilite singulièrement une exploitation rationnelle de terres arables."—*Eco. Rur.* p. 224.

APPENDIX.

Rate of Subdivision of Land in France.
(*See p.* 220.)

Although the statements in the text and notes of the preceding chapter, convey what I believe to be a correct estimate of some of the characteristics of French agriculture as signalized by many eminent authorities, it is well to mention that great difficulty seems to exist in obtaining perfectly accurate data with respect to the rate at which the subdivision of land has been going on of late years in France. As I have no personal acquaintance with the subject, I have thought it fair to subjoin an extract from the work of a very distinguished French writer who denies that the disintegration of landed property has either been so great or so disastrous as is alleged. He founds his conclusions on the results of a partial "recensement des cadastres" which took place in 1851. The justice of his views however, are, I understand, disputed.

"Tandis qu'en France la population générale, durant le laps de temps écoulé entre les anciens et les nouveaux cadastres, s'est accrue de 18 p. 100, le nombre des cotes foncières dans les localités où les opérations cadastrales ont été renouvelées ne s'est élevé que d'un peu moins de 11 p. 100, et, déduction faite de celles des cotes nouvelles qui proviennent, soit des aliénations de domaines publics, soit de distractions de portions du sol sur lesquelles il a été bâti, cette augmentation n'a certainement pas excédé la proportion de 7 p. 100.

"En ce qui touche les parcelles, le nombre n'en a augmenté que d'un peu moins de 1 et demi p. 100, et, comme il faut faire la part des parcellements dus les uns aux ventes de domaines publics, les autres à l'établissement de maisons et de constructions nouvelles là surtout où les populations se sont agglomérées davantage, il est vraisemblable que, dans les cantons et communes où le cadastre a été renouvelé, le territoire agricole ne contient plus autant de parcelles qu'il en contenait il y a trente-deux ans."

The point is but of secondary importance to our inquiry. Every one admits that the subdivision of land in France is frequently excessive, and no one would pretend that because a very minute comminution of the soil is compatible with agricultural prosperity in France, it would necessarily be advantageous in Ireland.

The Progress of French Agriculture.

No fairer statement of the progress of French agriculture can probably be found than in the subjoined passage from the work upon the subject by M. de Lavergne. Yet, though evidently anxious to take as favourable a view as possible, M. de Lavergne is forced to admit that France is still, "Three quarters of a century behind England."

"De tout ce qui précède résulte le tableau suivant pour le partage du produit brut par hectare.

	1789.	1815.	1859.
Rente du Propriétaire	12 fr.	18 fr.	30 fr.
Bénéfice de l'exploitant	5	6	10
Frais accessoires	1	2	5
Impôts fonciers et dîmes	7	4	5
Salaires	25	30	50
Total	50 fr.	60 fr.	100 fr.

"Ces progrès suffisent pour nous inspirer un légitime orgueil et une juste confiance dans l'avenir; mais nous ne devons jamais oublier qu'ils auraient fut être au moins doublés puisque nous avons perdu la moitié environ du temps écoulé depuis la révolution. Un pays voisin, chez qui les principes de 1789 ont été, malgré quelques exceptions apparentes, plus anciennement et plus constamment appliqués que chez nous, a fait dans le même laps de temps des progrès plus rapides encore. En 1789, le Royaume-Uni avait 13 millions et demi d'habitants; il en a aujourd'hui bien près de 30, sans compter plusieurs millions d'Anglais répandus dans les colonies; sa population a donc plus que doublé tandis que la nôtre ne s'est accrue que d'un tiers. Il ne nous a pas fallu moins de soixante dix ans pour défricher deux millions d'hectares de landes, supprimer la moitié de nos jachères, doubler nos produits ruraux, accroître la population de 30 pour 100, le salaire de 100 pour 100, la rente de 150 pour 100. A ce compte, il nous faudrait encore trois quarts de siècle pour arriver au point où en est aujourd'hui l'Angleterre."

Economie Rurale de la France, p. 59.
M. L. de Lavergne, 1861.

GENERAL APPENDIX.

In connection with the subject considered in the foregoing pages, the subjoined remarks by Dr. Longfield on the Irish Land Question are well worthy of consideration.

VALUATION.

The capacity of land employed in agriculture to yield rent depends on the excess of the annual produce above the annual outlay necessary to secure that produce. Every circumstance therefore, that tends to increase the amount or value of the produce, or that reduces the necessary or useful annual outlay, will increase the rent, or value of the land. No one, therefore, can form a correct judgment of the value of a farm by the mere examination of the land, however carefully and skilfully that examination may be made. But although the knowledge to be acquired by such an examination is not sufficient, yet it is a necessary preliminary to the formation of a correct judgment of the value of land.

Few persons are aware of the difficulty of this examination. It is not easy to compare several different farms as instruments of production, for the nature of the several products may be altogether unlike. One farm may be most profitably employed in raising wheat, another in fattening heavy bullocks, a third in flax, a fourth in green crops, turnips, mangolds, or potatoes. In each case it is the most profitable course of cultivation, according to the skill of the farmer that determines the value of the land. Its capacity under any less profitable course of cultivation has little or no effect upon the value. Thus, if we are to compare two farms which are most profitably employed as old pasture, it would be almost useless to know their relative powers of producing wheat or flax. Still the inquiry must be made, for it may turn out that the present mode of cultivation is not the best adapted to the nature of the soil. The land that at present yields indifferent wheat may produce admirable and profitable crops of flax, and thus enable the cultivators to pay a fair rent, and reap a handsome profit. The valuator must, therefore, be a skilful farmer, able to form a probable estimate of the results of the various modes of cultivation which may be adopted by a tenant of ordinary intelligence.

What is most generally proposed is, that every tenant should be entitled to a valuation of his farm, and to hold his land for ever at a rent to be determined by such valuation. Nothing can be more unjust than to substitute a valuation for a contract; but the injustice is not manifest at first sight, for the words appear fair. Why, it is said, should any tenant be required to pay more than the fair value for his farm? But every one who has any experience knows that nothing can be more uncertain and undetermined than the valuation of land. It is not uncommon to see two valuators differing enormously in their estimates, and yet neither suffering in reputation as if he had made a discreditable mistake. In this case all the mistakes would be made in favour of the tenant. If any mistake were made against him the remedy would be in his own hands, as he would not take the land; but indeed no such mistake would be made, for there would be a constant leaning in favour of the tenant. It is certain that the value as fixed under any tenant-right measure would be less than half the fair rent which a solvent tenant would willingly pay for the land. It is obvious that as soon as the possession of land ceased to be a subject of contract by mutual agreement, the valuators would have no average market value to refer to, and would form their estimates on the wildest principles.

Waiving for a moment all objections to the injustice of this proceeding, the question still arises, would it be of any benefit to the farmers as a class? Of course the individuals at present in possession would gain a pecuniary advantage, by being permitted to break their contracts, and confiscate the property of their landlords. But what would be the position of future tenants? A farmer has a lease for twenty-one years at a rent of £100 a year. By the proposed tenant-right he gets it for ever at a rent of £50. But if he or his son wishes to change his residence, and follow some other pursuit, does any man suppose that he will let it to a tenant, to have it valued on the tenant-right scheme? No. He would know that this would be to give away his property to a stranger. He will sell his tenant-right probably for £1500, and his successor will substantially have to pay not £50, but £125 a year for the land; viz. £50 for the rent, and £75 interest on the capital expended in the purchase of the tenant-right. Entering upon the land with crippled means, the capital that might have been more usefully employed in the cultivation of the soil having been expended in the purchase of the tenant-right, he will have reason to regret the change in the law which prevented him from dealing directly with the head landlord. The change as to all future farmers would be equivalent to a law, that no man should be permitted to occupy land as a farmer, except on the payment of a heavy fine. On the effect of this change on the cultivation of land there is not room for much difference of opinion. Adam Smith * thus describes the effects:—" Some landlords, instead of raising the rent, take a fine for the renewal of the lease. This practice is in most cases the expedient of a spendthrift, who for a sum of ready money sells a future revenue of much greater value. It is in most cases therefore hurtful to the landlord. It is frequently hurtful to the tenant, and it is always hurtful to the community. It frequently takes from the tenant so great a part of his capital, and thereby diminishes so much his ability to cultivate the land, that he finds it more difficult to pay a small rent, than it otherwise would have been to pay a great one. Whatever diminishes his ability to cul-

* Wealth of Nations, Book v. chap. 2.

tivate necessarily keeps down, below what it would otherwise have been, the most important part of the revenue of the community. By rendering the tax upon such fines a good deal heavier than upon the ordinary rent, this hurtful practice might be discouraged, to the no small advantage of the different parties concerned—of the landlord, of the tenant, of the sovereign, and of the whole community." This "hurtful practice," which Adam Smith wished to discourage by increased taxation, would under the tenant-right system become the necessary universal practice throughout all Ireland. No tenant could obtain the possession of land without the payment of a considerable fine, the only difference being that the fine should be paid to the preceding tenant instead of the landlord, a difference not affecting his interests, or the interests of the public. It would most usually happen that the fine or purchase money exacted would be so large that the incoming tenant must have recourse to a loan to raise the greater part of it. The condition of the new tenants would then be this, that he would hold his land for ever at a moderate rent, but on the other hand he would have been deprived of all the capital with which he could have cultivated it successfully, and in addition he will be subject to the payment of interest to the mortgagee of an annual sum which, with the rent he pays, would make at least the full value of the land. In any season of distress he would feel the difference between having the landlord or the mortgagee as his creditor. The labouring classes would be great sufferers by this change. The inferior cultivation of the land would diminish the amount of profitable employment for their labour, and reduce wages. The change would increase the disadvantages under which poorer men or men of small capital unavoidably labour. At present, if a man possesses a small capital, and some agricultural skill and energy, he may hope to procure a farm of sufficient extent to employ all his capital with profit. But on the proposed new system, he should expend the greater part of his capital in the purchase of a very small farm, and reserve a small remnant only for profitable employment At the same time the poorer man could never hope to rise above the condition of a common day labourer, as he never could save enough of money both to buy a farm and cultivate it.

And while no class of persons would derive any advantage from the proposed change, it may be fairly asked why should the landlords be robbed of their clear rights, for the benefit not of any class, but of the individuals merely who happen at present to be the occupying tenants? If the landlords are to be robbed it should be done for the benefit of the community at large, and not of any individuals; least of all, the individuals who alone would benefit by the proceeding. Their only claim is this: they say that too hard a bargain has been made. But no deceit has been practised on them, they entered into the contract voluntarily and ought to abide by it. But if they are entitled to any redress, the only just remedy would be to rescind the contract of which they complain to let them give back the land to the landlord, and be free from all future liability to pay rent.

THE CUSTOM OF TENANT RIGHT IN ULSTER.

In connection with the subject of tenant right I have thought it advisable to append a portion of my evidence on the Ulster Custom before Mr. Maguire's Committee in 1864.

* * * *

960. *Chairman.*] Is it your impression that agriculture is in a very flourishing condition in Ireland, or that it is in a very backward condition?—There can be no doubt that agriculture in Ireland is in a backward condition, and that it is more backward in some parts of the country than in others; but I think that even in the most advanced parts of Ireland the agriculture is inferior to the agriculture in the best districts of England and Scotland.

961. Would you say that agriculture is more advanced in the

province of Ulster than in other parts of Ireland?—I do not think it would do to say in Ulster generally, because there are parts of Ulster in which the agriculture is in as backward a condition as in any other part of Ireland; but the largest proportion of good agriculture in Ireland I should say was in Ulster.

962. In what portions of Ulster would you say?—In my own county, the county of Down, in Armagh, Monaghan, part of Antrim, part of Tyrone, and part of Donegal.

963. To what amongst other reasons would you attribute the more advanced condition of agriculture in those portions of Ulster?—I believe, but of course it is only my impression, and I cannot go beyond that, that the inhabitants of those portions of Ireland in which agriculture is superior are more industrious than the inhabitants of other parts of Ireland where agriculture is in a less forward state; and I also believe that the relations subsisting, and which have subsisted for years between the landlords and the tenantry in those parts where the agriculture is in a forward condition, have been upon the whole better than in those parts of the country where the agriculture is now in a less forward condition.

964. In those parts of the country to which you allude does the custom of tenant-right exist?—Yes.

965. Will you have the goodness to explain to the Committee what is meant by tenant-right?—Certainly. But perhaps, in connection with my last answer, in order that its effect may not be misunderstood if followed by the question which you have addressed to me, I think it right to state that I should not be disposed to attribute those good relations subsisting between the tenantry and the landlords of the north of Ireland to the existence of tenant-right, but that the existence of what is called the custom of tenant-right has been the consequence of those good relations.*

966. Is tenant-right a matter of recent origin, or has it

---

* Although the custom of Tenant Right has been established as a custom by the moderation and fair dealing of the Ulster landlords, the loyalty of the tenantry to each other has contributed to its maintenance. A landlord who was considered to have treated an outgoing-tenant with injustice would find difficulty in getting another tenant to take the farm.

existed for a considerable time in those counties?—I think the custom of tenant-right is a very difficult one either to describe or to explain, and perhaps very few people would be disposed to agree as to its historical origin. The custom may be, I think, thus defined: Tenant-right is a custom under which the tenant farmers of the north of Ireland, or, at all events, in those districts where that custom prevails, expect when they have occasion to give up possession of their farms, that their landlords will allow them to obtain from the incoming tenant such a sum as shall remunerate them for their improvements upon those farms. But at the same time, though I think that that is a perfectly legitimate definition of the custom of tenant-right as now understood, there is undoubtedly another element which exists, and which influences the operation which I have described. But the element is a very impalpable one, because, although of late, since the question has been agitated and the real elements of tenant-right have been analysed by public discussion, even the farmers themselves will describe their claim as a claim on account of improvements, there can be no doubt that the sums which were paid by the incoming tenant to the outgoing tenant very often had no relation whatever to the real value of those improvements, and the thing sold, instead of being called the tenant-right of a farm, which is now the term generally applied to it, used more commonly to be called the good-will of the farm, and under that designation I think a different thing would be understood than a payment made for the value of the improvements into the enjoyment of which the incoming tenant was about to enter. I think under the term "goodwill" would be recognised something approaching to what I may call "black mail," paid by the incoming tenant to the outgoing tenant, in order to induce the outgoing tenant not to interfere with his quiet possession of the farm.*

969. And do not you think that the existence of that sense of security is necessary to the proper development of the resources of the soil?—Yes, I think that the existence of the

---

* An incoming-tenant having paid an exorbitant sum to his predecessor, excused himself to Mr. Curling, on the plea "That he would sooner have his blessing than his curse." See Mr. Curling's evidence.

custom of tenant-right has upon the whole, in a certain sense, been a benefit to the north of Ireland, though in another sense it has not been a benefit. I do not think that I am prepared to balance the advantages or disadvantages which have resulted from that custom; but this I am quite prepared to say, that so far as tenant-right represents the custom under which the landlords of the north of Ireland have been in the habit of allowing the outgoing tenant to receive from the incoming tenant a fair compensation for the permanent improvements which he shall have placed on the farm during the time of his tenancy, and for which he shall not have had time to recoup himself, the custom has been an excellent one; but so far as tenant-right is a custom under which, without any reference whatever to the improvements into the possession of which the new tenant is about to enter, he has been in the habit of paying over to the outgoing tenant an enormous sum of money, amounting sometimes to 10, 15, or, I believe, even 20 years' purchase of the rent, the custom is a most unfortunate one.

970. Whatever uncertainty you might have as to the advantages or disadvantages of tenant-right are the Committee to understand you that you have no difficulty in forming an opinion as to the necessity of giving an industrious tenant compensation for improvements, in case of his eviction or the termination of his tenancy?—Certainly; I have a strong opinion upon that point. It seems to me that if a landlord invites a tenant to cultivate a farm, and if a general custom pervades the country, under which it is understood that a tenant at the expiration of his tenancy shall obtain a certain sum of money in consideration of his improvements, a moral obligation rests upon the landlord to see that a tenant who, we will say, expends a capital of £100. in the erection of a house, should, at the expiration of his tenancy, even though that tenancy should be of a great number of years' duration, obtain a fair amount of compensation.

971. Would you give him the full value of what remains of the improvement at the termination of his tenancy?—As a matter of private arrangement between myself and my own tenants, and as my private opinion, I am inclined to think that a tenant who has built a house, even though he should remain in the occupation of a farm upon which that house was built,

and in the enjoyment of the premises so constructed, for 60 or 70 years, would be entitled, at the expiration of his tenancy, to receive the actual amount which the buildings at that period might be worth; always provided that the landlord, before the house was built, or while the house was building, did not make any intimation to him that he was doing anything contrary to his wishes, or did not put him upon his guard. But in regard to improvements of a different description, such improvements as may be said to repay to the tenant the capital which he has expended, together with a fair interest upon that capital, within certain periods, I think that the scale of compensation ought to be regulated by such a system as I believe is adopted in Scotland and in England under similar circumstances.

972. Would you explain your views a little more fully with regard to such an improvement as a building, or other permanent improvement?—For instance, I think that a house probably at the end of 60 years, if kept in proper repair, would still be worth a very large proportion of the sum originally put upon it, and the tenant, on the supposition of 90 years being the proper term for a building lease, may not have had an opportunity of recouping himself for the expenditure which had thus taken place, as far as the house was concerned; or, again, we will take the case of a tenant who has settled on a very stony district; that tenant, at the time he originally entered into the occupation of the farm, will have found it worth almost nothing, but by dint of removing the stones, and either burying them or building walls with them sometimes, as I have seen them, eight feet broad and six feet high, will have converted what was comparatively worthless land into not very valuable land, but still land of a certain amount of value. I think, under those circumstances, that the tenant's claim would not lapse within the same period in which his claim for such improvements as draining, &c. would have lapsed, and that, therefore, a different scale of compensation must be applied to the one class of improvements from that applied to the other.

973. Would you, at the termination of his tenancy, consider the full value of the improvement, such as it then existed?— No. I think that even with regard to a case of that kind, you must admit the principle that the tenant's claim for compensa-

tion would undergo some amount of lapse; because it is to be supposed that when he made those improvements they were intended to be, and that they actually were, remunerative improvements, though it might take a longer term of occupancy for him to acquire the remuneration.

976. Do you consider that the want of that necessity for supplying a stimulus to the tenancy of the north of Ireland is to be accounted for by the existence of tenant-right which secures them, to a great extent, not only in the possession of their land, but in the enjoyment of the fruit of their industry?—I think that if the matter comes to be very closely examined, you must not attribute this feeling of security exactly to tenant-right; I think you must attribute it to the good understanding which has always prevailed between the tenants and the landlords of the north of Ireland, of which the custom of tenant-right is the exponent.

998. *Chairman.*] Is not that class of farms (small farms) on the decrease?—Yes, very much; for instance, the career of a tenant of that description is something of this kind. In the first place he has very frequently either run into debt, or exhausted his stock of ready money by the original purchase of his farm; he has probably a large family: if his sons grow up they do not like to go out as labourers, they prefer assisting him in the cultivation of the farm. He is not able to buy a sufficient number of cattle, and the limits of the farm are not sufficiently large to enable him to keep them with advantage. In all probability, he owes a considerable amount of money to his neighbours, and year by year he gets a little in arrear to his landlord. One year he perhaps pulls up a portion of that arrear; the next, he falls back into it again, and so it goes on from bad to worse, until at last he comes to me and says that he wishes to give up his farm.

1007. You do not think that a short lease is sufficient to compensate the tenant for his outlay in improving the land?—I think it is a self-evident proposition that the improvements of a farm being of two descriptions, the one self-compensating, and actually returning more than the original expenditure into the tenant's pocket, and the other not possessing that quality, a lease which would enable the tenant to recoup himself for one description of expenditure, would not be sufficient to enable him to recoup himself for his expenditure on the other description of improvement.

1027. *Mr. W. E. Forster.*] In the very interesting evidence which you gave us on Thursday, I understood your Lordship to say, that you considered that the sum paid for tenant-right in the north of Ireland might be considered as being paid for two things: first, for goodwill; and, secondly, for improvements?—Yes, I think so.

1028. I also understood you to state, that you did not suppose that benefit had followed from the payment for goodwill?—No, certainly not; the very contrary has been the result.

1029. With regard to these two payments, do you think it would be possible to apportion the proportion between the two of how much is paid for goodwill and how much for improvements?—Yes, I think that might be done by an analysis of each individual case; and I think that one may state, as a general rule, that the amount paid for goodwill diminishes in proportion to the value of the improvements; but perhaps I may be allowed to add, that although the sum paid under the title of goodwill represents a sum paid by the incoming tenant, for the purpose of conciliating the goodwill of the outgoing tenant, the real value which that payment represents is so many years' purchase of the difference between the fair rent and the rack rent.

1030. This payment for goodwill seeming to be very much the same as though it were a second rent charged upon the tenant; what is the effect of this second rent upon the first rent to the landlord; do you think that the rent paid to the landlord for land in the same condition where tenant-right exists, is lower or higher than where it does not exist?—I do not think that, if there were no payment for the goodwill, the rent would be higher; the difference is perceptible in the condition of the tenant and the narrower margin of his profits. The landlords in my neighbourhood, with whose practice I am acquainted, never seek to obtain a competition rent; their habit is to have their farms valued, either by their own agents, or by some professional valuer, and having ascertained the fair value at which the land might be let, they ask that rent for it. But, the rent having been thus ascertained, the competition for land is so intense that, although the landlord may say, "this is the rent which I consider right to ask for this farm," in nine cases out of ten, secretly and in spite of his endeavours, and the endeavours of his agent, the in-coming tenant will surreptitiously pay a considerable sum to the out-going tenant.

1033. But the result of your evidence would be this, would it not, that the tenant-right having, as you may say, two effects, one good, which is the payment for improvements, and the other bad, which is the compulsory payment for goodwill, yet that the good effect is so considerable that, upon the whole, you would consider the farmers are in a better position where tenant-right exists than where it does not?—I have already said that I should not like to strike the balance, but I am convinced that a great deal of good as well as a great deal of evil has resulted from the practice.

1034. That would seem to bring us to this certain result, would it not, that if we could arrive at the payment for improvements where tenant-right does not exist without the evils which flow from the payment for goodwill, that would have a very good effect?—Certainly.

1042. And I think I understood you to say, that you think it would be possible to facilitate that mode of settling the matter by the Government offering arbitration; has any mode by which that could be done occurred to your Lordship?—Yes; I think that one of the great difficulties in the way of arriving at a satisfactory adjustment of those claims proceeds from the absence of any independent authority to whom the landlord and the tenant could both refer a matter in dispute between them with equal confidence, and it certainly has occurred to me that if the Government were to establish, perhaps as an experiment, in two or three of the chief centres of Ireland, arbitrators of their own, men of recognised professional ability, and well acquainted with the practice of agriculture, and were to pay them such salaries as would enable us to secure the services of really eminent men, and that if those salaries were further to be augmented in proportion to the number of cases which they might decide, so as to make it an object with these arbitrators to give satisfaction in their decisions, both to landlords and tenants, a better result might follow. Then, in the case of a landlord and a tenant mutually agreeing to refer any matter in dispute between them to arbitration, these gentlemen might, without any difficulty or expense, come to the spot and go into the whole matter; but the landlord and the tenant having by mutual consent called in the services of an arbitrator, his decision should be binding in law, with perhaps a power of appeal in cases where considerable value was at stake. I think by this means we shall have done all that it is possible to do in this direction, because I am perfectly convinced that our only chance of success in facilitating such arrangements would be by not exciting the jealousy of the landlords, and by not placing the tenants in a position hostile to their landlords, because I regard a tenant who has made improvements on his farm without a lease, pretty much in the light of a woman who has made a runaway match without marriage settlements. The thing is done and cannot be helped; and, however much you may desire, if her husband treats her harshly, to alleviate her position, yet it is very well known that, generally speaking, interference does more harm than good. Therefore, in any measure of this kind, the great thing is to contrive some scheme which shall be recognised as a boon both to the landlord and to the tenant rather than as a measure introduced with the view of benefiting one of the parties to the detriment of the other. I think, perhaps, that if such machinery existed, there are many landlords who would be more ready to avail themselves of it. And I think, certainly in the north of Ireland, that the landlords would be more ready to avail themselves of it than the tenants. In any case the advantage would rest with the just man, whether he was a landlord or whether he was a tenant, because if the tenant makes an unjust claim the landlord can then apply this test and say, "Shall we go to arbitration?" If the tenant refuses, the landlord is then in a position to say, "Your claim can hardly be reasonable, because you have refused arbitration." If the landlord refuses, the tenant, at all events, can urge the same argument on his own behalf. And in that way public opinion, which I regard as one of the safeguards of society, and by which, in fact, some of the principal relations of mankind to each other are regulated, would be, to a certain degree, brought to bear on the settlement of the question; and I think that this is very important, for the very reason that, in Ireland, public opinion may be said scarcely to exist.

1043. Then the suggestion of your Lordship's, which is very valuable, appears to me to consist of this, that you would offer arbitration, it being distinctly understood that it was offered, but was not in any way compulsory?—Certainly; that is the vital principle of it.

1044. And do you consider that these advantages would flow from it; first, that competent arbitrators, which are difficult to find, would be provided by the Government; secondly, that an easy method would be provided, by which the legal value could be ascertained; and thirdly, that the Government would give all the weight of its authority and influence in recommending that compensation should be made for improvements?—Yes; I think so.

1045. You would consider, would you not, that one great advantage of this suggestion would be that it does not at all affect the principle of interference with property?—Exactly so.*

1053. In answer to some questions which were put to you by Mr. Forster at the commencement of your examination to-day, you stated, did you not, that you looked upon the sum paid in the north of Ireland for tenant-right as the combined result of goodwill and compensation for improvements?—Yes; but I do not think that the people who pay it attempt to analyse the transaction in their own minds; all they know is this, that the possession of a farm enables them to live in a manner suitable to their tastes, that it gives them a status of respectability in some degree analogous to the status which a gentleman in this country acquires by the posession of a landed estate, and that the desire for the possession of land is so ingrained in the imagination and in the nature of the people of Ulster that, without making any calculation, without asking

---

* If money were to be lent to the landlords for the purpose of compensating their tenants, it is evident that both landlord and tenant would have an interest in appealing to the arbitration of the Board of Works.

themselves the question, " What interest am I going to obtain
for my money, and what prospect have I of being able to make
a good living out of this farm?" they will pay whatever sum
is necessary to procure them the object of their desire ; but so
far from that sum having any reference to the value of the improvements, I think everybody acquainted with the north of
Ireland will admit that, as a general rule, the largest prices
are given for small farms which are utterly destitute of improvement.

1101. There not being any cottage upon the farm when the
landlord let the land to the tenant, and consequently the rent
of the land being in proportion low, do you think that as a
matter of course the landlord should compensate a tenant for
having put up, against his will, a small cottage upon a small
farm?—Yes, I think so, though of course the amount of his
claim would depend upon the duration of his tenancy ; but
even accepting the circumstances which you yourself have suggested, it would certainly follow, if the principle of compensation is to be accepted at all, that at the expiration of three
years his claim for compensation would be greater than it
would be at the expiration of 10 years.

1102. When the landlord lets the land to the tenant, seeing
that there is no house upon it, he lets the land at a rent proportionate to the want of accommodation which that land
affords to his incoming tenant ; therefore how can you say that
the tenant is entitled to ask for compensation from the landlord,
when the landlord, in letting the land to the tenant, has made
every allowance for the want of accommodation upon that land ?
—We will take a case ; here is an acre of land let at 15s an
acre ; if a cottage had been already built upon it, it would let
at 20s an acre. Therefore the advantage which the tenant has
obtained during the first year has been only 5s ; in the second
year another 5s ; and in the third year a third 5s and so on ;
but his expenditure during the first year will have been, we will
say, £50. It may be quite true, that at the end of a certain
period, the difference of the 5s in his rent will have recouped
the tenant for the £50. which he has expended; but it will
require a certain period of occupation for that operation to have
taken place, and therefore if his tenancy is determined within

a shorter period than would have been sufficient for the completion of that operation, I think that he would be entitled to compensation.

1057. But in the larger farms and the improved farms the price paid per acre is infinitely less than in the smaller and unimproved farms, is it not ?—Yes, certainly.

1058. And that I presume arises simply from the fact that there are fewer competitors in the one case than in the other? —Yes, there are fewer competitors, and those competitors are, generally speaking, men of great intelligence and sense.

1059. And therefore not ready to give an undue sum for possession if they do not see their way to make a profit of it ? —Yes.

1371. In Judge Longfield's examination he was asked, at Question 549, "Take the case of a tenant who had laid out a certain sum upon drainage, and was continued in possession of his farm for 15 years we will say, double the time which drainage is ordinarily given to repay him, do you think it would be fair that at the end of the 15 years, having doubled his money upon the expenditure originally laid out there, he should have a claim against his landlord," and his answer was, that he thought it was perfectly fair; do you think that a landlord is not entitled to any benefit from the expenditure of this money by the tenant, after the tenant has recouped himself from the original outlay a handsome interest?—If I possess a field in which for every half-crown a tenant sows there comes up a guinea, *i. e.*, 5s has been paid as rent, the 15s remaining in the tenant's pocket will not only include his original half-crown, but a fair interest upon it. Consequently it can be no injury to the tenant if, at the expiration of his tenure, the half-crowns remaining in the field should pass to the landlord. He has derived the benefit he anticipated from the use of the field; and it is quite clear that if you introduce a law declaring those half-crowns to be the property of the tenant, the sole result would be that the interest to be derived from the expenditure of capital on land being thus rendered by law far higher than would be the general rate of interest derived from the expenditure of capital in other ways, that circumstance would attract competition to the land, and the rent would consequently rise; the total result would be the same; *i. e.*, I should be offered 7*s* 6*d* for the use of my field, instead of 5*s*.

1137. And your Lordship has, in your own person, shown your disapprobation of the habit by purchasing up, in very many instances, the tenant-right of farms on your Lordship's property, have you not?—Yes; I think I have expended something like £10,000. or £11,000. in that way.

1138. You mean in purchasing up the tenant-right of holdings upon your Lordship's estate?—That is so. Where a tenant has gone to the bad, and has owed me a couple of hundred pounds for rent, in arriving at a settlement my agent has valued his improvements at so much, we will say at £100.; there would remain £100. which he still owed me. Under ordinary circumstances, if he had been allowed to sell his farm he would have received perhaps a couple of hundred pounds for it, and that £200, would have enabled him to pay me the arrears of rent due upon his farm: but wherever it is possible so to do, rather than allow the incoming tenant to pay a sum which, in my opinion, clearly represented no value, I sustained the loss myself, although the new tenant was eager to pay it.

1151. I think everybody concurs (at least I do, for one) that every fair compensation ought to be given to every tenant who has made *bonâ fide* improvement upon his holding; does your Lordship, however, base that view upon this, that by the law of England, and the law of Ireland too, all holdings between landlord and tenant are based upon contract?—Yes.

1154.—Supposing that a direct contract upon the subject has been made between the landlord and the tenant, do you not think that both parties are bound by that contract?—Supposing that you grant a lease for 14 years without any stipulation, but under the custom of the country, or in accordance with the practice which has always prevailed upon your estate, and the tenant expends £200. in building a house, I should say that at the expiration of his agricultural tenancy, which has been of the nature of a contract, there would remain a moral obligation upon you to compensate him for the money which he has expended in the improvements which he cannot carry away with him, and for which he has not been able to compensate himself; but with that exception, I should agree with what you have said.

1216. Do you think, speaking generally, that improvements upon an estate are best made by the landlord or by the tenant?—This is a point which I am very anxious to explain to the Committee. I think an impression generally prevails that the reason why the improvements are all made by the tenants in Ireland is, that the landlord has not got sufficient capital; and in a certain sense that is true; the landlords have not a sufficient capital to provide the population settled upon their estates with the conveniences necessary for cultivating those estates, subdivided as they are into small farms. But if it was merely a question of providing the estate with those farm buildings which are absolutely necessary to its cultivation, the landlords of the north of Ireland, as far as I am aware, would be perfectly able to provide them; and therefore the reason why they do not provide them is, because it would be unprofitable and undesirable that they should do so; because the tenant of a small farm wishing to erect a small farmhouse, is able to do so more cheaply by employing the odds and ends of his time, and the odds and ends of his materials. And I cannot give a better illustration of that fact than what occurred to myself just before I came over here. I was very anxious to build a large number of cottages upon my estate, and I wished to enter into some arrangement with my tenantry, under which those who wished to have a cottage built upon their farm, might have one on condition of a small addition being made to their rent. The cottage was to cost £100.; the rent of the labourer was to be limited to £2. 10s a year; and the farmer was to pay £1. a year, by which means my loss on each cottage would be reduced to £2. 10s a year, calculating the interest at 6 per cent. But my proposition was met by an offer on the part of the tenantry, that they should be allowed to build the cottages themselves, because they could do so much more cheaply.

1212. My question had reference, not to estates in so highly improved a condition as yours probably are, but to estates upon which the outlay of a very large capital was necessary; in such a case as that, do you not think that improvements on so larg a scale would, probably, be best effected by the landlord; in fact, would be effected cheaper, with greater judgment, and also with greater advantage to the estate?—I think it entirely depends upon the area of the farms. I think that if the farms are small, those improvements are made, certainly, more economically by the tenant, and perhaps with as good judgment, because, by long habit, he is thoroughly acquainted with every quarter of his little holding.

1230. From your knowledge of the tenant-right custom as it exists, do you think that it would be possible to embody it, or any portion of it, in a legislative enactment?—No, I think not. It seems to me that the moment you attempt to consign to an Act of Parliament any of the privileges exercised under the tenant-right you will make the position of the tenant far worse than it is under the undefined custom.

534. Do you think, speaking generally, that improvements are best made upon land by the landlord, or by the tenant?—I think they could be more cheaply made by the tenant, and in that way, the best, because I consider that improvement the best, which gives an example of its being profitable.

535. Why do you think that they can be best made by the tenants?—Because they have sometimes the aid of the labour of their own family, and sometimes they have the aid of the labour of those labourers whom they are bound to employ during the year, and then they can put them at their spare moments to this work, and take them away again when they want them for the farm.

1231. Then you think that any attempt, on the part of the Legislature, to embody this custom in Act of Parliament would have a tendency very much to weaken it?—Yes, I think so.

1232. And eventually to distroy it?—Yes, I think even the agitation that has taken place in regard to the custom has already weakened it; many people have regarded that agitation with extreme disfavour; but I myself have already thought it rather a beneficial circumstance, because the more those questions are agitated and examined, the more clearly right and wrong declare themselves; and I apprehend that the recent substitution of the term "goodwill," which formerly was in use, may be regarded as a result of the enlightenment of the opinion of the public in regard to this subject.

1233. Do you think that there is any wish on the part of the tenant class in the north of Ireland that an attempt should be made by legislation to embody this custom into a law, speaking from your knowledge of what your own tenants feel upon the subject?—I think I can prove unmistakably to the Committee what the feelings of the tenants are with regard to this matter. The Committee have done me the honour of referring to a speech I lately made to my tenants, and they will have seen that the proposals therein contained are as liberal as it could be expected that any landlord should make. Nevertheless, it was very evident that the instinctive inclination of those of my tenantry whom I consulted, and they were the most intelligent of them, was to allow matters to remain as they had hitherto been; that is to say, that they would prefer leaving their interests in my hands; and I apprehend the same feeling would also induce them to prefer to allow the matter to be regulated by custom, rather than by any legislative interference.

1234. Do you think, therefore, speaking generally, that any legislation that would have the effect of increasing the want of confidence between a landlord and his tenants would be very disastrous to the interests of the tenants?—I think so; I have compared a tenant, who has made improvements without a lease, to a wife without a marriage settlement; he is the weaker vessel, and in the long run, should a legal contest take place, he is likely to go to the wall.

1262. Is it within your knowledge that, in the north of Ireland, leases for very long terms, we will say on lives renewable for ever, or periods of that kind at nominal rents, are now in existence?—Yes.

1253. Is that a general mode of tenure; are there many cases of that kind within your knowledge?—On my own estate there are two areas held in perpetuity; and I am very sorry that I have not with me a return which has been made for me, from which the Committee will see that upon these areas, which have passed out of the landlord's control, the tendency to sub-division has been so intense that whereas the original tenants were only 12 or 13 in number, the lands in question now contain 55 or 56 independent holdings.

1264. The population has enormously increased upon the townland to which you refer?—Yes.

1265. Has it been found in other respects, for instance, as to the manner in which the permanent improvements, such as draining, fencing, and building have been effected, that on those long terms the improvement has been as much as we will say under an ordinary lease of 31 years?—No; to those long leases, which were very common in that part of Ireland, I attribute to a great extent the false position in which landlords and tenants now find themselves. At the time the leases were originally granted that tendency to subdivide was not very perceptible, and therefore the landlord did not introduce into his lease any clause against subdivision or subletting; but, during the course of the two or three generations which then ensued, this tendency to sublet and to subdivide developed itself, and by the time the lease terminated the landlord found himself compelled to deal with eight or ten, or perhaps even fifteen different occupiers, who all claimed an interest in the land; whereas his ancestor had originally only inducted one.

1340. Do not you think that the equity of the case would be satisfied by allowing a tenant, when he left a farm, to carry away some of those buildings from the place, for which he had paid out of his own pocket?—In order that I may not be misunderstood upon this point, I must ask leave to explain myself a little more clearly. What I intended to state was, that however small the improvement erected upon the farms might be, provided the improvement were necessary to the cultivation of that farm, it ought to be liberally dealt with by the landlord when the farm is about to pass into his hands, and for this reason, that if you were to deny a tenant's moral claim to compensation for such an improvement upon the ground of its no longer being of any use to the estate, which was about to pass into an improved condition, the same argument would hold good with regard to £100. worth of buildings expended upon a farm of 15 acres, or £200. worth of buildings expended upon a farm of 30 acres. Of course the point can be pressed in such a way as to render the tenant's claim to compensation infinitesimal, but its amount does not at all invalidate the argument as to the principle.

1474. I understand, in answer to a question, you attribute the prosperity of the north of Ireland to some peculiarity in the character of the people, they being more energetic and provident than the people of the south and west?—Yes; but my reply to that question was very guarded. I said it was my impression that such was the case.

1475. Do you not think that the comparative prosperity of Ulster might be considered as a necessary result of beneficent legislation rather than the result of energy in the people peculiar to that province?—I think it was the result of both; the one cause need not exclude the operation of the other.

1476. Is it not a fact that while Ulster prospered the rest of the country was impoverished?—Yes, it is the fact.

1477. And while the people of Ulster were thrifty and provident, the rest of the people of the country, to a great extent, were reckless and indifferent?—Yes, I think so; but at the same time I would observe that, during the last 30, 40, and 50 years, a period of perfect equality to all classes, the inhabitants of the north of Ireland have exhibited, I am inclined to think, a greater amount of industry and energy than the inhabitants of other parts of Ireland.

1478. How is that shown?—By the appearance of the country; by the appearance of the cottages in which the inhabitants live, and by the appearance of the inhabitants themselves; by absence of beggars in one district, and by the multitude of them in the other. But, at the same time, I do not wish to make such an observation in any invidious sense; I make that observation, not as an inhabitant of the north of Ireland, but as an Irishman, as much identified by ties of blood and affection with one part of the country as the other.

1479. Has it come to your knowledge that the great majority of the occupiers of land, in Ireland, are discontented with their position, which is one of tenancy at will?—As far as I am acquainted with the north of Ireland the very contrary is the case. Unfortunately the people of the north of Ireland are contented with being tenants at will; and I regard that as a mark of very great want of intelligence.

1480. Do you mean to say they would prefer to be tenants at will, to having leases?—Yes; I think they would.

1481. How do you account for that; do you think it is accounted for by any apprehension that if they took leases they might, perhaps, be obliged to pay more than the value, or a higher rental than they do now?—Certainly not; first of all, I think that that is to be accounted for by their want of intelligence as to the proper mode in which they should conduct their business, and in the next place it arises from the fact that the invariable justice which they have met with at the hands of their landlords has never forced upon their attention the advisability of insisting upon a lease. I think the proof of the correctness of my statement is to be found in the fact that the tenant-right of a farm, without a lease, would be sold for as high a price as the tenant-right of a farm with a lease. I may also add that during the last 15 years, except upon one occasion, I have never been asked for a lease, and yet all my tenants are tenants at will.

1482. But supposing in your own case, you were the occupier of land, with a house, would you be disposed to improve, if you were merely a yearly tenant, to the same extent as you would if you held for a longer term?—No, I certainly should not.

1483. When you give it as your opinion that, in these days, a man cannot live on a small farm, I suppose you mean that he cannot live on it and pay the rent which is likely to be demanded from him?—He cannot live on it and pay a fair rent—such a rent as the occupants of adjoining farms of larger extent are able to pay with advantage to themselves.

1484. Is it not the fact that the value of land in Ireland depends upon whatever the landlord chooses to ask?—That is over-stating the case; but there is no doubt that in the north of Ireland the competition for land is so great that a much higher price will be offered for it than the applicant is likely to be able to pay with advantage; that is to say, the tenantry will be content with a much smaller margin of profit than the tenants of either England or Scotland would be content with, or, in my opinion, my tenants should be content with.

1485. But although you say I may have over-stated the case

in my question, is it not a gross fallacy to assert that the tenants consenting to pay the rent demanded must be taken as an admission that the value of the land has been fairly estimated?—That is often the case, but even that assertion requires some modification. As compared with the skill of the tenant, the rent may be too high, though not too high as compared with the capabilities of the soil. It is difficult to explain; but here may be a farm occupied by an Irish tenant, without intelligence, without skill, and without capital. We will suppose that the rent he offers for that farm is as much as £2 an acre. The rent which his skill and intelligence and the small amount of his capital may enable him to pay may be only £1 an acre. Therefore, as far as regards that individual tenant, £2 an acre would be too high a rent for that farm. But another tenant might come with intelligence and skill, and with capital, and by the application of that intelligence, skill, and capital to that farm, he might, with the very greatest ease and advantage to himself, pay a rent of £2 an acre.

1487. That being so, of course he cannot be said to be a free agent?—We must modify that deduction. For instance, in the north of Ireland—because I am more at home in the north of Ireland—that would not be the case, for at this moment labour is so scarce that I consider the position of a labourer in the north of Ireland is better than that of a small farmer; consequently, if the owner of a ten-acre farm chooses to give up possession of his farm and adopt the occupation of a labourer, he can not only do so, but he can do so with very great advantage to himself and his family.

1488. If certain causes over which the tenants have no controul tend to lower the price of their produce, and to diminish their capacity to pay rent, must not the ruin of the small farming class be considered inevitable. Do you not think they have a right to expect that the Legislature should do something to preserve them, and to enable them to live in the country?—I am afraid it would not be advisable for the Legislature by artificial means to encourage a whole population to depend for their support on an industry capable only of sustaining a part of their number.

1498. I suppose you will admit that the tenants are the

best judges of what are their own interests?—In what respect?

1499. In respect, for instance, to whether security of tenure is better than insecurity of tenure, or in respect to whether they should pay more or less for the value of the land?—I should say certainly not, in the sense alluded to by the Honourable Member; and if he will allow me, I think I can furnish him with a very good illustration of how little the tenants are judges of what is for their own interest in these particulars; and I think I may be allowed to add that, in my opinion, some of those gentlemen who have undertaken to represent the interests of the tenantry, are also, to a great extent, unaware of what is really for the interest of that tenantry. In support of this opinion I will submit to the Committee certain facts which, I think, bear very directly upon this question. I think it right to tell the Committee that, until three days ago, I myself was unaware of the nature of these facts, and that they have only come to my knowledge in consequence of my having written to Ireland for information. In the centre of my property, but in two different parts of it, there exist two areas. By some fortuitous circumstance these areas, in the year 1745, were let in perpetuity; the one was let to six tenants, the other to seven tenants. The sizes of these separate holdings were on the one area 119 acres, 68 acres, 63 acres, 35 acres, and 21 acres. During the interval which has elapsed since 1745, the first of these farms has been subdivided amongst six tenants, the second amongst two, the fourth amongst six, the fifth amongst seven, and the sixth amongst four; so that the original six farms have now come to be 25 farms. Some of these farms are held by the co-heirs of the original tenants, but others are sub-let, and the rent upon those farms thus sub-let varies from 31s to 35s an acre; whereas similar land, forming a portion of the same townland, held under me at will, is let at 25s an acre. With regard to the other area, there were originally six farms, containing respectively 127 acres, 52 acres, 40 acres, 53 acres, 60 acres, and 29 acres. These six farms are now subdivided into 27 farms, and the rents now paid to the middlemen amount from 27s to 31s an acre; whereas upon my adjoining property the rent demanded is only 25s an acre. Thus the average size of these farms left to the control of a peasant proprietary has degenerated from 50 acres to 12 acres, while the rents have risen 30 per cent. above the price asked by the large landholder.* Now, I can give the Committee my word of honour that I never set my foot upon either of these areas. I was quite unacquainted with the number of sub-divisions which existed upon them; I was quite unacquainted with the rents paid by the tenants occupying them; I was only aware, by passing along the public road, from the general appearance of the district in question, that its cultivation was worse and the houses upon it in a more dilapidated condition than was the case on the adjoining parts of my property. I wrote to my agent, who, I may mention, although my tenants are almost to a man Presbyterian, is himself a Roman Catholic. I did not tell him with what view I required the information; I merely put upon paper the questions necessary to elicit the information I have now communicated; and I would venture to submit to the Committee my opinion that if by an Act of Parliament all the landlords of Ireland could be abolished to-morrow, and the farms let to their present occupiers, at whatever rent might be considered just, in the course of a certain number of years a similar operation would take place over the whole of Ireland (always, of course, with certain exceptions) as has taken place upon these two areas to which I have referred; that is to say, the present tenants would cease to be tenants, and would become landlords; they would exact a higher rent for the land than the present landlords exact; they would be less improving; the subdivision of farms would continue, and 50 years hence, if we could return to inspect the condition of the country, the then condition of the tenantry of Ireland would be worse than the condition of the present tenantry. The foregoing facts also confirm what I have already tried to explain, viz., that the lump sum paid by an incoming tenant to an outgoing tenant as goodwill,

---

* Colonel Adair gives a similar instance. In 1747 there were 63 tenants on a particular area, which is now occupied by 419 tenants and 374 cottiers. In 1747 each tenant enjoyed a farm of 110½ acres; whereas now the average size has been reduced to 16 acres.—*Ireland and her Servile War*, p. 48.

is nothing more than so many years' purchase of the difference between a fair rent and a rack rent. My rent of 25s an acre being from 35 to 40 per cent lower than the competition rent of 35s an acre paid on the adjoining area, a man who surreptitiously handed to my outgoing tenant £100. for the good-will of a 10-acre farm, would be in no worse a position than the adjoining tenant who pays a rack rent of 35s an acre. Thus the custom under which these good will payments are made is the exponent and the result, and not the cause of the landlord's moderation.

1500. Then, supposing that it is so, how do you account for this fact, that in several of the countries in Europe, where the peasants are owners of the land, agriculture is in a most flourishing condition?—It may be accounted for, I think, in this way: it seems to me, admitting the facts, which you state (which I believe to be the case), that there exists in Ireland an unreasonable tendency to subdivide the land; and that in other countries there are certain conditions which not only prevent that excessive subdivision of the land, but also that in these countries there are other modes of occupation which absorb the surplus agricultural population.

1501. Do you think that the anxiety to subdivide exists as much at the present time as it did formerly?—Not so much as it did formerly; because, I think, the landlords have done their best to check it.

1502. Do not you think the facility for emigrating, for instance, has also had a tendency to do so?—I think, probably, that has already begun, and will continue to operate.

1503. A farmer sees now that he can provide for his son differently than he did formerly, when he had nothing to do but to give him some land to farm?—I think that eventually emigration, which is now going on, and the development of the manufacturing industry of Ireland, and consequently the facilities likely to be afforded to the surplus agricultural population of providing for themselves by some other means than by subdividing the farms which their fathers occupied, will gradually reduce the presure upon the land; and that it is in that consummation that the true remedy for the unhappy condition of the agricultural population of Ireland is to be found, because by that means the tenantry will be placed in a position to make whatever bargains with their landlords they may think most conducive to their own interests, in the same way as those causes have already begun to render the labourer more independent of his employer. But I am afraid that a very considerable time must elapse before that result will be arrived at.

1507. What would you suggest yourself as an inducement?—I think that the chief inducement for a landlord to grant a lease would be the existence of a tenant with capital, skill, and industry; and that where they exist, the landlord, for his own interest, would at once grant a lease if the tenant insisted, as he should do, upon having a lease. There is one point to which you have referred in one of your questions upon which I think it right to add a word. You said that under the charter by which the undertakers in the reign of James the First, held their lands, provisions had been introduced, requiring them to let those lands at low rents, on long leases, and under favourable conditions. I replied that I had understood such to be the fact; but if I am right in supposing that you wish to infer from that circumstance that the present tenantry now occupying the districts formerly granted upon those conditions are legally entitled to such terms, I would remind you, as an historical fact, that a very large per centage of the present proprietors of the north of Ireland, are, in fact, the representatives of the very tenants on behalf of whom those conditions were made, and that consequently the conditions were complied with, and those on whose behalf they were imposed have reaped the advantages which it was intended they should obtain. Although all the lands I now possess formed a part of the original Clandeboye Grant,* 90 per cent of my property was acquired by purchase: the proportion I hold direct from the Crown is very small, and a similar process of disintegration and repurchase by the original grantees has taken place in respect to many of such grants. On the Clandeboye Survey of 1630, to which I have alluded, the names of the then tenants are not at all identical with the names of the present tenants, though the names of some of the

---

* No such condition as that alluded to by the Hon. Member was introduced into this Grant.

present adjoining proprietors are identical with the names of the then tenants. Moreover, though beneficial at that time, experience has proved that long leases would be anything but beneficial now, and every agriculturist will tell you that too low a rent is only less fatal to good cultivation than too high a rent.

1513. Mr. *Bagwell.*] I believe you have stated more than once, with reference to the size of farms, that consolidation was going on slowly in the north of Ireland ?—Yes, slowly.

1514. In fact, I gathered from your evidence, that where a small farmer wished to leave the country, or was unable to meet engagements, that then he would inform his landlord of the case; that he would look to the custom of the country of tenant-right, and that the landlord would have a veto as to the new incoming tenant?—The custom varies upon different estates; there are many landlords in the north of Ireland who refuse altogether to recognise the existence of the custom, who select their tenant, and take a special precaution that nothing should appear in the transaction as between them and their tenant in any way connected with the custom of the tenant-right.

1568. Will you explain the meaning of the term, "Set-off by the landlord," which you have used ?—There can be no doubt that, upon a very large proportion of the farms in the north of Ireland, although in the main the improvements have been executed by the tenant, the landlords have from time to time contributed to a certain extent towards those improvements. Of course it would be but just that whenever questions of tenants' compensation came to be considered, it should be competent for the landlord to plead such contributions as he or his ancestors may from time to time have made as a set-off to the claim of the tenant; and this set-off should not only include such counter-claims as those, but also where a tenant, by bad husbandry, has placed the condition of the land in a worse position than it was when he originally entered upon its occupation, that also should be regarded as a set-off in favour of the landlord. I may take this opportunity of stating as a reason why we ought to be very careful before we hurry the tenantry into any legal controversy with their landlords, that I am very much afraid if the claims of the tenant, and the corresponding claims of the landlord, were to be examined with the severity rigour which must be exercised by a court of justice, the claims of the landlord would very frequently not only counterbalance, but greatly exceed the claims of the tenant. I think that is one reason why the introduction of any hostile element into the relations of landlord and tenant would be prejudicial to the tenant. At present the landlords with whose practice I am acquainted, are very much disposed to deal liberally with their tenants, and not to insist very strongly on those pleas, which they might urge as a set-off against the tenant's claim, as of course they would be disposed to do if the matter were to come to a legal contest. Again, I have shown how it came about that under long leases the land was subdivided, and tenements erected upon such separate subdivisions. Before a legal tribunal, of course, a tenant could not claim for a building which he had erected on a subdivided lot under a lease, such an operation having clearly taken place without the landlord's connivance, and against his interest; but it is the practice of the landlords in the north of Ireland not to allow that consideration to enter into their estimation of the tenant's claim, consequently, I think that, generally, the practice of the landlord is, in this and other particulars I need not specify, more favourable to the claims of his tenant than the necessarily rigorous arbitrament of a court of law would be. For these reasons, I think the Legislature will do well to encourage and enable landlords (whether limited owners or owners in fee) and tenants to enter into contracts with one another, and to facilitate the adjustments of disputes when no contracts exist, by placing some simple and cheap system of arbitration within the reach of the agricultural interest.

SMALL *v.* LARGE FARMS.

I do not wish to pronounce dogmatically on the merits of small versus large farms; the very highest authorities are at issue on the subject,* but after a good deal of consideration, I have acquired a very strong impression :—

---

* "It is the general opinion of those who are equally well ac-

1. That the greatest gross produce is obtained from "la petite culture" as practised under short leases in East Flanders, though at a cost of labour in excess of what is required in England and Scotland to obtain almost equally large returns.

2. That in the abstract, grain crops are best grown on large farms, and leguminous and textile crops are raised with greater advantage on small farms.

3. That "la petite culture," when practised by tenants as distinguished from peasant proprietors, has a tendency to promote intense competition, and consequently is not conducive to the happiness of the agricultural population.*

---

quainted with both large farming and "la petite culture," that improvement is greatest under a due admixture between them."
Mill's Polit. Econ., Appendix G, (p. 192.) *Vol. I.*

"The question relative to large and small farms is one of the most puzzling and complicated possible, although a great number of writers on both sides have solved it with a promptitude which shows that they had only considered it hastily, and under a single point of view."—*Sismondi's Agriculture Toscane.*

Mons. de Lavergne when describing the Petite Culture in Flanders says, "This profitable mode of farming has one great drawback, which establishes the balance in favour of the English system —the excess of the rural population, which is in the ratio of 1 to 2½ statute acres. . . . . If Flanders produces more acreably than England, she produces only half as much relatively to the population. In the town of Lille *one-third* of the population are paupers, receiving public relief, and more than one rural district is equally pauperized."

* "Many witnesses are of opinion that the acreable rents of small farms are frequently higher than those of large, even under the same proprietors, and that large estates are in general let at lower rates than smaller properties."—*Dig. Dev. Com. p.* 756.

"Thirty shillings an acre would be thought in England a very fair rent for middling land; but in the Channel Islands it is only very inferior land that would not let for at least £4. and in Switzerland the average rent seems to be £6. per acre."—*Ibid. p.* 32.

M. de Laveleye is very persistent in this distinction when

4. That "la petite culture" when practised by peasant proprietors possessed of sufficient self-restraint and intelligence to deter them from excessive subdivision, or from burdening their little properties with extravagant mortgages, is a method of existence productive of great happiness, and calculated to promote a good system of cultivation, though probably yielding a less amount of gross produce than that obtained under the pressure of the tenancy system in Flanders.

5. That the foregoing conditions, though essential to the prosperity of "la petite culture," do not seem to exist to so great an extent as might be wished amongst the small proprietors either of France or Belgium, and could hardly be looked for in the present generation of Irish peasants of the South and West.*

---

advocating "la petite culture." Even Mr. Mill says that "la petite culture" cannot be fairly judged except when the cultivator is a proprietor.

* "Ainsi se multiplier dans le nord de la France, ces propriétaires pauvres que les paysans enrichis traitent assez durement en les désignant volontiers sous le nom de petites gens. Ainsi se recrute dans les campagnes un paupérisme non moins dangereux que celui des villes et des manufactures."

La Réforme Sociale, par M. F. Le Play, p. 388.

"Les enclaves de petite dimension, inférieures par example à deux hectares, sont un obstacle permanent à toute culture perfectionnée des bestiaux, les céréales, des plantes fourragères et industrielles."—*Ibid. p.* 400.

"Les exploitations de quelque étendue même quand elles restent aux mains d'un seul propriétaire, tendent à se subdiviser par une raison très simple: c'est que, morcelées, elles se louent beaucoup plus cher. Celles qui sont situées à proximité, des villages résistent difficilement à la plus value énorme que leur crée la concurrence des habitants agglomérés. Dans presque chaque commune, on trouve quelque corps de ferme qui, naguère loué en bloc de 70 à 80 francs par hectare, rapporte aujourd'hui de 120 à 150 francs parcelles de 10 ou 20 acres."—*Eco. Rurale, p.* 51, 52.

6. That where subdivision is pushed to an extreme extent, the consequences are disastrous.

7. That at this moment, a large proportion of the farms of Ireland, (nearly one-third of the total number of holdings being rated at less than £5 per annum, and two-thirds under £10) are below the average considered most conducive to agricultural prosperity in those countries where "la petite culture" is practised with the greatest success.*

8. That so far as we have experience of the past, it is evident that the occupiers of very small farms in Ireland are, and have been in a worse position than those who cultivated moderate sized holdings of twenty-five acres and upwards.†

---

* "Holdings in Ireland.—A Parliamentary return just presented, in pursuance of an order made on the motion of Lord Naas, gives a statement, in the first place, of the purely agricultural holdings in Ireland, 608,864 in number; 174,989 valued at £4. or under, 190,877 over £4. and under £10., 123,784 at £10. and under £20., 83,259 at £20. and under £50., 35,955 at £50. or upwards."

Extract from the Times.

"The Swiss peasantry, although almost universally landed proprietors, may be divided into two classes: those who are principally or exclusively agriculturists, and those who gain a livelihood chiefly by manufacturing industry. The farms of the former, except in the cantons of Berne and Tessin, and a few other districts seldom exceed 40 or 50 acres, but they are as rarely of less size than ten acres."—*Thornton's Peasant Proprietors, p.* 87.

"But in countries in which small farms abound their average size is frequently, perhaps generally, less than 24 acres: in France it appears to be 18 acres; in Jersey, 16; and in Guernsey, where land is more minutely divided than perhaps in any other part of Europe, is little more than 11 acres."—*Ibid. p.* 30.

Speaking of Flanders, M. de Laveleye says:—"Il est à remarquer que les fermes à un cheval d'une étendue de 11 à 12 (*i.e.* from 27 to 30 acres) hectares forment la moyenne culture et sont les plus nombreuses."—*Eco. Rur. p.* 49.

Evidence of Thomas Herrick, Esq., Land Proprietor.

† "With respect to the farming population, are the large farmers

That taking all these considerations into account, and making every admission which may be reasonably re-

getting richer?—The large farmers are always better off than the small farmers. There is no class so badly off as those small farmers, except the paupers; they are worse off than the labourers.

"What do you call a small farmer?—A man holding ten acres, up to twenty, I should say."—*Dig. Dev. Com. p.* 382.

Evidence of Adam Walker, Esq., Agent.

"Do you consider that the holders of large tillage farms are getting richer?—Yes, because they are improving in their style and mode of cultivating their land. That is confined to large farmers; the small farmers are not."—*Dig. Dev. Com. p.* 383.

Evidence of Rob. O'Brien, Esq., Agent and Land Proprietor.

"The small tenantry may be defined as those who handle the plough or spade themselves, and hold the largest portion of land in this country. A large portion of this class enjoy less comfort than if they were mere labourers with constant employment and well supplied with food, as they have not means to purchase manure for the land, and frequently let off the crops for two years, rent free, while they are obliged to make up the landlord's rent, till they can reimburse themselves with the corn crop."—*Dig. Dev. Com. p.* 383.

Evidence of Mr. Edmund Anthony Power, Farmer.

"With respect to the condition of the farming population, do you consider that the large farmers are getting richer?—Yes, I think they are. I think they are better off—we can have stock of the best kind. A tillage farmer must wait for the crops to grow, but a man who has cows can make butter and feed pigs.

"Are the small farmers getting richer?—No, there are too many of them."—*Ibid. p.* 384.

Evidence of Mr. William Robert Leckey, Farmer.

"With respect to the condition of the farming population, do you think the large farmers are getting richer?—I think they are; I think their condition is improving. They are better managers, and better tillers; they use better seed, and grow better crops than they did formerly.

"Are the small tenantry improving in their condition?—Some of them are. I do not think in a general way they can be said to be improving much, but several are."

quired in favour of "la petite culture," it is clear that the consolidation of farms in Ireland has not been in excess

Evidence of Anthony Strong Hussey, Esq., Land Proprietor.

" What is your opinion of the condition of the large farmers; do you consider that they are improving in their circumstances, or otherwise ?—I think, wherever they have adopted the new system of cultivation, they have very considerably improved; but the small farmers are in a very wretched condition.

"To what do you attribute the state of the small farmers ?— I think it is owing to the want of capital and the want of draining. Their lands want draining on every side, and it is very expensive."
Ibid. p. 384.

Evidence of Mr. Milhew, Farmer.

" Are the small tenants getting richer in the world ?—No, they are not, the subdivision of land is so great."
Dig. Dev. Com. p. 384.

Evidence of James Swan, Esq., Dispensary Surgeon.

" You think that a small farmer of five or six acres is worse off than a common labourer ?—Yes, I do; they have the greatest difficulty in paying the public rates.

" What is the usual food ?—Potatoes; and sometimes they get what they call a sprit, or sprat, or salt fish. I am intimately acquainted with their diet, and it is a fruitful source of chronic disease. Very few of that class are able to get milk; they are steeped in poverty; and though many of them go to market with their outside garments good, their under garments are bundles of rags."

Evidence of Geo. Robertson, Esq., Land Agent, Scotland.

" Is the rent which is paid by the crofters generally higher or lower than that paid by large farmers?—Generally higher: the agents generally take advantage of the competition for small quantities of land. I regret to say I have done this myself.

" Do you consider that a crofter paying the same rent which a farmer would pay for a large farm, can maintain himself and his family comfortably upon eight or ten acres, if he is an industrious man ? Yes, in a great measure; but much depends upon the adjustment and dove-tailing of the social system. Were you to make them all small crofters they would eat one another."—*Dig. Dev. Com. p.* 406.

of what was essential to the well-being of the agricultural class.

Evidence of Wm. M. Reade, Esq., Land Proprietor.

"What is your opinion of the class of farms most advantageous, all things considered?—From twenty to thirty acres is as good a farm as a landlord could wish to have on his estate.

"Do you see any strong objection to farms much smaller?—Yes, in this part. If there was any thing for them to do besides farming, it would be very well to have them more split; but it would be as well for them to have thirty acres to live with where they have nothing else for them to do."—*Ibid. p.* 410.

Evidence of Thos. Gerrard, Land Proprietor.

"Is it your opinion, that when a man holds less than ten acres he sinks below the level of an independent farmer?—Yes, that is my opinion."—*Dig. Dev. Com. p.* 411.

Evidence of W. Fetherston H., Esq., Jun., Secretary to Farming Society.

"Some landlords have a prejudice against small tenants; they think they cannot pay their rent. I think they pay as well as the larger ones, if properly managed.

"To what extent do you apply that?—If I was setting land I would never make a farm under twenty-five acres."—*Dig. Dev. Com. p.* 412.

Evidence of Rich. C. Brown Clayton, Land Proprietor.

"Farms averaging from twenty-five to thirty acres, on which a pair of horses are kept are best adapted to the circumstances of the occupiers here.......... On this, by careful management, a family may be maintained, and comforts procured equal to their requirements........ Those holding from five to twenty acres live in a condition little removed from the labourers, always struggling for an increase of land."—*Dig. Dev. Com. p.* 413.

Evidence of Wm. Blacker, Land Agent.

"I am in favour of such a subdivision of the land in both countries as the wants of the population may require."

Dig. Dev. Com. p. 400.

"Suppose you had room, what is the smallest division of land you would willingly make?—It depends entirely upon the capital and the means of the tenant I should like to have what would keep a pair of horses; that would be about fifty acres; from fifty to sixty English acres, or what would keep one horse, so that two neighbours could club together, and plough in partnership.—*Dig. Dec. Com. p.* 401.

" What is the quantity of land requisite for one horse?—From twenty to twenty-five acres would reasonably keep a horse for farming purposes, and it is very advantageous with us to have some animal of draught; they have to draw their turf a long way, and their lime, and this gives them extra employment.

" What would be the smallest quantity of land which you would give to a tenant for cultivation by spade labour?—The quantity I have mentioned is as small a holding as you could appoint for the support of a man and his family, and to keep a cow, because, unless a countryman, who has a wife and family, keeps a cow, he cannot manure his land, nor be in any comfort in his domestic circle." —*Ibid. p.* 401. (Mr. Mill also quotes this witness as a person of great authority.)

Evidence of Wm. Sharman Crawford, Esq., M. P. Land proprietor.

" What do you conceive would be the most desirable size for a farm, with reference to cultivation, if other circumstances allowed you to decide upon it?—With reference to cultivation, a tenant who has a farm of that size which requires horse culture, should have that size farm which would enable him to keep two horses, or else four horses, or such greater number as the ploughing of the land would require; the size of his farm should be such, as that he would not be required to keep horses which would not be fully employed; and my view is, that fifty Scotch acres would find employment for one pair of horses. But I am of opinion, taking another view of the subject, with regard to the interests of the population, that a smaller size of farm would contribute more to the prosperity of the population; and I think the highest degree of cultivation and production is obtained by spade labour."—*Ibid. p.* 401. . . . .

Evidence of H. Prentice Leslie, Esq., Land Agent and Landholder.

" To what extent have you been generally anxious to raise the farms?—My opinion is that a twenty-five acre farm is most desirable for the present condition of this country, and the circumstances of the people.

" When you speak of consolidation, you mean bringing farms up to that size?—Yes. But if a man had a thirty-acre farm, and a farm of five acres became vacant near to him, *I would rather that he had thirty-five acres, and do away with the small letting.*"—*Ibid. p.* 481.

(There is no sensible man in Ireland who would not agree with this witness.)

On the alleged Progressive Decline of the Prosperity of Ireland.

As it has been the fashion of late to describe Ireland as decreasing in prosperity, I append the concluding paragraphs from Dr. M. Neilson Hancock's admirable pamphlet on the subject, in which that theory has been refuted.

"The arguments for progressive decline have been confidently based on elaborate statistics; the most satisfactory way of testing the strength of such arguments is to examine fairly and fully the real tests of national wealth and prosperity, and to come to a decision, not by the mere criticism of mistaken or partial statistics, but by establishing the true state of the case by positive evidence, founded on a wide induction.

All the statistics I have examined appear to me to refute the theory of progressive decline, and to establish—1st, that there was in agricultural produce and other kinds of wealth a rapid progress in recovering from the effects of the famine. That this attained its height in sheep in 1854; in amount of Government stock held in Ireland, in 1857; in pigs, after considerable fluctuations, in 1858; in cattle and the total value of live stock in 1859; and in the deposits in joint-stock banks in 1859; in the total number of acres under crops in 1860; in the issue of bank notes, after some fluctuation also, in 1860; and in the railway traffic in 1861.

2nd. That omitting all account of investments in improving and reclaiming land, in manufactures, &c., the capital of the country appears to have increased, as judged by the tests of live stock, Government funds, bank deposits, and investments in railways,* from about £60,000,000 in 1841, to about

---

* In making this calculation, I have estimated the Irish portion of the capital in Irish Railways at £1,500,000 in 1841, £11,000,000 in 1859, and at £12,500,000 in 1862.

£120,000,000 in 1859, being an increase of 100 per cent.; and the decrease in these classes of wealth, since 1859, of about £8,000,000, still leaves their amount £112,000,000, or £52,000,000 more than in 1841.*

3rd. That the high average produce of all crops for four years, 1852-1855, seems to have been one of the chief causes of this prosperity.

4th. That the diminished average produce of all crops in the four years 1856, 1857, 1858, and 1859, seems to have led to a check of prosperity in some things, and, on the whole, to a diminished rate of progress in agricultural wealth; but, being years of reasonable plenty, and following on years of more than average plenty, the well-being of the people seems not to have been affected, except in 1859, in the case of those specially affected by the scarcity of hay and straw.

5th. That the still further diminished produce of all crops in 1860, 1861, and 1862, resulting from inclement seasons, with scarcity of turf in 1861, turned the diminished progress in wealth into a positive decline; and that the accumulation of the effects of three years' decline has produced a very serious diminution of national wealth and well-being—the losses of farmers in oats, wheat, potatoes, and cattle, in the three years, amounting to upwards of £26,000,000, or two years' rental.

---

* If we examine the corresponding progress made by England, omitting from the account whatever has been derived from her manufacturing industry and mineral resources, the comparison will be very much in favour of Ireland.

Statement of England's Agricultural Wealth in

	1815. £.	1856. £.
Land		
Tithes		
Manors	41,500,000	38,000,000
Fines		
Fisheries		
Farmers' Profits	21,700,000	24,224,443
	63,200,000	62,224,000

6th. That the losses in these years, though affecting indirectly all classes, have mainly produced pressure on the farmers, entitling them to a large amount of sympathy and consideration; and that the labouring classes, owing to the rise in wages, increase of employment since 1847, and abundance of foreign wheat and Indian corn at a low price, are suffering much less than was commonly anticipated."

Though the above remarks evince, beyond doubt, a steady tendency in Ireland towards continuous improvement and a rapid accumulation of wealth, they also teach us another lesson, viz.: that so long as the population of Ireland is solely dependent on agriculture the prosperity of the country will continue to be the sport of a fickle and precarious climate, and that the development of the manufacturing industry of the country is necessary to sustain and corroborate its agricultural system.

Comparison of the Rise in Wages and in the Price of Food.

It is contended by some eminent writers that though wages have risen, the increase in the price of the labourer's food has more than counterbalanced that advantage. Dr. Hancock discusses this opinion in the following sentences:—

"Some of those who support the theory of progressive decline admit the manifest fact of a great rise in money wages since 1846, but endeavour to destroy the effect of this admission by adding that the price of food has also greatly increased.

The average price of wheat in Dublin for seven years before 1846 was 30s 11d a barrel; and the average price for seven years, ending 1st November, 1862, was 30s 9d.

The rise in wages, without any rise in wheat, has brought household bread within the reach of a much larger number of the labouring classes.

IMPORTATION OF WHEAT AND FLOUR.

	Quarters in the Year.
Before 1846 (average of 7 years)	127,958
In 1860	1,383,609
In 1861	1,412,809
In 1862	2,112,715

In oats there has been a rise.

Potatoes are, in most years, much higher than before the famine, generally averaging about £4. a ton, while they formerly averaged about £2. a ton; but those who are too poor to consume wheaten bread, are no longer absolutely dependent on the potato. They have now what the law denied them before free trade—Indian meal, the present price of which is from 7s to 7s 6d per cwt., being about half the price of oatmeal.

The importations of Indian corn and meal were:—

	Quarters in the Year.
Before 1846 (average of 7 years)	11,007
,, 1860	1,317,514
,, 1861	1,970,988
,, 1862	1,773,255

If the cheap bread and cheap Indian meal is taken into account, the rise in oats and potatoes is prevented producing its full effect; so that the great increase in money wages is by no means counterbalanced by the rise in oats and potatoes.",

It must also be remembered that the difference in the rate of wages is not the measure of the difference of the change in the labourer's conditions: twenty-five years ago he only received payment at all on three or 4 days of the week. At the present moment his wages are not only higher, but he is in more constant employment.

CORK AND KERRY IN 1867.

The following pages contain some observations well worthy of consideration in connection with the subject under discussion. They emanate from Mr. Robertson, a very able agriculturist, who lately went over at my request to the South of Ireland, for the purpose of verifying, on the spot, some facts with respect to which I desired information.

Extract from a Report, by Mr. Robertson, on the Agricultural Condition of the Counties Cork and Kerry.

DURING my tour, the remark was over and over again made to me, if we only had "Fixity of Tenure" our farming would be as good as that in any part of the British isles. On one or two occasions I had the curiosity to inquire what was understood by Fixity of Tenure, and was informed that they understood that the tenant should hold his farm at the present rent as long as he continued to pay this rent. This outcry for "Fixity of Tenure" is not confined to the Tenant at Will holding under a grasping landlord, *but I have met with it on estates where the tenants would reject 21 and 31 years leases in favour of their present relationship with their landlords as Tenants at Will.* I regret that I have no alternative but to believe that the greatest portion of this outcry for "Fixity of Tenure" arises not from the laudable desire of protecting improvements made on the landlord's property, but from a desire to participate with the landlord in the ownership of the soil.

That a lease of moderate duration in the hands of an intelligent man offers great facilities for agricultural improvement, I admit, but I doubt the wisdom of granting them indiscriminately. Where a man is deficient in capital, deficient in intelligence or activity, I can fancy no greater punishment than giving him a lease. Many instances have recently come to my knowledge, where the position of the leasehold tenant is one of hopeless misery and destitution. Half cultivated fields, tumble-down houses, dilapidated fences, all testify to this. I believe that leases should be granted only to qualified tenants, men who have the means and will to profit by the security thus given to their outlay. *That long leases even when accompanied by low rents will not improve the agriculture of a neighbourhood, we have ample evidence to prove.* During the last few weeks it has been my lot to go over hundreds of acres of lands held on long leases at low rents. *These lands are invariably in the most wretched condition of cultivation;* where thirty years ago only one family was to be found, you now find eight or nine families living in mud cabins, obtaining from the land the means of a half savage existence; nearly all being in the same deplorable condition of abject poverty. *In spite of clauses against subletting and subdividing there is scarcely a holding with a lease of any duration which is not cut up and sublet.* These clauses have been found valueless in preventing this great abuse of property; these long leases are fast reverting to the original landlord; the land is in a frightful state of poverty; the cottages and cabins are in a sad state of repair; and the people themselves seem little removed from paupers. The condition of such properties is immeasurably worse than properties let under tenancies at will. Now, I neither condemn long leases or low rents, but I hold, that without the necessary amount of intelligence the effect on the occupant of the farm is detrimental to all agricultural progress. To give a lease without regard to the qualifications of the tenant is the most effectual plan of stopping all improvement.

I believe that in the more improved districts where men of intelligence and capital are located, landlords, in withholding leases, are doing great injustice to their tenants; we can fancy no position more disheartening, more calculated to stop all enterprise, or more antagonistic to all progress than the position of an intelligent enterprising tenant, holding as Tenant at Will, under an absentee landlord, this landlord represented by an agent ignorant of all agricultural knowledge. What under such circumstances can a tenant do, if he would pay his rent, educate his family, and live respectably, he must invest capital in his farm; the more capital he invests the greater he becomes dependent on the good will of his landlord, the better he farms the worse becomes his position, and the probabilities of his rent being advanced increase.

In most countries the duration of a lease is a matter of considerable controversy; I think I am not wrong in stating that the majority of the most intelligent farmers would gladly accept a lease for 21 or 31 years of their farm, and as a per centage on the capital they believe the landlord ought first to lay out on permanent improvements, would gladly pay a few shillings extra as increased rent. I can advise no step in my opinion more calculated to improve the agriculture of these counties than the giving of leases to all qualified to hold them : these leases being for a definite period, their duration depending upon the condition of the farm at the time the lease is granted.

On small holdings I do not think it advisable to grant leases. In both countries, these small farms, with few exceptions, are wretchedly cultivated. What these tenants want to protect in their outcry for a Tenant Right Bill I cannot imagine; as to improvements, in the majority of cases there positively is none, and there are not a few instances where I think the landlord is entitled to damages for the impoverished condition of the soil. If I occupied the landlord's position I would rather have the land in its unimproved virgin state as in its so-called reclaimed condition. On nearly all these small farms there is ample evidence of the occupier's want of capital and skill, on many the capital is not one-tenth of the amount it should be. We hear a great deal of the superior advantage of spade-culture, and of the great returns a farm yields when so cultivated; during the past few weeks I have gone over hundreds of these small farms, but in very few instances did I see any attempt at proper cultivation, whether these farms were held under lease or at will made little difference; it was only under the eye of the landlord or agent, or in close proximity to a town I saw any attempt to farm properly. I pointed out many instances to the occupant farmers where the expenditure of a few shillings or a day or two's labour would bring a large return; but I was almost invariably met with the reply, "Shure, if we did it, would not the rent be raised!" This is the common excuse for laziness and negligence amongst these small farmers. There may be cases where the landlord has raised the rent as the tenant's prosperity increased, but though I laid myself open for information of this kind I was not furnished with a single authenticated case, though I heard a great deal of the injustice of landlords in general.

These small farmers appear to make the distinction between outlay which is immediately remunerative and outlay which is only remunerative over a course of years; there are many improvements which are almost immediately remunerative; these any intelligent man would make whether he is a mere tenant at will or tenant for a term of years. That they are right, without sufficient security, in not investing capital in improvements "which take a long time to repay themselves," I of course admit.

Time appears of little moment amongst these small farmers judging by their attendance at markets and fairs.

If it is only a few pounds of butter, or a few eggs to sell, the farmer, his wife, and frequently a son or daughter must go to town 52 times a year, and with some it will occur oftener; what a serious charge against a small farm. The value of 52 days' labour for man, woman, and child, to say nothing of what they spend in town.

I met with a few instances of land being held by a number of families in common. The arable land in possession of each family varied from a quarter of an acre up to two or three acres, each family division being being marked out by heaps of stones. A fresh division of the arable land takes place annually. The grass land is grazed in common. On the land selected for cultivation they generally grow two crops of oats and two crops of potatoes, and then leave the ground for nature to cover it with a sward of grass, going to a fresh piece of land and repeating the process. After five or six years the abandoned land becomes covered with an indifferent sward of grass; this is grazed for a season or two when the foregoing process is again repeated. We need scarcely add that all the land thus managed is in a most exhausted condition. The arable land is all cultivated with the spade, horses seldom or never going near the land, not even to cart manure or remove the produce, this being almost entirely the work of the female members of the families of the occupants; manure to the land and produce from the land being conveyed in baskets on the women's backs. The cabins and cottages on such land are of the poorest description. *On one townland thus held I found 57 families resident where forty or fifty years ago but four resided; they were all very badly off, though the rent was very low.*

I found squatters settled in different parts of both counties. These people generally settle down on waste land from which turf has been removed, or on mountain sides, first, however, obtaining the consent of the occupying tenant. With the tenant farmer they generally make an agreement something like the following. They are allowed to have four acres of land; this four acres of land must be all reclaimed in five years. The farmers find them material for erecting their cabin, wood and straw for roof. They are to work for the farmer whenever required at a uniform wage of 1s per day, or if diet is allowed, "sour milk and potatoes," 6d per day. At the expiration of four years they will commence and pay the farmer a yearly rent of 12s 6d per statute acre. This agreement is greatly in favour of the farmer; not only does he command labour when required, but he makes a profit on this labour, if this labour is obtained only at 1s per week below the market price he still gains per annum 52s. This in itself is sufficient rent for the land occupied by the squatter; however, after the fourth year, as I have already stated, he gets a further return of 12s 6d per annum or 50s. The total amount of the farmer's outlay for building materials he allows the squatters seldom reaches £8. or £9.; by this investment he obtains a yearly return of over £5. per annum for land which previously brought him in no return. All allow that the position of these squatters is very unsatisfactory, they are very irregularly employed, *and it is generally just the season when they should be attending to their own crops that the farmer finds most need for their services.*

In both counties I found a general complaint of the difficulty in obtaining qualified agricultural labourers; plenty of labourers can be obtained, but they are of little use. *In one locality I heard farmers complaining that they could scarcely carry on operations from the difficulty in obtaining labourers, and was yet informed by a gentleman in the same locality, that on the morning of our visit he had had sixty applicants at his hall door for labour at 1s per day.*

Employment is very irregular, *the occasional labourer is frequently unemployed five or six weeks during the winter months, except in the neighbourhood of Cork;* these men's earnings will not exceed an average of 7s per week, out of this they must pay rent for cabin, &c. Regular labourers are paid in majority of cases 6s per week, and are allowed perquisites worth about 1s per week. These men have constant employment. Wages in the neighbourhood of towns have advanced fully 50 per cent. during the last 20 years. Although day labour is 50 per cent. cheaper in the north of Ireland, yet fully as much is paid for work done by task labour.

Small farmers rarely obtain more than two-thirds the value of their produce, there being no home consumption for this produce, before it reaches the actual consumer fully one-third of the value is consumed in carriage, commissions, &c.

There is a very large area of grass land in both counties which is in a very impoverished condition. The land is grazed year after year, young cattle are reared, and dairy produce sold; but nothing is returned to the soil. It will not be long before the Irish farmer experiences what the Cheshire dairy farmer has already experienced, that this system long continued in, will end in the total exhaustion of the land, and that before it can again be made remunerative a heavy outlay of capital will be required. It is only the high price of dairy produce which is now supporting the small farmers; let this price be reduced, or the produce lessened, and he will at no distant date have an entire disappearance of all farms less than 20 acres in extent.

Small farmers seldom make good labourers; they will only become labourers as a last resource; when thoroughly broken down they cannot realize the fact, that the respectable well-paid labourer occupies a better social position than the struggling small farmer. I think, however, if landowners would be firm there would be little difficulty in converting a great proportion of these small farmers into labourers. At present this is scarcely to be desired. Landlords must first fulfil their duty; capital must be invested in improvements before he can expect a labourer will receive anything like a sufficiency to maintain himself and family.

While the whole country is covered with fences, I scarcely see one worthy of the name. In looking over the ordnance map of county Cork I discovered one district containing an area of 540 acres, in which there was 320 fields; this gives an average of a little more than $1\frac{1}{2}$ acre per field. I do not hesitate in saying that in districts where farms of less than 50 acres prevail there is fully 10 per cent. of the land occupied with fences: many of these fences consisting of earth germ, with lime, good top-dressing for grass land. Their removal is, therefore, profitable to the tenant, not only for the 10 per cent. of ground rendered available, and the economy in cultivation, but also for the manure rendered available, so much needed on the grass land of these counties. A great deal of wood might profitably be planted in both counties.

In the foregoing remarks I have said little regarding the position of the larger class of farmers, though they also have much to complain of; still, I consider, they occupy no worse position than their brethren on the opposite side of the Channel. This class of tenantry are better able to make equitable arrangements with their landlords, and are consequently better off than smaller or more dependent farmers.

I have heard of many real and many sentimental grievances. In recording my observations I have endeavoured to be as free from bias as possible, taking my standard of comparison not from the condition of things on the English side of the Channel, but from observations I have made in the north of Ireland.

Feb. 1867. W. R. ROBERTSON.

A comparison of the profits of a small occupier in Co. Down, of average industry and skill, as compared with the earnings of a labourer and his family, in the same neighbourhood.

" MY DEAR MR. THOMSON,

" Have the kindness to calculate the probable profits of a farmer and his family cultivating a holding of ten acres in our County, as compared with the earnings of the same persons employed on wages, whether in town or country.   DUFFERIN."

MY LORD,

To give a definite reply to these questions it is assumed that the land is of *medium* quality, and that it is worked as is ordinarily done by the more intelligent of the small farmers on a five course shift. That

The father is aged	40
The mother	36
A son	15
A daughter	13
And a son	9

Common rotation—		
Wheat	2	acres
Oats	2	,,
{ Potatoes	1	,,
{ Turnips	1	,,
Hay	2	,,
And Grass	2	,,

	£	s.	d.
Produce of Wheat, 27½ cwt. @ 8/3	11	6	10
Oats 23 ,, @ 5/3	6	0	9
Straw off the above 4 acres	6	0	0
Potatoes, 4.4 tons @ 55/0	17	7	9
Turnips 9.2 ,, @ 11/6			
Hay 3.4 ,, @ 45/0	8	0	0
Grazing	4	0	0
	£52	15	4

Deductions—							
Rent @ 21/0 per acre				10	10	0	
Cess and P. Rates				1	0	0	
Seeds—Wheat	1	5	0				
Oats	0	16	0				
Potatoes	1	10	0				
Turnips	0	6	0				
Gr. & Cl.	1	3	0				
				5	0	0	
Manure				8	0	0	
Horse labour obtained in exchange for occasional assistance to a neighbour				0	0	0	24 10 0

Leaving this sum as representing profits
for the family . . . £28 5 4

Probable wages in a manufacturing town—
    Father per week . 8/0
    Boy . . . 7/0
    Girl . . 5/0   52 0 0

In favour of the income derived from wages
in a manufacturing town . . 23 14 8

Probable wages in an agricultural district
    Father per week . 8/0
    Boy . . . 5/0
    Girl . . . 3/0   41 12 0
Wages *from the farm as before* . . 28 5 4

In favour of the income derived from
wages in an agricultural district . £13 6 8

N.B.—The foregoing result might be somewhat modified by introducing flax as part of the rotation, but flax, though a highly remunerative product is a dangerous crop for a very small farmer to grow: it very often misses, and if it misses at all, it misses entirely, and inflicts a loss from which a ten-acre farmer finds it much more difficult to recover than a tenant of 25 or 30 acres of land. If flax were introduced into the rotation it might increase the profits of the farm from £3 to £4 per annum.

The amount of produce per acre, and prices relied on, have been taken from the actual statistics of the county, which show a higher rate of production than most other Irish counties.

I am, my Lord, &c.
M. THOMSON.

Of course it can be conceived that by the application of greater skill and more capital to the land, larger returns could be obtained, but the above is a fair representation of the *modus operandi* of an Ulster tenant labouring under no apprehension of insecurity. It is also to be noted that no charge, on account of tenant-right, has been entered against the farm, though in many instances it would form an important item in the occupier's expenses, amounting perhaps to one-tenth or even one-fifth of his profits.

TABLE XXIII.—Showing the Population in 1841, 1851, and 1861; the Number of Persons attending School and the Number and Proportion per cent. of those not attending School, in each year of age from 5 to 15, both inclusive.

Years of Age.	Population.			Numbers attending School.			Numbers not attending School.			Proportion per cent. at each age *not* attending School.		
	1841.	1851.	1861.	Week ended June 5th, 1841.	Week ended April 12th, 1851.	Week ended April 13th, 1861.	1841.	1851.	1861.	1841.	1851.	1861.
5	216,888	152,206	128,052	27,416	23,261	25,279	189,472	128,945	102,323	87	85	80
6	218,688	161,803	125,261	43,676	37,110	37,390	175,012	134,693	87,871	80	77	70
7	221,712	165,426	124,937	53,227	44,987	44,875	168,485	120,439	80,062	76	73	64
8	222,504	170,081	121,401	58,945	51,426	48,722	163,559	118,655	73,679	73	70	60
9	196,413	156,647	111,593	56,482	55,172	48,957	139,931	103,475	62,636	71	66	56
10	220,819	193,020	127,049	62,824	64,022	50,429	157,995	128,998	76,620	72	67	60
11	168,557	136,031	97,649	42,223	43,954	40,166	126,634	92,077	57,483	75	68	59
12	236,897	212,457	131,508	49,670	57,523	38,117	187,227	154,934	93,931	79	73	71
13	182,254	153,270	100,577	30,913	36,015	26,505	151,341	117,255	74,052	83	76	74
14	209,522	202,566	140,258	25,610	34,570	21,736	183,912	167,996	118,522	88	83	85
15	179,490	167,481	126,527	13,258	14,555	12,668	166,222	152,926	113,859	93	91	90
	2,374,044	1,873,958	1,334,792	464,254	460,595	395,294	1,809,790	1,410,393	939,428	80	75	70

Table showing the Density of Population.

In Ireland . . . 181 per square mile.
„ France . . . 177 „
„ Prussia . . . 171 „
„ Austria . . . 148 „
„ Scotland . . . 101 „
„ Spain . . . 90 „

Comparison of the Mineral Resources of Great Britain and Ireland:

Coal raised :—England . . 75,000,000 tons.
Scotland . . 11,000,000 „
Ireland . . 200,000 „

Annual Value.
Pig Iron :—Great Britain . £11,000,000
Scotland alone . . 4,000,000
Ireland . . . 0

Total Value in 1863.
Metals and Coals :—Great Britain £36,000,000
Earthy Materials „ „ . 2,000,000
Minerals and Coals :—Ireland . 500,000

In 1861.
Miners Engaged :—England and Wales 266,000
Scotland . 50,000
Ireland . 40,000
Industrial Classes :—England and Wales 4,828,399
Ireland 667,000

See "Causes of the Poverty in Ireland."—W. Jennings.

A distinguished geologist once told me that he considered the surface of Ireland had scarcely been scratched yet.

Deposits in Joint Stock Banks.

TABLE showing the aggregate Amount of the Private Balances in the Bank of Ireland, and of the Deposits in the Belfast, Hibernian, National, Northern, Provincial, Royal, Ulster, Union (Limited), Munster (Limited), and Exchange (Limited), Joint Stock Banks at the end of each year since 1840.

Year.	Total Amount.	Increase.	Decrease.
1840	£5,567,851	—	—
1841	6,022,573	£454,722	—
1842	6,416,795	394,222	—
1843	6,965,681	548,886	—
1844	7,601,421	635,740	—
1845	8,031,044	429,623	—
1846	8,442,133	411,089	—
1847	6,493,124	—	£1,949,009
1848	7,071,123	577,998	—
1849	7,469,675	398,553	—
1850	8,268,838	799,163	—
1851	8,263,091	—	5,747
1852	10,773,324	2,510,233	—
1853	10,915,022	141,708	—
1854	11,665,739	750,717	—
1855	12,285,822	620,083	—
1856	13,753,149	1,467,327	—
1857	13,113,136	—	640,013
1858	15,131,252	2,018,116	—
1859	16,042,140	910,888	—
1860	15,609,237	—	432,903
1861	15,005,065	—	604,172
1862	14,388,725	—	616,340
1863	12,966,731	—	1,421,994
1864	14,422,176	1,455,445	—
1865	17,050,552	2,628,376	—

W. NEILSON HANCOCK, LL.D.

TABLE SHOWING THE ACREAGE UNDER CROPS IN 1866.

	Acreage under each description of Corn Crop.					Acreage under each description of Green Crop.					Acreage under Hops, Flax, Fallow and Grass				
	Wheat.	Barley, Bere, and Rye.	Oats.	Beans and Peas.	Total of Corn Crop.	Potatoes.	Turnips.	Mangold.	Other kinds.	Total of Green Crops.	Hops and Flax.	Bare fallow or unoccupied Arable Land.	Clover under Rotation.	Permanent Pasture or Meadow.	Total Acreage under all kinds of Crops, Fallow, and Grass.
England and Wales	3,275,893	2,076,732	1,755,883	813,336	7,921,244	355,417	1,663,148	257,945	612,763	2,889,273	Hops. 56,576	870,857	2,552,809	10,255,748	24,546,507
Ireland	300,474	160,530	1,697,648	14,781	2,173,433	1,050,419	317,121	20,218	94,333	1,482,091	Flax. 263,659	28,060	1,600,495	10,002,058	15,549,796
Prov. of Leinster	112,689	112,536	429,023	5,816	660,064	213,289	97,732	10,662	27,996	349,679	7,326	12,018	581,081	2,472,144	4,082,312
,, Munster	120,002	33,660	311,727	1,968	467,357	264,549	91,423	7,073	26,276	389,321	4,151	7,491	454,596	3,277,877	4,600,793
,, Ulster	49,218	6,920	717,540	6,160	779,838	362,464	86,077	1,650	21,902	472,093	245,432	6,411	383,999	2,183,227	4,071,000
,, Connaught	18,565	7,414	239,358	837	266,174	210,117	41,889	833	18,159	270,998	6,750	2,140	180,819	2,068,816	2,795,191
County of Cork	39,160	17,309	134,889	35	191,393	90,988	41,161	3,186	10,785	146,120	1,479	2,095	124,563		
,, Kerry	1,765	4,771	27,005	37	33,578	34,838	5,679	252	3,109	43,878	773	470	67,184		
,, Antrim	7,713	329	81,016	3,705	92,763	53,661	8,594	111	1,975	64,341	27,929	870	68,592		
,, Down	23,558	1,149	117,671	968	143,346	58,667	15,988	433	3,973	79,061	51,769	642	60,064		

The mountain-pastures are excluded in the British Statistics of Agriculture, but are included in those for Ireland. The total extent of pasture in England and Wales may be taken at 17,800,000 acres.

TABLE SHOWING THE GROSS PRODUCE—IN TONS—OF THE ACREAGE UNDER CROPS IN 1866.

	CEREALS.					GREEN CROPS.					
	Wheat. Tons.	Barley, Bere, and Rye. Tons.	Oats. Tons.	Beans & Peas. Tons.	Total Tons.	Potatoes. Tons.	Turnips. Tons.	Mangold. Tons.	Total Root-Crops.	Clover, Hay. Tons.	Flax Tons.
England and Wales	2,325,458	1,869,059	1,448,603	707,602	6,350,722	1,368,355	16,797,794	3,069,545	21,235,694	4,339,775	..
Ireland	195,561	123,608	1,035,565	11,973	1,368,707	4,044,113	3,202,922	240,594	7,487,629	2,720,841	48,941
Province of Leinster	72,403	88,059	278,865	4,493	443,820	874,484	952,887	123,146	1,950,517	900,675	1,467
„ Munster	80,401	25,918	203,402	1,559	311,280	1,018,513	809,093	85,583	1,913,189	795,543	761
„ Ulster	34,576	4,342	407,204	5,282	451,404	1,431,732	989,885	19,305	2,440,922	710,398	45,481
„ Connaught	9,886	4,726	141,820	678	157,110	756,421	448,212	11,745	1,216,378	334,515	1,260
County of Cork	28,489	13,457	90,713	27	132,686	354,853	388,971	42,214	786,038	205,529	282
„ Kerry	1,244	3,685	15,393	35	20,357	135,868	55,086	2,923	193,877	110,853	117
„ Antrim	5,360	233	54,078	3,335	63,006	220,010	101,838	1,165	323,013	123,465	4,713
„ Down	16,196	695	67,366	760	85,017	258,134	147,089	4,243	409,466	102,108	8,752

NOTE.—The quantity in Bushels for the Cereals of England and Wales has been calculated by the data given in Mr. Caird's English Agriculture, and converted into tons on the weights per bushel given in Mr. McDonald's Farming and Estate Management. The Statistics of the Cereals and Root Crops of Ireland are calculated on the acreable averages of the Registrar General's Report, 1864-5, applied to the acres of 1866. There being no return of the acreable produce of Green Crops in England, it has been assumed *to be the same as in Ireland*; though such an assumption is probably unduly disadvantageous to England, and accounts for the rate of total acreable produce in England being below that of Ireland in the next table. In the acreable production of Cereals, of which we have accurate data in both kingdoms, England's superiority to Ireland is unhappily only too clearly established.

TABLE SHOWING THE GROSS VALUE—IN MONEY—OF THE ACREAGE UNDER CROPS IN 1866.

Per ton.	CEREALS.					GREEN CROPS.					MISCELLANEOUS CROPS.			Total value of all the crops.
	Wheat at £8. 5s.	Barley, &c. at £7.	Oats at £3. 5s.	Peas and Beans at £10.	Total value of Cereals.	Potatoes at £2. 15s.	Turnips at 11s 6d.	Mangold at 14s.	Other green crops at £6. (per acre.)	Total value of green crops.	Clover Hay at £2. 5s.	Flax at £50.	Hops at £15. (per acre.)	
England & Wales	19,185,098	13,083,413	7,605,163	7,076,020	46,949,626	3,707,976	9,658,731	2,148,681	3,676,578	19,191,966	9,764,494	none	848,640	76,754,726
Ireland	1,629,875	865,256	5,436,716	119,730	8,051,580	11,121,311	1,841,680	168,415	565,998	13,697,404	6,121,892	2,447,050	none	30,317,926
Province of Leinster	597,325	616,413	1,464,041	44,930	2,722,709	2,404,831	547,910	86,202	167,976	3,208,919	2,026,518	73,330	..	8,031,496
„ Munster	663,308	181,426	1,067,860	15,590	1,928,184	2,800,911	465,228	59,908	157,656	3,483,703	1,789,972	38,050	..	7,939,909
„ Ulster	285,252	30,394	2,137,821	52,820	2,506,287	3,937,263	569,183	13,513	131,412	4,651,371	1,598,395	2,774,050	..	11,030,103
„ Connaught	81,559	33,082	744,535	6,780	865,976	2,080,158	257,721	8,221	108,954	2,456,054	732,659	63,900	..	4,136,689
County of Cork	237,034	94,199	476,243	270	807,746	975,846	223,658	29,549	64,710	1,293,763	462,440	14,100	..	2,578,053
„ Kerry	10,263	25,795	80,813	350	117,221	373,604	31,674	2,046	18,654	425,978	249,419	5,850	..	798,468
„ Antrim	44,220	1,631	283,909	33,350	363,110	605,028	58,554	815	11,850	676,249	277,796	235,650	..	1,552,805
„ Down	133,617	4,865	353,671	7,600	499,753	709,869	84,576	2,970	23,838	821,253	229,743	437,600	..	1,988,349

TABLE showing the Tillage Acres, the Tillage Cultivators, and the gross annual value of the produce; also the annual value of the produce per acre, the annual value produced by each cultivator, and the number of acres he cultivates.

	Tillage Acres, 1866.	Tillage Cultivators. Census of 1861.	Gross produce on the acreable average production of 1864-5.	Annual value of gross produce per acre.	Annual value of produce to each Cultivator.	Number of acres to each Cultivator.
			£.	£.	£.	
England and Wales	14,290,759	2,229,117	76,754,726	5·3	62·4	11·6
Ireland	5,547,738	985,265	30,317,926	5·4	30·7	5·6
Leinster, Province	1,610,168	211,709	8,031,496	5·0	37·9	7·6
Munster „	1,322,916	253,364	7,239,909	5·4	28·5	5·2
Ulster „	1,887,773	339,705	11,030,103	5·8	32·4	5·5
Connaught „	726,881	177,618	4,136,689	5·6	23·2	4·1
Cork, County	465,650	84,582	2,578,053	5·5	30·4	5·5
Kerry „	145,883	34,643	145,883	5·4	23·0	4·2
Antrim „	254,495	36,912	1,552,805	6·1	42·0	6·9
Down „	334,882	47,717	1,982,349	5·9	41·6	7·0

From the foregoing Table it will be seen that the acreable produce in Ulster, where one man cultivates 5½ acres, is greater than the acreable produce in Connaught and Munster, where more men cultivate a smaller area; and that whereas in Ulster each cultivator extracts from the soil £32. 4s, in Munster and Connaught he only obtains £28. and £23. The same proportions will be seen to rule the rate of production when Antrim or Down are compared with Cork or Kerry.

Surprise may perhaps be occasioned by the rate of the acreable produce in Ireland appearing to be greater than the rate of the acreable produce in England. This is to be accounted for by our having been compelled to estimate the green crops of England according to the rate of production of green crops in Ireland, no statistics, except those which give the number of acres so cultivated in England, existing on the subject. But even though it be admitted that the same superiority of production which is evinced by the acreable yield of cereals in England extends to the rest of her cultivation, it is very evident that the difference in the agricultural prosperity of the two countries depends rather upon the excess of persons in Ireland amongst whom the produce has to be distributed than on the comparative inferiority of her rates of production. Indeed, it stands to reason, that both rent and wages being lower in Ireland than in England, if the rate of produce were anything like the same (and the difference in money value is probably much less than is supposed) the profits of the Irish farmer might be even greater than those of the English, notwithstanding his more distant markets.

If we assume that England is as superior to Ireland in the production of her green crops as in that of her cereals the rate of her gross acreable produce would have to be taken at something considerably above £5. 3s per acre, raising of course to a proportionate amount the annual value of produce to each cultivator. But probably the £11,000,000. worth of potatoes in Ireland are grown as skilfully as the £9,500,000. of turnips are grown in England, though it must be admitted that the predominance of our potato crop, and the restricted extent of our turnip cultivation may be an element of danger in the Irish system.

NUMBER OF ACRES IN EACH PROVINCE in 1851 and 1861; also the same reduced to proportions per cent.

Provinces.	Arable Land.		Plantations.		Towns.		Water.		Uncultivated.	
	1851.	1861.	1851.	1861.	1851.	1861.	1851.	1861.	1851.	1861.
	Acres.	Acres.	Acres.	Acres.	Acres.	Acres.	Acres.	Acres.	Acres.	Acres.
Leinster	4,037,717	4,079,130	101,776	102,218	18,712	20,063	52,009	52,009	665,997	662,895
Munster	4,310,452	4,538,054	103,665	106,347	14,238	13,176	151,381	152,157	1,484,843	1,257,987
Ulster	3,994,259	4,057,563	58,611	59,661	8,815	12,183	214,956	210,234	1,198,797	1,139,743
Connaught	2,460,153	2,790,078	40,854	48,371	3,825	3,814	212,864	213,064	1,674,347	1,336,713
Total	14,802,581	15,464,825	304,906	316,597	45,590	49,236	631,210	627,464	5,023,984	4,357,338
Per Cent	71·14	74·29	1·47	1·52	0·22	0·24	3·03	3·02	24·14	20·93

EXTRACT FROM AGRICULTURAL RETURNS.

Total extent under crops in Ireland in each year from 1817-1866.

Total extent under crops.		Year.	
5,238,575	in	1847	
incomplete	,,	1848	
5,543,748	,,	1849	Increase.
5,758,292	,,	1850	,,
5,858,951	,,	1851	,,
5,739,214	,,	1852	Decrease.
5,696,951	,,	1853	,,
5,570,610	,,	1854	,,
5,688,836	,,	1855	Increase.
5,753,547	,,	1856	,,
5,858,117	,,	1857	,,
5,882,052	,,	1858	,,
5,862,605	,,	1859	Decrease.
5,970,139	,,	1860	Increase.
5,890,536	,,	1861	Decrease.
5,753,610	,,	1862	,,
5,662,487	,,	1863	,,
5,676,321	,,	1864	Increase.
5,548,403	,,	1865	Decrease.
5,519,678	,,	1866	,,

This table proves that the annual extent of land under crops in Ireland is a perpetually-fluctuating quantity, regulated by prices, and by the character of the seasons, and that the alleged conversion of an enormous extent of the tillage lands of Ireland into pasturage is a delusion.

TABLE showing the NUMBER of HOLDINGS in each PROVINCE, in 1841, 1851, and 1861, arranged in CLASSES; with the INCREASE or DECREASE in each Class, during each decennial period.

EXTENT OF HOLDINGS.		LEINSTER.		MUNSTER.		ULSTER.		CONNAUGHT.		TOTAL.	
		Number of Holdings.	(+) Increase or (−) Decrease.	Number of Holdings.	(+) Increase or (−) Decrease.	Number of Holdings.	(+) Increase or (−) Decrease.	Number of Holdings.	(+) Increase or (−) Decrease.	Number of Holdings.	(+) Increase or (−) Decrease.
Not exceeding 1 acre,	1841,	Not ascertained.		8,488				6,273			
	1851,	16,017		8,825	+1,337	6,950		7,719	+1,446	37,528	
	1861,	14,447	−1,570	9,825		8,089	+1,139			40,080	+2,352
Above 1 to 5 acres,	1841,	50,110		57,857		102,215		100,254		310,436	
	1851,	25,711	−24,399	14,200	−43,657	29,709	−72,506	18,463	−81,791	88,083	−222,353
	1861,	23,848	−1,863	13,736	−464	28,458	−1,251	19,427	+964	85,469	−2,614
Above 5 to 15 acres,	1841,	46,039		61,753		99,605		45,402		252,799	
	1851,	33,051	−12,988	24,365	−37,388	85,176	−14,429	49,255	+3,853	191,854	−60,945
	1861,	29,515	−3,543	21,959	−2,406	82,053	−3,123	50,404	+1,149	183,931	−7,923
Above 15 to 30 acres,	1841,	20,688		27,611		25,219		5,824		79,342	
	1851,	26,006	+5,318	28,855	+1,244	57,651	+32,432	28,799	+22,975	141,311	+61,969
	1861,	24,226	−1,780	26,895	−2,050	57,660	+9	32,560	+3,761	141,251	−60
Above 30 acres,	1841,	17,943		16,665		9,665		4,362		48,625	
	1851,	38,096	+20,153	53,074	+36,409	37,813	+28,158	20,107	+15,745	149,090	+100,465
	1861,	39,384	+1,288	55,833	+2,759	39,464	+1,651	23,152	+3,045	157,833	+8,743
Total .	*1841,	134,780		163,886		236,694		155,842		691,202	
	†1851,	138,888	−11,909	128,982	−43,392	217,299	−26,345	122,897	−39,218	608,066	−120,864
	1861,	131,420	+7,468	128,158	−824	215,724	−1,575	133,262	+10,365	608,564	+498

* Exclusive of holdings under 1 acre. † The decrease shown in the ten years, 1841-51, is the decrease in the number of holdings above 1 acre and upwards, as the number of holdings under 1 acre was not returned for 1841.

Total Number of Farm or Land Holdings in Ireland, in 1841-51-61, 62-63, and 64; and their Extent in Statute Acres, in 1864.

Extent of Holdings.	No. of Holdings. 1841.	No. of Holdings. 1851.	No. of Holdings. 1861.	No. of Holdings. 1862.	No. of Holdings. 1863.	No. of Holdings. 1864.	No. of Statute Acres. 1864.
Not exceeding 1 acre,	134,314	35,728	40,080	43,716	46,096	48,653	25,394
1 to 5 acres,	310,436	88,083	85,469	84,463	82,451	82,037	288,916
5 to 15 acres,	252,799	191,854	183,931	183,031	180,145	176,368	1,836,310
15 to 30 acres,	79,342	141,311	141,251	140,218	138,540	136,578	3,051,343
Above 30 acres,	48,625	149,090	157,833	157,957	158,044	138,135	15,117,161
Total Holdings	825,516	608,066	608,564	609,385	605,276	601,771	20,319,924

Between 1841 and 1861 the number of holdings not exceeding 15 acres declined 55 per cent, while those above 15 acres increased 133 per cent.; between 1841 and 1861, the farms from 15 to 30 acres have nearly doubled in number, and in the same period the farms above 30 acres have increased from 48,625 to 157,833.

Table of HOLDINGS, 1841 to 1864, from the Registrar General's Returns.

Size of Holdings.		Leinster.	Munster.	Ulster.	Connaught	Total.
		Number.	Number.	Number.	Number.	Number.
Above 1 to 5 Acres	1841	50,110	57,857	102,215	100,254	310,436
	1851	25,711	14,200	29,709	18,463	88,083
	1864	23,103	12,901	27,565	18,468	82,037
		Decrease.	Decrease.	Decrease.	Decrease.	Decrease.
Increase or Decrease in number between 1841 and 1864		27,007	44,956	74,650	81,786	228,399
Rate per cent.		53·9	77·7	73·0	81·6	73·6
Above 5 to 15 Acres	1841	46,039	61,753	99,605	45,402	252,799
	1851	33,058	24,365	85,176	49,255	191,854
	1864	28,532	20,780	78,826	48,230	176,368
		Decrease.	Decrease.	Decrease.	Increase.	Decrease.
Increase or Decrease in number between 1841 and 1864		17,507	40,973	20,779	2,828	76,431
Rate per cent.		38·0	66·3	20·9	6·2	30·2
Above 15 to 30 Acres	1841	20,688	27,611	25,219	5,824	79,342
	1851	26,006	28,855	57,651	28,799	141,311
	1864	23,447	25,421	56,257	31,453	136,578
		Increase.	Decrease	Increase.	Increase.	Increase.
Increase or Decrease in number between 1841 and 1864		2,759	2,190	31,038	25,629	57,236
Rate per cent.		13·3	7·9	123·1	440·1	72·1
Above 30 Acres	1841	17,943	16,665	9,655	4,362	48,625
	1858	38,096	53,074	37,813	20,107	149,090
	1864	39,351	55,819	40,418	22,547	158,135
		Increase.	Increase.	Increase.	Increase.	Increase.
Increase or Decrease in number between 1841 and 1864		21,408	39,154	30,763	18,185	109,510
Rate per cent.		119·3	234·9	318·6	416·9	225·2
Total	1841	134,780	163,886	236,694	155,842	691,202
	1851	122,871	120,494	210,349	116,624	570,338
	1864	114,433	114,921	203,066	120,698	553,118
		Decrease.	Decrease.	Decrease.	Decrease.	Decrease.
Increase or Decrease in number between 1841 and 1864		20,347	48,965	33,628	35,144	138,084
Rate per cent.		15·1	29·9	14·2	22·6	20·0

TABLE showing the Number of MEN, WOMEN, and YOUNG PEOPLE employed on 11 FARMS in ENGLAND, abridged from the "Hand Book of Farm Labour," by John Chalmers Morton. London, 1863.

No.	Tillage. Acres.	Pasturage. Acres.	Men.	Women.	Girls and Boys.
1	910	15	20	0	22
2	900	120	30	12	15
3	660	100	33	3	13
4	260	0	12	8	4
5	550	0	26	20	15
6	310	110	8	10	0
7	200	100	14	4	5
8	400	40	16	4	8
9	2004	430	96	40	20
10	408	280	25	12	8
11	500	225	31	14	17
	7102	1420	310	127	127

NOTE.—Men employed as above 310

Women and Young People (each individual in this category is taken as the equivalent of ¾ of a man, their average wages being in that proportion to the men's wages) . 190
                                                                                                            ───
                                                                                                            500

Which in the proportion of 8 men to tillage for 1 man to pasturage, gives 14·5 acres of tillage to each cultivator.

N.B.—In the Table at p. 154, it has been calculated that in England one man is employed on no more than 11 acres. It will be seen that Mr. Morton's figures give the proportion as one cultivator to 14·5 acres: but as two-thirds of the holdings in England are under 100 acres, the farms cited by Mr. Morton would hardly give a correct general average.

THE COST OF HAND-POWER.

The subjoined extract appears in *Morton's Handbook of Farm Labour:*—

"A man will dig 8 perches of land, or say 2,000 square feet nearly a foot deep, in a day. In doing so he lifts probably three-quarters of it through about a foot in height—that is to say, he lifts 1,500 cubic feet, weighing at least 150,000 lbs., one foot high, in ten hours' time, and to do it therefore he must maintain upon the average a lift of 250 lbs. per minute all that time. Of course, in addition to the mere lift, there is the labour of cutting off this earth from the firm ground to which it was attached. In my second case, then, this portion of his labour is very much reduced. Three men will lift 100 to 120 cubic yards of farmyard dung, and fill it into carts, in 10 hours' time. The 33 to 40 cubic yards which fall to each man's share, at 12 to 14 cwt. apiece, weigh 50,000 lbs., and this is lifted over the edge of the cart, or 4 feet high—equal to 200,000 lbs., lifted daily 1 foot high, or 330 lbs. per minute. This is one-fifth more than in the last case. Now, take a third instance, in which there is no labour in detaching the weight from any previous connexion. A man will pitch in an hour's time an acre of a good crop, tied in sheaves, to an average height of full six feet on the cart or waggon. Straw and corn together, such a crop will weigh more than two tons, say 5,000 lbs. In doing this he therefore lifts 300,000 lbs. one foot high in ten hours, or 500 lbs. per minute. My fourth case is of much the same kind. One man and five boys or women, equal as regards wages, and I will therefore assume equal as regards power, to three men, will throw into carts, upon an average of Swedes and mangel-wurzels, three acres of a good crop, say 70 tons in all, in a day of nine hours' length. They lift these 150,000 lbs. four feet, being equal to 600,000 lbs. one foot; or 200,000 lbs. apiece in nine hours' time, which is about 370 lbs. a minute. These four cases indicate the mere force of a man then, at a cost say of 3d an hour, as equal to a lift of 250, 330, 500, and 370 lbs. per minute; the two former being cases where the load has to be detached as well as lifted, and the third being performed under the influence of good harvest fare. But now compare this, even in its best case, with the duty of the steam-engine—namely, the lift of 33,000 lbs. one foot high per minute for 3d or even less per hour; and compare it with the actual average performance of the horse, 16,000 to 19,000 lbs. lifted one foot per minute for 5d an hour. In order at the best rate named to do the work of the steam-engine, 66 men would be required at a cost not of 5d but of more than 15s per hour; and in order to do the work of the horse, 32 men would be needed, at a cost of 8s instead of 5d per hour. It is plain that if we can take much of the mere labour of the farm out of the hands of the labourer, and put it into the hands of steam power for its performance, there is an enormous amount of saving to be made in the cost of agricultural production. It is plainly folly in the labourer to think that as regards the mere labour of the land he can compete with either steam-power or horse-power. Strength of body is desirable, and sinew hardened by long practice in hard work has a considerable marketable value—for that, however hardly it may sound, is the aspect of the matter in which the interests of the labourer most directly appear—but it is clear that for sheer lift, and the mere putting forth of force, horse-power, and still more that of untiring steam, must grind the soul out of any body that shall pretend to competition with it. It is in the cultivation not so much of mere strength of body as of skill and intelligence that the safety of the labourer lies, and in his capability of education he is perfectly secure."

EMIGRATION.

As the aspect in which I regard the emigration of the embarrassed Irish tenant, as well as my opinion on the desirable limits of population in Ireland, have been a good deal misrepresented, I insert the following extracts from former speeches on the subject.

Extract from a Speech in the House of Lords, 16 *March,* 1866.

"But it may be objected, if only the resources of the country were to be developed, occupation might be found for all these millions. That I at once admit. I believe the soil of Ireland is capable of sustaining a population as large as it has ever borne; and that a hundred fountains of wealth have yet to be unsealed. . . . .

"Depend upon it, as soon as conditions favourable to its development again exist, population will recreate itself; and perhaps there is no race in the world which has given such unmistakeable evidence of its expansive power."

Extract from a Speech by Lord Dufferin at a Tenant's Dinner, April, 1865.

"Gentlemen, it is undoubtedly a sad thing to watch the tide of noble-hearted, free, and energetic men, year by year, flocking from the shores of Ireland to seek a better future on more abundant soils. But, gentlemen, I confess, a still sadder, and to my mind a more terrible, spectacle presents itself whenever I see a patient, industrious tenant, hopelessly struggling on year after year, encumbered with debt contracted on the Tenant-right of a farm too small for remunerative cultivation, and surrounded by promising boys and girls, whom his necessities confine to the drudgery of field labour, and whose minds are gradually becoming spell-bound by the same unhealthy craving after a patch of land which originally tempted their father to his ruin. Such a sight, I say, is, to my mind, the more painful of the two; for whereas in the one case we can picture to ourselves the emancipated emigrant manfully working his way in the world until at last his efforts are crowned with affluence and success, in the other we can only look forward to the gradual but sure approach of still more bitter disappointment, and a deepening degradation in each succeeding generation."

NUMBER OF EMIGRANTS IN EACH YEAR.

Provinces and Counties.	1851-57.	1858.	1859.	1860.	1861.	1862.	1863.	1864.	1865.	Total number of Emigrants from May 1, 1861 to Dec. 31, 1865.			Per-centage of Emigration 1861-65 to Population in 1861.
										Males.	Females.	Total.	
Leinster	197,963	10,161	11,841	13,366	8,576	11,368	15,020	19,790	20,524	157,916	150,693	308,609	21·2
Munster	364,763	18,503	19,715	27,428	22,404	33,452	54,870	48,397	37,426	318,316	308,642	626,958	41·4
Ulster	241,146	29,179	38,150	27,790	21,323	14,115	22,497	19,853	22,301	232,685	203,669	436,354	22·8
Connaught	114,715	5,760	7,464	8,172	5,124	6,244	17,815	18,121	12,477	97,422	99,470	196,892	21·6
Not stated	15,274	734	3,429	7,865	5,865	4,938	7,027	8,008	8,769	34,174	27,735	61,909	··
Total	933,861	64,337	80,599	84,621	64,292	70,117	117,229	114,169	101,497	840,513	790,209	1,630,722	28·1

Extracts from a Report by Mr. Robertson on the Rate of Agricultural Labour in Co. Cork.

My Lord,
    In as few words as possible I will endeavour to state the result of my observations on the condition of the agricultural labourer in the County of Cork.

As might have been expected, the wages given in and around the City of Cork, are fully 20 per cent. above the wages given in the country districts.

The following may throw some light upon this subject. They are a number of questions I put to the various agricultural authorities, resident in different parts of the county, in some cases fully twenty miles apart. The answers here represent the opinion of the majority of the persons questioned :—

What are the weekly wages of agricultural labourers in your locality, are they entirely paid in money, or have they perquisites?

Ans. They get 7s, a free cottage, one load of coals per annum, one pair of shoes, " at Blarney." These are regular hands, and employed all the year round.
Probable gross weekly value, 8s 6d.

Do. They get 6s or 7s per week, have no perquisites. Best men sometimes allowed a free house: but this the exception. " Dunmanway, 40 miles west of Cork."

Do. They get 6s or 7s per week, are generally allowed free cottages. " Bandon, 20 miles west of Cork."

Do. They get 8s per week, have no perquisites. Best men allowed free cottage. " Four miles south of Cork."

Do. They are paid 7s per week if free labourers. If squatters they are paid 1s per day by the farmer on whose land they have squatted. In some cases the farmer provides a cottage for the family, and boards the labourer in his own house, paying him 6d per day. "Millstreet and Kenturk, 40 miles north-west of Cork." . . . .

Have wages advanced during the past 10 years?
Yes, *in many localities* 50 *and* 60 *per cent.*

Is there a good supply of properly qualified agricultural labourers?
No. There is great difficulty in obtaining skilled workmen, especially in poor districts.

To what is this deficiency to be attributed?
The removal of best men into districts where machinery is employed, (*farmers in these localities being able to pay better wages* for intelligent men,) emigration, education, increased facilities for travelling, &c.

In the case of occasional labourers, what time do you suppose they are unemployed?
For five or six weeks during winter. . . . .

The occasional labourer, is in a most unfortunate plight, in most cases he is a squatter, and is bound to assist the farmer, on whose land he is squatted, whenever his services are required, at a uniform rate of 6d per day and his food, or 1s a day without food. They generally have four or five acres of land round their cabins, which they cultivate. Few are employed during more than six months of the year, during the remainder they are either idle or occupied on their own patches of land. As the farmer pays a uniform wage, he takes good care only to employ these labourers when the weather is favourable for outside labour, during unfavourable weather the labourer being left to his own resources. . . . .

The farmer has thus at hand always plenty of labour, which he can command at all seasons of the year, as the squatter only holds possession of his cabin and ground as long as he keeps faith with the farmer.* Round some of these cabins the three or four acres of reclaimed ground is in a fair state of cultivation. The cabins are, however, invariably in the most wretched condition, and generally littered all round with a mass of decomposing animal and vegetable matter, the general receptacle for all kinds of refuse. . . . .

I spoke to several farmers regarding the condition of these

* See p. 5.

poor people. The following is the substance of these conversations.

They are in a bad condition these squatters. Do you not think their position might be improved?

Well, they are, but I don't see what can be done for them; they are of great use to the country, half of the cultivated land round here has been reclaimed by them.

What proportion of their time do you suppose they are employed by the farmer?

In some cases two-thirds, but the majority only half time.

What do they do during the remainder of the year?

Reclaim the bits of ground round their cabins.

Do you think what they obtain from the farmer, and what they produce on their own ground will be worth 8s. per week all the year round?

Certainly not, except under very favourable circumstances. Few have had a day's work during the past three or four weeks. *Even in summer they have a great deal of lost time:* they go to a farmer, but if the day turns out wet they are sent home.

Do you find such labourers useful and obliging workmen?

They are obliging enough; but are careless, unskilful workmen; require constant supervision; they are difficult to teach; *being their own masters during half of the year* are difficult to manage.

Then you think, if they had no land, but had good cottages, and were regularly employed, it would be better both for themselves and the farmer?

Certainly. But who is to reclaim the land?

Well, if the landlord was to reclaim large tracts himself, employed these men as labourers, letting the land at a fair rate of interest on his outlay, would not the land be far more satisfactorily improved, and these people in a far more satisfactory condition?

Yes; but farmers would have to pay more wages, and they can scarcely live as it is.

Well; but if your labouring population were better paid, and better housed, do you not think a larger quantity of farm produce would be consumed in the locality, and would not the 15 or 20 per cent. saved in conveyance to a market more than pay this extra cost of labour?

Possibly it might.

The squatter holds generally by the same term as the farmer; or as long as he keeps the terms of his contract with him. At the expiration of a lease, fifteen or twenty of these squatters' families are sometimes found resident on a farm. Here a difficult problem presents itself—what is to be done with these poor people? They cannot be turned adrift, and it would not be judicious to make them tenants. Out of compassion, in many cases, they have been recognized as tenants; but this has been a very unfortunate step for the country—a race of pauper-tenants has been created, with farms of five or six acres. *These persons, feeling themselves elevated above their previous position, refuse to work for their former employer, excepting as fancy or necessity may dictate.* . . . .

Round Killarney I found a large population who have very migratory habits. During spring and summer these people go into the agricultural districts north and north-west, returning to this locality during the winter months. At the present time these people are in a very unfortunate position: work of all kinds is very scarce, and the average wages is only about 1*s.* per day. . . . .

Bad as is the condition of the agricultural labouring man, the condition of the female employés on farms is even worse. Their wages are lower and they work as hard, in many cases, harder than the men; carry on their backs, in wicker baskets, manure to the fields; go to the bog and carry home turf, &c. . . . .

I would, in conclusion, only add, *that it is not the low rate of wages in these parts, which causes such sufferings to the labouring class, but the uncertainty and irregularity of their employment.* If regularly employed, I believe they would be more comfortable on 6*s.* per week than under present circumstances, though, at times, they may earn 8*s.* or 9*s.* per week. When a labourer loses work for two or three weeks together, it takes a large weekly pay to make him a fair average through the year.

W. R. ROBERTSON.

MEM. *as to the former and present rate of Wages in the County of Down, by Lord Dufferin's Agent.*

Labourers pay-sheets have been continuously passing through my hands for the last 38 years, and during that time, and especially since 1846 or 7, the rate of wages paid to the agricultural labourers has been gradually increasing until it has reached 1s. 6d. a day or 9s. a week, which is the present standing rate of wages for ordinary labourers in constant employment; *but able-bodied, active and handy labourers can readily command, and are at present earning* 1s. 8d. *a day, or* 10s. *a week*; and mason's assistants, quarrymen or drainers from 1s. 8d. to 2s. per day; indeed for the last eighteen months or so I have been paying (20 miles from Belfast) to a "squad" of constant labourers 2s. a day. In harvest and other busy seasons 1s. 6d. to 2s. per day, *with their victuals,* is not at all uncommon.

The food of the labourer now is altogether different from what I recollect it; and although the simple diet he was then accustomed to was perhaps as wholesome as the higher standard he can now afford, yet there can be no doubt whatever but that his present dietary is more suitable, as enabling him to endure with less fatigue the toils that labour imposes upon him. In fact, his condition is in every respect bettered; his food is improved and his clothing improved, for neither the price of the one or the other has at all kept pace with the rise in wages—many of the necessaries of life being now cheaper than when his wages were at the lowest.

The half yearly wages paid to a general farm labourer, boarded and lodged in the house was, in 1830 and for many years afterwards, £3. to £3. 10s, and now the same class of servant is paid from £6. to £8. for the same period. It was a very common custom to let the reaping of the corn crops by the acre: 5s to 6s used to be the price given, now it cannot be got done under 10s to 12s per acre.

April, 1867. MORTIMER THOMSON.

POSTSCRIPT.

MR. BUTT'S PAMPHLET.

SINCE the foregoing pages were sent to press, I have had the advantage of reading Mr. Butt's recent work, entitled "The Irish People and the Irish Land." In that publication Mr. Butt has been good enough to notice my letters to the *Times*, and to contest my facts and opinions with a freedom I am only too glad he should have used, but with less candour than I might have expected.

As I am anxious my pamphlet should be at the service of Members of Parliament before the adjourned debate on Lord Naas' Land Bills, I do not propose to enter into any lengthened examination of Mr. Butt's very able and interesting volume; but I must be allowed to notice one or two sentences in which he refers more immediately to myself.

The first passage it is necessary to quote is the following, p. 51—

"Before I do so I must claim your lordship's permission to offer some observations upon the letters of Lord Dufferin. . . . .

"It is only in a third letter that Lord Dufferin incidentally notices the 'Plea for the Celtic Race.' Before noticing the second letter I claim your lordship's permission to offer some observations on the third.

"I cannot say that, in this letter, Lord Dufferin has even made an attempt to answer me. I gather, indeed, from the way in which he alludes to it that his lordship had not then condescended to read the tract upon which he commented. In his third letter he observes that—

"'It has been objected I have mistaken the nature of the accusations directed against the landlord class in Ireland, who, *I am informed*, have been ruthlessly gibbetted, not exactly on account of their own acts, but as representatives of those bygone generations to whose vicious mismanagement of their estates the present misfortunes of the country are to be attributed.' . . . . . .

"As, in a subsequent part of the letter, Lord Dufferin does me the honour of mentioning me by name, I presume that I am 'the writer' referred to in this passage, and that this is intended as a criticism on the 'Plea for the Celtic Race.' The very language of the reference, 'I am informed,' implies that Lord Dufferin had formed his opinion of the tract upon the opinion of others. I did not need, indeed, that reference to assure me that this was so. It was, I believe, impossible, if he had read it, for a writer as intelligent and able as Lord Dufferin so completely to misunderstand — equally impossible for one of his station and character so entirely to misrepresent.

"If, as I have reason to believe from his subsequent letter, Lord Dufferin has since read the 'Plea for the Celtic Race,' I am sure he will admit that it would not be fair to describe me as having 'ruthlessly gibbetted' Irish landlords, or 'gibbetted' them at all. My whole argument was that 'the landlord of 100 years ago' was, as Lord Dufferin describes him, the creature of circumstances. I never once alluded to any management, vicious or otherwise, of the estates of a century ago."

In reply to these observations I have much pleasure in assuring Mr. Butt that he is not the writer to whom I alluded in the passage he has quoted. It was the anonymous author of a very able article in the *Daily News*, of Dec. 12, whom I described as proposing to "ante-date our responsibilities;" and, so far from implying that Mr. Butt shared his opinion, I endeavoured to refute it by a quotation from Mr. Butt's own pamphlet.

Mr. Butt next objects to my view of the injuries inflicted on Ireland by the commercial restrictions of the last century. Of course the point must always remain a matter of opinion. It cannot be proved by a rule of three sum; but if Mr. Butt has any confidence in the judgment of Mr. Cobden and Mr. Bright, I would refer him to the opinion of those two gentlemen. Mr. Cobden has stated that but for the suppression of her trade and commerce, Ireland might have been as prosperous as England; and Mr. Bright, in his speech at Dublin, has said that, but for the development of her manufacturing resources, England might have been as miserable as Ireland. If any weight is to be attached to these two authorities, the matter is reduced to something very like a mathematical certainty.

Mr. Butt objects that for the last 80 years the trade of Ireland has been free, and that ample time has been given to the South to rival the North in manufacturing prosperity. I would venture to remind him that within the same period the South has been the scene of two attempts at rebellion, and the theatre of a perennial agitation, and that such circumstances are unfavourable to industry and to the investment of capital.

Mr. Butt further complains that I have not taken into sufficient account the confiscations of former times, and the religious hostility which prevailed between the owners and occupiers of the soil.

I have never proposed to myself to review the political history of Ireland, for the simple reason that I did not consider that any change in the destination of existing property could be justified by a reference to transactions which took place in the days of Elizabeth, Cromwell, and William; nor that any practical purpose could be served by reviving ancient animosities of race.

With regard to the wrongs inflicted on Ireland by the penal code, I could be as warm, if not as eloquent, as Mr. Butt; and I sincerely hope that before long we shall see the Catholic clergy of Ireland placed on a footing of perfect equality with their brethren of the Protestant communities. But I abstained from enlarging on these topics because they were unconnected with the subject of my immediate inquiry. Moreover, it is not true that the fact of their landlords being Protestants, deteriorated the *economical* condition of the Irish tenant to the extent which has been implied. As Mr. Butt himself has admitted, and as Mr. Gregory, in his recent most able and statesmanlike speech, has still more distinctly told us, it was rather from the exactions of the middleman than from those of the head landlord, that the tenant suffered: but the middlemen in general were of the same race and religion as their tenants; nor do I imagine would any one dream of asserting that any difference of religion has rendered the relations between Mr. Herbert and his tenantry less friendly than those which prevail between the tenantry of the Kenmare estate and Lord Castlerosse. A government of religious ascendancy must always prove demoralizing, both to the rulers and to the ruled; but if the landlord of former days was imperious, it was not because he was a landlord, but because he was a member of a dominant sect, though, as a landlord, he would undoubtedly be afforded more ample opportunities of displaying this weakness in his character. But it is unjust to describe as peculiar to the landlord, failings which were the offspring of Acts of Parliament, and were more or less common to every member of the Protestant establishment.

The next statement of Mr. Butt's, to which I shall refer, is the following, p. 105:—

"*I am still unwilling to part with Lord Dufferin's third letter without noticing two passages of no little significance; one, in which he avows himself the apologist of exorbitant rents; the other, in which I think he acknowledges his enmity to Ulster tenant right.*"

The first part of this sentence I need not dwell upon. If it affords Mr. Butt any satisfaction to disseminate such an assertion amongst our fellow-countrymen, of course I cannot prevent him. I would only suggest that a gentleman who can put such a gloss on a writer's language will hardly prove an impartial guide through an historical enquiry, or the complexities of an economical analysis. With regard to my opinion of the tenant right in Ulster, I can add nothing to what I have already said: I simply dissent from Mr. Butt's description of its origin, its nature, and its effects.

I now come to a point of considerable importance, to which Mr. Butt has alluded in the subjoined terms, p. 124:—

"Lord Dufferin then points attention to the fact that a greater number of emigrants go from Ulster than from any other of the three provinces of Ireland. . . . . . .

"It is easy for any man to look wise in quoting figures; but it often happens that exactly as he looks wise he is really foolish.

"It will scarcely be credited that Lord Dufferin makes out his representation by leaving out of account the relative proportion of the population of Ulster to that of the rest of Ireland. It is not necessary to use more words than those which are requisite to make this clear.

"By the census of 1861 the population of the whole of Ireland was, in round numbers, 5,700,000; that of Ulster was 1,900,000; about a third of the entire. The total emigration from Ireland in the year 1864 was 114,908 persons, in round numbers, 115,000. Of these, Ulster ought, in proportion to its population, to have supplied 38,500. The number of emigrants for that year from Ulster was 19,815. Leinster, with a smaller population, supplied the same number. The population of Connaught is not one half that of Ulster, yet the number of its emigrants was very nearly the same.

"Let us compare the population and the emigration from Ulster and Munster in the years 1864 and 1865. These figures are few and simple, they can be understood by every one. By the census of 1861 the population of the two provinces was as follows:—

| Ulster | . | . | . | 1,900,000 |
| Munster | . | . | . | 1,500,000 |

"If, therefore, emigration were in proportion to population, the emigrants from Ulster would have exceeded those from Munster in a proportion of 19 to 15, that is, by a little more than one-fourth.

"How stand the facts as to the last two years. The emigration of these two provinces was as follows:—

	1864.	1865.	Two Years.
Munster	48,387	37,426	85,813
Ulster	19,853	22,302	41,635

"So that the actual emigration from Ulster, with a population of 1,900,000, was not one-half of that from Munster, with a population of 1,500,000. In proportion to the population, the emigration from Ulster was 41 out of 1,900, or little more than two per cent., in Munster it was 85 out of 1,500, or very nearly 6 per cent.

"It cannot be said that the last two years are exceptional. The summary of the returns which, since the year 1851, he has, with marvellous skill and industry, obtained; in the fifteen years ending with the year 1865, the emigration from these two provinces was as follows:—

   Munster 626,968
   Ulster 436,000

"In proportion to the population the emigrants from Ulster do not number one-half of those from Munster.

"And yet from these very figures Lord Dufferin rushed recklessly to the conclusion that want of security of tenure could not be the cause of emigration, because it was as great from Ulster, where tenant right prevails, as from the other provinces of Ireland. . . .

"' Lord Dufferin has proved,' is the language in which this burlesque upon all statistical argument was, and is still cited by the defenders of the present system of Irish land tenure, at the English and even at the Irish press. There never was such an instance of the credulity with which the rash assertions of a man of rank are accepted by some portions of the public as proof.

"This extraordinary fallacy—respect for Lord Dufferin prevents me from saying blunder—was detected and exposed by Mr. Dalton, the gentleman who, under the name of 'Philocelt,' has written so ably in the columns of the *Daily News*. Every one seemed to acquiesce in the imposing array of Lord Dufferin's figures, until the publication of Mr. Dalton pointed out the palpable error upon which *the* argument was based."

I do not propose to notice the personal allusions which Mr. Butt has introduced into his argument, but I must point out that, by taking the years 1864 and 1865 to the exclusion of all the preceding ones with respect to which we have information, and by comparing Ulster with Munster to the exclusion of the other two provinces of Ireland, he had educed a result calculated to give a very incorrect impression. In the passage of my letter, to which Mr. Butt has applied the language I have quoted, I had simply stated that, although immediately after the famine, the emigration from the South was in excess of that from the North, during the last 14 years, the amount of Ulster's contribution to the general emigration had been greater than that of either Connaught or Leinster, and in the ratio of 23 to 28, as compared with the average of the four provinces; in fact, I repeated a statement which, any one who chooses to look, may find in Thom's Almanac. I did not go further into the matter, because when once I had shown that there had been an enormous emigration from Ulster, I had proved all that I wanted to prove, viz.: that a large emigration from a particular district did not constitute a *primâ facie* case of landlord oppression.

It was not necessary for me to enquire whether the ratio

of the emigration, either to the entire population or to the occupying population, was greater in Ulster than in the other three provinces; but as Mr. Butt will see in my present compilation I have done so, and the result proves not only that the *absolute* amount of the emigration from Ulster has been greater than that from either Leinster or Connaught, but that it has also been greater proportionately to the respective populations of two out of the three provinces brought into comparison, as will be apparent from the subjoined table :—

TABLE showing the population of the provinces of Ireland in 1861, the emigration from 1st of May, 1851, to 31st December, 1865, with the percentages of emigration for that period to the population of 1861 :—

	Population.	Emigration.	Percentage.
Leinster	1,457,635	308,609	21·1
Connaught	913,135	196,892	21·6
Ulster	1,914,236	436,354	22·8
Munster	1,513,558	626,958	41·4

Mr. Butt has taken the two particular years which are the most favourable to himself and the least indicative of what has really occurred during the last fourteen. I have no doubt he has acted in perfect good faith, nor need he feel distressed at having fallen into such an error. It was natural enough he should have taken the last two years for his standard. If, however, he had happened to take 1861 he would have found that during that year not only had the emigration from Ulster been greater in proportion to its population than that from Leinster or Connaught, but that it has been nearly twice as great, and but very little less than that from Munster.

$$\frac{\text{Ratio of Emigrants from Leinster in 1861}}{\text{To Population of Leinster in 1861}} = \frac{8,576}{1,457,635} = 0\cdot 56 \text{ per cent.}$$

$$\frac{\text{Ratio of Emigrants from Munster in 1861}}{\text{To Population of Munster in 1861}} = \frac{22,404}{1,513,558} = 1\cdot 15$$

$$\frac{\text{Ratio of Emigrants from Connaught in 1861}}{\text{To Population of Connaught in 1861}} = \frac{6,124}{913,135} = 0\cdot 67$$

$$\frac{\text{Ratio of Emigrants from Ulster in 1861}}{\text{To Population of Ulster in 1861}} = \frac{21,323}{1,914,236} = 1\cdot 1$$

If again he had chosen the years 1858 and 1859, he would have found the proportionate emigration from Ulster not only more than double that from Connaught and Leinster, but even larger than that from Munster.

$$\frac{\text{Ratio of Emigrants from Leinster in 1858 \& 9}}{\text{To Population of Leinster in 1861}} = \frac{22{,}002}{1{,}457{,}635} = 1\cdot 5 \text{ per cent.}$$

$$\frac{\text{Ratio of Emigrants from Munster in 1858 \& 9}}{\text{To Population in Munster in 1861}} = \frac{38{,}218}{1{,}513{,}558} = 2\cdot 5$$

$$\frac{\text{Ratio of Emigrants from Connaught in 1858 \& 9}}{\text{To Population of Connaught in 1861}} = \frac{13{,}224}{913{,}135} = 1\cdot 4$$

$$\frac{\text{Ratio of Emigrants from Ulster in 1858 \& 9}}{\text{To Population of Ulster in 1861}} = \frac{67{,}320}{1{,}914{,}236} = 3\cdot 5$$

The only safe way is to take the entire period about which we have information, as I have done on the preceding page and in the body of my work.

If I might venture on a further suggestion in reference to this subject, it would be that knowing—as Mr. Butt must know—how difficult it is, with the best intentions, to manipulate statistics fairly, he should be more considerate in his language when he has, or rather thinks he has, convicted an opponent of a mistake.

With regard to his omission of all mention of Leinster and Connaught, when he is criticising my comparison of the emigration of Ulster with the emigration from the rest of Ireland, I can hardly speak with the same equanimity. If the proportionate preponderance of emigration has been greater in Ulster than in two out of the three other provinces of Ireland, surely it would have been right to have noted that fact, and not simply to have confined the comparison to the *one* province out of the three where the reverse was the case.

Even Mr. Dalton does not handle this point quite fairly when he lays such stress on the fact of the emigration from Ulster with its far larger population being below the average of the emigration from the whole of Ireland, for he neglects to mention that it is the predominance of the emigration from a single province (Munster) which swells the general average of the kingdom to a figure above that reached in Ulster. The argument was that the Irish emigration was composed of farmers fleeing from the oppression of their landlords. I replied, "the emigration does not consist of the class you imagine, nor is it occasioned by the causes you allege. If it were there ought to be scarcely any emigration from Ulster. But as it happens the emigration from Ulster is, whether taken absolutely or in proportion to its population, greater than that from two of the other three provinces, and within 18·6 per cent. of what it is even from the third." This was a perfectly clear and unassailable position.

The case as put by Mr. Dalton would only have significance if it had been his intention to prove that the landlords of Munster were pre-eminently wicked. But this is not his object. What he, or at least those gentlemen, who are opposed to the view I have taken, want to prove is that the exceptional circumstances which prevail in Ulster have impeded emigration; but as the emigration from Ulster has been greater than that from Leinster or Connaught, their argument breaks down.

The next passage from Mr. Butt's volume to which I must take exception is the following, p. 143 :—

"In passing, let me say that I cannot admit that which Lord Dufferin assumes, that it has been an advantage to the country to turn out every man who held a farm under 'fifteen acres.'"

I would venture to ask Mr. Butt to point out the sentence in which I have said any thing of the sort. I have, indeed, quoted passages from the evidence of gentlemen who are known to be strong partizans of the tenant, which show that 15 acres is the smallest area over which they themselves would extend the protection of a lease, or on which they considered a man and his family could live with comfort, and I argued from this evidence, 1st. That it was not surprising that, as a consequence of the potato failure, the number of farms in this particular class should have diminished; and 2ndly, that as there were still in Ireland upwards of 300,000 holdings below 15 acres (a size described as precarious by Bp. Keane), it was fair to conclude that the landlords had not carried their alleged policy of consolidation to any excessive lengths. But to invest this very reasonable and fair argument with the meaning Mr. Butt seems to attach to it, is not a justifiable way of discrediting even a landlord, while to imply, as he does imply, that the tenants who have disappeared out of this category, *have been turned out because they held less than 15 acres of land*, is a grave misrepresentation of facts.

If Mr. Butt thinks that holdings of 5, 10, or even 15 acres are not rather small, let him argue the matter with those gentlemen who have pronounced a different opinion, and more especially with Mr. Dalton,* from whose pamphlet he has so frequently quoted, and who has pronounced the subjoined dictum on the subject.

"All sorts of calculations have been made as to what should be the minimum size of a farm. Experience is, after all, the best guide; and mine, which has been tolerably extensive, tells me that a farmer of average intelligence and industry can thrive on a farm of 20 statute acres of land of medium quality; some on much less; but 20 acres is a safe *minimum*."†

As it happens it has never occurred to me to fix a minimum size of farms, though I have stated more than once, that I did not think a 10 acre farmer was likely to prosper, and that a man with 25 acres and upwards would have a better prospect. As to my recommending that a tenant should be evicted, or rejoicing that a tenant had been turned out *because* he had only 15 acres, it is an imputation which I do not think it necessary to disavow.

I now come to Mr. Butt's observations on what I said in my letter to *The Times* with regard to the rate of wages in the South and West of Ireland. As ten pages of his work are devoted to the exposure of the incorrect statement I

---

* Mr. Dalton is the author of the able letters signed Philocelt, which appeared in the *Daily News*, and although I thought, and still think, that on one occasion I had reason to complain of the inference drawn by Mr. Dalton from a passage in a speech of mine on emigration, which that gentleman had quoted separately from its context, I have great pleasure in recognizing the ability, and fairness with which he has put forward his views, with which it is with regret I disagree.

† It is perhaps well that I should note a subsequent observation of Mr. Dalton's with reference to a very modest intimation of what my own experience had led me to think on the same subject.

"In sober truth all this dogmatizing on the size of farms, so much in vogue at the present day, is unprofitable work,—the very charlatanry of agriculture. One might as well discuss the abstract size of a shoe, as the abstract size of a farm."—'*Irish Peers and Irish Peasants*,' an answer to Lord Dufferin and the Earl of Rosse, by *Gustavus Tuite Dalton*, p. 25.

certainly made on this subject, I cannot quote all his observations, but since he complains that I have never rectified the error in *The Times*, though I at once did so in the *Daily News*, I do not hesitate to perform the necessary penance, and Mr. Butt shall himself be the executioner. At p. 148, Mr. Butt says:—

"Those who believe that emigration has proved a blessing to the Irish people, at least to that portion of them who have remained at home, must of necessity contend that the outgoing of the labouring population has bettered the condition of the labourer who remains. Lord Dufferin, in support of his argument, describes in very strong terms the improvement. He actually goes the length of stating that

"'THE IRISH LABOURER HAS ALREADY RISEN FROM A SERF TO BE HIS EMPLOYER'S EQUAL!'

"Again he asserts that the evicted tenant has been converted from a struggling farmer into 'a well-paid labourer.'

"Again, 'the wages of labour have doubled within the last fifteen years.'

"And finally, he clearly and unequivocally asserts that throughout the South the wages of agricultural labourers "RANGE FROM TEN TO TWELVE SHILLINGS, OR EVEN FOURTEEN SHILLINGS, A WEEK.' . . . . . .

"I need not say it is not easy for a private individual, unacquainted practically with rural affairs, to ascertain the average rate of wages throughout Ireland. Still I made such effort as was in my power. . . . . . .

"I need scarcely say that this state of facts is entirely irreconcilable with the plain and literal meaning of the passage I have quoted from Lord Dufferin's letter in *The Times*. His statements have been challenged by Mr. Dalton in a letter to the *Daily News*. Lord Dufferin in a letter to that journal of the 24th Jan. thus explained, or qualified, or retracted them.

"I hope I will not be accused of 'ruthlessly gibbetting' any landlord, past, present, or to come, if I place in parallel columns that which Lord Dufferin wrote, and that which we now know he meant:—

"'When I was in the West of Ireland, fifteen years ago, the rate of agricultural wages varied from half-a-crown to five shillings a week. Ever since it has gradually advanced, ranging in the South and West, from ten shillings to twelve shillings, or even fourteen shillings a week; while in the North THE LABOURER is almost absolutely master of the market, and can dictate what terms he pleases.'—Lord Dufferin's first letter.

"'What I alluded to when I named ten or twelve shillings a week was, not wages of the ordinary farm servant—though I admit I had inadvertently used the word agricultural in the previous sentence—but of the best description of unskilled manual labour. . . . . I myself have been paying from 1s. 4d. to 1s. 6d. a day.'—Lord Dufferin's second letter.

"The explanation certainly invites criticism. I have too often admired, on other subjects, the happy elegance of Lord Dufferin's light and graceful style not to feel an interest in the comparison between these two sentences. We know that the mistake proceeded from the 'inadvertent' use of the word 'agricultural,' in the previous sentence.' The 'previous' sentence is, 'When I was in the West of Ireland, fifteen years ago, the rate of agricultural wages varied from half-a-crown to five shillings a week.' The next sentence—' It gradually rose until.' As a full stop intervenes, its intervention is perhaps to be considered, in courtesy to the monarch of punctuation, to constitute two sentences; but a full stop never yet divided words which looked more like a continuation of one. 'Fifteen years ago the rate of agricultural wages varied from two-and-sixpence to five shillings a week. It rose.' What varied, and what rose? 'It' seems very like a mere repetition of 'the rate of agricultural wages.' This unfortunate 'it' is the point of the whole confusion—a huge mistake has hid itself in that little word. 'It' plainly means 'agricultural wages,' but 'it' does not mean 'it;' but when 'it' is mentioned 'it' means the wages of the best 'unskilled manual labour,' whatever 'it' may be.

"I confess I cannot see why in the explanation the farm 'servant' is introduced. He is not exactly the personage whom we had known in the previous statement as the agricultural 'labourer.' Neither his position or his wages are the same. But images elude our closest observation as they glide into each other in the marvellous disappearances of that dissolving view in which all that Lord Dufferin said so exquisitely vanishes into something that he meant.

. . . . . .

"If Lord Dufferin is to be judged, as every public writer, no matter what may be his rank or his ability, must be judged by that which he has published and deliberately given to the world; it is difficult to suggest an excuse for the carelessness of this statement. The real wages are little more than one-half of that which Lord Dufferin assured the English people Irish labourers were receiving. The statement was made with all the circumstantiality of time and place. 'Fifteen years ago, when I was in the West.' It pledged Lord Dufferin's personal knowledge to a part of the statement, it appeared to pledge it to the whole. And this was done in a controversy in which Lord Dufferin had volunteered to come forward as the impugner of the accuracy of others—to convict Mr. Maguire and Mr. Bright of having inaccurately represented to the people of England the condition of Ireland. For a misrepresentation so wonderfully incorrect in its general statement—so marvellously, I might almost say, miraculously, put together, as to convey a wrong impression in every detail of the combination of its words—nothing in Lord Dufferin's explanation furnishes anything like a sufficient excuse."

There can be no doubt that Mr. Butt, on this occasion, has me at his mercy, and he is evidently not inclined to spare his advantage, for he comments on the point with all the irony and indignation, of which he is so great a master, through several closely printed pages of his book. The words I wrote certainly did imply that the rate of *agricultural* wages had advanced from half-a-crown or five shillings a week to ten, or twelve, or even fourteen shillings, in the South and West; and such a statement would be incorrect, though not quite so incorrect as Mr. Butt alleges. But that this misrepresentation was either the result of dishonesty or of ignorance I hope to be able to disprove.

As, perhaps, it may be remembered, I had occasion, on the 16th March last year, to make a speech in the House of Lords on the state of Ireland. That speech, together with some other compositions of my own, was afterwards published in the form of a pamphlet; and a great portion of my letters to the *Times* consisted of passages which repeated the substance of that volume. In the speech to which I referred occurs the following sentences, which in the pamphlet were accompanied by the note now attached to them.

"If we look to the labourer, we shall find a corresponding cause for congratulation. At this moment, in my own county, the wages of an ordinary labourer averages from 1s 4d to 1s 6d a day —in harvest time he cannot be hired under 2s or 1s 6d, and with his food supplied. Railway labourers can get from 10s to 12s a week, and carpenters and masons, etc., from one to two pounds; the actual increase in the rate of agricultural wages being estimated by Judge Longfield at from 25 to 80 per cent. between 1844 and 1860."*

* I have received several letters from different parts of Ireland, assuring me that I have understated the rise in the price of labour. See also *Pall Mall Gazette*, March 31st, 1866.—"The rapid in-
"crease in emigration has produced a great increase in the wages
"of the labouring population. In Kerry they have reached their
"highest, viz., 12s to 15s a week. In Cork—present rate 10s ; with
"present prospects as to emigration, labour is likely to command
"this price."

Now, in reading this extract, the candid reader will see that in writing the sentence which Mr. Butt has taken such trouble to denounce, I intended to put into as condensed a form as possible, the statement made in my speech in the House of Lords. The necessity of crowding what I wanted to say into the space suitable to the columns of a newspaper, has occasioned even graver misconceptions of my meaning, though not through so palpable an infelicity of expression.

Unfortunately, in this instance, the apparent import of my observation was not even ambiguous, for the qualifying epithet, "agricultural," had slipped into the preceding sentence, and, of course, applied to whatever followed.* If I had used the phrase "the price of labour has advanced from its former rate of five shillings a week to ten or twelve, or even fourteen shillings a week," the statement would have been true, though many people would have derived from it a different impression from that which I wished to convey. What I meant was this, that when I was in the South of Ireland during the famine years, and, again, two or three years later, I found that the Southern labourer was not paid more than from 6d to 8d a day, and that even at this rate, he could not obtain anything like regular employment. At the present moment, he has frequently a chance of earning from ten to twelve shillings a week, and, consequently, his position is greatly improved. Even as a common agricultural labourer he receives twice as much as he used to do. In the North he sometimes gets more than twice as much; and, if I am to believe my tenants, he has become a very exacting personage to treat with. This was the sum and substance of what I meant to say. A slip of the pen gave a different character to my sentence. When this was pointed out to me, I acknowledged my error in the *Daily News*, and only refrained from doing so in the *Times*, because I looked forward to setting the matter right in the republished edition of my letters, when I could do so at full length, without occupying the space of a newspaper with a subject of personal rather than of public interest.†

---

* The distinction between an agricultural labourer and an ordinary labourer must always be very indefinite. A navvy, a hodman, a drainer, belong to the same class as the agricultural labourer. They differ rather in the subject of their employments than in their personal qualifications.

† So afraid was I of all exaggeration, that I understated the rate of wages (12s a week) I myself have been paying to my best men during the last year and a half.—*See Mem. by my Agent, p. 376.*

Mr. Leone Levi has lately issued a valuable book on the wages of the working classes. At p. 41, Chap. Agricultural, Mr. Levi says, that in 1860, agricultural wages in Ireland averaged 7s 1½d: that they have been rising ever since, and that allowances included they may now be estimated at 14s a week in England and Scotland, and 10s in Ireland. This, I admit, appears to me too high an average.

Mr. Butt asserts, that the average rate of agricultural wages throughout Ireland does not exceed seven shillings a week. On turning to pages 279, 280, it will be seen that this statement does not quite agree with the authorities there quoted; while on page 280 my original statement is fully confirmed. That I was correct in putting the former rate of the labourer's earnings at from half-a-crown to five shillings a-week will be seen by a reference to page 37.

The only other remark of Mr. Butt's which I think it necessary to notice is the passage in which he objects to my theory that at the determination of a tenancy, during which the occupier has had time to remunerate himself for his expenditure, the landlord is entitled to re-enter into possession of his property.* Now Mr. Butt proposes to impose upon us the obligation of letting out our estates on leases of 63 years. Does he intend that at the expiration of that period the land is to be restored to our controul, to be let, if it should so please us, to other individuals than those who may at that time be in occupation of it? If he does, he accepts my theory, for he would hardly argue that a future tenant can be changed at the expiration of a 63 years' lease, but that an actual tenant under a lease of equally long duration, and at even a more beneficial rent than that which he proposes to attach to his new tenures, should be invested with a more permanent interest. If he does not, his plan consists not of a system of 63 years leases, but of a scheme for transferring in perpetuity the property of Ireland from its present owners to their tenants. And if this is his intention he should have the manliness to say so.

---

* The more the matter is considered the more inconceivable it is to me how any man can dispute this point. I will take the case of an individual farm which I am now about to deal with. For some years past it has been in my own occupation; part of it was incorporated with my park; I have put it into pretty good order. I am now about to let it on a lease of 21 years. On what principle of equity or justice can it be pretended that a tenant who hires this farm for a specified term of 21 years, is entitled to hold it for a longer period, if at the expiration of our contract I should wish to let it to a more desirable occupant. It is now mine. By what rhetorical hocus pocus can it be rendered his and not mine?

The question of compensation for improvements depends on a totally distinct principle.

I have now touched in a very imperfect manner upon some of the salient points which have attracted my notice during a hasty perusal of Mr. Butts' pamphlet, but before taking leave of this part of the subject I must venture to express my regret at a device which has been adopted by Mr. Butt, and which is hardly worthy either of himself or of the audience his eloquence and talents will always enable him to command, viz.: that of endeavouring to invest an adversary's words with an obnoxious meaning, which no candid person could attach to them. I have already noted how Mr. Butt has described me as apologising for rack rents, and rejoicing over the expulsion of every tenant of 15 acres: a single additional instance will suffice to explain my meaning. At page 213, Mr. Butt has introduced the following observations:—

"In another letter he actually claims for the landlord the right of turning off his tenants exactly as he would his farm servants whenever he chooses to consider them deficient in energy or skill:—

"'It is a mistake to imagine that non-payment of rent is the only 'circumstance that can justify evictions. Any one acquainted with 'the management of land is aware that an unskilful farmer, even 'though he pay his rent, may do his landlord's property more harm 'than an industrious tenant who is occasionally in arrear. Few 'things are more liable to deterioration than land, and the value of 'a field may be as completely annihilated for a certain number of 'years as that of a house off which you have taken the roof. Now, 'one of the landlord's most important duties is that of insuring the 'consummate cultivation of his estate, and to hold him up to obloquy 'because he makes a point of *weeding his property of men whose want* '*of energy, or skill, or capital* renders them incapable of doing their 'duty by their farms, and replacing them by more suitable tenants 'is hardly reasonable.'

"According to this theory, the tenant is, in fact, to be a species of bailiff or deputy of the landlord; the landlord's chief duty being not to benefit his tenants, but to ensure 'the consummate cultivation of his farm,' and for this purpose to 'WEED OUT' the tenants when they fail in the energy, the skill, or the capital that is necessary for that purpose. If this be not an approach to the 'metayer' system it certainly makes the landlord the superintendent of the cultivation. But I protest I think this is very like an open avowal of a policy of extermination; it is so if extermination be necessary for the discharge of the chief duty of the landlord, the ensuring of 'the consummate cultivation of his farm.'"

Selecting the word "weeding" from the foregoing very innocent passage (which he describes as "an avowal of a policy of extermination"), Mr. Butt takes it up and plays with it, and cavils at it, and educes inferences from it with a practised skill which no one can admire more than myself. Yet the animus displayed by Mr. Butt towards the indolent or unskilful tenant is even perhaps more hostile.

" I propose to bind the tenant to proper cultivation of the farm, and to the maintenance of all improvements ; and, in the event of his failing in either of these conditions he incurs, in like manner, the forfeiture of the interest which the statute confers upon him." —*Fixity of Tenure, by C. Isaac Butt, p. 5.*

Should his bill ever become law, does he intend to inaugurate a fresh crusade against those landlords who take advantage of the power with which he now proposes to invest them, if they remove from their estates those tenants who fail to fulfil the statutory conditions upon which they hold their land?

Mr. Butt comments upon my remarks as if this process of "weeding" could only be applied to tenants at will. If this were the case, it would be indeed a reason against the granting of leases, but as every well drawn lease contains covenants against burning the land and exhaustive cropping, the lease-holder is as subject to the avoidance of his tenancy for improper cultivation as the man who holds from year to year. Those who are acquainted with the management of property are aware that an intelligent agent knows pretty accurately the position of every tenant on the estate, and that he cannot commit a grosser dereliction of duty than to allow a bankrupt tenant to go on year after year making up his rent out of a succession of flax or corn crops taken off the same field, or with money borrowed from his neighbours. Under such circumstances the most merciful alternative open to a landlord is to step in and terminate a hopeless struggle, which, if prolonged, would only plunge the unfortunate cultivator into deeper debt, and occasion a still further deterioration of the land.

I do not propose to continue my observations on Mr. Butt's work further. Mr. Butt is much too formidable an adversary to be dismissed in a few short sentences; he writes with great power and eloquence, he is evidently actuated by the most sincere and benevolent motives, and he brings to the discussion of the subject a considerable acquaintance both with the past history and present condition of Ireland. No one should think of forming a definite opinion upon any of the questions involved in the present controversy without a patient study of his works; but they should not be read without a careful investigation of what has been said by those who disagree with him. He does not state his opponent's case fairly. Like a mediæval necromancer he moulds a waxen caricature of his adversary, and then amuses himself with running pins into the misshapen " eidolon " or roasting it over a slow fire. To pick out the version of one's argument, which is reproduced in his clever pages, is like trying to trace one's image in a shattered mirror. The brilliant surface is all blurred by flaws, false lights, and sharp splinters, while here and there you catch a detached feature, which you would never guess to be the reflection of your own countenance.

I confess I consider it a misfortune for the country that Mr. Butt should have embarked on the disastrous mission in which he is engaged. Its effect will be to render the landlords jealous of the pretensions of their tenantry, and to make the tenants distrustful of the designs of their landlords, to frighten the English mortgagee, and to discourage the investment of capital.* At the same time I am perfectly ready to enter with Mr. Butt into the examination of all these questions with the most perfect composure. If he considers it would be for the advantage of the country that the owners of property in Ireland should be converted into mere rent chargers, with an almost inappreciable interest in the welfare of their former tenantry and the improvement of what were once their estates, it is certainly advisable that the fairest and most dispassionate consideration should be accorded to his arguments. If he would prefer, as some very respectable persons seem to desire, that the landed gentry of Ireland should be abolished with or without compensation, there is no reason why we should not talk the matter over, and consider the results from every point of view. The possession of land in Ireland is neither so lucrative an investment, nor its management so agreeable an employment as to render the prospect of its acquisition by the State as intolerable a calamity as it might be considered in other countries.

---

* Money has always been from ½ to 1 per cent. dearer to the Irish than to the English proprietor. Of late I am told British capitalists will not look at Irish securities.

Having served for many years as a text to the local agitator, the Irish landlord has now been promoted to the dissecting table of the philanthropist and the speculative philosopher. His head, his heart, and his bowels of compassion are opened, analyzed and lectured over. His origin is accounted for on the Darwinian theory, and the fate of the Palæozoic monsters is predicted for him. Every warmhearted gentleman in the country, or rather in the towns, whose imagination has become excited over Irish newspapers and Irish debates, considers himself entitled to offer him advice as to the management of his property and the regeneration of his moral nature, while men like Lord George Hill, and a hundred others, who have devoted their lives and fortunes to reduce to order the chaos, into which the uncontrolled instincts of the peasantry had converted a great portion of the island, are gravely told that their exertions have depopulated the country, and that they and their fellows, as the representatives of "*Landlordism*," (a new crime invented for the occasion) are a public nuisance to be abated with the utmost despatch.

We will endeavour to submit to this discipline with patience and good humour, to follow out as far as we can the suggestions which are offered to us, and to continue in a humble way to do our duty to the best of our ability toward those in whose happiness we have a traditional concern, and with whose prosperity our own material welfare is incorporated. But there are some among us, members of either house of Parliament, upon whom are imposed even graver obligations, viz: those of guarding the rights and liberties of all classes of the community, and upon these will devolve the responsibility of protecting the property of the country from such assaults as those to which I have had occasion to refer in the foregoing pages.

MR. HILL'S ARTICLE ON IRELAND

IN

'QUESTIONS FOR A REFORMED PARLIAMENT.'

I HAD scarcely finished the perusal of Mr. Butt's volume before my attention was called to a very interesting article on Ireland by Mr. F. H. Hill.

This paper is written in a spirit of genuine liberality. With many of Mr. Hill's opinions I cordially concur, and if I dissent from the contents of his concluding pages, it is rather on account of the incorrectness of his data than with any fault I have to find with his general argument.

At page 18, Mr. Hills says:—

"Since 1851 nearly two millions of people have left Ireland, not intending to return. Within certain limits this movement was necessary and healthy. Its effects were for a time visible in the higher wages and improved modes of living of the labouring poor, who were better clothed, better housed, and better fed than before; in the increase of the deposits in the joint-stock banks and of the investments in Government stock and other securities; and in the multiplication of the signs of business enterprise. The evil days were believed to be over: and a new era was thought to have commenced. These favourable symptoms, however, have during the last dozen years become less and less marked, and now they have nearly disappeared. Irish agricultural prosperity reached its highest point in 1855, fostered by exceptionally favourable seasons, by the new capital, and new spirit introduced through the agency of the Encumbered Estates Court, and by the removal of a surplus and half-pauper population, which had increased the consuming mouths without multiplying the productive hands of the country."

This admission narrows the question very considerably. If the immediate effect of emigration has been "to raise wages, to improve the mode of living of the labouring poor, who were better clothed, housed and fed than they were before,"—the only disputable point remaining is the exact moment when the process to which Mr. Hill himself attributes these beneficent results may have ceased to be productive of good.

Mr. Hill seems to consider the tide ought to have turned in 1859:—

"This progress continued, though at a slackening rate, until 1859. From that time to the present, there has been retrogression rather than advance."

And he proceeds to detail the data which have led him to this conclusion.

It is the accuracy of these data which I venture to dispute.

First, Mr. Hill asserts on the authority of Mr. Cliffe Leslie, a gentleman to whose courtesy, candour, and talents I am glad to have this opportunity of paying a tribute of admiration, that the rate of agricultural wages in Ireland, North and South inclusive, does not exceed a shilling a day over the working year, while he adds on his own authority *that it has actually declined since* 1859. In reply, I can only say that my own experience and the information I have acquired on the subject does not confirm this opinion; nor, were such a fact established, should I be disposed to accept low wages as a proof of an undue diminution in the number of the labouring population.

Mr. Hill then appeals to the poor-law returns, and taking one of what he himself describes as a series of "exceptionally favourable seasons," viz., the year 1858, he compares it with 1866, and because more persons were in receipt of relief at that latter date, he argues that this excess of pauperism has been occasioned by the concurrent emigration having diminished the wages fund of the country; but he does not note with sufficient distinctness that the increase of pauperism did not take place until two years after the year he mentions, that it was occasioned by a series of bad seasons commencing in 1859 and ending in 1863, that from 1852 to 1856 the percentage of paupers to population was higher than it is at present, and that during 1864 and 1865, down to the period he quotes, there has been a continual diminution in the number of persons in receipt of relief, as will be seen on a reference to the subjoined table.

---

* Mr. Hill says 20,000 more. I cannot understand where he gets this figure. According to the official returns the average number of persons in receipt of relief amounted to 45,790 in 1858, and to 53,917 in 1865, which shows an excess in 1865 over 1858 of 8,000 instead of 20,000.

TABLE shewing the average daily number of Poor in receipt of relief during the year in Workhouses in Ireland, from 1862 to 1865, with percentage of same to population.

Year ending 29th Sept.	Total number in Workhouses.	Per-centage to population.	
1852	166,821	2·60	decrease
1853	129,401	2·06	"
1854	95,190	1·54	"
1855	79,211	1·30	"
1856	63,235	1·04	"
1857	50,665	0·84	"
1858	45,790	0·76	"
1859	40,380	0·67	"
1860	41,271	0·69	increase
1861	45,136	0·78	"
1862	53,668	0·93	"
1863	57,910	1·01	"
1864	56,525	0·99	decrease
1865	53,917	0·95	"

So far from "there having been on the whole a steady increase of pauperism during the last ten years," as asserted by Mr. Hill, there has been a continual decrease of pauperism during the first four and the last two years of the series he refers to.

Considering the disturbed state of the country during these two last years, a less favourable result might have been expected.

Mr. Hill then recurs to the old story of the conversion of tillage into pasturage, "*which has been in progress in Ireland during the last twenty years,*" a perfectly inaccurate statement, as will be seen on referring to the table at page 363, and he adopts Mr. Dalton's dictum that "the increase in the number of holdings above 15 acres has been generally effected in the worst possible way, a ten acre farmer has been converted into one of 20 acres by the Procrustean process of stretching him;"—a conjecture which a moment's reflection might have told Mr. Hill is quite incapable of verification, and which implies that the land agents of Ireland do not know their business nor the landlords their own interest. If he wishes to test the accuracy of Mr. Dalton's observation let him try to "unstretch" the alleged victims of the experiment, and see what the twenty-acre farmer will say when it is proposed to dock him of half his holding.

But this is not the only opinion Mr. Hill has borrowed from Mr. Dalton. He actually asserts that the productive energy of Ireland has declined during the last five and twenty years. Those who have watched the great advance which many of the tenantry of Ireland have been making in skill and knowledge of their art during this period will be inclined to smile at such an assertion. But as figures are quoted, let us examine their bearing on the question.*

---

* TABLE showing the average rates of produce of the principal crops to the statute acre in Ireland, from 1847 to 1865:—

	Years.	Wheat. Cwts.	Oats. Cwts.	Potatoes. Tons.	Turnips. Tons.	Flax. Stones, 14lbs.
Ascertained by Constabulary.	1847	16·5	14·7	7·2	15·5	48·0
	1848	11·3	13·3	3·9	14·3	38·4
	1849	13·3	13·3	5·6	16·1	39·6
	1850	11·0	13·5	4·6	15·7	39·4
	1851	12·5	13·8	5·1	15·9	38·6
	1852	13·8	14·4	4·8	15·9	41·4
	1853	14·5	13·8	6·4	16·4	40·2
	1854	14·8	15·4	5·1	15·8	37·6
	1855	14·3	13·7	6·4	16·6	38·6
Ascertained by Constabulary, and revised by Poor-Law Guardians.	1856	13·0	12·8	4·0	12·9	28·3
	1857	12·5	12·6	3·1	12·5	23·7
	1858	13·5	12·6	4·2	12·9	30·7
	1859	13·3	11·6	3·6	10·7	25·3
	1860	11·5	12·6	2·3	8·3	29·6
	1861	9·0	11·2	1·6	10·2	24·4
	1862	8·1	10·3	2·1	10·1	25·9
	1863	13·5	12·8	3·4	11·9	31·9
	1864	13·3	12·1	4·1	10·3	34·2
	1865	13·0	12·3	3·6	9·9	25·2

Mr. Dalton founds his opinion on the fact that the return of the average rates of produce to the statute acre in 1865 is considerably less than that given for 1847; but 1847 was the first year during which these rates of produce were estimated, and it is well known the operation was performed with less precision than was subsequently attained. Under any circumstances, a glance at the table will show either that too high an estimate was made, or that 1847 was an exceptionally prosperous season, and by no means a fair representative of the rate of production over a lengthened period, as will be observed by comparing it with the very next year in the list.

The only fair way of learning anything from such a table is to break it up into groups of years, and then to compare the average rate of produce during these successive cycles.

TABLE showing the average Rates of Produce of the principal crops to the statute acre in Ireland, in cycles of three years, from 1848 to 1865.

Cycles.		Wheat. Cwts.	Oats. Cwts.	Potatoes. Tons.	Turnips. Tons.	Flax in stones of 14 lbs.	
1848, 49, 50	Ascertained by Constabulary.	11·85	13·36	4·70	15·36	39·13	
1851, 52, 53		13·60	14·00	5·43	16·06	40·06	
1854, 55, 56		14·03	13·96	5·16	15·10	34·83	
1857, 58, 59	Ascertained by Constabulary and revised by Poor Law Guardians.	13·10	12·26	3·63	12·03	26·56	An excess of rain fell in these years.
1860, 61, 62		9·53	11·36	2·00	9·53	26·63	
1863, 64, 65		13·26	12·40	3·70	10·70	30·43	

N.B. "The estimates of produce were made differently before 1855 and after 1856. In the earlier periods the produce was esti-

* *Note by Mr. Thomson on Flax Cultivation in Ulster.* The decrease in the produce of the flax crops is owing in a great measure

mated by the Sub-Inspectors of Constabulary, in November in each year. Since 1855 the produce is estimated by the Constabulary in January or February, after each crop, in Poor Law Electoral Divisions, and corrected according to opinions of Poor Law Guardians. In 1855 the opinion of the Poor Law Guardians was to some extent used in checking the returns of the Constabulary; in 1856 both systems were used. *The tendency of taking the opinion of the Guardians has been to lower the rates of produce"*—Vide *Tables of Estimated Acreage Produce*, 1856 : Dr. N. Hancock, p. 24.

The result obtained by this method is very different and much more significant than that deduced by Mr. Dalton from the capricious comparison of a single year at the commencement of a long series with a single year at its end. It clearly shows that any fluctuations in the annual rate of production are to be attributed to the varying chances of the seasons, and not to an alleged continuous decline of Irish agriculture, which is neither in accordance with our statistics, nor our experience.

Mr. Hill next lays considerable stress on the fact of the comparative deficiency of pasture in Ulster, but he neglects to mention that the stiff clay lands of a large proportion of that province, including Antrim, Down, Monaghan, Armagh, and Derry, are quite unsuitable to anything but tillage.

He then compares the average size of farms in the four provinces, without making any allowance for the obvious fact, that large tracts of pasture lands in a given area must necessarily swell the average size of all the farms within that area, and he particularly instances Armagh, where the average size of holdings is only 14 acres ; but he abstains from noting that there has been a greater decrease of population to the square mile in Armagh than in any other county of Ireland, and that so far from there being a larger

---

to the fact that, up to 1847, and for some years later, flax seed was only sown on land peculiarly adapted to the growth of that plant, while in recent years the prices realized for flax were so tempting that the seed was sown on land not at all suitable for the purpose, and which was at the same time foul and exhausted. This told also on the Oat crop, for the additional exhausting crops introduced between two manured ones, was seen to tell more or less unfavourably on the produce of all.

proportion of small farms in Ulster than in the rest of Ireland, there is a larger percentage of holdings from 1 to 5 acres both in Connaught and in Leinster than in Ulster, and that even of holdings from 1 to 15 acres the percentage in Ulster is less than it is in Connaught and within 7 per cent. of what it is in Leinster.

TABLE showing the per-centage of Holdings from 1 to 5 acres, and from 1 to 15 acres, to the entire Holdings of the respective Provinces.

	Leinster.	Munster.	Ulster.	Connaught	Ireland.
Entire holdings in 1864	114,433	114,921	203,066	120,698	553,118
1 to 5 acres	20·1	11·2	13·5	15·3	14·8
1 to 15 acres	45·1	29·3	52·3	55·2	46·7

He then goes on to state that the purely agricultural emigration from Ulster has been smaller than that from any of the other provinces of Ireland,* a gratuitous assumption which cannot be deduced from the statistics upon the subject (see pp. 382, 383) ; and he concludes his observations by assuring us, on the authority of a correspondent of the " Daily News," that there are proportionately fewer cultivators to the acreage under cultivation in Ireland than in England, and that the agricultural class in Ireland cannot number at this moment more than 650,000 persons, a proportion which, allowing one occupant to every farm in the island, would leave each tenant a fifth of a labourer to assist him in its cultivation !†

---

* If by " purely agricultural emigration," Mr. Hill means actual cultivators, his guess is probably correct, for the simple reason that there are fewer cultivators to the area cultivated in parts of Ulster than elsewhere; if, however, he means the sons and daughters of farmers, I see no reason why that should be the case, except so far as the manufactures of Ulster may enable some of them to find employment at home.

† The total number of holdings in Ireland in 1864 was 601,771. See p. 366.

In undertaking to pilot a reformed Parliament through the rocks and shallows of Irish politics, Mr. Hill would do well to take soundings on his own account. He will then be able to buoy the channel with beacons in which the public will be able to place more confidence than in those which he has now borrowed for their guidance.

It is a general misfortune when a gentleman so intelligent as Mr. Hill, is led astray by inaccurate information.

THE END.

WILLIS, SOTHERAN & CO., PRINTERS, 42, CHARING CROSS.

www.ingramcontent.com/pod-product-compliance
Lightning Source LLC
Chambersburg PA
CBHW051736300426
44115CB00007B/586